African Studies
and the
Undergraduate
Curriculum

African Studies
and the
Undergraduate
Curriculum

edited by

Patricia Alden
David Lloyd
Ahmed I. Samatar

LYNNE
RIENNER
PUBLISHERS

BOULDER
LONDON

Published in the United States of America in 1994 by
Lynne Rienner Publishers, Inc.
1800 30th Street, Boulder, Colorado 80301

and in the United Kingdom by
Lynne Rienner Publishers, Inc.
3 Henrietta Street, Covent Garden, London WC2E 8LU

Library of Congress Cataloging-in-Publication Data
African studies and the undergraduate curriculum / edited by Patricia
    Alden, David Lloyd, and Ahmed I. Samatar.
    Includes bibliographical references.
    ISBN 1-55587-445-2 (alk. paper)
    1. Africa—Study and teaching (Higher) I. Alden, Patricia, 1945– .
II. Lloyd, David, 1941– . III. Samatar, Ahmed I. (Ahmed
Ismail)
DT19.8.A358 1994
960'.071'1—dc20   93-50942
                                                                 CIP

British Cataloguing in Publication Data
A Cataloguing in Publication record for this book
is available from the British Library.

Printed and bound in the United States of America

⊗   The paper used in this publication meets the requirements
     of the American National Standard for Permanence of
     Paper for Printed Library Materials Z39.48-1984.

Contents

Acknowledgments

This book owes its existence to the collaboration of many individuals whose efforts have built a strong program in African studies at St. Lawrence University in Canton, New York. Our acknowledgment begins with those who, over two decades, have sustained our Semester in Kenya, with warmest appreciation for the excellent direction given by Paul Robinson and Howard Brown. We also thank the Kenyan faculty who have taught in our Study Abroad program; in particular, Micere M.G. Mugo and Njuguna Ng'ethe, who as visiting scholars at the university pressed the case for the further development of African studies.

By the late 1980s a core of dedicated colleagues had established a minor in African studies. Under the leadership of President Patti McGill Peterson, and with her unstinting support, faculty members were encouraged to develop a proposal for external funding to further strengthen our program. President Peterson presented our ideas to the Ford Foundation, where Dr. Peter Stanley, then director of the Education and Culture Program, assessed the merits of our proposal, sharing with us the benefits of his critical acumen and administrative experience. We thank Dr. Stanley and the Ford Foundation for their strong conviction that the study of Africa at the undergraduate level is as important now as it was at the dawn of the enterprise, more than four decades ago. Special appreciation also goes to Marlene Guzman, director of Corporate and Foundation Relations at St. Lawrence, whose numerous abilities include the talent for turning the less-than-orderly ideas of faculty members into successful proposals.

The culmination of our three-year grant from the Ford Foundation was a conference, African Studies and the Undergraduate Curriculum, held at St. Lawrence University in October 1992. For additional support for the conference we also thank the Fund for the Improvement of Post-Secondary Education. The essays presented as chapters of this volume have been developed from papers presented at the conference. They owe much to the interaction of all who attended. We are grateful to the authors of the essays for the generous effort they extended to make the conference successful and the volume as useful as possible. We also thank some forty other teachers of African studies who attended the conference, and particularly those who traveled farthest, representing our Kenya program. Three scholars from Africa, Micere M.G. Mugo, Njuguna Ng'ethe, and Obioma Nnaemeka, invited to critique the conference, provoked vigorous debate. A lively panel that presented student perspectives on the teaching of African studies was organized by David McWethy; it included Elizabeth Garland, Francoise Cromer, Andrew Dabalen, and Marc Perry. Two students who assisted with conference logistics deserve special recognition: Sara Wilkinson and Santosh Abraham.

Thanks go to Dean Robert Schwartz for granting a course reduction to one of the editors to work on this book; to Rene Murphy in Instructional Technology; to Laurie Olmstead in Word Processing for her expertise in producing final copy; and to Vickie Perrin, secretary of the English Department, for assistance with the conference and the book. We also thank Lynne Rienner Publishers for their generous interest and support and superb assistance in editing the volume. Finally, on behalf of our university, David Lloyd and Patricia Alden want to thank Ahmed Samatar for his enormous energy, dedication, and creativity over the past eight years in developing African studies at St. Lawrence. As he moves on to a distinguished new position, he will be sorely missed.

P. A.
D. L.
A. I. S.

Introduction: African Studies Within U.S. Liberal Arts Education

Patricia Alden, David Lloyd & Ahmed I. Samatar

If then a practical end must be assigned to a University course, I say it is that of training good members of society. Its art is the art of social life, and its end is fitness for the world.
—John Henry Cardinal Newman[1]

The function of the university . . . is to be the organ of that fine adjustment between real life and the growing knowledge of life, an adjustment which forms the secret of civilization.
—W.E.B. DuBois[2]

Every hour that passes brings a supplement of ignition to the crucible in which the world is being fused. We have not had the same past, you and ourselves, but we shall have, strictly, the same future. The era of separate destinies has run its course.
—Cheikh Hamidou Kane[3]

This volume is in a sense travel literature: it reports on intellectual and physical journeys across the globe and across disciplines—those territories into which the realms of knowledge have been carved. The essays are maps, reflective of both a changing geography and a changing curriculum wherein the old relationship of center and periphery is challenged. They report on long-standing and newly developing trade routes of intellectual and cultural exchange and suggest alternative ways of structuring an education intended, in an adaptation of Newman's phrase, to fit students for the world.

The work of scholar-teachers in widely disparate fields, the essays reflect important debates about the direction African studies should take within undergraduate education. Africanists, once considered specialists at the margins of the undergraduate program, increasingly play a critical role

1

in constructing core curricula, vigorously engaging the central concerns of liberal arts education. The present volume attests to the particular contributions that African studies has made, and continues to make, to rethinking both the aims and the means of liberal learning.

Journey is an apt metaphor for the educational process. The student travels out from the self, encountering new experiences and ideas, liberating the imagination from the singularity of personal experience and local environment. Yet this expansion, opening the eyes to the world, simultaneously affords a new perspective on the self. Knowledge of the other makes possible knowledge of the self and, furthermore, obliges us to consider ourselves in relationship to that world that lies beyond the self. While the study of any subject can inaugurate such a journey out from the self, the study of other cultures, and perhaps particularly the study of distant cultures like Africa's, constitutes an especially demanding engagement with this process.

A journey to Africa—and we stress in this volume the value of physical travel as an accompaniment to the intellectual voyage—ensures that students will confront difference in every sphere: in the environment and in cultural adaptations to it; in political and social structures, esthetic norms, moral ideals, and religious intuitions; and in human bodies. Such differences directly challenge students' ideas about the naturalness and inevitability of their own worlds and allow them to see their own societies as but one possible form among many.

But the confrontation with difference fosters a recognition of what is shared and enduring in human experience. Material circumstances vary, but students recognize the endless resourcefulness of people coming to grips with fundamental aspects of the human condition: the need for physical, mental, and spiritual nurture; the blessing of birth and the inevitability of death; the distribution of necessary and often scarce resources; the desire for power and control along with the consciousness of vulnerability. Such recognition fosters not merely tolerance for but an affinity with the plural cultures across the globe.

Knowledge of the other; knowledge of the self: the journey to Africa supports both projects. But most urgently it pushes students to consider the relationship between the two: between self and other, West and non-West, "developed" and "underdeveloped." African studies is a way of studying Africans; but it is also, even more significantly, a way of studying the processes of globalization.

As the twentieth century comes to a close, countries and cultures are being pulled toward each other at a pace more furious, and with consequences more fundamental, than was the case even half a century ago. This thrust toward the increasing integration of the aspects of the human world is propelled by diverse forces: transnationalization of production, finance, and information; new technology such as satellites, computers, and fiber optics that enable an unprecedented compression of time and a dramatic reduction of space. But such processes lead not just to integration; rather, in an acutely dialectical fashion, they engender disintegration and fragmentation. Scholars have used the words "combined and uneven development" to describe this process: *combined* underscores the articulation of an expanding, essentially Euro-American, commercial and industrial order with the livelihoods of peripheral nations; *uneven development* points to the resulting imbalance in the costs and benefits of the relationship. As the pace of globalization has accelerated, so also have the forces of disintegration. We see this in the decomposition of the vast territory of the Soviet Union; in ethnic and nationalist strife around the world; in ecological crises; in huge population movements of refugees and émigrés; and in the deterioration of the material conditions and cultural integrity of many nations in the South—and also, increasingly, in the North.

Africa represents in starkest form some of the consequences of the contemporary processes of globalization and the attendant paradox of integration and disintegration. Economic development in Africa staggers; technology and markets tie Africa ever more closely to a West-dominated order, which results in the increasing diffusion of African cultures and values. Environment is threatened by market forces as well as physical changes on the planet, with whole cultures being forced to the brink of extinction. Travel to Africa and study of Africa bring students face to face with some of the sharpest contradictions of global interdependence. The urgency of the problems engenders a sense of social responsibility; an awareness of the need to develop global *civitas*—to reconsider the terms of coexistence and relationship on the planet. As Cheikh Hamidou Kane forcefully reminds us, "The era of separate destinies has run its course."

If African studies confronts students in a particularly urgent way with the global forces shaping the planet, it can also foster a sense of agency, directly involving students in participatory, problem-based research, as several chapters in this volume attest. Students come face to face not just with African problems but with Africans working on those problems. They test their Western theories, explanations, and methodologies alongside African frameworks, and in the common effort to produce better solutions and better models, both African and North American students stand to gain much. In this way, African studies can become a model of genuinely intercultural education that emphasizes exchange and dialogue.

Why should Africa suddenly become optimal material for realizing intercultural education? Precisely because our past approaches to learning about (and coexisting with) Africa have been so evidently flawed. Joel Samoff argues, in Chapter 2, that *we*, the subjects of the learning process, have scrutinized *them*, the objects, without imagining that we might learn from African knowledge systems or from African views of the West. Because in the late twentieth century there is so much evidence that this model of (non)relationship has had disastrous consequences for Africa, African studies offers a particularly effective base from which to urge that our ways of organizing knowledge and learning need to be changed. Moreover, as many of the chapters argue, incorporating African materials into traditional disciplines has challenged the adequacy of fundamental assumptions, methodologies, and practices in several fields. Whether we are rethinking from within the epistemology dominant in much of the West or juxtaposing Western and African knowledge-constructs, students' awareness of the historical situatedness of all paradigms is sharpened.

Our argument is not simply that the study of Africa is compatible with, or even supportive of, the goals of liberal arts education; rather, we make a more emphatic claim: that African studies provides an especially direct engagement with those processes of globalization that are rapidly transforming our world; that African studies affords a particularly striking context in which to contemplate the consequences of these world processes; and that African studies encourages students to explore what their relationship has been, and what it ought to be, to the world. Africa challenges students not only to understand but to act; to assume responsibility, with others, for creating a different relationship between self and other, between West and non-West, between center and periphery. The development of African studies represents one of DuBois' "fine adjustments" between life and the knowledge of life. It is an adjustment that may indeed bring us closer to "the secret of civilization."

AFRICAN STUDIES AT ST. LAWRENCE UNIVERSITY: LOCAL AND NATIONAL CONTEXTS

A decade ago, historian Robert McCaughey wrote of international studies and general education that it was "an alliance yet to be." His detailed review of the separate lines of development of these two academic enterprises ends in 1978, when Harvard College instituted a Foreign Cultures requirement as part of the core. McCaughey at that time speculated whether "international studies faculty elsewere [might] be persuaded that they too have an important stake in the shape of the undergraduate curriculum at their institutions?"[4] In the spring of 1990, the Association of American Colleges coordinated a national project, funded by the National Endowment for the Humanities, entitled, "Engaging Cultural Legacies: Shaping Core Curricula in the Humanities." The program aimed at including more non-Western or multicultural materials in general education courses. The 250 institutions that participated in the Cultural Legacies program (St. Lawrence University among them) attest to the considerable activity on many college campuses in the past decade to forge connections between international/area studies and the core curriculum.

The development of African studies at St. Lawrence University, linked to the larger issue of international studies, exemplifies significant national trends in undergraduate education. We also think our institutional history may be instructive in other respects, for those involved in international education and area studies did not ride an irresistible wave. The momentum the faculty has been able to sustain at a small, selective, geographically remote college testifies also to skillful program-building over several decades.

Situated in northern New York state, near the Canadian border, St. Lawrence University began as early as the 1930s to think internationally, developing cooperative education projects with Queen's University in Canada. This led to the establishment of a widely recognized program in Canadian–U.S. relations. In the postwar period, St. Lawrence, along with many other colleges, instituted a number of language-immersion programs abroad, tied to the Modern Languages Department. In the mid-1970s, the Government Department inaugurated first a summer and later a semester program in Kenya for students who had a comparative or international focus in their social science major. One or two other departments sponsored similar international semesters that complemented their major. These developments again reflected national trends toward more off-campus experience. Throughout the 1980s in U.S. higher education, a consensus emerged that an international perspective was critical to a serious liberal-arts education.[5] The potentially transformative value of international education for the undergraduate student was expressed at St. Lawrence in a 1989 "White Paper on International Education":

> Undergraduates tend to view their own cultural milieu as the natural culmination of the mainstream of history. The unspoken corollary is that other cultural traditions are outside of the mainstream, and, therefore, at best, flawed imitations of a grander tradition. Cultural chauvinism is a natural sentiment; it is also a mortal enemy of liberal education. . . . Serious study of other cultures improves students' understanding of themselves, provokes students to reexamine their own culture, and develops in them a critical tolerance for other points of view and for the diversity of humankind. Liberal education with an international perspective also includes some study of major issues and human developments which transcend individual cultures, sometimes uniting and sometimes dividing them. Study of such issues can give students an expanded sense of their obligations and capacity to perform, and can thereby prepare students for responsible adulthood in the larger world.

Responding to the developing national consensus, a small number of the St. Lawrence faculty began to push the college toward greater commitment to international studies. The faculty voted to add a non-Western course to graduation requirements, predicated on the recognition of a growing, interdependent global community. Only one course was required, however. Some thought this manifestly inadequate to achieve the stated objective that all students, regardless of academic major, will have "some understanding of another way of perceiving the world." Others saw this as a strategy for gradually adding non-Western courses (and faculty to teach them) to the college. About the same time, area programs in African, Asian, Latin American, and Caribbean studies were being developed. In 1987, the university centralized the administration of its eleven Study Abroad programs: for the first time, a director of International Education had primary responsibility for developing a coherent curricular context on campus that would support international study, for recruiting international students and visiting scholars, and for developing extracurricular programming.

African studies on campus grew largely as a consequence of our particularly strong Semester Abroad program in Kenya. Between the mid-1970s and 1990, over nine hundred students, about half of them from St. Lawrence and the rest from more than thirty other colleges and universities, had participated in this extraordinary program. Comprising language training, rural and urban homestays with Kenyan families, academic course work, and special field studies/internships, primarily taught by faculty from the University of Nairobi and Kenyatta University, this cross-cultural encounter challenges students to deepen their understanding of Africa and its peoples, to explore the complex and changing roles of Africa in the global context, and to examine critically their personal values and beliefs.

Realizing the large demands this program made on the people and facilities of Kenya, and searching for ways to reciprocate, St. Lawrence University started a scholarship fund through which two Kenyan students each year are matriculated at the university. A few years later, St. Lawrence also initiated a fellowship for a Kenyan to complete a master's degree in education while teaching Kiswahili on the main campus. This language training enabled students to achieve some facility in the major lingua franca of the region before participating in our program abroad, as well as, once in East Africa, to gain a much deeper appreciation for African peoples and cultures.

During the early 1980s, in order to strengthen the links between our campus and the Kenya program, two Kenyan faculty affiliated with our Abroad program, Dr. Micere Mugo and Dr. Njuguna Ng'ethe, were able to teach on the St. Lawrence campus. Both of these educators enriched the academic climate of international studies and were instrumental in convincing the university to create some permanent positions for Africanists. The objectives were to better prepare students for the Kenya program, to further those students' education on return from that experience abroad, to offer a wider range of courses, and to build a stronger understanding about African studies within the wider academic community. Subsequently, two

Africanists, one in history and one in political economy, were hired. To-gether with other faculty who had offered occasional courses in Africa, they constituted a critical mass that could then lobby for a more coherent structure beyond a random offering of courses within a number of dis-parate departments. A new, interdisciplinary minor in African studies was approved in 1987, organized around the theme of development. By then, Asian studies had become a combined major, and another interdisciplinary minor was subsequently approved in Latin America and Caribbean studies.

These area studies programs provided in-depth knowledge of the his-tory, philosophy, religion, geography, politics, and artistic expressions of non-Western cultures. They were also envisioned as interdisciplinary and, as some strenuously argued, transdisciplinary, although the debate on how to identify and build these attributes continues. In fact, in many institu-tions where such area studies efforts have been successful, established aca-demic departments have remained suspicious of these innovations, not sure of their ultimate impact upon the curriculum and budget.[6] At St. Lawrence, these tensions have been mitigated by requiring all faculty in area studies to be based within a department. There, they meld their disci-plinary expertise with their aspiration to teach beyond departmental boundaries. However, faculty in African studies are sometimes squeezed by having to divide their time between departmental and area studies de-mands. Lacking departmental status, the area studies programs can neither hire nor tenure independently; and their development is to a considerable degree dependent upon maintaining cordial relations with department chairs and the chief administrators of the university.

In the late 1980s, faculty members at many colleges were keenly aware of a new climate of fiscal austerity. There were declining student enrollments, cutbacks in both private and federal funding for higher edu-cation, and growing disillusionment among many faculty at rapidly disap-pearing employment prospects. Demoralization threatened to undermine hard-won achievements in internationalizing the undergraduate curriculum.[7]

To counter this climate, the African studies faculty at St. Lawrence were encouraged to seek external funding to support new initiatives. The generous grant the university received in 1990 from the Ford Foundation indicated a growing concern at the national level about the deterioration in financial and institutional support for intercultural education, particularly at the undergraduate level. The success of the St. Lawrence proposal was an indicator that much of the future effort in this country to educate a wider populace as to the importance of cultural empathy and new forms of cooperation and conflict resolution would be taking place within the un-dergraduate sphere.

In addition to funding faculty and student development, the Ford grant supported a national conference on the role of African studies in under-graduate education. In October 1992, sixty scholars, all with considerable experience in teaching U.S. undergraduates, attended a four-day forum held at St. Lawrence University. The major goals were threefold: (1) to link African studies to the national debate about how and why we should expose students from North America to materials and perspectives from cultures other than their own; (2) to make a significant contribution to the assessment of the current state of African studies at the undergraduate level; and (3) to focus on new developments within and across the disciplines, as well as on new pedagogical approaches, in African studies. The fruits of this national conference are presented in this volume.

ORGANIZATION OF THE BOOK
AND OVERVIEW OF THE ARGUMENTS

Part 1, "Interculturalism and African Studies," has three chapters, each offering a distinct perspective on the relationship of African studies to the rest of the undergraduate curriculum. In Part 2, "Reassessments and New Directions," ten chapters review developments within the disciplines that contribute to African studies. In Part 3, "Programs Abroad," four essays describe different models for study-abroad programs. Part 4, "The Evolution of Undergraduate Programs in African Studies," includes an overview from a director of a Title VI-funded African studies center and perspectives from four institutions engaged in developing different structures for their African-content courses. In Part 5 the editors assess the directions for African studies proposed by the contributors.

The twenty-three chapters of the book offer significant areas of consensus and of disagreement about future directions for African studies. In Chapter 1, Gregson Davis draws upon his own, culturally complex, positioning. A Caribbean scholar of African descent, much of his work focuses on Greek and Roman literature. In "Between Cultures: Toward a Redefinition of a Liberal Education," Davis argues for abandoning reified notions of discrete cultures, invented traditions, and canonical hierarchies: he would replace these with an emphasis on the dynamic interactions of cultures throughout history. Culture is inherently "agonistic," a process of continual "contestation and synthesis, competition and fusion." He endorses attention to the predicament of liminality, the necessity of living between cultures that provokes a continual redefinition of self, and urges that the study of culture should aspire to a catholicity both temporal and spatial, historical and geographical. With considerable experience in the recent academic battles over the future of so-called Western civilization, Davis, the classicist, challenges the notion of "the classics" as foundational texts of Euro-American culture. He envisions humanities courses that, no longer privileging the West, illuminate the fundamentally interactive and constructed character of all traditions: courses that help students to appreciate the cultural wealth of the globe.

If Gregson Davis offers a persuasive invitation to share a common heritage, Joel Samoff, in his "Triumphalism, Tarzan, and Other Influences: Teaching About Africa in the 1990s" (Chapter 2), reminds us how emphatically and persistently Africa has been made to represent *the other* in the West, an *other* occasionally exotic but far more often "primitive," "underdeveloped," "crisis-ridden," and "dependent." Teaching about Africa, for Samoff, involves challenging these stereotypes; questioning the sources of "knowledge" of Africa; getting students to "address critically what is presented to them as fact." For both Davis and Samoff, teaching African material becomes an opportunity for students to unlearn a number of certainties; to see, in stark ways, the West's myth of its own "development" in contrast to Africa's "underdevelopment."

Samoff stresses that what students can learn about Africa is conditioned by those economic and political frameworks within which Africa is perceived as increasingly marginal. Even as he anatomizes the inadequacies of modernization theory, Samoff suggests its dominance within the social sciences. What students know about Africa is the continent's painful struggle to modernize and democratize along the lines of the triumphal Western model. Samoff's is, in several respects, a bleak assessment of the barriers to breaking out of the we/them paradigm (*we* being the West, the subject directing knowledge and development; *them* being Africans, the objects of study and of aid efforts). African studies continues to play a heroic, though possibly inadequate, role, challenging conventional views of Africa, teaching respect for the value of non-Western perspectives, questioning whether "blaming the victim" is ever an adequate explanation, and positioning students to appreciate "Africans as actors, not simply objects." The goals of the field, as Samoff conceives them, are clearly appropriate for, indeed central to, a humane, liberal education. The goals are most likely to be reached, Samoff argues, by restoring the legitimacy of traditional area studies. Holistic and particularistic knowledge of places and peoples is the best safeguard against the imperial ambitions of Western theory in its guise of universal science.

In a critique of Samoff's chapter, William Martin (in Chapter 3) sketches quite a different future for African studies. Where Samoff sees, and rues, Western "triumphalism," Martin sees, and celebrates, chaos and uncertainty, which open up radically new possibilities in African studies. He writes: "We are witnessing the collapse of an old order predicated on U.S. hegemony, global expansion, and the promise of nation-state . . . development. From North to South it is evident that progress and well-being are no longer a national affair, which leaves standing naked the *enduring* global relationships and inequalities that have so long been denied." Just as nation-states and Western development models seem unable to deliver economic progress or justice, so the academic disciplines on which modernization depends for legitimacy and rationalization (political science, economics, sociology) are also exposed as no longer being conceptually

adequate. Amid the breakdown, new phenomena demand our attention—
and demand different kinds of analyses. Africanists have always been
noted for their multidisciplinary approach to problems, but Martin suggests that at the present juncture this traditional flexibility is no longer adequate. Revitalizing traditional area studies programs might seem to answer the calls for multiculturalization of the curriculum; but this approach,
in Martin's view, would continue the insularity of nation-state analysis and
obscure those global or world-relational phenomena that yoke the disparate histories of continents: these should command our attention in the
next century. Desperate conditions in the periphery, and especially in
Africa, together with the evident breakdown of the promises of modernization in the core, force upon us a different kind of analysis. Africanists
are well positioned to begin this analysis, one that will build quite a different foundation for African studies. No longer would Africanists serve as
interpreters of the *other* to the West, much less as "promoters of illusory
development and democracy"; rather, they would provide leadership for
study that illuminates the "increasingly shared and unequal history" of the
planet. Africanists would become teachers not of *area* studies but of *world*
studies.

What Davis, Samoff, and Martin share is a rejection of a form of intercultural study that amounts to little more than the inclusion of exotic
and unfamiliar material into an otherwise unchanged curriculum. All three
insist on the transformative power of non-Western or nontraditional material—material that, by its presence, brings into focus the interactive and relational character of cultures and histories.

Part Two of the book, exploring the impact of African and Third
World material within established disciplines, opens with a chapter entitled "Transnational Cultural Studies and the U.S. University," by Neil
Lazarus. In it he asks whether "postcolonial" literatures can appropriately
be studied within an English department; or whether, as Gayatri Spivak
has argued, we need to shift these texts into area-studies programs where
they can be studied alongside indigenous languages and appropriate theory. Contra Spivak, Lazarus argues that traditional English departments
urgently need the cultural studies approach he envisions: what's good for
George Lamming is also good for Herman Melville, and if *In the Castle of
My Skin* should be considered in the context of cultural transformations,
all the more reason to develop a similar perspective on works like *Moby
Dick* that have been monumentalized, and, thus, dehistoricized. Lazarus
makes a particular brief for cultural production that is situated between the
First and Third Worlds, problematizing the opposition between a nativist
essentialism and a monolithic hegemony of "the West." Contra Ngugi wa
Thiong'o (on the language question), he sees writers like Achebe and
Soyinka using English to express perspectives that derive neither wholly
from Africa nor the West: perspectives produced from the interactivity of

cultures. Such texts, and other cultural practices, are "emergent," in Raymond Williams's sense, and thus transformative.

Patrick McNaughton alludes to this interactivity of cultures in his (Chapter 5) response to Lazarus, "I Think You Should Hear Voices When You Look at African Art." In teaching, McNaughton conveys the multiple ways in which artifacts are perceived and used within African communities as well as within the extended world of art consumption. While teaching "traditional" material, McNaughton insists that all art is "in a perpetual state of emergence"; always contributing to a discourse about art, and more broadly about culture, that is always "becoming." We should try to hear as many voices in that conversation as possible. African art challenges colonial and neocolonial stereotypes about African societies and prepares students to hear a real conversation about reciprocal cultural exchange. "Artworks become instruments [through] which individuals and cultures constantly reinvent each other." The very resistance of art historians, when faced with the divergences of African material, to revise their fundamental conceptions about their discipline makes McNaughton the more emphatic about the value of "keeping our teaching centered in disciplines." At the same time, the presence of a strong African studies program at Indiana University, where McNaughton teaches, has provided essential conditions for teaching and research, among which is contact with Africanists in other fields.

Lazarus and McNaughton share a fundamentally optimistic view of the capacity of their disciplines to become hospitable to non-Western materials. Paul Stoller's response (Chapter 6) suggests that a postmodern and transnational culture may be way out in front of the academy. As his vignette about the Songhay at 125th and Lennox Avenue makes clear, hybrid cultural practices surround us at every turn. He doubts the capacity of the academy to "confront the inadequacy of longstanding categorical assumptions" in the face of such rapid change. Specifically, he notes the distance still maintained by disciplinary constraints between "quotidian" culture and the arts and suggests that the African cinema may become the most effective bridge between high and popular cultures.

Two social scientists interested in postmodern phenomena (Stoller and Martin) find common cause with two humanists (Lazarus and McNaughton) to this extent: all four have considerable faith in the capacity of cultural workers at the periphery to resist the hegemony of the West, not by retreating into a nativist essentialism (opposing indigenous tradition to Western canon) but by working in a genuinely intercultural spirit, borrowing ancestors, languages, and technology to make myriad voices heard.

Part Two continues with essays by an economist and an historian. In Chapter 7, economist Ann Seidman draws upon her extensive engagement with development issues in Africa, suggesting a pedagogy designed to overcome the we/them opposition that Samoff deplores. Students need to understand that economic forces have a global impact and affect livelihoods, ecologies, and cultures in South and North; they also need to step across disciplinary boundaries as they analyze economic problems, and, most of all, they need to become engaged as students and as citizens. Seidman recommends "participatory problem-solving learning"; another way of saying, along with McNaughton, that students should learn to hear many voices. Ideal learning, according to Seidman, will center around real economic problems, with their complex human roots, rather than around hypothetical models of the market. Students (and researchers) should listen to those most directly affected and connect local issues with global causes. She suggests a variety of ways in which American students can be engaged with Africans in studying economic issues, connecting their analyses and solutions to development issues in their own (North American) communities. Classroom and field study thus model the kind of social and intellectual relationships that Seidman endorses.

In her response (Chapter 8), Sara Berry begins by delineating several ways in which African studies has evolved genuinely interdisciplinary problem-solving strategies and productive comparative approaches. She also notes that collective participation does not ensure consensus and offers the realistic caution that African studies teachers should be prepared for conflict as well as collaboration. Seidman's examples of participatory learning largely assume a shared model for rational problem solving. As with Berry's reservation above, Seidman perhaps underestimates the possibility for ultimately conflicting epistemologies that preclude consensus.

In Chapter 9, "From Periphery to Center: African History in the Undergraduate Curriculum," Thomas Spear argues persuasively for the central importance of African studies in today's academy. First, African historians have had of necessity to develop a diverse repertoire of research methodologies, borrowing from anthropology, archaeology, linguistics, and other disciplines in order to recover and reconstruct the hitherto "hidden" histories of ordinary peoples who have left no written records. In this respect, African history has influenced the practice of social historians of every continent. Because the writing of African history so often dramatically foregrounds the issue of cultural bias, it is especially valuable in fostering cognitive development, prompting students to move from a naive confidence in the "truth" of their sources to a critical understanding of the situatedness of every historian. The particular contributions of Afrocentrism extend these questions about ideology, ensuring that the study of distant lands has direct relevance to contemporary U.S. students grappling with racial division in their society.

Spear cautions that the current interest in multiculturalizing the curriculum can sometimes amount to a reductive "lumping [of] people together into a single indistinguishable category of *other* that promotes a sense of a monolithic mass of *them* opposed to *us*." This ultimately works at cross-purposes to the goals of area studies in challenging stereotypes and presenting an informed appreciation for the distinctiveness of cultures. In this respect, Spear and Samoff both view the traditional organization of area studies as serving an important pedagogical function.

Lidwien Kapteijns, in a commentary (Chapter 10) on Spear's views, observes that while African historians have done excellent work in social history, foundational problems such as the way Africa continues to be partitioned in textbooks (most notably, the separate treatment of North Africa) have not yet been adequately addressed. Lack of theoretically rigorous periodization also contributes to "analytical chaos" in the field. More strenuously than Spear, Kapteijns urges the view that African studies in the academy is always part of a political struggle over who controls history: Africanists must remain alert to this question and be prepared to learn from, as well as to critique, Afrocentrist thinking.

Focussing on the sciences, in Chapter 11, Ben Wisner suggests how provocative the linkage between the sciences and African studies might be. Teaching science *from* Africa (that is, indigenous knowledge) constitutes a critique of Western assumptions not only about Africans but about science itself; and about the companion terms, progress and development. Like Seidman, Wisner emphasizes the value of a problem-solving rather than a disciplinary approach, both in the classroom and in the field. Technological "solutions," like economic ones, need to be intimately connected to environment and human culture. Researchers and community members must participate in exploring development strategies: again, many voices should be heard. Wisner identifies several critical areas that could be explored in science courses, including water and soil resource-management, agricultural and zoological research, engineering, energy, and health. He offers abundant case study and bibliographical references in each area and draws extensively on African scholars' work.

Celia Nyamweru (Chapter 12) offers some reservations about Wisner's emphasis on "hybrid science" that incorporates indigenous and Western knowledge. She reminds us that a great deal of science, as it is done in the West, is practiced in Africa, by Africans, to preserve and to develop their environment. North American students, she argues, benefit from a (Western) scientific understanding of the physical world of Africa; Africans continue to do "pure" research in Africa that benefits the global community. We should not limit our view of African science exclusively to the applied or problem-based issues that Wisner addresses.

In the final essay of Part Two, Gretchen Walsh offers a valuable overview of the essential library resources needed to sustain an undergraduate program in African studies. She evaluates critical reference works and suggests budgetary realities for journal and monograph acquisition as well as a process for collection-building. She also indicates how new computer technologies can both assist and frustrate student research in African Studies.

Part Three shifts the focus to undergraduate programs that support African studies, offering perspectives on the strengths and liabilities of different models for study in Africa. Each of the four chapters speaks to a concern, articulated in Part Two most urgently by Ann Seidman and Ben Wisner: the value of having students working collaboratively with Africans on real problems. This experiential learning, grounded in well-designed field study, is at the heart of St. Lawrence University's Semester in Kenya. The philosophy and structure of this program are described (Chapter 14) by its directors, Paul Robinson and Howard Brown.

In Chapter 15, Sandra Greene, for many years director of Kalamazoo College's in-university program for study in Africa, highlights several difficulties experienced with this type of program, which offers extended cultural immersion. Her thoughtful discussion of the challenges to students entering an African culture are relevant for any program director. In Chapter 16 Joseph Pickle describes his and Zimbabwean Solomon Nkiwane's efforts to establish a new Study Abroad program for the Associated Colleges of the Midwest. And in Chapter 17, Neal Sobania reviews a number of issues facing any institution considering or currently participating in an Abroad program in Africa. Central among these are questions of how such programs are impacting on African universities and how U.S. institutions can reciprocate with opportunities for African students and faculty.

Part Four, on the evolution of the undergraduate programs, begins with James McCann's overview on the role of Title VI-funded African studies centers. Skeptical that the recent interest in multiculturalism will strengthen undergraduate study of Africa, McCann stresses the role of African studies in shifting the conceptual frameworks that underpin both interdisciplinary and discipline-based teaching.

McCann's call to "infuse Africa into the existing curricula" has a remarkably apt response in Louis Tremaine's report (Chapter 19) on how African texts have been incorporated into the University of Richmond's core curriculum. Tremaine, whose work at Richmond engages him in developing the university's focus on African studies, nevertheless argues for equally valuable work *beyond* the enclosure of a program—the work of "infusing Africa" in the larger curriculum.

Jack Parson, in Chapter 20, details the development of an African studies minor at the College of Charleston, which was achieved amid many restrictions, budgetary and otherwise. Parson stresses the need to tailor the program to the particular institution and environs. He also discusses the value of experiential learning in the U.S. classroom. Parson himself accomplishes this through simulations. Arthur Drayton (Chapter 21) reports on a longer history of the development of an African studies program—that at the University of Kansas, which grew from a Black studies program established in the 1960s. Kansas has consciously linked African and African-American program development; the College of Charleston has equally thoughtfully separated them. Both writers reflect on the relationship of African courses to African-American students and to issues of race in America.

In the final contribution to Part Four, Thomas Hale describes the Association of African Studies Programs, an umbrella organization that serves as a valuable resource for institutions that have, or that are considering building, programs in African studies.

In their concluding remarks (Part Five), Lloyd and Samatar identify and expand upon five major concerns shared by the contributors to this volume: we have tried to connect these concerns to the larger debate—that of the internationalizing of curricula. We suggest the most promising areas for further research. We intend our remarks to help strengthen undergraduate education, both by crystallizing the most salient contributions of African studies and by widening the dialogue in new directions.

NOTES

1. John Henry Cardinal Newman, *The Idea of a University* (Notre Dame: University of Notre Dame Press, 1982): 134.

2. W. E. B. DuBois, *The Souls of Black Folk* (New York: Signet Classic, 1969 [1903]): 117.

3. Cheikh Hamidou Kane, *Ambiguous Adventure* (London: Heinemann, 1972 [1963]): 79.

4. Robert McCaughey, in *Liberal Education*, vol. 270, 1984.

5. Cf. Ernest Boyer, *College: The Undergraduate Experience in America* (New York: Harper & Row, 1987); Barbara Burns, *Expanding the International Dimension of Higher Education* (San Francisco: Jossey-Bass, 1980).

6. Cf. Martin Staniland, "Who Needs African Studies?" *African Studies Review* 26, 3/4 (1983): 77–97.

7. Cf. McCaughey, in *Liberal Education,* 368–372; Richard Ralston, "The Struggle for African Studies: A View from Wisconsin," in *Issue: A Journal of Opinion*, XVII, 1 (1988): 41–44; David Wiley, "Academic Analysis and U.S. Policy Making on Africa: Reflections and Conclusions," in *Issue: A Journal of Opinion* XIX, 2 (1991): 38–48.

PART ONE

Interculturalism and African Studies

1

Between Cultures: Toward a Redefinition of Liberal Education

Gregson Davis

The topic I address in this chapter—multiculturalism in the undergraduate humanities curriculum—has functioned, in one form or another, as an unacknowledged subtext in my career as a university teacher; and it did so long before the term *multiculturalism* became fashionable. This has changed. Recent developments in the movement for undergraduate curricular reform, which has advanced far more rapidly than most of us dared to hope, have served to propel the topic in my consciousness from subtext to text; and it will be a main objective of this chapter to offer a few summary reflections on what this overt shift might entail for the traditional concept of a "liberal education."

At the outset, however, I wish to impart a peculiar inflection to the very notion of *multiculturalism* that constitutes the focal concept around which this book is organized. I do not hesitate to suggest the term *intercultural* in place of *multicultural.* This substitution of *inter* for *multi* is a provocative strategy on my part: I intend thereby to address certain fundamental issues in the contemporary discourse on culture from a different angle of vision. As a point of departure for my contribution, therefore, a brief preliminary rationale for my use of *intercultural* will be in order. I hope to make it clear that I am unequivocally committed to the basic educational principles that underpin the multiculturalist agenda.

A brief autobiographical prelude will help to place this personal inflection of terminology in perspective. As a native of a former British island colony in the Caribbean who went abroad to pursue a classical education as an undergraduate at Harvard, I was impelled by cross-cultural shock at a relatively early stage in my intellectual formation to a radical, critical engagement with the concept of culture. The secondary-school system to which I was exposed in my Antiguan childhood (a system that was deliberately modeled on the elite British public school of a kind to warm the heart of a Matthew Arnold) was not merely Eurocentric; it was even more blatantly *Anglocentric,* in its representation of what was of superior value and importance in the history of civilization. It was only after I had, through the U.S. institution of the General Education program, which was then in its heyday at Harvard, become more than superficially acquainted with the (for me) novel discipline of cultural anthropology that I came to an intellectual critique of Eurocentrism as it shaped the teaching of such subjects as history and literature. For a West Indian of African descent who had already assimilated a good portion of the Greek and Latin classical canon, the exposure to the study of African cultures, in particular, through the lens of anthropological theory, enabled me to see beyond, and ultimately to begin to exorcise, the elements of European, and, more narrowly, British chauvinism that had come to dominate my precollege conception of the evolution of human cultures. In my ongoing effort to "decolonize" my mind of the distortions perpetrated by the Western assumption of a "civilizing mission," I was more or less obliged to reexamine at close range the interaction between the dominant European cultures and the dominated African and indigenous ones in the arena of the New World historical experience; and in so doing, I gradually arrived at a revised perception of culture as a site of dynamic intersection. In fine, I came to regard the colonial paradigm of intercultural exchange, with its mixture of contestation and synthesis, competition and fusion, as in some deep sense representative of a process that is basic to human culture in general when viewed in historical perspective.

I shall return to the question of historical versus ahistorical approaches to intercultural study when I take up the question of comparative literary studies. For the moment, I wish to round off my first item of autobiographical testimony with a short quotation of a favorite passage from a Caribbean poet who frequently adumbrates the theme of cultural liminality. The opening lines of Derek Walcott's lyric poem, "Homecoming: Anse La Raye" (from his collection of early poems entitled *The Gulf*[1]) eloquently sum up the situation of the colonial student of European canonic texts:

> Whatever else we learned
> at school, like solemn Afro-Greeks eager for grades,
> of Helen and the shades
> of borrowed ancestors,
> there are no rites
> for those who have returned.

The phrases *Afro-Greeks* and *borrowed ancestors* take us right to the core of the issue of acculturation (or, as the francophone tradition would have it, assimilation) as it relates to the predicament of most colonized peoples—represented, in this case, by an anglophone West Indian pupil trying to identify with the heroic figures of Homeric narrative. At the same time, they draw ironic attention, as only the words of a master poet can, to a cultural predicament (to borrow an apt expression from the title of a book by James Clifford[2]) that, I shall contend, is by no means restricted to the experience of subject peoples in a colonial or postcolonial context.

Intercultural, then, is a designation that, in one of its major connotations, focuses attention on the relationship between cultures in such a way as to emphasize process and interaction. Whereas *multicultural* may often conjure up a plurality of distinct, even static, entities that coexist, to varied degrees of uneasiness, within a given society (usually if not invariably the United States), *intercultural* may more readily invoke an image of a dynamic interchange whereby cultures continually define and redefine themselves in relation to each other and where hegemonic roles are challenged and contested.

Before I go on to elaborate on the fluid nature of cultural self-construction and its ramifications for undergraduate education at the university level, it may be appropriate for me to interpose yet another strategic caveat pertaining to the ideal scope of the term *multicultural.* If I am not mistaken in my reading of the cultural scene, the term *multicultural* as it has gradually crystallized in our academic lexicon, has come to signify the particular configuration of cultures and subcultures that preponderate in the contemporary United States. To the extent that it seeks primarily to rectify the historical under-representation of minority cultures in the U.S. undergraduate curriculum, the multicultural movement tends to focus on the task of recuperating those cultural contributions that have been neglected and devalued by the regnant culture. Such recuperation is an activity that should continue to be pursued with vigor, if only because it has already yielded up some buried treasures (in the sphere of letters, for example, it has led to the rediscovery of such authors as Zora Neale Hurston). In the long run, however, if we circumscribe our multicultural horizon to the North American cultural aggregation (which, incidentally, is constantly shifting in response to ephemeral patterns of emigration), are we not opening ourselves to the charge of parochialism, which is but a step removed from the chauvinism we deplore? In rebuttal to this objection, we may resort to the facile defense that the United States is, after all, a microcosm of world culture/s—a line of defense that has the effect of fortifying our own more or less narcissistic preoccupations. Be that as it may, multiculturalism, as an alternative to an ethnocentric humanities, will, in my view, be radically impoverished if it fails to embrace a genuinely global and historically elastic perspective. In correcting the abuse of under-representation of minority voices, we need to avoid falling into the trap of an unconscious parochialism that assumes the United States to be the world, however seductive the half-truth of a microcosm might be. In a society in which we routinely refer to what is a strictly national sport competition as a World Series (I allude, of course, to the so-called national pastime of baseball), it is especially important that we enlarge our tacit presuppositions regarding "the world" so as to encompass remote cultures that are not merely non-European, but extra-American.

I am not, I hasten to add, arguing for a purely *quantitative* expansion of our cultural reach. It would be absurdly impractical and self-defeating to insist on achieving a global perspective by the sheer addition of foreign cultures to our nationally restricted repertory. What I have in mind is a basically *qualitative* change in our outlook that would encourage us to transcend our tendency to cultural chauvinism as we go about the crucial task of redefining the contours of a liberal education. In a word, I am proposing that a truly transnational, rather than a parochial, conception of *multi* should determine the scope of our educational turn to the study of other cultural traditions. To be comprehensive in a meaningful way, such a turn should also extend beyond the confines of the contemporary world to encompass past models of intercultural representations. This broader view of multiculturalism merges with another connotation of *intercultural* that I will also be concerned to sponsor; i.e., the systematic comparison of symbolic forms (e.g., literary texts) from alien cultures that are historically unrelated to our own or to each other.

In both geographical and temporal reach, then, the new humanities curricula should, in my judgment, aspire to a catholicity that is perceived as central rather than marginal to their purview. At the very least, we can make our integration of minority cultures the point of departure for more extended transcultural excursions. For instance, the study of African-American cultural forms should stimulate us to relate them (following the lead of Herskovits) to their African origins, while of course we remain fully cognizant of their transformations in the New World crucible; similarly, the analysis of Asian-American cultural expressions should lead us to take a closer look at Japanese and Chinese traditions. Ultimately, the study of these foreign cultures in their own terms should supersede our immediate need to relate them to our national preoccupations with the relative viability of the myth of the melting-pot.

I have thus far presented the case for a more global multiculturalist agenda at a level of generalization that seems pertinent to the requirements of the topic, and I could easily surrender to the rhetorical temptation to remain entirely at such a nebulous level. On the other hand, even sweeping generalizations, however appropriate, might well benefit from more concrete substantiation in terms of their main curricular repercussions. Since my academic identity is, and has been for over two decades, split in the form of a joint appointment in the disciplines of classics and comparative literature, it might be expedient for me to focus my advocacy of intercultural approaches by drawing on my personal involvement in the praxis of curricular reform. What I have to say about literary studies and, more specifically, about the links between classics and comparative literature will, I trust, provide a framework from which one may readily extrapolate to other domains of inquiry and pedagogy.

In its simplest institutional manifestation, comparative literature presumes the study of at least two literary traditions, whether or not they happen to be historically affiliated. When we look at actual academic practice, however, the situation is generally far more circumscribed with respect to the range of traditions than one would suppose from sheer principle. To be sure, I am limiting my ken to what is normal in most of our elite institutions (and several outstanding exceptions spring to mind as I write); but it is by and large the case that comparative literature programs and departments in the United States are disproportionately oriented toward the all too familiar ambit of European literary traditions. Although I have not compiled the relevant statistical evidence to support this statement, I would venture to assert that the typical comparative literature program continues to be dominated by professors and students whose primary research interest lies in the literatures of the major European countries (French, German, English, Italian, Spanish, Russian). This Eurocentrism is a phenomenon that has been endemic to comparative literature from the very inception of the field, as a cursory glance at the preoccupations of the founders of the discipline will readily confirm. A global multiculturalism, then, ought in principle to have characterized the discipline from its early foundations. The perpetuation of a narrowly Eurocentric range of traditions is, however, indefensible at this historical juncture. I wish to stress, however, that multiculturalism in regard to literary studies should require no special pleading on moral or political grounds; nor need there be any resort to condescending gestures on the part of European scholars to the sensitivities of neglected ethnic groups. To be blunt, it has become more and more obvious to any serious student of world literature that Europe can no longer claim (if indeed it could ever legitimately so claim—but that's another story!) to be the sole fountainhead of great literature. It is by no stretch of the imagination an act of charity on the part of Western academic institutions to recognize the outstanding achievements of such writers as Chinua Achebe, Wole Soyinka or Gabriel Garcia Marquez, to name three conspicuous examples. Even the Nobel prize committee (a major instrumentality of canonization in our time) is beginning to close the gap between ideology and reality in the domain of international recognition. So it is important that we acknowledge that the current call for a drastic revision of the traditional Great Books curricula to reflect a non-Eurocentric perspective is not, at bottom, a call for a trendy allegiance to "political correctness" that might somehow lead to a cheapening of the canon, but quite simply a belated demand for an unbiased, culturally open perusal of the best that contemporary literature has to offer. The idea that the inclusion of, say, a Soyinka play in a comparative survey of drama is merely a sop to political pressure is, to put it mildly, nothing short of scandalous. Fortunately, most major comparative literature departments, including that at Cornell where I currently teach, have gone a long way toward expanding the canon of their Great Books courses to install works by leading non-European writers.

If comparative literature appears prima facie vulnerable to the charge of a narrow Eurocentrism, where does the study of Greek and Roman literature stand in relation to the issue of global representation? The question may at first sight seem woefully irrelevant. Are not the classics, by philological convention, limited to a particular area and historical time span, and is not the modern academic field akin to an "area study" in which various subdisciplines are brought to bear on a distinctly bounded geographical and cultural-historical period? The rhetorical question does not imply a straightforward and uncomplicated answer. It is by no means clear, for instance, that classical literature is, in some quintessential sense, *European*. It is certainly undeniable that European scholars have not only passionately admired ancient Greek culture but have gone a long way toward appropriating it wholesale as regards the point of origin; the veritable "aetion" of their own evolutionary myth. The concept of Western culture, however, as such pioneering works as Edward Said's *Orientalism*[3] and Martin Bernal's *Black Athena*[4] have recently underscored, is a relatively recent historical construct. Western (occidental) culture is, of course, necessarily defined in an epistemologically polar relation to an Eastern (oriental) conceptual entity that is, to say the least, slippery, amorphous, and riddled with ludicrous stereotypes. The myth of a Western culture (I use the word *myth* in its value-neutral, anthropological sense) that originates in ancient Greece is basically, as we have come around to admitting more openly, a European invention. (The analogy with the invention of "Africa" has become evident from the seminal work on the subject by V.Y. Mudimbé.[5] In its need for a prestigious myth of origin as a necessary ingredient in its own self-definition, the European academy, led by a vanguard of classical philologists, proceeded to invent Greece—a Greece that invented everything Europe considered superior in its own civilization—including, of course, the mind itself, as reflected famously in the title of Bruno Snell's influential twentieth-century book, *The Discovery of the Mind (Die Entdeckung des Geistes)*.[6] German philologists of the post-Enlightenment and early Romantic periods, as Martin Bernal has brilliantly documented in volume one of *Black Athena*, fabricated a Greece that, like Athena emerging fully formed from the head of Zeus, came to be seen as supremely endowed and independent at the moment of its miraculous appearance. "Hellenomania" aside, the idea of Greece as the inventor of such hoary fields of inquiry as philosophy or such venerable arts as sculpture and architecture is, as we are increasingly aware, a patent distortion and, interestingly enough, one foreign to the thinking of the ancient Greeks themselves, who openly acknowledged their profound debt to older civilizations, such as that of Egypt. In short, Europe's quest for its own identity induced it to construct a myth of Greece that was congruent with its emerging self-image and lent prestige to its presumptive origins.[7]

Once the Greeks ceased to be regarded as *other* and were redefined as *self*—albeit a childhood self—those aspects of ancient Greek culture (including its literary products) that were deemed most alien to so-called Western culture had to be either downplayed or reinterpreted in ways that made them more readily assimilable. Those of us who are routinely charged with teaching the Greek and Roman classics in translation to the nonspecialist undergraduate are only too familiar with the pedagogic impulse to stress sameness rather than difference in making the texts accessible to our audience. We understandably strive to portray an Achilles or an Odysseus as an archtetype of Western man, and in so doing we often find ourselves erasing, ignoring, or explaining away features of those exemplary heroes' behavior we regard as incongruous with civilized norms. It is all the more important, therefore, that we periodically remind ourselves of just how different and alien the ancient Greeks actually were. I shall always fondly remember a casual remark of the distinguished classicist Sir Kenneth Dover—a remark that he uttered from the sidelines during the impassioned debate at Stanford University on the issue of the content of a required set of courses on Western Culture, as it was then still called. After listening to repeated references by speaker after speaker to a Western canon that claimed the ancient Greeks as its founding fathers, Dover was heard to remark quite dispassionately words to the effect, "I have never really thought of the Greeks as Western anyway." For a good many within earshot, the offhand remark about the non-Western character of Greek culture had shock value, coming, as it did, from one of the most acclaimed contemporary classical scholars—one with impeccable credentials for a claim to intimate knowledge of ancient Greek society. Dover's shrewd, though unorthodox, observation forces us to confront our most entrenched assumptions about the constitution of our literary canons, our preconceived notions concerning West and East, and between cultural self and other.

It would be an intriguing exercise to reconceptualize Greek and Roman literature as non-European in certain fundamental respects; and to reread Hesiod, Homer, and Aeschylus in this light. In my experience in teaching Hesiod's *Theogony*, for instance, I came to the by no means original realization that Hittite, as well as more remote, ancient Near Eastern, motif parallels for the myth of divine succession provided a valid context for interpreting the violent, intergenerational conflicts between gods of the Greek pantheon. My further explorations of recurrent motifs in mythical narratives across cultures (on which there is a large accumulation of scholarly literature from diverse disciplines) soon brought home to me how shallow is the surprisingly widespread notion that Greek myths are somehow superior, sui generis, and essentially incomparable. In the case of the Hesiodic narrative, it is only through systematic comparative analysis, in fact, that we can arrive at a plausible account of the strangeness of some of the major episodes (e.g., the castration of Uranos). Our unrepressed, initial experience of "strangeness" is the reaction that Dover was recuperating from in his provocative remark quoted above. Paradoxically, we recoup a different sense of familiarity with Hesiod's story when we begin to grasp structural similarities (in the role of the sky-god) between the Hittite and archaic Greek cosmogonic accounts. We are drawn, in short, to revise our initial impression of strangeness at the point where we discover the recurrent motifs that Hesiod's text shares with other non-European mythographic traditions.

A word of personal testament is appropriate here. When I was asked in the mid-1960s to teach a general undergraduate course in Greek mythology at Stanford University, I immediately changed the title of the course to Comparative Mythology and proceeded to juxtapose and analyze, with the collaboration of the students, examples of mythical narrative patterns from a wide variety of cultural traditions. This mode of cross-cultural comparison of motifs depended, in large part, on a typology that was, at best, conveniently elastic. The course approached the *Homeric Hymn to Hermes*, for instance, by a circuitous route that led us to narrative traditions as remote from each other as the Dahomean, Ashanti, and Native American; and in these we found the trickster variously (and respectively) named Legba, Anansi, and Coyote. In short, by converting a standard course on Greek mythology into one on comparative mythology, we were able to make far better sense of the many opaque motifs in the Greek narratives. At the same time, we were continually on our guard against the trap of treating non-Western texts merely as a detour on our way to a deeper comprehension of the Western literary monuments. The preservation of a nonhierarchical approach to the comparative study of traditional narrative poses the most serious challenge to the multiculturalist agenda.

I have appended this report of personal engagement with minor curricular reform to the insightful comment of Kenneth Dover in order to underscore a larger point (or rather two related points) about Eurocentricity and the classics. The first is that by recategorizing classical literature as *other,* we are already taking a small but significant conceptual move away from the Eurocentricity and the "borrowed ancestors" referred to above in Derek Walcott's trenchant poem. Whether or not we are Americans of African descent, we certainly do not need to annex an archaic Greek ancestry in order first to defamiliarize, then eventually to refamiliarize, aspects of Homeric epic or Greek tragic drama. The second point is that, in attempting to conceptualize the *other,* we are inevitably drawn into illuminating, though theoretically hazardous, cross-cultural comparison. The net effect of this double strategy is to call into question the pernicious habit, to which we too often fall prey, of studying a particular cultural tradition or set of traits in isolation.

In regard to the critique of a narrow, isolationist approach, I cannot resist introducing yet another personal anecdote by way of illustration. One of my more vivid memories of the turbulent 1960s is of running into a West Indian friend one day on the U.C. campus at Berkeley (where I was a graduate student) and hearing him greet me with obvious relish in the following manner: " Well, hello Gregson! How are things going in Greco-Roman ethnic studies?" At a time when ethnic studies programs were coming into being and, simultaneously, becoming the target of negative criticism, my friend's quip cleverly exposed the ingrained cultural chauvinism that often insidiously invades older disciplines such as classics, no less than emergent ones. Consider, for example, the blithe assumption of a unilinear evolution that underlies the term *antiquity,* or, as the German philologists would say, *Altertum.* Whose antiquity, we are entitled to ask, are we referring to? By renaming a certain isolated and fundamentally ethnocentric approach to classical studies as "Greco-Roman ethnic studies," my friend went straight to the heart of a matter I have been elaborating in various ways under the aegis of the construction of cultural identity. His terse formulation of the issue carried a special resonance for a budding West Indian classicist with comparatist aspirations who grew up in the intercultural arena of a postcolonial society.

I have been contending that Eurocentricity is, at a deep level, detrimental to the scientific study of both classics and comparative literature. To clinch the point in regard to classical literature, I would now like to reinvoke the well-known controversies surrounding the oral nature of Homeric epic poetry. I do not have the space to retell the intriguing story of how the classicist, Milman Parry, and his collaborator and follower, A.B. Lord, revolutionized the study of Homeric verse by demonstrating its significant affinities with oral composition.[8] Parry and Lord, it is worth remembering, did not confine their pioneering research to the internal evidence provided by the texts of the *Iliad* and *Odyssey.* What gave their thesis its enormous explanatory power was, above all, their extensive comparative study of oral epic versemaking. As is well known to students of Homer, Lord continued to build on Parry's theoretical insights by erecting a formidable edifice of empirical evidence for the widespread use of metrical formulas on the part of living bards working within the Serbo-Croatian epic tradition. No more spectacular vindication of the comparative avenue to literary study can be imagined than the illumination that the work of Parry and Lord shed on central aspects of the age-old Homeric Problem (e.g., the question of how a supposedly illiterate bard could have composed epic poems on the scale of those in the Homeric corpus). Their research revealed the workings of the oral formulaic technique, whereby a bard is able to compose extemporaneously by utilizing a repertoire of fixed repeated phrases (formulas) that conform to convenient metrical units. The key to their dramatic success in establishing Homer's affiliations (whether vital or vestigial is still a matter of moderately heated dispute) with the techniques of oral composition lies, I need hardly stress, in their systematic cross-cultural comparison of contemporary epic performances. Their story may stand as a parable for the intrinsic value of investigating literary forms from a comparative perspective. To be sure, the Parry-Lord thesis has, and always will have, its detractors, and several later revisionists have attempted to disprove the essential orality of the Homeric poems. Nevertheless even the most hardened skeptics would admit that Homeric studies have gained immeasurably in this century from having been exposed to the comparative methods pioneered by the Parry-Lord school of investigation. Adherents of "Greco-Roman ethnic studies" will no doubt continue to proclaim the inferiority of contemporary Serbo-Croatian epic bards to the incomparable Greek Homer. Their judgment on this score is no doubt tenable and widely taken for granted. In pronouncing these verdicts, however, such critics betray their primary interest in erecting cultural hierarchies rather than in understanding the interplay between similarity and difference among variants of a virtually universal narrative genre. The ultimate irony resides in the paradox that, even for those determined to trumpet what they perceive as cultural hierarchies, it is apparent that one cannot logically arrive at a just understanding of what makes the Homeric cultural monuments unique or original without prior comparison of their techniques and thematic organization with those of other exemplars of the genre of heroic narrative. In sum, it is only by widening our horizons to include an examination of what a given culture shares with others that we derive a more sophisticated and accurate assessment of its peculiar inflections.

I have chosen to illustrate my point about the merits of comparative methods with reference to a seminal Greek text. Apart from the mere accident that my own interdisplinary identity bridges classics and comparative literature, there are substantive historical reasons why the status of classics as a discipline may be an appropriate vantage-point from which to reassess and revise the notion of a liberal education. As many readers are aware, the very conception of the humanities is derived, through the mediation of Italian Renaissance thought, from the classical idea of the *studia Humanitatis* as formulated principally in the writings of Cicero. The study of the Greco-Roman intellectual tradition was, for a long stretch of time in post-Renaissance Europe, regarded as the cornerstone of a liberal education, and although the discipline of classical philology now occupies a far less exalted role within the typical humanities curriculum, a vestige of its former status persists in the form of survey courses in the Western cultural tradition in which the foundational Greek and Latin texts are presented in translation. Since the Homeric poems are widely seen as inaugurating the Western canon, I have found it strategically useful to treat the issue of the value of multicultural investigation in reference to their exegetical history.

I have held up the example of the comparative investigation of oral epic poetry as one model for intercultural literary studies. With this model, cultural products of societies that are historically unrelated (and, in the striking case of ancient Greece and contemporary Serbo-Croatian, vastly separated in time) are juxtaposed in order to disclose commonalities as well as differences of technique and form among oral bards operating within a presumptively universal genre. Since the global extensiveness of oral epic traditions has been copiously documented by literary scholars and cultural anthropologists (the work of Isidore Okpewho in regard to African epic is a case in point), the genre provides an exceptionally fertile ground for scrupulous intercultural comparison of both so-called Western and non-Western forms.[9]

Though I have been advocating the usefulness of gross generic frameworks (such as "oral epic") as the basis for global comparisons, I do wish to sound a note of warning with respect to the compatibility of such literary-generic categories. The very notion of genre has come to be regarded as notoriously elusive in recent critical theory and many literary scholars (myself included) have been analysing ways in which poets ancient and modern have articulated generic boundaries as a first move in a larger dialectical strategy that involves the transgression and even the obliteration of such boundaries.[10] Even if we set aside such caveats and assume, for strictly operational reasons, that genres are stable entities at some level of abstraction, we are still faced with the unsettling fact that they tend to be, in practice, nuanced in culture-specific ways. The repertoire of "literary" genres in any given culture is likely to show distinct peculiarities, and we risk becoming overly tendentious in our typological generalizations when we indulge in intercultural analogies. In their classic study of Dahomean narrative, for example, Melville and Frances Herskovits admonish us against the facile assumption that our narrative categories correspond with those of other cultures, despite superficial similarities.[11] If narrative typologies differ from culture to culture, then the theory as well as the practice of transcultural generic analysis is deeply problematic. Such strictures should not, however, deter us from undertaking global comparisons altogether; rather, as the authors of *Dahomean Narrative: A Cross-Cultural Analysis* themselves show, uniqueness is more clearly grasped against the background of broad considerations of universality and its limits (see for instance their penetrating critique of the archetypal theory of myth in the work cited). As Fredric Jameson has phrased it in a remark on the methodological problem posed by cross-cultural comparison:

> Differences can only be established within some larger preestablished identity: if there is nothing in common between two cultural situations, then clearly the establishment of difference is both pointless and given in advance. What this means is that if Identity and Difference are fixed and eternal opposites, we have either a ceaseless alternation, or a set of intolerable choices.[12]

The employment of generic frameworks across cultures, however sophisticated and nuanced, poses, as we have seen, special intrinsic problems;

but so, it must be admitted, do all other universalist avenues to comparative literary studies. So the major challenge we face in extending the traditional canon lies in sustaining the theoretical juggling act that requires us to be attentive to cultural difference while risking exploration of features that cultures appear to share. This Janus-faced attitude to intercultural discourse becomes an absolute imperative for a humanist enterprise of the scope and boldness we are trying to envisage here. Among well-tried alternatives to a gross generic approach are modes of analysis that employ a thematic, as opposed to a formal, principle of organization of culturally disparate material. Whether we choose to experiment with fundamental themes or genres, however, we need to discriminate carefully between comparative methods that are synchronic (and hence basically achronological) and ones that are diachronic (and hence oriented toward questions of historical development and interconnection). Themes no less than genres provide opportunities (as well as perils that should not be downplayed) for horizontal juxtaposition of texts that ignore time-periods and historical context (e.g., a thematic framework might justify the study of the Babylonian epic of Gilgamesh alongside, say, the Hebrew narrative of David and Jonathan, or a Polynesian creation myth alongside an ancient Egyptian cosmogony). On the other hand, it is equally important that we find ways of balancing such synchronic paths of exploration with approaches foregrounding cultures that have interacted in the historical continuum. It is this latter byway of intercultural study that I broached at the very beginning of my talk and I would now like to return to sketch some of its advantages by way of approximating a conclusion.

In the sphere of diachronic study of cultural interrelationships, an exciting and challenging area of research and teaching is one that has acquired the overarching label of Postcolonial Studies. Here again I naturally draw upon my personal involvement in francophone Caribbean literary studies, in which European colonization of non-Western societies has provided a framing historical experience that invites scholarly investigation into the strategies that cultures use to define self and other. There has emerged in the latter half of this century an impressive new canon of Third World writers (to use a possibly moribund expression) from excolonial polities whose works often thematize problems of cultural identity in a context of conflict between Western and non-Western. I have already cited the example of Derek Walcott's short lyric poem, "Homecoming: Anse La Raye" to illustrate the plight of the aspiring "Afro-Greek." Walcott has also given us, in his 1990 magnum opus, *Omeros*,[13] a vast narrative canvas that positively revels in the exploration of such elusive issues as cultural analogy and differentiation, the specification of what is essentially human, the epistemological necessity of defining the self in relation to an other, and the everpresent, postmodern question of canonicity. And within my own specialty of francophone Caribbean poetics, I have found the oeuvre

of Aimé Césaire to be a representative focal point for the critical examination of intercultural thematics, such as cultural hegemony and resistance
to assimilation.[14] It is perhaps the inevitable outcome of our assigning priority to the postcolonial matrix of literary production that works like Césaire's masterpiece, *Cahier d'un retour au pays natal* (rendered in an excellent recent translation by Eshleman and Smith as *Notebook of a
Return to the Native Land*) should move from the periphery to the center of our revised undergraduate syllabuses in world literature courses.[15]
I confess to a certain feeling of vindication at the prospect that other
postcolonial literary texts, such as Jean Rhys's *Wide Sargasso Sea*
(which some of my generation began to include in our literature courses
in the mid-1960s) have now achieved the status of modern classic in a
humanities literary curriculum that is increasingly amenable to foregrounding intercultural issues (and here of course I fold in feminist
perspectives on canonic Western texts). One of the main advantages of
postcolonial literary studies is that it does not entail the wholesale dis-
placement or replacement of older canons, but rather it raises issues
(some new, some perennial) that can be tackled only by intertextual comparison between Western and non-Western norms and values. We are
thus obliged, if we take the overt intertextual clues seriously, to read
Rhys's *Wide Sargasso Sea* in dialogic relation to *Jane Eyre* (the plot of
the former uses the latter as its point of departure); or, to take another
example, we are made to read Césaire's play, *A Tempest,* in conjunction
with Shakespeare's *The Tempest* (whose underlying themes and dramatis
personae it explicitly interrogates and transforms).

In conclusion I want to suggest that the intercultural discourse I would
place at the very center of a reshaped humanities curriculum cannot hope
to avoid superficiality unless it is firmly grounded in the insights and intellectual tools of cultural anthropology. Why, the reader may well ask, do
I propose to privilege a particular discipline (viz., anthropology) at the expense of a panoply of other candidates in the academic spectrum? The
repositioning of cultural anthropology within the ideal scheme I am es-
pousing is far from arbitrary; indeed, it follows logically from commitment to multiculturalism of the global variety. Anthropology is precisely
the discipline that has made the concept of culture and the description of
difference central to its theoretical and empirical agenda. Seminal ideas
such as cultural relativism (the move to dethrone cultural hierarchies that
I first encountered in my undergraduate experience, via Ruth Benedict's
classic and elegant exposition in *Patterns of Culture*[16]) will necessarily
come to the fore in an interdisciplinary critical discourse that focuses on
our unexamined assumptions about notions like *civilized* and *primitive*. It
goes without saying that the project of realignment I am helping to promote would be gravely handicapped if it did not rely on collaboration between disciplines, and a common denominator of such collaboration will

surely be the contribution of a discipline that has concerned itself with the central problem of cultural sameness/difference.

In terms of my own double vantage-point in literary studies, I am content to observe that there appears to be a convergence in progress between the critical discourses of literary and ethnographical studies. In the not too distant past we literary scholars regularly turned to anthropology for theoretical guidance in understanding (for example) the intersection of literature and ritual. Thus, in coming to terms with the widespread phenomenon of ritual possession, I have myself have come to rely in the classroom on ethnographic accounts of ecstatic religions, such as Haitian vodun cults, in order to make sense of a certain dimension of Euripides' play, *The Bacchae*. Incidentally, Wole Soyinka's brilliant adaptation of *The Bacchae* under the title, *The Bacchae of Euripides: A Communion Rite* constitutes an artistic contribution to the discursive intersection of literature and ethnology.[17] Recent research on the part of classicists into the construction of sexuality in ancient Greece (I refer to the exemplary work of the late Jack Winkler, for instance) has clearly profited from anthropological insights and investigative premises.[18] What we are now beginning to witness in the convergence of which I spoke can perhaps better be characterized as a mutuality of influence. As more and more literary scholars are gravitating toward "cultural studies," there is a simultaneous awareness among many cultural anthropologists of the similarities between ethnographic description and fictional narrative, and leading theoreticians in the field, such as Clifford Geertz, have been pointing out the usefulness of literary theory (especially narratology) as applied to the stories that anthropologists construct in order to give coherence to the conceptions of the *other*.[19] This convergence in regard to the theoretical preoccupations of two important disciplines promises to blur even further the lines that artificially compartmentalize the traditional fields of study in the humanities. Are we being unduly optimistic if we reach the conclusion that we may be on the verge of inaugurating an era in which the configuration of disciplines in our academic institutions will be fundamentally transformed?

NOTES

1. Derek Walcott, *The Gulf: Poems* (New York: Farrar, Straus, Giroux, 1970).
2. James Clifford, *The Predicament of Culture: Twentieth-Century Ethnography, Literature and Art* (Cambridge, Mass.: Harvard University Press, 1988).
3. Edward Said, *Orientalism* (New York: Pantheon Books, 1978).
4. Martin Bernal, *Black Athena: The Afroasiatic Roots of Classical Civilization*, vol. 1 (New Brunswick, N.J.: Rutgers University Press, 1987).
5. V. Y. Mudimbé, *The Invention of Africa: Gnosis, Philosophy, and the Order of Knowledge* (Bloomington: Indiana University Press, 1988).

6. Bruno Snell, *The Discovery of the Mind: The Greek Origins of European Thought,* trans. Thomas G. Rosenmeyer (Cambridge, Mass.: Harvard University Press, 1953).

7. Bernal, *Black Athena.*

8. Albert B. Lord, *The Singer of Tales* (Cambridge Mass.: Harvard University Press, 1960).

9. Isidore Okpewho, *The Epic in Africa: Toward a Poetics of the Oral Performance* (New York: Columbia University Press, 1979).

10. Gregson Davis, *Polyhymnia: The Rhetoric of Horatian Lyric Discourse* (Berkeley and Los Angeles: University of California Press, 1991).

11. Melville J. Herskovits and Frances S. Herskovits, *Dahomean Narrative: A Cross-Cultural Analysis* (Evanston, Ill.: Northwestern University Press, 1958).

12. Fredric Jameson, "A Brief Response" in *Social Text* (Fall, 1987).

13. Derek Walcott, *Omeros* (New York: Farrar, Straus, Giroux, 1990).

14. Gregson Davis, *Non-Vicious Circle: Twenty Poems of Aimé Césaire* (Stanford, Calif.: Stanford University Press, 1984).

15. Aimé Césaire, *The Collected Poetry,* trans. Clayton Eshleman and Annette Smith (Berkeley and Los Angeles: University of California, 1983).

16. Ruth Benedict, *Patterns of Culture* (Boston: Houghton Mifflin, 1934).

17. Wole Soyinka, *The Bacchae of Euripides: A Communion Rite* (London: Methuen, 1973).

18. David Halperin, John Winkler, and Froma Zeitlin, eds., *Before Sexuality: The Construction of Erotic Experience in the Ancient Greek World* (Princeton, N.J.: Princeton University Press, 1990).

19. Clifford Geertz, *Local Knowledge: Further Essays in Interpretive Anthropology* (New York: Basic Books, 1983).

2

Triumphalism, Tarzan, and Other Influences: Teaching About Africa in the 1990s

Joel Samoff

The meanings are clear. The assertions are aggressive, arrogant, and unqualified. After a brief stint as a beacon of developmental progress, Africa is once again portrayed as the archetype of backwardness, decay, and dissolution. In this final decade of the twentieth century, that portrayal is the one our students are most likely to encounter and with which we and they together must grapple.

"Colonialism's Back—and Not a Moment Too Soon," screamed the headline in the Sunday *New York Times Magazine*.[1] "Let's face it: Some countries are just not fit to govern themselves," the subtitle explained. Hailing the revival of colonialism, the author defends external intervention and direction as not only practical but also morally correct: "The civilized world has a mission to go out to these separate places and govern," he writes.[2] The article did, also, refer to the disarray in eastern Europe, but it stressed, "it is obvious that Africa, where normal government is breaking down in a score or more states, is the most likely theater for such action." In case the message was still not clear, an accompanying graphic portrayed a large, white hand hovering powerfully (helpfully? menacingly?) over disembodied, darker-colored forearms rising from a desolate and feature-less terrain.

This self-congratulatory and condescending certainty finds frequent expression in the 1990s. We've won, George Bush, the president of the United States, regularly reminded his audiences during the national elec-toral campaign of 1992. Not only have we won, he insisted, but we are the standard against which others measure themselves. More because they could not claim direct responsibility for the victory than because they doubted that it had occurred, his major political opponents sought to asso-ciate themselves with this triumphalism, not challenge it.

The *we*, of course, referred to "true Americans"; that is, what the politicians like to describe as the "patriotic, God-fearing, loyal citizens of this country." Mostly very white or at least thoroughly assimilated, this *we* is counterposed to a poorer and generally darker-skinned *other,* some of whom live next door. In the early 1990s, perhaps the most visible of the *other* lived in Europe, the pitiable but not unsympathetic victims of Communist rule. But the most extreme *other*—the measure of the unchanging primitive, the disease, the disarray, the disorder, the decay to be avoided— were African. It was there that one found evidence of decivilization and regression toward barbarity.[3] That *other* is not white.[4]

In its early stages this triumphalism is seemingly boundless. The precipitous dissolution of Communist rule is interpreted as the inevitable victory of the United States over the Soviet Union, capitalism over socialism, the market over planning, good over evil. Even the 1992 Olympic Games, where the athletes of the former Soviet Union actually did quite well, was generally depicted in the United States as a contest between the United States and the rest of the world. "Our way" prevailed over theirs, we are reminded, because it is inherently better. Even more: everything that can be linked to socialism, however tenuous the link, is clearly flawed, precisely because of that link.

It is in this setting that U.S. undergraduates study Africa at the end of this century. What they study, and how they study it, is influenced much more by what is happening in the world—or rather, by how global events come to be generally interpreted and understood—than by a deepening knowledge of Africa or improved theories and methods in the social sciences. Arrogant triumphalism is of course not the only source of contemporary wisdom; it is useful, therefore, to review briefly the experiences in teaching about African politics.[5] For that, it is helpful to review the transitions in addressing a concern central to the social sciences: *Who governs?*

First, though, a comment on this chapter. I am concerned here with teaching about Africa in the social sciences in undergraduate settings, and I shall draw heavily on experiences in the fields in which I have been most directly involved: political science and education. There are grounds here for both excitement and dismay. The challenge is, of course, enormous, since most students at U.S. universities know little about Africa; or rather, most—while having strongly held opinions—have neither very conscious nor very visible understandings of Africa. Although on the first day of an introductory course on Africa most students will assert they "know nothing" about Africa, in fact, terms like *tribe* and *chief* and stories about Zulu warriors will make perfect sense. I want, therefore, to address that challenge, especially by focusing on the context for (and influences on) teaching about Africa.

Most of us who teach about Africa, I believe, are not primarily concerned with transmitting information. Rather, we try to organize our courses to require students to grapple with information. We know that our students will encounter a good deal of confusion and misinformation about Africa, and we want to help them become competent consumers of both specialist and popular sources. We also know that most of the writing about Africa that they will see is by non-Africans who are for the most part white and male. We know that much of the information-base on which our students will draw is tinged with racism and the other legacies of colonial rule or is steeped in the prejudices of the present. This knowledge, and perhaps our sense of pedagogy, leads us to insist that our students address critically what is presented to them as fact. We urge them to read skeptically; to question authority. As instructors, we must do no less. It is to that task that this chapter is addressed. Its fundamental subject is not teaching but learning.

I shall not be primarily concerned here with pedagogy and instructional methods. My sense is that, in general, Africanist academics tend to be somewhat more innovative and creative in their classes than most of their colleagues. They are more likely to draw on the findings and insights of disciplines other than their own; to incorporate novels, films, life-histories, and other sources whose origins lie outside the social sciences, and to emphasize student discussion and classroom interaction. I hope my comments here will encourage, not discourage, my colleagues, but I shall leave the how-to-do-it issues for another discussion.

I should also note here three apparent points of departure from many of my colleagues. First, I consider students' lack of accurate systematic information about Africa, and their internalization of misunderstandings and confusions, to be a challenge and an opportunity, not a major problem. Second, I take the integration of knowledge to be primarily the responsibility of students, not instructors. Stated simply, I do not think it is possible for instructors to organize a course that successfully integrates all that we try to address—diverse and conflicting information, contradictory sources, varied national and subnational experiences, multiple themes, different and perhaps incompatible perspectives, alternative emphases, and more—and still effectively meet the needs of students with their own expectations, priorities, and learning styles. Hence, rather than try to prepare a thoroughly and consistently integrated package, I seek instead to develop a *coherent approach* that emphasises inclusiveness and diversity and that challenges students to integrate what they hear and do; to take charge of their learning more generally.

Third, I am convinced that the fluctuations in student interest in Africa are only marginally a function of the strategies and approaches of teachers about Africa. Clearly, an active program of courses and other campus activities may attract a few additional students, just as the departure of prominent faculty may lead students to enroll elsewhere. The creation or elimination of an African studies program will of course also affect enrollment. But over the longer term, what matters most in this regard is what happens outside the university, not within it. When the liberation struggle in South Africa became more visible, registration for all sorts of

Africa courses increased. There may even be a reasonably direct correlation between the percentage of space and time in print and televised news allocated to Africa and enrollment in social science (and other?) courses on Africa.

Since undergraduate courses on Africa generally pay limited attention to research and research methods, I shall not address them extensively here. At the same time, it is clear that we need to explore critically the links among research, methods, and instruction. If we and our students are to be effectively critical, we must constantly examine how we know what we know. We must be especially skeptical about what seems most sure. Consequently, we must address approaches, what underlies them, and what motivates them.

Teaching is a complex process with many faces and dimensions. In part, it is an architectural process, concerned with structure, order, and materials. It is also a managerial process, with responsibility for simultaneous, multiple, overlapping, and often at least partly incompatible activities. At times its mode is imagination, stepping outside *what is* to understand it better. Done well, its manner is interactive, with shared and shifting initiatives and responsibilities. Its outcome is never entirely predictable, since if successful it empowers learners to share control over goals and directions. For these reasons, a chapter on teaching about Africa must meander a bit. As in the classroom, there will be chance encounters to follow up, even though they lead us at a tangent from the main line of the discussion. And, again as in the classroom, it will seem fruitful periodically to retrace our steps, to return in more detail to a point introduced earlier. That is not to suggest that there is no order here, for there certainly is; rather it is to note at the outset that I have favored function over form, content over organization.

I begin, then, with a retrospective overview of teaching African politics. The transitions there, I believe, tell us a good deal about how social scientists have addressed Africa, and perhaps a bit about why. Following that review I shall comment on the knowledge base for teaching about Africa and on transcending its limits. I shall conclude by highlighting several major challenges we face.

TEACHING AFRICAN POLITICS:
A RETROSPECTIVE OVERVIEW

The exploration of who rules in Africa has generally fallen within the responsibilities of the department of political science or government. The most common strategy has been to locate the African politics course among other courses on comparative politics. The underlying orientation in that compartmentalization is shared by many of the other social sciences: it is of interest, and perhaps instructive, to compare patterns of government (or social structure or the organization of production) in different countries. The corollary presumption is that Africa is a subset of that subset of the study of politics. African politics are fundamentally different in some important way from politics elsewhere; and at the same time they are sufficiently diverse to permit comparison of the different patterns across the African continent.

Academics are forever debating how they organize themselves and their departments. That should not be surprising, since jobs, careers, and reputations are all potentially at stake. It is not uncommon for there to be a good deal of bloodshed when political scientists try to reach agreement, or at least a generally accepted decision, on how their particular knowledge-domain is to be structured. Although the agreed division is always defended in rational terms, in practice what emerges is often largely a compromise among competing interests. So, indeed, for comparative politics. In many departments of government or political science (that terminology is itself regularly contested), comparative politics turns out to mean those faculty who study other countries. (Studying the interactions among other countries—international relations—is generally allocated its own compartment.) Although comparativists may claim to have a common approach or methodology, or aspire to define one, in practice what is common is their interest in places, people, and events outside the United States. The situation is similar in comparative education. There, too, notwithstanding the professional associations and journals, the fundamental and enduring commonality is the foreign focus. Within comparative politics, the most common division has been simultaneously ideological and pragmatic. The usual approach is to categorize countries as democratic or socialist or developing. Those can be, and usually are, of course, overlapping and nonexclusive categories. In this usage, *democratic* really refers to the countries of the North Atlantic (and did so even when Portugal and Spain were certainly not democratic) and Japan; *socialist* refers to the (former) Soviet Union, its allies in eastern Europe, and China; and *developing* refers essentially to the countries of the southern hemisphere. This categorization roughly corresponds to the division of the globe into the First, Second, and Third Worlds. Africa has always been among the developing countries.

The contextual point here is an important one. For the most part, African politics have been treated as a special case, or at best a set of special cases, that warranted a unique location in the study of who rules and how. Almost never do African countries appear as cases in point in courses on the legislative process, or the judicial system, or elections, or public opinion, or interest groups, or local government. Here is a clear consequence of Africa's role as the *other*. It is not easily integrated into the constructs we use to analyze ourselves. And as might seem appropriate in a setting where many people regard Africa as a country rather than a continent, instructors in African politics courses are expected to include in their teaching nearly all (but not quite all) of the continent.

Here it is important to note this is *not quite all,* for it bears on the sort of external influences to which I shall return in more detail later. In many universities, Africa was, and is, understood to mean sub-Saharan Africa, or more accurately, Africa except for those countries generally considered North African. In this, universities followed the pattern of the U.S. Department of State, which assigns North Africa to the Middle East. The organizational scheme that seemed to make sense to those charged with protecting U.S. geopolitical interests was also assumed to make sense for studying Africa on the campus. That orientation is annually reinforced by the World Bank, which in its publications on Africa and its regular Development Reports specifies such a scheme. For example:

> Most of the discussion and all of the statistics about Africa in this study refer to just thirty-nine countries south of the Sahara, *for which the terms Africa and Sub-Saharan Africa are used interchangeably.*[6]

For the most part, significant objections to that scheme have been infrequent, spasmodic, and generally muted. Some scholars do see this usage as a systematic effort to de-Africanize the older societies of northern Africa, along with their recognized achievements in art, architecture, education, language, productive activities, trade, and international relations. Whatever the motives, rarely are students offered a systematic explanation for why Africa's own sense of itself—the membership of the Organization of African Unity—should not guide instruction in U.S. universities.

Surveys of African Politics Courses

We get a glimpse at what happens in courses on Africa in two surveys undertaken by Mark DeLancey and his colleagues.[7] These teams surveyed instructors of courses on African politics, first in 1978 and again in 1987, asking them what they did and why. Several of their findings stand out. On the one hand, there were striking similarities. Nearly all of the surveyed instructors had multiple purposes in organizing their courses. Beyond developing a basic overview of African politics, the instructors also sought to dispel myths about Africa, increase knowledge of Africa more generally, develop cultural awareness, expose students to alternative theories and methods, and develop research and analytic skills. Three-quarters of the instructors surveyed reported extensive use of novels and films. Nearly all reported relying heavily on student discussion. External events influenced the contents of these courses in two ways. First, the increased political activity in South Africa during the 1980s corresponded with increasing

attention to South Africa in these courses. That, in turn, may have been associated with the increased interest in Africa and increased enrollment that
the surveyed instructors reported. Second, the general orientation of U.S.
politics and interests seems to have influenced both how instructors organized their courses and where they conducted their own research. Most of
these courses focused on sub-Saharan Africa. And these instructors concentrated their research in the English-speaking countries that DeLancey
and his colleagues characterized as generally pro-West or capitalist in their
policies.

There was striking diversity in the findings. There was, for example,
relatively little agreement on the books to be used. In the 1987 survey, no
one book was assigned as a text in more than 12 percent of the classes. For
a single basic course on African politics, forty-two professors assigned
181 different texts. A request to list the two or three most important books
on African politics revealed a comparable diversity. One book was listed
by 20 percent of those surveyed in both 1978 and 1987, but no other book
appeared on more than 12 percent of the lists in 1987.

From the Exotic to the Pitiable

The glimpse provided by these surveys begs for a somewhat fuller discussion of teaching African politics. I shall address especially what seem to
me to have been the most important changes over time, with particular attention to the interplay between events outside the classroom—both within
and outside academia—and what goes on inside it. To focus our attention,
I shall limit myself to selected themes. Many points in this discussion warrant extended attention: that would require a book, not a chapter.

The depiction of Africa and the general approach to studying its politics in U.S. undergraduate classes have changed with the times. The earliest efforts, through the 1950s and early 1960s, were guided by the comparative perspective developed largely by anthropologists. Whether
formally trained or experientially educated or simply self-designated, they
provided most of the basic source information. Africa was exotic but
nonetheless orderly. One could usefully compare societies with complex
structures of authority with other societies that seemed to have no central
officials at all. That comparison could then be integrated into explanations
for African behavior during and after European rule.

Anthropology provided the approach as well as the data. Having assumed responsibility for the primitive in their split from sociology in the
nineteenth century, anthropologists offered a well developed methodology
that emphasized extended and close observation, attention to detail, and
accurate recording of ostensibly unimportant events. To develop an adequate understanding of what was observed required a close familiarity
with people and their lives, including a mastery of their language and often

participation in their social events and rituals. Field-workers of this sort were necessarily holists. Comprehending patterns of social interaction required a basic knowledge of the local history, economy, politics, and cultural expression.[8]

During the era of European rule, anthropology and sociology (understood broadly) provided much of the academic terminology and legitimacy for the distinction between *we* of Europe and the *them* of Africa. (The grammatic shift from subjective to objective case is not accidental.) As referring to the primitive and the backward became politically offensive or simply unfashionable, new ways of specifying the distance between the modern *we* and the backward *them* became prominent. Perhaps most visible among the academics were the dichotomies introduced by Parsons and their offspring: affectivity vs. affective neutrality, self-orientation vs. collective orientation, particularism vs. universalism, ascription vs. achievement, diffuseness vs. specificity. African societies need no longer be termed primitive or backward. Instead, they were particularistic, ascriptive, diffuse, and so on. The *we/them* differentiation also appeared in the everyday language of describing Africa: empire/state/nation vs. tribe; emperor/king vs. chief; prince/lord/duke/viceroy/marquis/knight vs. headman; priest/minister/bishop/archbishop/pope vs. juju man/ritual priest/witch doctor/shaman; doctor vs. witch doctor; chemist/pharmacist vs. medicine man; clothing vs. dress/costume; hut vs. house; and more. From language that had justified the colonial enterprise (modern vs. primitive) we had progressed to language that entrenched the exotic, though rather more subtly.

Note here that in this era, African politics highlighted what were described by the European colonial powers as two divergent orientations toward the primitive: assimilation/direct rule/France and trusteeship/indirect rule/England. For the former, the Enlightenment provided the sense that industrialization, westernization, and modernization marked progress. The backwardness of Africa was a condition to be overcome. For the latter, the guiding image was that of the noble savage corrupted by contact with modern society. Both views, however, maintained the *we/them* dichotomy. Both assumed a great distance between the *we* and the *them*. In practice, colonial policies differed far less than their philosophies of justification seemed to suggest.

In the energy, excitement, and optimism of the decolonization of Africa, exotic Africa became *emergent Africa*. With the fetters of European rule eliminated, the potential seemed unlimited. The legacy of backwardness did remain, of course. It was now regarded as tradition, which was both noble and anachronistic. Though occasionally delayed and dismayed by the practices of the past, the peoples of Africa could now employ their imagination, creativity, and energies to construct new societies. Most students of Africa questioned neither the emergence nor its general direction. And in the euphoria of that era, most foresaw a relatively rapid narrowing of the *we/them* gap.

As the behavioral revolution swept the social sciences, emergent Africa became *modernizing Africa.* The presumed tension between tradition and modernity now warranted primary attention. Notwithstanding furious debates about stages, paths, and alternatives, the general sense was that everyone understood what being modern meant. For most, though of course not all, becoming modern meant becoming more like the societies of the North Atlantic, especially the United States.[9]

For the dominant perspective in the social sciences, particularism was backward, both in African societies and in research methodology. The language of functionalism offered universal terms like *rulemaking* and *interest aggregation.* Since these functions had to be performed in every society, they could become the tools for comparative analysis. It was less important for scholars to know a particular society well than to understand these constructs, presumed to be universal. Although many of the professors who managed this transition in the study of Africa had secured their own positions as African area studies expanded rapidly, they were transforming the instructional and research agendas in ways that were eventually to undermine much of the case for area studies. The rationale for offering courses and degrees on Africa, after all, went beyond the assertion of Africa's uniqueness to insist on the importance of a multi-disciplinary holism. But behavioral social science emphasized the universality of approach and method, not the specificity of time, space, and society.

It is important to note here that students of Africa as a group have never quite digested the clarion call for quantification that has been central to the behavioral revolution. Some scholars, of course, have relied heavily on evidence in quantitative form. But Africanists on the whole have recognized that nearly always the available quantitative data are not up to the analytic tasks for which they are commonly used. The saga of the Nigerian census is a clear case in point. The count taken in 1962 was politically unacceptable, since it would have deprived the north of its majority of parliamentary seats. A recount in 1963 reported a growth in population of nearly 25 percent, surely impossible. Yet the population figures produced by the 1963 census became the official numbers on which subsequent planning, and international statistical comparisons, relied. The saga was repeated in the 1970s. If the margin of error in the total population may be as large as 10–20 percent, then the margins of error in all data that rely on that number (for example, education spending per capita) are likely to be larger than whatever variation one observes in a particular variable. When that occurs, we cannot tell whether or not a significant change has occurred. Then what? We can ignore the precepts of sound research, announce to readers that the data are flawed, and proceed to ignore the problem and present findings as if the data were not problematic; or we can turn to other sorts of information. Africanist social scientists have followed both strategies, though, I believe, unlike colleagues who study other areas, more the latter than the former. What have not emerged, however, are innovative approaches to seriously incomplete and flawed data, specifically tailored to the African setting.[10]

The critique of modernization that emerged in Latin America had Africanist advocates as well. Especially as it became clearer that the initial postcolonial optimism about rapid modernization was not matched by substantial and visible improvements in the standard of living, modernizing Africa became *dependent Africa*. It did not make sense, the critics argued, to search for the causes for Africa's problems entirely within Africa: that is blaming the victim, finding that the cause of poverty is being poor.

Whatever was happening, it was argued, was largely the result of the interactions between Africa and the rest of the world, and especially of the incorporation of Africa into a global system largely on terms set outside Africa. The underdevelopment of Africa was neither a historic legacy nor an aberration. Rather, it was the foundation for the development of Europe. In this sense, underdevelopment was an ongoing process, not a state of being. For much of Africa, the situation deteriorated daily. The common example was unequal and declining terms of trade. A tractor that could be purchased for, say, one ton of an African export would cost two tons or more a decade later.

Explanations delimit solutions. If the problem was the relationship with Europe, then intensifying that relationship could only make things worse. The appropriate development strategy was not further integration into a global economy dominated by the North Atlantic countries but limiting that integration, expanding inter-African links, and then reshaping the global economy itself. For the modernizationists, all the talk about imperialism and alliances across the southern hemisphere was a distraction from the major business at hand: national development. For the *dependistas*, there was no tension at all. Reforming the international economy, which required combating imperialism, was a necessary element of any development strategy.

The notion of a dependent Africa relied on the assumption that there was more than one path to development, however defined. African states were not simply immature versions of what the states of the North Atlantic had become, destined to follow along the same path, though perhaps somewhat more rapidly. Rapid industrialization in the Soviet Union and Eastern Europe and agricultural transformation and the elimination of famine in China seemed to provide concrete evidence that Africa had an alternative to following the advice proffered by the countries of the North Atlantic and the transnational organizations they dominated. By the late 1970s, Cuban support to the government of Angola seemed to confirm the viability of noncapitalist development strategy under harsh conditions.

Here was a small, island state, long under the thumb, or heel, of the United States, able with Soviet support not only to protect itself against invasion but also to send its troops halfway around the world to stand up to a U.S.–South African alliance.

The disarray of Eastern Europe in the late 1980s, however, was interpreted by most observers to mean that there was only one path after all. The implication was clear, it seemed. The Eastern European economies had failed so badly that their leaders saw no alternative but to privatize, to replace planning with markets. That failure tainted anything even vaguely associated with socialism. To continue to insist on public ownership, or to focus as much attention on redistribution as on production, or to allocate substantial resources to ostensibly nonproductive social services was to perpetuate poverty.

During the same period, the economic situation became much more difficult for most of Africa. Some observers were quick to point to socialist initiatives, in some areas, as principal causes of economic problems; but in fact, the economic distress was widespread. Countries with very different microcircumstances—different patterns of colonial rule and decolonization, different political institutions, different forms of accountability and responsibility, different ideologies, different regional interactions, different development strategies—had very similar macroexperiences. To explain problems that affect nearly all African countries by things African is to claim that at the root is something uniquely African. If not the climate,[11] then it must be the genes.[12]

This combination was devastating. Alternative development strategies that once appeared promising lost credibility. Economic distress became financial crisis that could only be managed, it seemed, by additional foreign aid. Increased reliance on external assistance brought with it ever more explicit advice, now formalized as conditions. Securing national aid became more dependent on maintaining good relations with the transnational organizations dominated by the United States, the country whose leaders claimed credit for their global triumphs. Dependent Africa had become *crisis Africa* and then *pitiable Africa*.

An aside. It is tempting to infer from the contemporary crisis that Africa failed to follow the development advice it received, or that development advice was inadequately or incompetently administered. Many African governments, however, followed that advice. While there were, of course, disagreements about timing, phasing, and details, African countries adopted many of the basic development recommendations proffered by one or another of the external agencies on which they relied. There has been at least as much continuity in following that advice as there has been consistency in the advice itself. Both advisers and governments have changed their minds, often dramatically; and both have had little patience with their critics; hence, it is striking how little development, of the sort projected, there has been. This is too complex a story to pursue here, but whatever lack of progress is observed cannot be entirely a function of failures on the African side of that development connection. It is simply not possible that the advice was uniformly good and the implementation always flawed.

Overloaded, Besieged, Undemocratic

It is useful to conclude this overview of teaching African politics by returning once again to the common contemporary rendering of the African state. Since the current debates among the students of African politics are too recent to have been reviewed and discussed extensively, it is useful both to note what is being said and to indicate what seems problematic. There are two important threads here: one emphasizes the state's incapacities; the other focuses on its authoritarian character and nondemocratic origins.

For many commentators, the developmental state in Africa has become the overloaded state or the besieged state.[13] The argument is straightforward and has regularly been advanced by the modernizationists. Demands on the state have expanded far more rapidly than its capacities. That imbalance is compounded where the state is expected to play a major role in organizing and managing the economy. Overloaded, the state proves unable to fulfill even its more limited functions. Incapable of staffing the schools, or supplying the clinics, or maintaining the roads, the state is besieged by an angry populace. Threatened and powerless to relieve the fundamental pressures, its leaders respond with coercion and repression. Participation in civic affairs is limited or entirely prohibited. The resulting authoritarianism is defended in terms of a need for national unity in the face of multiple crises and, perhaps, vicious enemies. It is justified as well in terms of the essential importance of expertise. Development is a matter for those who know what they are doing, not illiterate villagers. Heartened by the downfall of authoritarian leaders elsewhere, the populace reinvigorates its protest, overloading and besieging the state still further.

There are several problems here. Some are terminological. For example, in this perspective, *state* sometimes means *country*. At other times, perhaps in the same text, state means *government* or its officials or those who actually hold power, whether or not they have formal positions. What is most problematic here, however, is that the analysts are once again looking for explanations entirely within Africa. The limits on a government's capabilities (what makes it "overloaded") have as much to do with the country's international role as with its national policies. The Zambian government, for example, has been so dependent on sale of copper that a chart of the economy's health looks very much like a graph of the world market price of copper. And certainly, those in power in Mozambique were besieged far more by foreign attacks and pressure than by the local citizenry.

The second thread reflects the rediscovery of the importance of politics. For much of Africa, effective politics secured independence and then came to be regarded as threatening. The leadership that was borne to power by a mobilized populace began to fear that mobilization. Political competition was regarded as an obstacle to national unity. An alliance between a technocratic-administrative elite and whoever held power (which in many countries was the military) felt especially vulnerable to a politicized public. The end of the 1980s witnessed a rediscovery of politics, both within Africa and among students of African politics. The key term has been democracy, usually taken to mean multiparty competition. Surely a step forward. Or is it?

Much of this new fascination with politics has a limited vision. It seems more concerned with refurbishing the functionalism of the 1960s (emphasizing the importance of mechanisms for aggregating and articulating interests) than with enabling people to govern themselves. It relies heavily on the sense that rules and practices in the North Atlantic, and especially the United States, are the models to be emulated, though some proselytizers for democracy in Africa caution against the adoption of the distinctly undemocratic features of U.S. politics. What Africans hear is, "You have failed in your development, but we have succeeded. Now you should go and do as we have done, or as our rules specify we should be doing. That is not perfect, but it is certainly preferable." The principal focus of attention is on elections, the primary symbol of democratic practice. Democratic elections are deemed to require parties, preferably not too many, to integrate divergent interests into a coherent organization that is capable of governing.

Troubling here is the heavy focus on institutional arrangements. To assess the democratic character of a particular country, observers pay attention to the number of parties, the rules that govern the creation of new parties and their candidates' participation in elections, the autonomy of the judiciary from executive control, the independence of the media from government direction, and the like. It seems reasonable to consider as more democratic those countries where the relevant laws make it easier for new parties to present their programs and support their candidates, other things being equal. But very often, other things are far from equal. Hungry and malnourished people, for example, are less likely to be able to negotiate the legal procedures required to stand for election, however open and encouraging they may be, than their better-fed neighbors.

To put this concern somewhat differently, it is puzzling to find a list of criteria of democraticness that has no mention of access to economic resources. The formal legislation may permit anyone to start a newspaper; but in practice, the resources required to begin publication may make it impossible for all but a few to do so. The administrative rules may formally permit anyone to bring a case to court; but the complex procedures and substantial fees for filing a charge may make the courts unavailable to a good part of the citizenry. How, then, to determine which country is more democratic if it is only institutional arrangements that matter?

This orientation is a hallmark of liberal democracy. The principal concern is with institutional arrangements. Apprehensive about relying on the intentions and wills of those in power, liberal democracy emphasizes the framework and the rules that are, in principal, independent of particular officials. Earlier, the study of African politics seemed to have gone beyond that institutional focus. It was at least as much concerned with outcomes as with laws, rules, and procedures.

An analogy may be useful. How to determine if a race is fair? One approach is to focus on the rules. Are some runners unreasonably precluded from entering the competition? Do some runners start sooner or in front of the others? Are some runners permitted special assistance not available to others (advance knowledge of peculiarities of the course? drugs?)? The race organizers may go further to insure that all runners have had comparable training and arrive at the start with equivalent equipment. If all of these arrangements are fair, then one can, in this view, safely conclude that the outcome is fair. Having established an equality of opportunity, the organizers can presume the fairness of the result. What, though, if one observes after a number of races that one set of runners has a much higher success rate than the others even though whatever makes them a set should confer no special advantage? Suppose the left-handed runners, or the blue-eyed runners, consistently win more often? What if the winning runners are lighter skinned or come from more affluent families? That result should make us wonder about the fairness of the race. We might well infer that the race favored one group over another in a way that had not been foreseen in our attention to the arrangements. But we would discover that only if, in addition to looking at the arrangements, we also focused on the outcomes. What seems to be equal opportunity may, in practice, not be equal at all.

Perhaps the race analogy is too distant from politics. Let us turn to a labor-discrimination case in the U.S. courts. Several years ago, a group of female employees sued the principal U.S. telephone company, claiming they had not been promoted or not received salary increases because senior officials discriminated against women. The charged officials rejected that claim. They presented to the court a forest of paper to show that, in each case, the procedures they used were fair and not discriminatory. In its judgment, the court did not point to a discernible systematic pattern of discrimination in the numerous cases reviewed; rather, the court decided that, where women constituted nearly all the workforce at the lowest level, half at the middle level, but only a minuscule proportion at the very top, it was reasonable to infer that there was discrimination. Apparent equality of opportunity was not adequate. The inequality of outcomes was itself sufficient evidence of discrimination, even if one could not point directly to the discriminatory practices, and even if those who discriminated were not entirely aware of the general consequences of their actions.

The implications for the efforts to assess democracy seem obvious. We might have expected that the experiences of the past few decades would have demonstrated the inadequacy of the institutional focus. Just as the apparent equality of opportunity is at best only a partial yardstick for measuring fundamental equality, so access, openness, and autonomy of political institutions are at best only a partial set of criteria for measuring democracy.

The continued dominance of the nation-state as the key unit of analysis is also problematic in this era. Nonstate actors, both transnational and subnational, are clearly important and influential. Might peasant organizations, literacy movements, unions, women's leagues, cooperatives, and many other institutional arrangements not play a central role in *African* democracy? And as integration at the global scale renders less significant the political terrain controlled by the leaders of particular countries, might regional organizations, to take just one example, not prove to be the most stable foundation for *African* democracy?

Perhaps what is most perceptive in this recent attention to parties and elections is the recognition of the role of politics in establishing and maintaining the legitimacy of both the system of government and those who hold office; that is, what is at issue here may be legitimacy more than participation. If so, then the risk that elections will be a facade to obscure and shield continued governance by a small elite is great. Elections, ostensibly democratic, may be staged in an effort to restore a legitimacy undermined by sluggish growth, increasing unemployment, and the consequences of these failures for nutrition, health, and the quality of life. Ultimately, the legitimacy of the African state and its officials is dependent on improving the standard of living. If that improvement continues to be heavily dependent on circumstances and events largely beyond Africa's control, a renewal strategy, indeed any development strategy, must envision reforming that relationship. Elections may, but do not necessarily, move in that direction. An authoritarian regime may be able to retain power if its political base sees an improving, or at least not deteriorating, standard of living. Where that standard appears to decline, elections may confer the legitimacy that prosperity no longer provides. But unless elections are accompanied by the sort of participation that enables citizens to control their state, voting will quickly become a facade. Perhaps fashionable, but not functional, such elections would do little to fulfill the promise of Africa's development.

This odyssey through teaching about African politics is instructive. From the exotic to the pitiable, from the modernizing to the dependent, but always the *other*. At least in the earlier perspective it was possible to see the uniqueness of Africa's contribution to the world and to an understanding of it. In the current image of Africa-the-helpless, Africa-the-impotent, Africa is of general interest primarily as a recipient of charity.

This rapid decline has been accompanied by a transition in the guiding social science. Three decades ago, it was the knowledge and approaches of the anthropologists that informed the study of Africa. Today they have been displaced by economists. Indeed, by the 1990s economics had become the ideal type for social science. Explanations of why communities maintained their solidarity came to look remarkably like cost-benefit analysis. It became more important to hold the context constant ("all other things being equal") than to explore its peculiarities and idiosyncrasies. What was highly rewarded was not the depth of familiarity with a particular society or situation but how rapidly one could model it. The point here is not that anthropology is in some fundamental way better than economics; or that either discipline is inherently better suited to guiding our study of Africa; rather, I have sought to highlight the transition and to note that each offers a different way of knowing and proposes a different role for the student and observer.

My concern here has been to lay a foundation. Teaching about Africa in the 1990s requires addressing not only what students know and do not know about Africa, but also what we ourselves, as teachers, know, do not know, and think we know about Africa.

THE KNOWLEDGE-BASE

This review of teaching about African politics in the past has clarified the construction of the knowledge-base that will be used in teaching about Africa in the future. I want now to address several other components and characteristics of that knowledge-base, all of which inform, and thus condition and constrain, what we do and how we do it.

The Invention of Africa

To begin this part of the discussion, it is essential that we recognize the Africa that *we*—in the sense in which I have been using that term—have invented. Most important, the invention process is ongoing.

Mudimbe[14] makes this case powerfully, detailing exactly how early Africanists, primarily missionaries and anthropologists, created, characterized, and stereotyped Africa. Indeed, colonialism coevolved with anthropology as a discipline. That is not to say that all anthropologists were apologists for colonial rule, but rather to note that both colonial rule and early anthropology reflected the ideas of their times and that each influenced the other. It is also to note that as they sought to justify their conquests and subjugations, colonizers often employed the descriptions and categories of the anthropologists. Some anthropologists took it as their duty to support the colonial effort. Others asserted their duty was to avoid criticizing it: "Whether [those who control colonial policy] are doing right or wrong is a question for moral philosophy, not for social anthropology."[15]

Central to both enterprises was the absolute insistence on two conceptually and empirically different sorts of society and people: primitive and modern. Anthropologists assumed responsibility for describing the primitive in scientific terms, but they were never solely concerned with description: they generally sought, as well, to characterize and explain—asserting that they understood it better than anyone else—the transition from primitive to modern. One scholar, writing in pre–World War II times, asserted: "Anthropology, which used to be the study of beings and things retarded, gradual, and backward, is now faced with the difficult task of recording how the 'savage' becomes an active participant in modern civilization."[16]

At first, Africans were essentially subhuman; or perhaps prehuman: paganism, nakedness, and cannibalism were their defining characteristics. Intervening in their societies to civilize them, it could then be argued, was not only reasonable but a moral responsibility of the Europeans. Over time, the *primitive* became simply *underdeveloped*. Europeans could then either justify transforming their societies in order to modernize them or denying them access to the status and rights of European society in order to preserve their ostensibly uncorrupted state and permit them to develop at whatever was thought to be their own pace. In practice, Europeans often did both.

Creating Africa was necessarily a complex process. To provide content to the backwardness of Africa required specifying a moral order of sorts: hierarchies of values and authorities, and economic, social, and political institutions (including tribe and tribalism). All of that had to be associated with the people, activities, and social relations that one encountered in Africa. Africa did, after all, exist. Africa-the-backward had roots in both that Africa and the Africa that was being fashioned by its European interpreters. The more they considered themselves the bearers of European social science, the more those interpreters insisted they could distinguish the true Africa from the Africa that had already been deformed by its contact with the (more powerful) outsiders. Since they were best able to make that distinction, they insisted, they were true-Africa's only reliable interpreters.

My point here is not to indict anthropology. As I suggested above, the receding role of anthropology has had, I believe, unfortunate consequences for African studies more generally; rather, my concern is to highlight the interconnections between the state and the academy in that earlier era to sensitize us to its links now.

The impulse to invent and describe the primitive in order to define ourselves is extraordinarily powerful and influential. That, it seems to me, is the most powerful lesson of this part of the story. We need *them* in order to be clear about *us*. We indicate who *we* are by differentiating ourselves from this *other,* and our pride and self-respect (and therefore self-confidence) are in large part a function of that distance. To maintain our sense of self, that distance must be maintained.

> A conversation of "us" with "us" about "them" is a conversation in which "them" is silenced. "Them" always stands on the other side of the hill, naked and speechless, barely present in its absence. Subject of discussion, "them" is only admitted among "us," the discussing subjects, when accompanied or introduced by an "us," member, hence the dependence of "them" and its need to acquire good manners for the membership standing.[17]

It is worth stressing again that this invention is necessarily an ongoing process, not simply the legacy of a misguided moment in the European past. The examples surround us. To take just one, from a publication that arrived in my mailbox as I was preparing this chapter:

> Six million proud people defend a culture rich in history and tradition. Fighting the invasion of industrialization . . . shielding their magic and mystery from the techno-terrors of modern society. Can they protect this lifestyle? Or must they surrender to the promise and the pain of a new prosperity?[18]

This advertising copy appeared in one of the most modern of our magazines—a magazine for computer owners, for people willing to invest in electronic communication. It was an advertisement for IQuest, a collection of some 850 databases. Set under a picture of a young boy with a shield (a boy I presume to be Zulu-speaking), the ad's big type proclaimed: "You could go to Udombo to learn about the Zulus. Or you could GO IQuest." So here, amid information about the latest research techniques that search rapidly through collections of data—the most contemporary sort of news, that is available to its audience even before it reaches print—what do we find? First, we encounter an attractive child attired in what many people would describe as tribal regalia. Second, our attention is directed toward the enduring mystique of the implacable tension between tradition and modernity. Third, we find a war, between tribal people on the one side and the invasion of industrialization and the technoterrors of modern society on the other. And fourth, we find *Zulu,* a symbol intended to evoke a combination of pride, strength, and primitiveness.

What we do not find is a hint that much of the Zulu-speaking population lives in urban and semiurban areas and wears clothing rather like that of the magazine's readers. We do not find the suggestion that some

Zulu-speakers are engineers, or bankers, or industrialists; people who benefit from and advocate modernization, who do not decry it. And we do not find a glimmer of the contemporary conflict in South Africa, where the principal terror is that created by the state, not modernization; and where at least some Zulu-speakers have been thoroughly implicated in spreading that terror.

The point here is straightforward. The invention of Africa is a process, not an event in our distant past. It goes on daily, in settings that are diverse and too numerous to count. It is far more pervasive than systematic instruction by expert Africanists in universities or elsewhere. As this primitive Africa is regularly reinvented, it legitimizes treating Africa as it is depicted. And as Internet plays its role, it creates a new cast of experts who can become more active participants in the reinvention process as they share their new knowledge with others. After all, many more people will see the advertisement than will take the trouble or spend the money to look up *Zulus* in IQuest's databases.

The Restoration and Durability of Modernization

I have already pointed to the durability of notions of modernization in political science. Since those ideas reach across the social sciences, and even into the humanities and physical sciences, it is essential to explore their significance further. Some of the proponents of modernization are now less extravagant and arrogant in their claims; some are even defensive. Indeed, several prominent orators have offered eulogies for the modernization perspective. But reports of its passing have remained premature; and its theoretical precepts have proved strikingly durable.

The modernization ideology has several major components. As I have noted above, the initial—and generally unstated and undefended—premise of the ideology locates the sources and causes of Africa's problems within Africa.[19] Contemporary poverty, for example, is to be explained in terms of the distant past (a historical legacy of rudimentary technology and small-scale societies); or the climate (the abundant tropical bounty stimulates neither hard work nor invention); or the missing factors of production (insufficient capital/technology/skills to develop local resources fully); or early socialization (maternal dependence, subjugation of self to group); or attitudinal orientation (a stoic passivity, even fatalistic submissiveness, in the face of adversity); or psychosocial mindset (low need for achievement); or inefficiency and corruption; or in terms of some variant or combination of these themes.

A second component of the ideology of modernization development deals largely with technical-administrative process. In this understanding, development is fostered by rationalizing the use of scarce resources, supplying requisite capital, skills, and technology at critical junctures, and using state power to reward those who engage in desired behaviors. Development has to do with applying knowledge and manipulating inputs, which for the most part are regarded as technical and administrative tasks. The reliable performance of those technical and administrative tasks is deemed to require well-oiled machinery and smoothly meshing gears: in the parlance of politics, relative stability and manageable conflict, and not society-wide popular mobilization and the sharp clash of competing programs, or the energetic confrontation of incompatible interests, or conflict among antagonistic classes.

A third theme is that managers of this technical-administrative process are expected to be a modernizing middle class.[20] Only that class, imbued through its education with the requisite skills and socialized to value individual economic and social mobility, can shoulder the burden of national reform. Acting in its own interests, it can initiate and, more importantly, manage broad social transformation. The elites of the old order—whether aristocrats, feudal lords, leaders whose authority was drawn from lineage, clan, and ethnic formations, conquerors and other successful generals, or designated inheritors of the colonial mantle—lack the combination of competence, vision, and drive necessary for the construction of a new order. Peasant political mobilizers, trade union militants, radical critics of imperialism, and neocolonialism—like politics in general—are all regarded as obstacles to progress.

From tenets two and three comes a fourth theme: the preferred political form is liberal democracy, in which citizen participation is indirect and limited and in which expertise reigns supreme. Unlike other societies where education is much more widespread and where groups critical of public policy can advance their own experts, the very narrow base of education in most of Africa means that to favor expertise is to exclude the mass from serious policy debate and decisionmaking. As Fanon perceptively predicted, however, where the new postcolonial African leadership failed to become a modernizing middle class, authoritarian rule would prevail over pluralistic politics. In practice, only a few efforts to maintain liberal democracy in Africa have survived. Elsewhere, it decayed as the postcolonial leadership thought they no longer needed it; or it crumbled as its facade of participation failed to generate the political legitimacy necessary to sustain it; or it succumbed to those who proclaimed the necessity of centralized direction and control as they discarded the constitution and seized power.

From this perspective, empowerment, democratic participation, and collective liberation have for the most part been regarded as inimical to modernization's agenda, at least in the short term. Circumstances have changed, however. For at least some modernizationists, the practical benefits of democratic practices now seem to outweigh their increased burden on African governments. One lesson from recent African experience is that governments that are not regarded as legitimate by their citizens are unable to implement the modernization agenda. The difficulties in fulfilling the conditions attached to what has come to be called structural adjustment assistance have made that painfully clear.

Briefly, as the quality of life deteriorated for many Africans during the 1980s, their governments ever more energetically sought external aid. By the 1980s, the experts of the major transnational financial institutions, especially the World Bank and the International Monetary Fund, were convinced that they understood clearly what had to be done. Special foreign aid, not linked to specific projects, and increased foreign assistance in general, became available, on the condition that African governments adopted a series of economic policies (often termed *liberalization*). Although the specific policies to be adopted varied a bit from one setting to another, in general they emphasized substantial devaluation, decreased direct government role in the economy, especially in productive activities, reduction in the size of the civil service, encouragement of foreign investment, and support for privatization of many activities, including public services. Nearly everywhere, the implementation of these policies meant new or increased fees for social services (for example, for medical treatment) and increased prices for consumer goods (often through the elimination of subsidies for staples). Nearly all African governments found at least some of these policies unpalatable. Some found them impossible to implement. Rapidly increasing food prices led to urban riots in Egypt and Zambia, for example.

The lesson seemed clear. A government with an insecure popular base could not successfully restructure the national economy. Restoring legitimacy thus became central to the modernization agenda. That, in turn, broadened the support for multiparty competition, elections, and other popular initiatives.

I do not mean at all to suggest here that all who advocate and study democracy are simply modernization instrumentalists: that is certainly not the case. What is clear, I believe, is that modernizationists who earlier sought to limit popular initiatives because they overwhelmed government capacity and rendered more difficult the imposition of unpopular policies are now convinced that the absence of popular support is even more problematic. What is not yet clear is how they will respond when, among the new parties, they find socialists who call for more, not less, government role in the economy, or populists who reject outright major elements of the modernization program.

Finally, it is important to note that this ideology of modernization has, to a significant extent, been internalized not only by Africa's elites but also by its populace at large. Education provides a clear example. On the one hand, popular demands for expanded access to education are often fundamentally conservative in their orientation. By and large, parents are not searching for a new society but rather for better access to the old order. Admission to postprimary schools is valued not because it portends fundamental social transformation but rather because it holds the promise of increased income, job security, and an improved standard of living. On the other hand, parents are often passionate defenders of their own exclusion from educational policymaking. The experts should make such decisions, say the members of the district educational planning committee as they ratify a proposal presented by officials of the ministry of education. Or, we must support the headteacher who knows better about these matters, comment the members of the school committee as they agree that major elements of school policy need not be brought to their attention. My point here is not that popular demands are inherently conservative or that all peasants acquiesce in their exclusion from decisionmaking; it is, rather, that the ideology of modernization operates within as well as on the African populace. The very people who are served least well by this ideology are also its purveyors.

An ideology of modernization, however attractive and however much internalized, could hardly sustain on its own an arrangement of this sort. In Africa, that ideology is linked to a particular pattern of postcolonial politics: the conditioned (peripheral capitalist) state.[21] Governed by a class whose political base lies in its control over the administration rather than in its creative role in the economy,[22] the conditioned state in Africa remains responsive to the needs of its external allies and requires sharp limits on popular participation; that is, the ideology of modernization is not simply the legacy of European rule or earlier development thinking, or even of foreign governments and international agencies: it is as well an ideology that is critical to an administrative governing class and that is, therefore, incorporated within the institutions of the conditioned state. Internalized and institutionalized, its influence is both subtle and powerful.

We would err, however, were we to underestimate the significance of external support for this orientation. That support is multifaceted, sometimes obvious but often indirect and largely unseen. Foreign assistance agencies, for example, may be explicit in their insistence on support for a modernizing middle class (access to education, recruitment to senior positions, provision of a comfortable lifestyle) as a condition for grants and loans. At the same time, support for individualism, private competition, and depoliticized administration may be so deeply embedded in their curriculum that it escapes the critical attention of the African students in North Atlantic, especially U.S., universities. As those students become middle-level and senior decisionmakers in their own countries, the orientation that they have internalized sets the boundaries within which policies are made. Radically different conceptualizations simply do not appear on the agenda. To put it sharply, technicians called on to repair an internal combustion engine do not spend their time thinking about solar power:

photovoltaic cells are simply not in their toolkit. And economists called on to adjust the prices of externally marketed commodities do not analyze incomes in terms of the generation and appropriation of surplus value: their kit, too, lacks the tools to make that possible.

There has been, then, a return to the perspectives of the late colonial and immediate postcolonial era. The earlier critique, which once seemed to carry the day, has been largely discarded, at least for the moment. Itself stimulated and nurtured by decolonization and national liberation struggles, that critique—focused on underdevelopment and dependence—insisted that the explanation for Africa's situation could not be found solely, or primarily, or even largely, within Africa. Rather, fundamental causes had to be located in the global complex, particularly in the relationships between Africa and the rest of the world.

Although fundamentally shaken by that critique, modernization has proved resilient and durable. Now, as then, explanations for poverty in Africa focus on factors of production, ethos, mind-set, cultural values, and the like. The causes for Africa's poverty are to be found in Africa, with, apparently, some minor input from the global setting. Remedies for the current problems are also to be found within Africa: better planning, more rational economic decisionmaking, governmental or other institutional reform, multiparty elections, privatization. Much of the writing has returned to offering advice to Africans. We have progressed a bit, however: now the corpus of commentators includes a few Africans, nearly all educated and socialized in North Atlantic institutions. In its tone, that writing speaks to Africans who are deemed incapable of adequately analyzing their own situation and incapable of converting analysis into action. These incapabilities are assumed to be logically prior to issues of physical capacity, resource deployment, and capital investment.

The powerful critique of the dependency and world-systems literature—to the effect that explaining poverty in contemporary Africa requires attention to Africa's role(s) in a world system and the institutionalization of those global connections within Africa—is widely noted—and, except in its broadest sweep and most superficial form, commonly ignored. The international order is a given; a background condition, like the glass of the test tube in which the experiment is conducted. In practice, of course, the international order is part of Africa's foreground, not background: an energetic chameleon, not an immutable landscape. To continue the test-tube analogy, closer inspection may reveal that the tube is made not of nonreactive glass but rather of durable, poisonous lead. The deterioration of those who ingest the experiment's products may then stem more from that lead than anything they do or fail to do. And even as the situation worsens, actions within the vessel may reshape the content's form and rearrange its structure. To take as given what are potentially primary causes is to exclude them from the policy (and research) discourse. What is unseen and undiscussed will surely not be the focus of policy attention or public action.[23]

What We See, What We Say

Teaching about Africa continues to be encumbered by images and words that at best confuse and distract and at worst themselves become the instructional agenda. Here, then, is a third major component of the knowledge-base for teaching about Africa in the 1990s. I shall limit myself to two examples.

Tarzan, Tarzan, and more Tarzan. A few years ago I developed an introductory course on Africa that relied heavily on film. To supplement what we did in class, I asked the participants in the course to search the weekly television schedules for images of Africa. An unforeseen benefit of that supplementary work was that we could analyze the weekly compilations to see what images of Africa got the most airtime.

About half the class expected wildlife/nature images to dominate. The rest of us were divided: some expected to find that conflict would be most often depicted; others were sure that pictures of hunger and starvation would appear most often. We were all wrong. In fact, it was the Tarzan image that appeared the most often, followed by "George of the Jungle" (an animated Tarzan spoof). A collective third was feature films (Abbott and Costello/Bob Hope in Africa; the brave white hunter's quest in darkest Africa; Humphrey Bogart/Sidney Poitier intrigues in African settings). A brief follow-up survey two years later found a similar pattern.

By its nature, our survey of images of Africa on television in the San Francisco Bay Area does not permit grand generalization. We surely missed some programs, and we never arrived at an unimpeachable strategy for determining the total number of televised hours, since that varied from one community to another and depended on whether or not viewers had cable connections. Nor did we have information on what people watched rather than what was broadcast. The finding nevertheless was dramatic. In the late 1980s, in one of the largest television markets in the United States, casual viewers saw more of Tarzan than any other image of Africa. For the most part, the Tarzan image was of the earlier series of films (one channel had a weekly rebroadcast of one of the old films). But there were also the more recent productions, both live-action and animation.

Consider what the Tarzan image portrays: Here is a white man, dropped suddenly in the middle of Africa, who is soon able to do nearly everything better than anyone else in sight. He can outfight all opponents, run more quickly, swim faster, shout louder, escape danger more readily, and recover more rapidly than the local people he encounters. He can communicate effectively with the animals, enlisting their support regularly. He is also able to communicate with all the people he meets, even though they are apparently unable to understand each other. He can tell the good guys from the bad guys at first glance, both black and white. A metaphor for modernization.

Words matter. Our methods of describing that which we study have an influence on how we understand it. The constructs we employ to study Africa reflect contexts, conventions, and, ultimately, social relations. At the same time, the language we use rarely has clear, unambiguous meanings. Words do not stand alone like unique prominences on an uncluttered plain. Their meanings vary from one time to the next, from one setting to another, even within a single conversation.

Often, the words we use privilege some explanations while obscuring others. Although sometimes that process is conscious and crude, more often it is subtle, nearly invisible. What seems descriptive is in practice delimiting, perhaps analytically disabling. It may be politically disabling as well. T. Minh-ha Trinh stated strongly: "Language is one of the most complex forms of subjugation, being at the same time the locus of power and unconscious servility."[24] Recall my list above that contrasted the terms used for similar phenomena in Europe and Africa (see subsection, "From the Exotic"). To supplement that list, consider a few examples of rather more complex terms.

• *Subsistence farmer/farming.* One of the dichotomies most frequently applied to Africa is that of subsistence vs. cash crop farming. At first glance, the distinction is clear: some farmers eat what they grow; others sell what they produce. Each strategy is then associated with different economic goals and general life-situation. That understanding, however, is both empirically and analytically problematic. In practice, no farmers are entirely self-sufficient. All must buy implements, household goods, or clothing. All must turn to the market for at least some of their needs, and this, in turn, requires having something to sell. Equally important, farmers often do not know at the beginning of the farming season whether or not they will produce enough to have a surplus to sell; hence, they must be prepared for both outcomes: having too little harvest to survive, or having a surplus to sell.

Analytically, *subsistence* was a useful construct when it was used to understand not who would consume the produce but rather how the farmers made their decisions about what to plant, how much to plant, how much labor to invest in planting and tending the crop, what indebtedness (in whatever form) to incur. In that usage, *subsistence farming* suggested a local horizon and relative inattention to events beyond the family and immediate community and especially to distant markets. But there are extraordinarily few, if any, farmers of this sort in contemporary Africa. *Subsistence farming* in this sense disappeared long ago.

All African farmers keep an eye on the market. To do otherwise would be terribly shortsighted and perhaps suicidal. In addition to prices, farmers must also monitor their access to credit, the availability of transportation, seeds, fertilizer and the like, and more. A farmer may produce for local consumption in one year and for more distant consumption in another; or do both in the same year. Because of market uncertainties and because the quantity of the harvest will in part be determined by factors beyond the farmer's control, producers may not be sure, when they plant, where their harvest will be consumed. For local communities to function effectively, markets must exist to accommodate excess production and even to provide for inadequate production.

In short, while the construct *subsistence farmer* fits well with the traditional side of the traditional/modern dichotomy, it fits much less well with the realities of contemporary Africa. It suggests a category of self-sufficient farmers unaffected by markets and by the global economy—a category that simply does not exist. As generally used, this construct does not help students understand the extensiveness and pervasiveness of the colonial experience. Nor does it assist them in recognizing the integration of Africa into the global economy and analyzing its consequences.

• *Food vs. cash crop.* This dichotomy, an extension of the notion of subsistence farming, provides a second example of encumbering language. It is common to distinguish those African farmers who produce food (to be consumed locally) from those who produce crops for cash (to be sent to the market). As I have suggested above, in practice this distinction, too, is both empirically and analytically problematic.

These are, of course, not exclusive categories. In practice, many (though not all) food crops have a cash value. In practice, some of the crop may be consumed locally and some sold in the market. It may well prove useful to consider the extent to which farmers are dependent on or insulated from markets, both local and distant. But contrasting food with cash-crop production simply obscures the important underlying issues.

Together, *subsistence farming* and *food vs. cash crop* assert a duality in African agriculture. Once again we find the differentiation between more and less advanced, modern and traditional, or, as has become fashionable, formal and informal.

• *Informal sector.*[25] This term refers to economic activities not fully recorded in official records and statistics, including but not limited to petty commerce, street vendors, sidewalk artisans, roadside auto mechanics, and the like. This usage is in part a legacy of the construct, *dual economy,* and as such perhaps marks its return to legitimacy. The notion of a two-sector economy has its roots in the duality of modernization, the assertion of the critical importance of the distance between the *we* and the *them,* and the expectation of incessant individual and collective turmoil fueled by the fundamental incompatibility of the old and the new. This perspective became more widespread and more comfortable to Europeans as they imposed their rule on Africa. Entrenched in various justifying ideologies—the rationalizations of Christian participation in the slave trade as well as the subsequent official philosophies of colonial rule—duality fit quite well with the other baggage that Europeans took with them to Africa. It captured what seemed to Europeans to be an unbridgeable gulf between cultures, and its utility was ostensibly confirmed by the readily apparent differences between rural and urban.

It is not surprising, therefore, that much of the literature of Africa's independence era characterized African economies as dual, constituted by the inherently uneasy cohabitation of modernity and tradition. The modern sector produced for export, included European administrators, company representatives, and educated Africans, and aspired to the values, patterns of interaction, and lifestyles of contemporary Europe. The traditional sector produced for local consumption (*subsistence*), included the mass of the African population, and struggled to maintain the values, social networks, and daily customs of a distant past.

The duality assumed in that early literature was sharply challenged. As critics of this perspective demonstrated the extent and solidity of the links between these ostensibly sharply distinct sectors—especially the flows of labor, small-scale commodities, and wages—the popularity of the construct waned. Where dual economy focused attention on separation, incompatibility, and distance, the critics emphasized the integration of Africa into a global economy and the incipient homogenization of cultures.

Within the analytic framework that assumed Africa's dual economy, *the economy* came to mean the modern sector: registered firms, wage employment, and taxpaying citizens. In the national statistics, the much more extensive but presumably anachronistic and disappearing exchanges organized around local production and consumption went largely unrecorded. In this regard, attention paid recently by scholars and policymakers to the informal sector brought an important corrective to the study of the economies of Africa. The unregistered and unrecorded were accorded a new legitimacy. Their durability and rationality were formally recognized.

That very recognition, however, restored duality to the center of economic analysis. Yet, this usage is, in part, a process of labeling that characterizes as qualitatively different, and often of lesser significance, those economic activities that economists and other social scientists for many years did not study carefully and still find it difficult to study systematically and that governments found, and find, harder to regulate and control.

In fact, as is increasingly widely acknowledged, the economy of the informal sector is neither very informal nor invisible. Patterns of employment are reasonably clearly structured and supported by a rich institutional network. There are hierarchical chains of authority, functional specialization, reliable sources of credit, and often even small-scale bureaucracy.

Nor are these activities marginal to the national economy. In many, perhaps most, African countries, most employment is in activities labeled informal, and those activities are integrally connected to the rest of the economy through wages, purchases, credit, labor deployment, and the like. The streetcorner merchants and the women who sell baked goods at factory gates are surely not invisible. Mechanics who earn a living repairing automobiles under the shade of trees could not survive if their services were hidden; indeed, they may well advertise. Even the official enumerators have no trouble finding them when that is their goal.

That economists and others have not been as successful in documenting these activities does not require employing terminology that reinvigorates the notion of duality and suggests their lesser significance for the economy as a whole. That governments within and outside Africa have increasingly recognized both the importance of these activities and their limited ability to regulate and control them does not render the practices of the unregistered economy unique or warrant considering them to be invisible. Nor does their invisibility to officialdom indicate that the entrepreneurship that unregistered producers and merchants manifest and the business skills they employ are in some fundamental way different from those of their registered counterparts.

The point here is not that there are not important distinctions among patterns of economic activity or that we do not need terms to differentiate social behaviors; rather, that many of the terms currently in use mystify more than they clarify. To demystify them requires more than simply selecting other terms. Piercing the mystique involves tracing their origins, locating their roots in a particular understanding and approach, and then encouraging and enabling students to comprehend what they read by specifying their own perspective.

The Academy

The above subsections—on inventing Africa, on enduring notions of modernization, and on the ubiquitous images that stereotype and generally deprecate the African experience—are all part of the knowledge-base for teaching about Africa in the 1990s. The academy itself—universities, colleges, research institutions—and especially its changing character constitute a fourth component of that knowledge-base.

The decline of area studies. In the 1960s, area studies were a central part of the effort to save U.S. higher education. The successful Soviet launch of the first artificial earth satellite, Sputnik, in the late 1950s highlighted the successive failures of the United States to orbit its own satellite. By the end of the decade, there seemed to be widespread agreement that the quality of U.S. education had deteriorated, and that schools, colleges, and universities in this country were falling behind those elsewhere. At the same time, U.S. foreign policy seemed to be in disarray. The decolonization of Africa was perceived as creating openings for the Soviet Union to extend its influence. The unsuccessful invasion of Cuba was regarded as a failure of U.S. intelligence, U.S. military capability, U.S. resolve, or all three.

One (small) part of the solution adopted then was to strengthen research and instruction on those parts of the world little known and little studied in the United States. A primary vehicle for this funding was the defense appropriation, specifically the National Defense Education Act. Increased government funds were accompanied by new foundation support, especially from the Ford and Rockefeller Foundations. One result was the rapid expansion of (foreign) area and language studies. Major beneficiaries were public institutions, especially in the Midwest, that could create new centers. These were soon larger than the older centers on the East Coast. Many senior colleagues of contributors to this book secured their first academic positions in this era.

With the creation of these new centers came efforts to redefine knowledge-domains to justify treating Africa as both a focus for study and a quasi discipline, with its own approaches and methods. The pattern varied from one institution to the next, but in many of the most visible universities it became possible for undergraduates to devote a good deal of attention to Africa, and perhaps to graduate with an African studies major.

By the 1990s, the tide was moving in the opposite direction. Now, as then, there is the widespread sense that something is wrong with U.S. higher education. Now, as then, world events are forcing a fundamental rethinking of U.S. foreign policy. But this time around, area studies, and Africa in particular, do not seem to be central to the solution. A major difference, of course, is that this time around the U.S. leadership is not apprehensive about losing an international contest. Rather, it is confident that it has won. Certainly, what had once seemed to be a contest for influence in Africa is now considered to be no contest at all. Soviet and Chinese direct support have been greatly reduced. Communism seems to have lost its position on the anti-imperialist moral high ground as well as its influence in the dust and mud of everyday activities. The would-be socialist states, after years of direct attack and destabilization, are now in such disarray that they seem willing to do whatever is demanded to avoid complete collapse. To the extent that the improvement of higher education requires attention to foreign areas, it is Europe, and what is termed as the Pacific Rim, that warrant increased funding, not Africa.

The earlier period also saw the creation and expansion of Black studies centers. The environment for that expansion had elements both outside and inside the academy. The external context was the energized civil rights movement of the 1960s and the resultant increased public and policy attention to discrimination. The larger number of black students on college and university campuses (though they were still few in absolute terms) generated the critical mass necessary to focus curricular attention on the black experience.

Alas, only a few of the Black studies centers established or expanded during this period were planted in ground sufficiently fertile to enable them to flourish. Even where financial support was adequate, academic recognition and administrative sustenance were not. In many universities, these centers were regarded by the university leadership and much of the faculty primarily as political and scholarly concessions, not initiatives with great research and pedagogical potential. Although a few of these centers have flourished and distinguished themselves intellectually, many have seen declining enrollment, support, and respect. Some no longer exist.

It is not possible here to explore the causes for the difficult situation of Black studies on U.S. campuses, or to try to sort out the responsibilities of national policymakers, university administrators and faculty, and black students and staff in that regard. Surely it should not surprise us that those living and studying the black experience find things difficult on as well as off the campus. More directly relevant to this book is that only rarely have effective links been established between African and Afro-American studies. In many universities, these were separate departments or centers or institutes, each with its own faculty, staff, and students. Notwithstanding frequent references to common interests, there was a good deal of mutual suspicion. Often they saw each other as competitors for resources and recognition. Often each felt threatened by the other. Generally created and managed by established white faculty, the African studies centers worried that they would lose students and legitimacy to Black studies. Often begun and administered by younger, less well-established faculty, Afro-American studies centers were anxious about losing what they saw as a major part of their academic agenda and with it academic recognition and respect. By the 1990s, in most universities both had lost ground.

Beyond the diminished attention to Africa, area studies have, I think, declined more generally. Notwithstanding all the fuss about political correctness and leftist professors (or perhaps as a result of it), it is the disciplinary departments that have been more successful in articulating their perspective, not the area studies centers. It is the specialists, not the holists, who are held in highest esteem and who have the most influential voices. The preeminent goal is to be able to say something about, say, peasants—peasants everywhere—without necessarily being about to say a great deal about peasants somewhere, or a particular group of peasants.

Economics as social science. As I have suggested, accompanying the decline of area studies has been the emergence of economics as the model social science. This increasingly influential and powerful role for economics stands on two legs, one within and the other outside the academy. In their ideal form, the methods of economists correspond well to the direction social science has been moving over the past several decades— the first leg. The focus is on causal relationships, established by drawing on law-like statements about patterned regularities and exploring the connections among precisely defined factors. Previous research, for example, may be taken to have established that in a specified set of circumstances, an undervalued currency will have particular and specifiable consequences for independent farmers who grow crops that are sold for export. Within that carefully mapped terrain, one may then study the effects of raising or reducing the price paid to the farmer for that crop. Factors that are deemed extraneous to the relationship at hand can be ignored. Factors that may affect the relationship being studied are either assumed not to vary ("other things being equal") or to vary randomly (thereby having no systematic influence) or are controlled by the researchers. Finally, the restricted set of factors to be examined ("the variables") can be studied. Ideally, those factors can be changed in some orderly way, either by careful choice of locations, times, or farmers sampled, or by simulating the variation based on the information available. Expectations about causality (hypotheses) can then be rejected or supported. The longer-term goals are to increase the number of law-like statements that are generally accepted as sufficiently well supported to serve as the foundation for research and perhaps policy and to broaden their field of applicability.

For many scholars, this orientation defines the social scientific method. The ultimate standard is the controlled experiment, in which all of the factors can be manipulated by the experimenter. Since that is rarely possible for social scientists, the challenge is to approach that ideal as closely as possible.

To turn to the second leg, the current preeminence of economics also stems from its role as the social science deemed to have the most important practical consequences. Many people, both inside and outside the academy, understand the value of social science primarily in terms of what used to be called social engineering: how to make society function better; how to improve people's lives, or resolve conflict, or reduce environmental degradation, or. . . . Generally, economics is perceived as more closely related to that objective, and better able to achieve it, than any of the other social sciences. Put crudely, history may help us learn a bit from the past, but the lessons are often too distant from or unclearly related to current experience to be directly useful. Extensive interpretation is required, and since the interpreters often disagree with each other, lessons with clear practical utility rarely emerge. Political science has the potential to improve how we govern ourselves (or how our governors manipulate us), but that potential has rarely been reached. Here, too, disagreements among the interpreters undermine the vitality and utility of the advice they offer.

After all, political scientists have not been able to help us understand, let alone do much about, one of the most striking characteristics of the democracy we market to the rest of the world. Elections are considered the foundation of contemporary democracy. Yet, barely half the U.S. populace votes regularly, and in local elections in many areas, not even a quarter of eligible voters show up at the polls. Besides, since the Vietnam War and Watergate, public distrust of politicians and cynicism about the political system generally has become the order of the day. If politicians are not to be trusted, those who advise them are even less worthy of our time and attention. The parade of stereotypes could continue. Psychology may help a few individuals to sleep better, or a few employers to recruit new personnel more efficiently, or marriages to last longer; and it may fill out our knowledge about exactly how short-term memory works. But improve society more generally? And so on.

We live in an era and in a society in which the principal unit for measuring our well-being is money. It follows that those who study production and wealth, for which money is also the most common measure, will and ought to have the most to say about how to improve that well-being. That role reaches beyond our own society. In addition to the ponderous analytic weight of economics as the preferred way to look at things, there is also a developmentalism in viewing the world, especially the Third World, that makes economic growth the only satisfactory measure of progress.

Perhaps this as it should be. As I have argued elsewhere, I do not think so.[26] Whatever one's own position, the challenge for teaching about Africa is twofold. First, we need to recognize the preeminent role of economics as a choice rather than a given and to identify its manifestations and consequences. Second, we need to help students not only to explore different perspectives but also to understand that there are alternative ways of knowing and that the rules for how we know what we know are neither ordained nor immutable but are themselves derived from particular approaches and theories.

On methodology and approaches. Here, then, is a third dimension of the academy that is part of the setting for teaching about Africa: the push toward a social scientific method, ostensibly detached from its theoretical foundation and universally applicable. If we learned *the* scientific method in high school biology, why not expect to find at the university level a rather more complex but comparably universal social scientific method? That the procedures for validating claims to knowledge are a function of more or less public policy rather than the result of an atheoretical, impartial, scientific process is clear. That most social science courses operate as if there were only one reasonable and reliable way of accomplishing that validation is equally clear.

None of that is very new, and creative instructors have been wrestling with it for a long time. What is more recent, though, is the relentless push toward broad propositions, generalization, and fundamental causes, especially in studying development. The corollary is reduced attention to case studies, detailed observations, and to the absence of fundamental causes, or rather, to the very large consequences of very small events.[27]

Only partially obscured by the mountain of paper that the development business generates, a striking tension is materializing. On the one hand, for most observers the world seems ever more uncertain. At the same time, development decisionmakers insist on ever higher levels of certainty before they will release funds and undertake programs. It gives one pause. Or it should. Although it is pervasive, this tension between the constrained certainties in the world we observe and the demand for nearly unqualified certainties in development is not immediately apparent. The push for certainty has its roots in the zealously energetic efforts of many social scientists to emulate what they regard as the rigor and precision of the physical sciences. Ironically, however, the model that is to be emulated is a caricature, never really typical of the process by which knowledge is created in the physical sciences and certainly not so today. Beyond its limited correspondence with actual practices, that model has limited heuristic value for the social sciences, since it obscures rather than reveals the role of the scientist and promotes an inflated sense of certainty and precision. At what are generally acknowledged to be the frontiers of knowledge in the physical sciences, this model, with its evolutionary, linear accumulation of discrete bits of knowledge organized into deterministic inferences and deduced conclusions, is sharply at issue.

Many authors have recognized the fundamental inaccuracies of this image of the physical sciences and its obfuscating impact on the social sciences. Yet even as scholars work to demystify that image and draw on the insights of recent theory and research in the physical sciences, among students of Third World development there is a strong push to rescue linear determinism from its senility. As external funding agencies have become increasingly influential in setting the research agenda and specifying how it is to be addressed, the breadth of imagination has been narrowed, and accountability, both scientific and political, has been curtailed.

Social scientists' search for regular patterns and reproducible results confronts a remarkable cross-disciplinary convergence of understandings that points to discontinuities and unpredictability in many domains. Paleontologists, geochronologists, and linguists reject the image of a steady and stately evolution in favor of a series of spasmodic spurts. Infinitesimal, often random events turn out to have global, even galactic significance. Assuming an orderly moment of initial creation, cosmologists scan the skies and record a decidedly disorderly arrangement. Instead of an even distribution of celestial bodies, they find clumps of stars. Even the clumps are not smoothly distributed. Galaxies occur in clusters separated by vast voids. At a still larger scale, clusters of supergalaxies are similarly unevenly distributed. To explain the apparent emergence of disorder from order, cosmologists reach to cosmic strings, ruptures in the fabric of space-time, and wormhole tunnels to alternative universes.

Some economists eagerly appropriate mathematicians' theories of catastrophe and chaos to analyze markets and money. Conventional categories like solid, liquid, and gas become inadequate in a world of semicrystals, superconductivity, and tunneling electrons that seem quite regularly to appear in two places at the same time. Quantum mechanics postulates uncertainty and constructs reality from mathematical probabilities. Its categories and entities are averages, highly reliable in general but frustratingly uninformative about the behavior of unique individual entities. To a degree that is discomforting to many, the ostensibly objective reality depends on the initiative and activities of the observer. The exact characteristics (*state, spin, form, velocity*) of a particle can be known (in the usual sense of that term) only when someone bothers to try to find out. Even then, increased precision in determining one characteristic reduces the precision of the determination of the others.

Humanists, too, grapple with uncertainties and discontinuities. For many, high culture is no longer uniquely privileged and therefore cannot provide a secure vantage point, a solid standard for examination and measurement. Validated within its local domain, each perspective asserts its authority and legitimacy. Rootlessness favors disassembly and deconstruction, not synthesis.

Political analysts, like meteorologists, can be certain only when looking backward, and often not even then. For both, correct understandings are validated by congruence with observable events. For both, prediction is potentially a confirming process. Both can offer at best limited confidence in short-range predictions and even less over the longer term. The consumers of their knowledge find equally dissatisfying a 40 percent probability of rain and a 40 percent probability of a military coup. Explanation and understanding must envision a large, and enduring, degree of uncertainty.

Across the domains of knowledge, then, there is increasing recognition that small events may have large consequences. As in the clash of the earth's tectonic plates, movement is abrupt and spasmodic, simultaneously constructive and destructive. The creation of knowledge itself is characterized more by occasional unique insights than by the accumulation of small, connected understandings. It is not that scholars have given up their search for pattern and regularity in their respective domains. They surely have not. Especially energetic is the effort to explain how order spawns disorder, and since the disorder is apparently not random, to explain what orders it. That effort, too, occurs in many different disciplines and across disciplinary boundaries. How did the orderly Big Bang become clumps and clusters? How did relatively undifferentiated human groups generate the complex patterns of differentiation and discrimination that characterize contemporary societies? Perhaps the most dramatic outcome of addressing these puzzles is the increasing recognition of the importance of nonlinearities and discontinuities. Writing in *Discover* magazine in 1989, Stephen Jay Gould pointed out:

> It cannot be coincidental that all the mathematical advances catching public attention over the past decade—from René Thom's catastrophe theory, to Ilya Prigogine's bifurcations, to Benoit Mandelbrot's fractals, to the current surge of interest in chaos theory—have the common property of producing large and rapid changes in the overt forms of things from small alterations in the underlying formulas that generate them.[28]

Note that the chaos of chaos theory refers not to a patternless jumble but rather to the process by which small perturbations produce tidal waves. Imagine two airplanes flying side by side along nearly identical paths. Clearly, a divergence in their routes that is initially too small to be measured will eventually have the two airplanes flying away from each other and reaching very different destinations. Recall the perhaps apocryphal story of the ingenious bank official who managed to have the thousandths of a cent lost to rounding transferred to his account. Depositors who reviewed their statements saw nothing missing when the bank's 6.33 percent interest rate added $49.18 to their $777.00 balance. But the embezzler was pleased to see $0.0041 deposited to his secret account. A nearly perfect crime, it seemed. No one lost anything, but he soon became quite rich. Collecting the fractions of a penny that were beyond the precision that the bank maintained made him a millionaire, at least temporarily. Or consider the efforts to establish precisely the orbital paths of the planets in our solar system, each influenced by all of the others and directly and indirectly shaped by forces outside the solar system. Modern computation technology permits a high level of precision over a short time-horizon. But as the orbital paths are projected into the future, irregularities that are too small to be recorded at the outset reduce the precision that is possible. The system is termed chaotic because far enough into the future it is impossible to determine exactly what will happen; or more accurately, the farther from the initial conditions, the greater the uncertainty. Precisely because the system is chaotic, improved instrumentation and more rapid computation can never resolve the uncertainty.

Uncertainties of this sort inexorably impose themselves on both the theory and practice of social science. The potentially enormous significance of initial conditions highlights the contextual and situational specificity of our findings. The inaccuracies and large margins of error in the data on human behaviors that compound these uncertainties ought to make us cautious, tentative, and skeptical in our interpretations. Recognizing these uncertainties and discontinuities ought to, and sometimes does, carry with it a healthy humility in our efforts to extend knowledge and the limits of what is knowable. To approach that from another perspective, as the search for understanding confronts the frontiers of knowledge, careful observers become increasingly cognizant of the roots and limits not only of their knowledge, but more importantly, of their ways of knowing.

Even as scholars and practitioners become increasingly aware of the extent and importance of uncertainty, however, the development business demands ever greater certainty. Let us pursue for a moment the recent history of development research. Much of contemporary social science shares a common set of premises. There is a fundamental order to social interactions; that order is discoverable through the application of (social) scientific methods; that order explains much, though not all, observed behavior; knowledge about that order can be used to structure or change society, though individual social scientists may or may not be interested in doing so.

In addition to sharing these premises, developmentalists share a common objective: to use their understanding of the underlying order to reform society; that is, to make things better in some form or other. Some social scientists, of course, explicitly reject this objective and deny that it guides their work. In practice, however, this reformist impulse, the origins of which lie in liberal individualism, is implicit in much of standard social science. Even those who insist that their scholarship is not influenced by this determination to make things better often justify their work in those terms. Hence, the principal task for students of development—in Kuhn's terms, normal science—is to develop a set of statements about the relationships among the major units of the economic/ideological/political/social system. Those statements are to be falsifiable and testable empirically. Wherever possible, short, simple, more encompassing, and unqualified statements are to be preferred to longer, more complex, less encompassing, and qualified statements. For at least some social scientists, these statements have, or should have, law-like characteristics.

Implicit in the ethos of planning and management that is pervasive among developmentalists is the belief that rational resource allocation requires reliable knowledge about whatever behaviors and relationships are deemed important in a particular setting. Do investments in primary education yield a higher rate of return than allocations to universities? Do expanded agricultural extension services significantly increase the appropriate use of fertilizers and pesticides? Is external supervision more effective than increased internal accountability in reducing cooperatives' inefficiencies and wastage?

Initially, small local studies provide partial and tentative answers to these and other questions. But the pressure for broader generalization and higher levels of confidence is relentless. As the results from limited studies are accumulated, their conditions and caveats are discarded, and the confidence with which their findings are presented is compounded. The possible becomes likely; likely outcomes become, simply, results; and eventually, and sometimes very quickly, a cascade of certainties generates the sort of simply stated and largely unqualified statements that are then used to advocate and defend particular courses of action. Rather than uncertainty and humility, we find certainty and arrogance.

In short, this demand for precision and certainty has two principal sources. One resides in the rules for the creation of knowledge that have come to dominate the social sciences. The second reflects the imperatives of lending institutions and their increasingly important role in research on development.

To understand what people do and why, we need to know something about what they have done. Rarely, however, are social scientists direct observers of all of the events of interest to them. Hence, most often we rely on information that someone else has collected, more or less systematically, usually for some other purpose. The behavioral revolution in the social sciences, with its shrill cries of "falsifiability!" and "reproducibility!" has pushed us toward the sort of information that can be recorded and stored in quantitative form. It has pushed us as well toward increasingly complex, and perhaps sophisticated, techniques for exploring relationships within that information.

Note here the powerful but often little recognized influence of the prevalent computation strategies. To the present, most computing in the social sciences has been digital. High-speed combinations of relatively simple bimodal choices—*on/off, yes/no, either/or*—permit the manipulation of massive volumes of information. Miniaturization and other technological advances have produced extraordinary increases in speed and capacity. Beyond the raw processing capabilities, digital representation of information has important advantages for social scientists. For example, ambiguities in categorization are either explicitly precluded or organized into contingent connections through which individual paths are unambiguous. For another example, consider the resistance of digital communications to distracting and confounding small errors. A telephone conversation across a digital connection with extensive interference remains clear. The receiving apparatus need determine only whether the received signal is high or low. It is not confused by a signal that is a little bit higher than other lows, or slightly lower than other highs. Like its counterparts in the digitized reproduction of music, it filters out the unevenness, restoring the original purity and clarity.

Actual voices and symphonies, however, have more than two states. Indeed, their range varies in infinitesimal increments. The analog world is at best imperfectly captured in its digital representation. However sophisticated the sampling techniques, some information is lost. Similarly, when social scientists are constrained to construct categories that are mutually exclusive, the disadvantages of excluding inconsistency and ambiguity may outweigh the value of the apparent resulting clarity. The variations in temporal and spatial context that go unrecorded because they are smaller than the units of measure employed may prove to be critical to inference and interpretation.

Of course, even the most advanced techniques can at best provide only partial remedies for inaccuracies and inconsistencies in the original data. Indeed, careful scholars regularly include a caveat at the beginning of their publications, calling readers' attention to gaps and other problems in the data they use. Unfortunately, often even careful scholars proceed to ignore their own reservations, developing arguments that rely on data-characteristics and/or a level of precision not found in the original data.

The insistence on certainty in an uncertain world—that is, a setting that is chaotic (in the sense explained above) and where the relationships that matter most are likely to manifest sharp discontinuities—is neither liberating nor rejuvenating. The cascades of certainty that constitute research on development neither wash away ignorance and confusion nor irrigate the seedbeds of local imagination and initiative. Instead, as it becomes a set of largely externally defined rules specifying acceptable courses of action, research disorients and imprisons. Even worse, the prisoners themselves become the warden and jailers.

Several implications follow. First, humility: we need a much clearer sense of the limitations of our understandings and of their partial and conditional character. Second, we need to discard the model of understanding as the result of an incremental accumulation of discrete knowledge in favor of a recognition of a world characterized by discontinuities and small results with large consequences. Third, we need to reject the current model of cloistered or proprietary research in favor of an openness both to alternative approaches and methods and to critical scrutiny. For that to be fruitful, fourth, we need self-consciously to protect and nurture the critics. And fifth, in this era of political democratization, we need to institutionalize the accountability of those who provide development advice to those who are expected to benefit from it.

REVISING THE KNOWLEDGE-BASE:
TRANSCENDING (AND TRANSFORMING) ITS LIMITS

I have been concerned thus far with the knowledge-base for teaching about Africa in the 1990s and especially the more and less visible constraints it imposes on us and our students. That knowledge-base is of course not static. Even as we seek to correct and revise it, what we know, or think we know, about Africa continues to respond to events and ideas on and off the campus. I want here to highlight four major currents, again both political and intellectual, that shape the thinking and teaching about Africa early in this final decade of the twentieth century.

Socialist Disarray and U.S. Triumphalism

There is a grand—and instructive—irony in the contemporary triumphalism. As Przeworski puts it:

> Neoliberal ideology, emanating from the United States and various multinational agencies, claims that the choice is obvious: there is only one path to development, and it must be followed. . . . Yet if a Martian were asked to pick the most efficient and humane economic systems on earth, it would certainly not choose the countries that rely most on markets. The United States is a stagnant economy in which real wages have been constant for more than a decade and the real income of the poorer 40 percent of the population has declined. It is an inhumane society in which 11.5 percent of the population—some 28 million people, including 20 percent of the children—lives in poverty. It is the oldest democracy on earth, but has one of the lowest voter-participation rates in the democratic world, and the highest per capita prison population in the world.[29]

October of 1992 highlighted yet another triumphalist irony. The United States marked five hundred years since 1492. For much of the New World, Columbus's voyage was an early moment in the process of European conquest and colonial rule. Half a millennium later, what were we to celebrate—or mourn? Do our students understand the cultural confusion over this anniversary? Do they recognize what is at stake in the confrontations over the role and consequences of the arrival of Columbus and his crews? Do our courses help them acquire knowledge to address these issues?

Some observers see the orderly march of history in the apparent self-destruction of socialism and the seemingly inexorable success of capitalism. That self-congratulatory triumphalism is surely shortsighted. Indeed, we may be witnessing not the terminal decay of socialism but the struggles of its rebirth amidst the debris of statist authoritarianism. More likely than the enduring impregnable hegemony of a single country is an era of innovation and experimentation. With new institutional arrangements will come new tensions and power relationships, perhaps with dramatic rapidity. Surely the future will be no more linear or unidirectional than was the past. Only faith, not reason, can sustain the conclusion that efforts to construct a democratic social order without private property have been definitively defeated. Insisting that there is only one path to development—*ours*—this triumphalism tells us that there is no need to explore alternative routes; indeed, no point in doing so. The perception of victory seems to make legitimate the ethnocentrism and arrogance of the U.S. regard for Africa.

At the same time, this triumphalism makes it difficult to explore socialism and socialist movements in Africa. It considers communism even less worthy of study, other than as a historical example of a flawed ideology and its unfortunate influence. How, then, to help undergraduates understand why the South African Communist Party appears to be vibrant and healthy and why children in South Africa regularly rename their schools after its leaders? Are they all simply ignorant or hopelessly confused? Or is there a content that the triumphalism obscures?

Afrocentrism

Most Africanists see themselves as advocates for Africa. Among their colleagues, both African and non-African, they may be quite critical; some have been outspoken in their opposition to tyrannical rulers, official corruption, and abuse of authority. At the same time, Africanists recognize the extent of the misinformation about Africa that is widely accepted as knowledge. Consequently, however critical they may be, for the most part Africanists also assume responsibility for presenting Africa accurately, for keeping Africa on agendas from which there is risk that it will disappear, and defending Africa against the epithets and charges directed toward it. As they do so, however, most continue to treat Africa as *them*. And in most U.S. colleges and universities there has been a visible distance between these Africanists, most of them white, and their colleagues for whom Africa is *we*. As I have noted, in few institutions has there been a serious attempt to integrate African and Afro-American studies; in fewer still have those attempts been successful.

For many years, a group of scholars has sought to relocate the center of gravity in the study of Africa. That effort has had multiple strands, including emphasizing the African contribution to European societies, to science and scientific inquiry, and to education and recording and transmitting knowledge. Revising the history of contacts between Africans and others in turn has consequences for what happens in the classroom.

Even though this Afrocentrism remains a small voice in a very noisy room, some instructors have found it threatening. In part, that has to do with an implicit or explicit challenge to the legitimacy of a largely white African studies faculty. In part, that is perceived as a challenge to the entire academic edifice by a small group of faculty and students who may appear to be claiming that commitment is more important than expertise, and that the accepted procedures for accumulating knowledge are suspect. In part, of course, there are also the tensions I noted above about access to resources.

Generally unstated but equally powerful here is a confrontation about the *we/them* relationship and how it is specified; or rather, who specifies it. Afrocentrism is explicitly critical of the distance between *we* the instructors and *them* the Africans. If that challenge were entirely a matter of perspective and analytic framework to be debated in academic settings, it would be serious but not terribly threatening. But that challenge is not solely intellectual: it is also a challenge to the white academic establishment's own self-definition. Not only is its expertise questioned but its ownership (some would prefer to call it guardianship) of the *them*—that *them* by whom we define ourselves. If *we* are no longer able to specify the *them*, then how can we know who we are?

To put that in more conventional terms, characterizing people, societies, and cultures as uncivilized, or backward, or less developed is central to specifying what is unique about us. We define ourselves in large part in terms of what we are not. For much of the United States, what we are most clearly *not* is Africa. To learn that Africa is not really as we have been describing it undermines our claim to be more modern or further developed; and if we lose control over defining Africa, then our society might turn out to be the one that is backward and less developed; even uncivilized.

In recent years, the assertion of this Africa-centered perspective has reached beyond the study of Africa. Much of the study of what is commonly called Western civilization in U.S. colleges and universities pays little attention to Africa. Yet it is clear that African societies influenced what was to become Europe early in its history, that Africa played a major role in preserving and extending the knowledge of ancient Greece and Rome during the tribal wars of Europe's Dark Ages, and that Africans have been a significant part of the population of the New World for several hundred years. An Africa-centered orientation thus requires revising not only how we teach about Africa but, equally important, how we teach about ourselves.

Feminist Scholarship

No systematic observer in Africa could miss the central role that women play in production as well as reproduction. Yet, for much of the twentieth century, observers described, analyzed, and explained Africa as if that were not the case. History was recorded in terms of which men did what. Characterizations of the economy and the development advice that ensued assumed that the model producer was a male.

Two decades ago teachers had a limited choice of books that explored and highlighted the activities and lives of Africa's women. For some topics and themes, there was little that was readily accessible. That is certainly no longer the case. Relevant publications are numerous, diverse, varied in their presumptions about prior knowledge and level of sophistication, and easily available.

There are two major threads in this literature. First, both feminist authors and others have sought to detail and decipher women's roles. The task has been to revisit places and events to fill in the part of the story omitted in accounts in which women are hardly visible and certainly not central to the action. The parallel effort has been to integrate women more fully into official and unofficial development programs. Although often this writing talks about "bringing women into" history or development, of course women were never *out*. Insisting that scholars address women's roles, relocating women and their activities to the center of attention and action, and recognizing African women as interpreters and not simply the interpreted has dramatically transformed our understanding of some events and relationships and will surely have a similar effect on many more. For some instructors, this thread is already woven into the fabric of their courses. For others, there is a long way to go.

The second thread has to do with the radical intellectual contribution of feminist scholarship. I use the term *radical* here not to refer to political orientation or practice but to emphasize the fundamental challenges to ways of understanding—to social science more generally—that have emerged from and been nurtured by feminist scholars.

Consider, for example, the social construction of gender. Studies of the social construction of ethnicity are numerous and diverse: they have been and continue to be widely debated. The most influential of those studies inform not only how we understand Africa but also how we study and teach about it. Much more recent is the parallel set of studies on the social construction of gender. But even those have for the most part not yet taken up the challenge of imaginative feminist scholarship, since in practice they address gender roles, not gender itself. We take for granted the meaning of gender. We assume we know the meanings of female/woman and male/man. But do we? Here, too, the critical scholarship suggests we know rather less than we think we do and that most of us are unaware of our own ignorance.

Feminist scholarship charges us with two related but distinct tasks as we teach about Africa. One is to establish and illuminate the role of women in Africa and to employ gender as an analytic construct across the wide range of topics we address, largely within the framework of contemporary social science. The second is to focus on the ways that social science itself is fundamentally flawed or incomplete precisely because its intellectual and human organization reflect the gender hierarchies and inequalities of the societies in which it has developed.

The Conjunction of Development Assistance and Research

Although this chapter is not directly concerned either with development assistance or research on development, both influence teaching about Africa. As I have suggested, not only research findings but perhaps even more important its methods shape our understanding and often our pedagogy. We are accustomed to thinking of social science research as the responsibility of scholars, conducted in reasonably public and well documented ways, and reviewed by competent peers in the competition for support, in seminars and conferences, and in publication. What is missing from that picture is the extensive research on Africa commissioned and sometimes conducted by the agencies that provide development assistance. Though generally much less visible and frequently not critically evaluated by informed and experienced outsiders, that research has come to play a major role in what we know about Africa.

That the state funds research and influences its agenda should not surprise us. After all, many of the early European visitors to Africa had funding directly from their governments or indirectly through academic societies. The close connections between the colonial enterprise and the social science of that era are equally clear. That earlier experience, unfortunately, seems not to have sharpened our critical faculties. It is useful, therefore, to note very briefly the forms and consequences of this conjunction of development assistance and research. Education will provide the case in point.[30]

As African countries have increasingly sought external assistance to support not only new but also continuing education programs, the agencies providing that support have come to play a major role in both setting the education agenda and determining how that agenda is set. The World Bank has come to be the lead agency in that role. How to choose among the alternative policies that compete for support? Where failures abound and success stories are scarce—and available resources are scarcer still—which policy directions are to be pursued? It is in this process of specifying education strategies, both large-scale and small-scale, that the funding becomes a principal determinant. In the contemporary context, research becomes the visa required to cross funding's frontier. The prevailing understanding, indeed faith, that education is a complex undertaking whose organization and management are best left to relevant experts limits popular participation in discussions of education policy. It also privileges those among the experts who are most successful in characterizing their recommendations as supported by relevant research. In the face of an unmet and in most places still expanding demand, the absolute shortage of funds advantages those who are most successful in attracting external resources to support their recommendations. Together, research and funding constitute control, sometimes challenged and occasionally deflected but rarely rejected or overturned.

The manifestations, consequences, and problems of this conjunction of funding and research are multiple. Especially problematic are the ways in which this conjunction influences and constrains the education and development discourse, legitimizes weak propositions, entrenches flawed understandings by according them official status, seeds and fertilizes theoretical and analytic fads, and treats education primarily as technique and administration. In the conjunction of funding and research, scholarship becomes a proprietary process. The investors have the determining voice in the selection of topics, researchers, and methods, limit access to source materials, and often control the dissemination of findings. Consequently,

the process of knowledge-creation is obscured, mystifying the power relations embedded in the research and thereby in the programs it supports.
Perhaps not entirely aware of their own role, scholars become advocates
not only for particular understandings of development and underdevelopment but also for a particular sort of global order. Equally corrosive of innovative, thorough, and reliable research is the absence within this financial-intellectual complex of the critical review and peer scrutiny of
academia. Consequently, research that would not withstand broad exposure and critical examination entrenches selected approaches and methods,
filters explanations, and legitimizes particular courses of action. Ortho-
doxy masquerades as pluralism. Obeisance to research obfuscates the decisionmaking process, obscuring its basic assumptions and cloaking its
politics with the accoutrements of scholarly inquiry. Enmeshed in the techniques and administration of proprietary research, perceptive and well-
meaning individuals lose sight of the larger issues at stake. Obliged to cast
their comments in the language and form of this special sort of research,
even critics are distracted.

Recognizing this conjunction of development assistance and research
carries two implications for teaching about Africa. First, we must be a lot
clearer about the sources of what we take to be knowledge about Africa.
Correspondingly we must enable and encourage our students to ferret out
the biases and flaws, not only in research of the sort to which we are accustomed but also in this research that is much less visible and accessible.
Second, beyond competent academic consumerism, we must focus our
critical attention on this conjunction itself, addressing both its substantive
and methodological consequences.

CHALLENGES ON MANY LEVELS

The challenges in teaching about Africa are multiple. At one level they
have to do with information and misinformation, often a great deal of the
latter. At another level they have to do with recognizing the ways in which
larger events, both inside and outside the academy, constrain and condition
teaching about Africa. At yet another level they concern the ways in which
teaching about Africa is intertwined with the issues of race and identity
that trouble our society. Transcending the specifically Africa content of
our courses, several other challenges seem to me to stand out.

It is essential that young people in the United States recognize that
there are perspectives on the world other than our own. All teaching of
course must deal with things that are not quite what they seem, or even
that are quite different from their appearance. Beyond that, I suggest, those
who teach about Africa must be especially concerned with the "seeming"
process. African experiences will often turn out to be unfathomable if they

are forever filtered through a screen that is largely Western and white and predominantly male. It is not that Western white males are structurally incapable of understanding Africa, any more than, say, de Tocqueville was unable to understand the early United States because he was French and an outsider. Rather, it is to argue that we cannot assess their understandings until we can also hear African voices.

To put that differently, effective teaching about Africa requires that our students engage Africa. To engage Africa, they must grapple with Africa and Africans as actors, not objects. For Africa to be a continent of cartographers, not simply places that are mapped, it must inform how we understand it. Africa must not only be the focus of our attention but must also guide how that attention is directed and structured. Whether or not Afrocentric, our courses surely must be Africa-centered.

And that, in turn, requires that our students develop the ability to approach the world along pathways that consciously and purposefully reflect perspectives quite different from those with which they are comfortable.

A second challenge is to help our students understand that *blaming the victim does not constitute an explanation*. Competent teachers about Africa have long ago ceased treating Africa and Africans as museum exhibits on display.[31] Yet, explaining Africa solely in terms of things African is doing precisely that, in a rather more insidious form. The ready assumption that if there is a problem in Africa its causes are to be found in Africans' culture, or psyche, or habits, or social structure reinforces the sense of an Africa somehow insulated from the rest of the world, whether enriched or impoverished by its history and traditions.

Consider, for example, what has happened to education planning in much of Africa. Faced with high and increasing demands for schooling and sorely limited resources, education planners have regularly sought external assistance. Experienced at their craft, many of Africa's education planners tune their plans to the aid they think will be available. If, say, the Swedes are thought to be interested in adult education, then on their arrival, Swedish aid officials find proposed plans for expanding and improving adult education. When the Swiss arrive, the local priority may seem to be higher education. Planning becomes marketing. Although education planners may have their own sense of what needs to be done, without resources nothing will get done. It is surely quite reasonable for them to adjust what they describe as their major priorities in terms of their understanding of the sources of funds available. One result of this strategy is apparently contradictory objectives and priorities. Another may be lack of continuity and consistency in pursuing an agreed course of action. A third is the effort to transfer funds from the projects for which they were formally allocated to other activities that have higher local priority but that were not directly funded. Observers often seek to explain these results in terms of planners' limited education and experience, unfamiliarity with relevant techniques, opportunism and corruption, and the like. Clearly, however, the transformation of planning into marketing makes sense only in terms of Africa's integration into a pattern of global interactions, a pattern whose primary dynamic lies largely beyond Africa's control. To focus on planners' incompetence is to miss the point.

A third challenge is to *restore the legitimacy of area studies.* The holism of students of Africa is potentially a very powerful lesson for their social science colleagues. But as I have suggested, that holism has increasingly been displaced by an intellectual particularism. For our students, it must be clear that to understand African politics, it is necessary to develop solid knowledge of Africa's history, organization of production, patterns of social relationships, cultural expression, and more.

Finally, we need to help our students understand that *to learn about Africa is also to learn about ourselves.* Our apparently insatiable need to continue to define ourselves by inventing and substantiating a darker-skinned *other*—the racism of our own society—is central to every course on Africa. To fail to recognize that, and to address it critically, undermines whatever else we do.

NOTES

1. Paul Johnson, "Colonialism's Back—and Not a Moment Too Soon," *New York Times Magazine,* 18 April 1993: 22–23, 43–44.

2. Ibid: 44.

3. There are many code words in this story. *Civilized* is one of them. Behavior that does not fit one's own moral code, or even one's sense of good and bad, is more easily disparaged if it is termed uncivilized. Over time, *civilized* had become the shorthand for good, progressive, modern, enlightened, humane, just and democratic. *Uncivilized* is brandished like a spray gun that paints large areas in a few sweeps: it is used regularly to relegate much of humankind to the depths of the universal dustbin. Were its consequences not so tragic, it would be amusing to note that countries that guarantee all their citizens access to health-care resources, or that have abolished the death penalty, or done away with corporal punishment in schools are considered uncivilized compared with the United States.

4. As we shall see, the efforts to shape and reshape the contours of the relationships between Africa and Blacks resident overseas sometimes are, and ought to be, important influences on teaching about Africa. Notwithstanding those efforts, even for much of the black population of the United States, the measure of the primitive, the unmodern, the not-yet-fully-civilized is distinctly black.

5. As is always the case, generalizations that focus attention on major relationships and the trajectory of change at the large scale necessarily omit and distort at the small scale. For the purposes of this discussion, it is reasonable to consider common orientations and practices while recognizing the diversity and disagreements among those who teach about Africa.

6. World Bank, *Education in Sub-Saharan Africa: Policies for Adjustment, Revitalization and Expansion* (Washington: The World Bank, 1988): viii. (Emphasis added.)

7. Mark W. DeLancey and Christopher Herick, *African Politics in American Universities and Colleges: A Survey of Purposes, Methods, and Materials,* Institute of International Studies Occasional Paper No. 1 (Columbia, S.C.: University of South Carolina, 1979); and Mark W. DeLancey, December Green, and Kenneth J. Menkhaus, "African Politics at American Universities and Colleges: A Survey of Purposes, Methods and Materials" (paper presented at the African Studies Association annual conference, Denver, Colo., 1987).

8. The approaches and methods of anthropologists are of course far more complex and systematic than this suggests. My concern here is simply to highlight the characteristics of an approach to studying Africa that was influential at an earlier moment and that has since been significantly eclipsed. The introspective analyses of anthropology and its methodologies are numerous. Three that I have found insightful are Peter Rigby, *Persistent Pastoralists: Nomadic Societies in Transition* (London: Zed Books, 1985); George W. Stocking, Jr., *Colonial Situations: Essays on Contextualization of Ethnographic Knowledge, History of Anthropology* (Madison: University of Wisconsin Press, 1991); and Renato Rosaldo, *Culture and Truth: The Remaking of Social Analysis* (Boston: Beacon Press, 1989).

9. It is striking that a similar presumption has featured so prominently in the discussions of post-Gorbachev Europe. After all, *we* had won without a war, in large part because *they* wanted their societies to be more like ours. From this perspective, the promise of video recorders had prevailed over guaranteed jobs, low-cost housing, and affordable basic consumer goods. The attractiveness of that tradeoff was taken to prove not only the superiority of *our* system but also the universality of modernity.

10. There are of course exceptions. I have addressed some of the data problems in "The Facade of Precision in Education Data and Statistics: A Troubling Example from Tanzania," *Journal of Modern African Studies* 29 (December 1991): 669–689.

11. In fact, the climate is a common factor for much of Africa, where agricultural production is almost entirely dependent on adequate and timely rainfall. Put crudely, when the rains are sufficient and timely, all development strategies work, and success can be attributed to whichever is being employed at the time. When the rains are too light or too heavy, or come at the wrong time, no development strategy works, and failure can be blamed on whichever is then in practice.

12. At its root, identifying the nature, characteristics, and behaviors of the poor as the causes for poverty necessarily devolves to a genetic explanation. If the circumstances in which they live lead the poor to behave in ways that perpetuate their impoverishment, then it is those circumstances—local, national, global—that cause poverty, not something inherent in the poor. To insist that the poor are poor because of who they are, however disguised, sanitized, beautified, and situationally conditional that claim may be, is to assert a genetic basis for differences in wealth and their consequences.

13. A recent succinct commentary of this sort is *The State and the Crisis in Africa: In Search of a Second Liberation* (Uppsala: Dag Hammarskjöld Foundation, 1992).

14. V. Y. Mudimbe, *The Invention of Africa: Gnosis, Philosophy, and the Order of Knowledge* (Bloomington: Indiana University Press, 1988). T. Minh-ha Trinh broadens and extends this argument in *Woman, Native, Other: Writing Postcoloniality and Feminism* (Bloomington: Indiana University Press, 1989).

15. E.E. Evans-Pritchard, *Social Anthropology and Other Essays* (New York: Free Press, 1962): 119–120, quoted in Mudimbe, *The Invention of Africa,* 68.

16. B. Malinowski, in B. Malinowski et al., *Methods of Study of Culture Contact in Africa* (Oxford: Oxford University Press, 1938): vii, quoted in Mudimbe, *The Invention of Africa*, 20.

17. T. Minh-ha Trinh, *Woman, Native, Other: Writing Postcoloniality and Feminism* (Bloomington: Indiana University Press, 1989): 67.

18. From an advertisement for IQuest, a collection of databases, available electronically through CompuServe in *CompuServe Magazine* 11, 9, September 1992: 1. A box in the advertisement referred to *Facts on File,* perhaps the source of this quotation: a modestly extensive search, however, did not find this text there. By then, of course, my account had been billed and the advertisement had served its purpose.

19. That this premise informed research conducted at the end of the colonial era is less surprising than that it is so pervasive in research more than three decades later.

20. It is striking that both the modernizationists and many of their critics agree on the critical role of class. As early as the late 1950s, for example, Fanon asserted the importance of a modernizing middle class, even as he argued that the African nationalist leadership would fail to become just such a class (Frantz Fanon, *The Wretched of the Earth* [New York: Grove Press, 1963]).

21. I use here the terminology developed in Martin Carnoy and Joel Samoff, *Education and Social Transition in the Third World* (Princeton: Princeton University Press, 1990), especially chapter 1–3 and 10. Public policies are conditioned by the nature of the peripheral role that these countries' economies play in the world economy, by the corresponding enormous influence that the dynamic of metropolitan capitalism has on their development process, and also by significant noncapitalist elements in their own political systems. Note that *conditioned* differs from *dependent* in its emphasis on the internalization of many of the structural characteristics and much of the ideology of the world capitalist system, the role of local resources, the development of local social movements, and the emergence of a local class structure in determining the organization of production, the nature of political formations, and the relative importance of specific contradictions within the peripheral state.

22. I use *class* here in the common but somewhat imprecise sense of the local segment of the ruling-class alliance that exercises the functions of government but that can rule only with the support of external owners of production. In this sense, the bureaucracy governs but does not, by itself, rule. Although the bureaucracy is not a class simply by virtue of its political position or its corporate interests, it behaves as a class, or more accurately as a fraction of a class, as it exercises its authority on behalf of the entire ruling-class alliance.

23. In this sense (of a perspective so deeply embedded in a society's institutions and practices that it is scarcely noticed, rarely examined, and hardly ever challenged) the ideology of modernization can be termed *hegemonic.*

24. Trinh, *Woman, Native, Other,* 52.

25. Several other terms have also been used to label this phenomenon, including *parallel, invisible, hidden, subterranean, underground,* and *second* economy.

26. Especially on social science methodology, "Class, Class Conflict, and the State in Africa," *Political Science Quarterly* 97 (Spring 1982): 105–127; "On Class, Paradigm, and African Politics," *Africa Today* 29, 2 (1982): 41–50; and "Chaos and Certainty in Development" (Buenos Aires: XV World Congress of the International Political Science Association, 1991).

27. I draw here on ideas initially presented in the paper listed in Note 26, "Chaos and Certainty in Development."

28. Stephen Jay Gould, "An Asteroid to Die For," *Discover* 10 (October 1989): 64.

29. Adam Przeworski, "The Neoliberal Fallacy," *Journal of Democracy* 3 (July 1992): 46.

30. I summarize briefly here points that are developed more fully in my "Research, Knowledge, and Policy in Assistance to African Education: The Financial-Intellectual Complex" (Buenos Aires: XV World Congress of the International Political Science Association, 1991).

31. Alas, that has not disappeared entirely; and perhaps it gains legitimacy from Africa's current problems and public image. Challenging that practice, particularly in one's own work, is difficult. My point here is that those who succeed in getting past that problem face an even more daunting challenge.

3

Deposing Tarzan, or Teaching About Africa in the Post–Cold War Era: A Commentary on Joel Samoff

William G. Martin

If we were to start with Joel Samoff's challenges for teachers and students of Africa (in the concluding pages of the last chapter), we may all quickly, I think, find agreement. Few would find fault with statements that "It is essential that young people . . . recognize that *there are perspectives on the world other than our own.*" Or that we are challenged "to help our students understand that *blaming the victim does not constitute an explanation*"; that we need to "*restore the legitimacy of area studies,*" and to help students understand that "*to learn about Africa is also to learn about ourselves*" (emphasis in original). Such conclusions parallel the themes and conclusions of other chapters in this volume, which strongly emphasize the inherently critical character for Euro–North Americans of learning from a culture other than their own.

As the body of Samoff's essay makes eminently clear, however, his assessment moves well beyond agreements on the ability of African courses to counter Euro-North American provincialism. The strategy is straightforward, if rarely encountered: an analysis of long-term trends in two key areas: (1) the practice of how we teach about Africa, with particular emphasis on the politics of Africa; and (2) the construction of both a body of knowledge regarding Africa and teachers of it. From these considerations come the call to reorganize the field and its teaching, targeting a critical reinsertion of socialism, an African-centered perspective, feminist scholarship, and a revision of the relationship between scholars, research, and their institutional supports.

It is a complex and sweeping set of arguments. I suspect however that most readers would find, as I do, that the overall tone and direction of the argument lead to a stark and bitter interpretation: despite the critical perspective provided by area and African studies, the study and teaching of Africa, like the continent itself, faces a dismal future. This is not a conclusion I share, despite the fact that I find myself in substantial agreement with most of Samoff's arguments. I even agree, furthermore, with the openly stated assumption that underpins this conclusion; namely, that "over the longer term, what matters most . . . is what happens outside the university, not within it."

To take this approach can lead, as I hope to demonstrate, to a quite different set of conclusions. For while we may agree—versus the standard assessments—that African studies and the teaching of Africa may be in crisis, this represents, in my view, a rich opportunity to shed the constraints imposed by the construction and teaching of Africa as formulated during the last forty years. This is an opportunity to be explored, if not in every detail celebrated—and not simply a series of grim facts and bleak trends to be deplored. And this has, moreover, direct and radical implications for undergraduate teaching.

I can only briefly sketch this argument here, posing four questions that organize and follow from Samoff's analysis: (1) What provides the global context for the study and teaching of Africa in the next decade? (2) How do we and our undergraduates understand and study Africa, particularly in the social sciences? (3) What is the future of African studies and the teaching of Africa? And (4) How do we move beyond *we* and *them*, Africa vs. United States, in the academy, the social and historical disciplines, and African studies?

TRIUMPHALISM—OR THE END OF THE COLD WAR LIBERALISM?

What [U.S. undergraduates] study, and how they study it, is influenced much more by what is happening in the world—or rather, by how global events come to be generally interpreted and understood—than by a deepening knowledge of Africa or improved theories and methods in the social sciences.—Samoff, Chapter 2 of this book.

What is the global context for the study and teaching of Africa in the next decade? In answer, Samoff paints an easily recognizable picture: U.S. students confront a world in which "triumphalism is seemingly boundless": the United States stands victorious in the epoch-making contests of the Cold War, with naked capitalism winning the battle against communist/socialist/nonaligned states and movements. Gone, it would appear, are the prospects of any alternative development strategy to full integration with and subordination to the North Atlantic countries. Increasingly, we are told, there is only one path forward: an obeisance to the free market, the world financial community, and the dictates of the North. For Africa, the trends are even more negative: a wholesale collapse beyond dependency to the pitiful state of supplicant for aid. In Samoff's words: "Dependent Africa had become *crisis Africa* and then *pitiable Africa*."

As Samoff's arguments stress, we have indeed entered a new global phase, where the framing issues of the past generation no longer hold sway. Whether and to what extent this implies a wholesale victory of the North, however, remains in my view very much an open question. Indeed, I would derive an alternative analysis. What we are witnessing, I believe, is not the loss of the possibility of alternative, autonomous paths by states beyond the Euro–North American center of the world economy, much less a return to modernization theory (of which more below), but a collapse of the legitimacy of the Euro–North American global project in its cultural, economic, and ideological forms. Swept away are a variety of illusions, from the promise and ideology of capitalist progress, to the expectations that national developmental models can deliver enhanced well-being.

I can only briefly sketch this line of argument here. As we shall see, however, it has substantive implications for the United States, U.S. undergraduates, and our relation to Africa. Rather than focusing upon present triumphalism, one might begin by recalling that the Cold War was made possible and sustained by the construction of an adversary relationship with "Communist" states and movements. At one swift stroke, the end of the Cold War has thus removed the ideological underpinnings of U.S. world leadership. At the same time, the structural basis of U.S. leadership is also in tatters, as is all too evident from the daily evidence of continuing global stagnation and the reemergence of rival core powers/regions. Undergraduates have no problem recognizing the uncertainties these entail: gone are the halcyon days of a stable global order pivoted on the United States—and the prosperity (and jobs) that it assured.

I can hear the immediate objections: but surely none of this displaces the unprecedented power of the North in general and the United States in particular over the South and Africa. At the level of policy analysis, and in particular the IMF/World Bank/USAID consortiums, this is true. Yet at the level of the construction of an understanding of North-South relations, almost all the old certainties are disappearing. For over thirty years, prosperity within a Cold War framework locked in a "liberal" vision of developing the South on Northern models. In essence, the patterns were dictated by a single framework with two variants: nation-state development on the basis of Western, modernization models, or nation-state development based on communist/socialist models (the intellectual and political roots of this developmentalist paradigm must, in this discussion, be set aside). Even the most radical movements and their supporters were entrapped within this framework, seeking to attain through the capture of state power an independence that would, in the end, fail to provide the promised development.

In both "capitalist" and "communist/socialist" cases, the fundamental premise was that national development was assured. This was, as we now know, a grand illusion; as any number of studies have shown, the gap between rich and poor on a global scale has steadily increased across at least the last five decades.[1] Indeed, it is not too difficult to argue that the modern capitalist world represents, by comparison with previous social systems and civilizations, an epoch of unprecedented inequality, poverty, homelessness, famine, and violence.[2] Nothing makes this clearer than the more recent confrontation of these realities on the part of East Europeans and Russians, as the effects of global stagnation have finally shaken their regimes and the illusive promises of "capitalist" development have become evident (and belatedly, one must note, by comparison with Africa, Latin America, and Asia).[3]

In summary, and by contrast to Samoff's reading, I would offer a quite different assessment of recent events on a world scale. Far from heralding the victory of the West, we are witnessing the collapse of an old order predicated on U.S. hegemony, global expansion, and promise of nation-state (Western or Eastern-led) development. From North to South it is evident that progress and well-being are no longer a national affair, which leaves standing naked the *enduring* global relationships and inequalities that have so long been denied.

This conclusion is, particularly in my abbreviated presentation here, a highly interpretative one. It may be illustrated more concretely by examining Samoff's argument in relation to the knowledge-base of African studies and the organization and teaching of Africa at the undergraduate level.

TARZAN AS HOMO ECONOMICUS: THE KNOWLEDGE-BASE

How do we and our undergraduates understand and study Africa? In the wake of "triumphant" capitalism it is easy to discern, as Samoff unearths, a refurbishing of traditional images of Africa, the poor and pitiful *other*. One need look no further than the popular magazine racks. As the cover and lead story of the 7 September 1992 issue of *Time* illustrates all too well, the political and economic condition of Africa easily calls forth images of decay and disaster. Even where prospects are brighter, as in the demise of minority rule in South Africa, one constantly confronts the presentation of Black on Black Violence versus a white world of responsible leadership, signified not only by de Klerk but white radicals (as in the September 1992 issue of the magazine of youth-style, *Details*, where the discussion of opposition to apartheid is restricted to young white radicals' rejection of conscription). As for the reach of such images, one needs only to note that both magazines are of course also sold in South Africa.

As the rich, triumphalist West is now placed against Africa, Samoff tells us, *traditional* becomes once again *primitive;* and the primitive becomes the underdeveloped; and the West—the West is the model for all peoples aspiring to liberal democracy and development. Translated into academia, the result, Samoff argues, is the refurbishing of modernization theory, the collapse of alternative paradigms and paths to Western-led development, and the rising domination within African studies of the discipline of economics due to its role as the model, scientific discipline. Apart from the fact that stereotypes endure,[4] the world that Samoff describes is unrecognizable and univocal. It is a world I find neither in the discipline within which I am employed (sociology), the social sciences and humanities, African studies, nor my classrooms. In each of these arenas one finds, far from a resurgent hegemonic perspective, uncertainty and challenges from multiple perspectives.

One could reject these out of hand as simply unruly and noisy voices, shortly to be swept away, as patriarchal, core-centered perspectives reassert themselves. If we move beyond the realm of contested interpretations of contemporary global or classroom events, however, what we find is a fundamental collapse of the intellectual and ideological pillars that have sustained, for well over a century, not just ethnocentric images but our conceptual and theoretical understanding of the modern world.

Recall the construction of the social sciences in the nineteenth century: cutting across increasingly divided disciplines was a shared premise of the belief that the British industrial revolution, the French Revolution, and the Enlightenment generated the secular, modern, capitalist world. From abstract and ahistorical models of this process came the founding theories and concepts of economics, political science, and sociology (history being left to deal with "the past," and anthropology with the non-Western).[5] Samoff illustrates quite well the post–World War II development of this framework, moving from Tönnies' *gemeinshaft-gesellschaft* distinction to Parsonian pattern variables and their application in the social sciences and the study of Africa. Part and parcel of this process was the increasing attempt, again as Samoff stresses, to model the study of the social/economic/political upon the supposedly objective, universal, and rigorous models of the natural sciences (in crude presentation, the quantitative search for replicable, law-like models of human behavior).

In the flowering of the Cold War, the result was stages of development theories, including both Western modernization and Eastern Stalinist models. Abstract and ahistorical models of the USSR and/or Western states' development were simply constructed and then applied as conceptual, theoretical, and planning guides for "developing" states. As many in African and other area studies programs have noted, these constructions were fundamentally flawed—and not simply in their attempt to apply Northern models to the South, which was relatively easy to perceive, but in their basic assumption that development in the capitalist epoch could ever be isolated within national boundaries. In this respect, their basic Eurocentrist constructions were false, not only for the South but for any historical understanding of the North as well.[6]

No matter where one turns, the combination of shattered national models of progress and development are increasingly evident. One need not refer only to the increasing intellectual and popular awareness in the South of the effects of global relationships in order to perceive this. For equally evident are the uncertainties and inadequacies of the social sciences themselves as they apply to even the North, built as they have been on models promising and predicting unlimited progress and growth. Since at least the mid-1970s, it has been apparent that Keynesian solutions are wholly inadequate to address stagnation in the North, leading to a fruitless search for an alternative paradigm. In a similar vein, sociology's inability to offer solutions to "social problems" has been noted and decried by many, not the least by those who see research funding declining as a result.[7] Prospects in political science may be brighter, as the "democratization process" in the Western vein now holds sway; I leave this arena to Samoff, only noting as he does that democratic practice in the North seems increasingly problematic to locate, while Northern models of electoral democracy are being challenged in the South (and indeed have only limited allegiance on the part of Northern policymakers).

Approaching the South, the open failure of the social scientific models based upon conceptions of progress and linear, Western, nation-state models of national development are evident everywhere. Highly striking is the disappearance of the "economics of development." As even the conservative *Economist* has highlighted, "Economists are interested in growth. The trouble is, even by their standards, they have been terribly ignorant about it. The depth of their ignorance has long been their best-kept secret" (4 January 1992: 15). We now speak of "development economics": it is hard to tell which word should be the adjective, which should be the noun. No one, least of all the World Bank, speaks any longer of the prospect of natural capitalist development leading to increased standards of living and well-being for the 80 percent of the world's population that live outside core areas of the world economy. Even discussions of industrialization and its benefits have largely disappeared for Africa. Economics may be the model "scientific" social science, yet there is little sign— and here I simply cannot understand Samoff's argument—that it has come to dominate either the study or teaching of Africa.[8] As for "democracy" in the South, it is evident both that its expressions will take forms that are increasingly unpalatable to the North, and that core models are being forcefully challenged by scholars rooted in more activist traditions in Africa, Latin America, and Asia.[9] Indeed, to abandon a developmentalist, national framework in favor of a global relational perspective, reveals a quite different process, whereby state formation in core areas is continuously matched to state deformation in peripheral areas. As for sociology, the relatively small group that attempted to apply Northern, national models to the South is disappearing from the scene.[10]

None of this denies a central point underwritten by Samoff, namely that practitioners of social science are well-entrenched and will continue to attempt to resuscitate the paradigms to which they are committed. One does not need to be a postmodernist, however, to perceive the growing chaos within the social sciences.[11] It has become increasingly difficult to defend, much less resuscitate, nineteenth-century theories, concepts, and disciplinary boundaries: the canons are encircled; the disciplines are leaking like sieves; and scholars are scrambling for new foundations upon which to validate their work. If this applies to the understanding and management of the Euro–North American economy/polity/society, it applies with even greater force to the South, including, most notably—but not only—Africa. Across the disciplines, and particularly within the study of areas and peoples beyond the borders of dominant core states, we are indeed watching nothing less than an incipient crisis in the epistemological, ideological, and historiographical bases of modern social science.

A revival of the hegemony of modernization theory across the disciplines seems quite implausible set against these trends. In parallel fashion, the institutional and political certainties that underpinned the modernization epoch are also absent: unchallenged U.S. hegemony and financial power, the Cold War project, the belief in social engineering to generate full employment and industrialization, the promotion of state power and governing classes in the South, and so forth.

The implications of the present conjuncture for both African studies and the teaching of Africa are direct. As will become evident, I am less sanguine than Samoff and other contributors about the former, and more optimistic regarding the latter.

FUTURE DIRECTIONS
FOR TEACHING AFRICAN STUDIES

What is the future of African studies and the teaching of Africa? On the one hand, Samoff makes the case for signs of decline, noting that African studies is no longer high on the agenda of either policymakers or universities. In many departments—and it would seem political science is a major case here—retiring area specialists are far more likely to be replaced by generalists steeped in core-centric concepts and models. Recent surveys of Africanists on this matter seem to confirm this.[12]

On the other hand, there are good grounds to argue that African studies and courses on Africa in the United States, while suffering from some retrenchment, actually are the recipients of steady funding and increasing enrollments. One could go further: federal funds for at least the Title VI Centers have been increased; in 1992, Congress approved a new, $150 million trust fund for international studies and exchanges (controlled, one must note, by the Department of Defense); and interest in African materials are clearly at the center of curriculum debates. By contrast to the position of African studies in Britain, for example, U.S. Africanists are in a position of undoubted affluence,[13] as can be seen by the flow of British scholars to the United States.

How to make sense of the conflicting evidence? Deciphering contradictory data and projecting present trends will hardly help here. To place African studies in a longer viewpoint, and specifically the disciplinary and global trends sketched above, leads, however, to disquieting conclusions. One might first note—as do Samoff, Spear, and other contributors—that African studies, by right of its area focus and multidisciplinary approach, has managed to avoid much of the provincialism associated with the post–World War II growth of the social sciences. Despite this, it must be stated that African studies was firmly constructed as part and parcel of Cold War realities, global expansion under U.S. leadership, and the necessity of responding to African nationalism and the civil rights movement. As is quite well known, the vast increase in federal and state support for area studies was readily justified in terms of the global contest between the United States and the Soviet Union and the rise of African nationalism.[14] From this conjuncture flowed the predominance of modernization models across the social sciences and their application to the Third World and Africa by leading scholars such as Rostow (economics), Apter (political science), and van den Burghe and McClelland (sociology). As Rostow emphasized, the task was to construct developmental models for the Third World and Africa that could counter the allure of rapid growth and industrialization on the Soviet model. The result was that, as area studies and programs grew, Africa became the preserve of Africanists, bifurcating the United States from the continent—even as most Africanists struggled to make the relationship one of *we* and *them,* as contrasted with United States versus Africa. Eclipsed in the academy as part of this process were many African-American scholars who had hitherto operated amidst a disdain for the study of African cultures. (This was not, of course, the case in Europe, where citizens of the colonial powers had long dominated the field.)

As should now be apparent, both the global and intellectual logic for these pillars of African studies have been removed. The search for a new justification is well revealed by the successive attempts to wring support from the government and the university. In large part, this has been a search for a place in educational reform efforts: do we cast ourselves as leaders in the effort to internationalize, globalize, or multiculturalize the curriculum? None of these jury-rigged efforts are, in my view, likely to be very successful given the current construction and practice of African studies. Far better, it seems to me, to confront the basis of the field over the last generation and seek to move beyond it. To fail to do so will most likely shunt the existing structure and practitioners of the field into an ever more isolated and shrunken fortress.

To recognize and abandon past constructions will assuredly entail difficult times for Africanists. Yet the opportunities are myriad. Certainly the interest in Africa on university campuses—both in my limited experience and in light of my informal questioning of colleagues across the country— has never been higher. Certainly the symbols of Africa have never figured as prominently (both positively and negatively) in popular culture—from music to literature to clothing (particularly in youth and hip-hop culture). As anyone familiar with this at the level of the undergraduate or youth population can immediately recognize, these interests are expressed from and through groups traditionally held outside the ambit of African studies; that is, African-Americans, and especially African-American youth. Set against this, and for all the reasons Samoff details, the legacy of the construction of African studies has largely been undertaken by white male scholars, often fearful that their field of inquiry will suffer the fate they see handed out to Black studies programs in the 1960s and 1970s.

This is not, however, solely an issue of the racial character of the membership of the academy and African studies. For all the reasons sketched above, the definition of the field's subject matter, concepts, and models have operated to prevent any recognition of the relationship between the United States and the continent. As I have argued at some length above, the very construction of models of economic/social/political development rested upon the assumption that the history and development of Europe and North America could be discerned on their own, and then applied to the societies outside core areas of the world economy. If my analysis is correct, the collapse of the federal and global pillars that sustained the construction of African studies is directly matched by the demise of organizing conceptions and methods of inquiry. The result is that African studies and the teaching of Africa has no future but to move beyond past patterns, including the definition of its subject matter, framing issues, and larger community.

BEYOND TARZANIAN DEVELOPMENTALISM

How do we move beyond "U.S. and Africa" in the study of Africa, particularly in the social sciences? Lest the above comments appear too abstract, I will give a few, highly restricted examples drawn from my own teaching of undergraduates (The preparation of new Africanists in graduate programs I necessarily set aside here). Since my initial appointment as an assistant professor of sociology in 1986, I have regularly taught two introductory courses concerned with Africa: "Introduction to Modern Africa" and a special section of "Introduction to Sociology" centered on African materials (versus the U.S.–centered, developmentalist approach and texts). Each of these courses is distinctly different, in view of different audiences and subject matters. (I set aside the much smaller undergraduate and graduate seminars I teach on Africa and other subjects; for example, courses on South/Southern Africa, the capitalist world economy, the industrializing Third World, world-historical methods, and so forth.)

In each case, there has been a clear growth in student interest, expectations, and knowledge brought into the classroom. In the instance of the "Introduction to Modern Africa" course, it was taught, through the mid-1980s, usually to thirty to forty students, even during the campus divestment campaign, which ended in Spring 1986. South/Southern African courses in this period held more interest than Africa generally. Recent enrollment has been around 120 to 240 per semester, with students closed out of the course during early registration (during the previous semester). The expansion to such numbers has meant an unhappy transition from a small lecture-discussion format to lectures and formal discussion sections led by teaching assistants. This has required the commitment of new teaching assistant resources from both my dean and the sponsoring department, with class size now limited by the level of TA support. The student body has changed as well, from overwhelmingly white to a range of 50 to 90 percent students of color (and this on a predominantly white campus). The "Introduction to Sociology Through Africa" course, although restricted to smaller numbers, has met a similar response. In short, despite new faculty and courses on Africa at the University of Illinois, we simply cannot meet demand for these and other African courses—and this includes an expanding attention to diaspora studies and courses by faculty associated with the Afro-American Studies and Research Program.

It is not simply that student interest in Africa has grown: if this were the case, we could simply call for additional staff and courses. But across all such courses one sees the impact of the arguments given above regarding the nature of the social sciences, the present conjuncture, and the study of Africa. In each case, the need to abandon past organizing concepts and theories is evident. Take, for example, sociology: Can one with any validity present *society* as the primary organizing tool for the study of the present, or the past four hundred years? Certainly not if *society* is a national construct, as is most commonly posed in introductory sociology texts. The confusion (terminological incoherence) is apparent when one finds a study of the United States supplemented with a single chapter on "other societies." In some textbooks "globalization" is described as a *recent* process. The absurdity of this is apparent to students of Africa, familiar with the enslavement and colonizing processes that transformed Africa, the Americas, and Europe. It is not too difficult to perceive that other concepts, such as the European-led movement from "*gemeinschaft* to *gesellschaft*," or the diffusion of a "nuclear family" model, also fall by wayside. One could make the same commentary regarding political science and economics. Can we seriously organize our subject matter and materials—whether teaching about Africa or Europe/North America—through the notions and concepts of equally independent, autonomous, sovereign states or national economies?

Particularly pertinent for political scientists and sociologists is the tracking of evolutionary scales of political systems and societies—the very essence of modernization theory and its contrasts of modern vs. traditional and Euro–North American vs. South. In each and every case, students and instructors must quickly confront the social and historical construction of Africa in relation to the West. As suggested above, this is easily perceived and demonstrated in relation to the emergence and expansion of a capitalist, world economy. It is no less apparent when one deals with images, concepts, and values. Take for example the issue of stereotypes, a topic common in Africa courses. Students have no difficulty in accepting our standard criticisms. It is easy for them to accept the common critique: the stereotypes represent a pejorative and ethnocentric depiction of Africa. All the teacher needs to do is to rely upon well-socialized beliefs regarding the rise of equality, fraternity, and liberty as part of the rise of the West. But to move beyond this is more difficult. To confront racism and sexism as *modern* creations—that is, not artifacts of pre-Enlightenment, traditional, or primordial societies—opens up very disquieting and volatile discussions.[15] And to push further raises even more disquieting inquiries. Ask, for example, if academics have historically done any better: Where do the concepts of *tribalism* come from? Why did African scholars object, so long ago, to such conceptions (long before it became fashionable to talk about *the invention of tradition* in the Western academy[16])? When and how are concepts like *nation-state, ethnicity, race,* and, most importantly, *Africa* formulated and reformed? These are not simply pejorative terms, but concepts whose very definition relies upon national models of progress that separate Europe and North America from Africa. In short: abandon the national unit and Western visions of progress, and the ranking and comparing of isolated capitalist societies, polities, and economies, and the heart of the traditional, reigning frameworks themselves disappears. Need I say more regarding *comparative politics* or *cross-national, comparative sociology*?

Such an abandonment (of treating Africa as either an isolated continent/collection of states, or a negative reflection of the developed North) leads to equally startling implications for the study of civilizations prior to their forced incorporation into the capitalist world. As notions of a linear, evolutionary scale of societal development disappear, students can imagine alternative and more civilized forms of social existence—both in pre-capitalist and (a potential future) postcapitalist times.

If we proceed in this manner, we are led well beyond calls to be more interdisciplinary, more multicultural. If the conceptual and theoretical constructs of our disciplines rest on shaky ground, the teacher quickly discovers that the division of intellectual labor into disciplinary compartments is a major obstacle to understanding Africa, its relation to the United States, or any social system. Linking together segments on the polities/economies/ societies of Africa only compounds the problem, making it impossible to grasp the often transnational construction of social/economic/cultural/political relationships, concepts, and identities. Similarly, an approach to multiculturalism that simply adds a segment on Africa to an existing curriculum or textbook serves only to reinforce separation—between Africa and other civilizations and, in the modern period, of the world into watertight, national compartments.

To push beyond reform efforts toward a truly world-historical, transcultural perspective necessarily upsets more than the stereotypes that students bring into the classroom: it also challenges the fundamentally uncritical consciousness that is formed by living in an ahistorical culture predicated on national success stories. For students this means, rather than taking the dictation of accepted facts and theories, entering a world of great uncertainty. Nowhere is this more evident than in the debates that emerge over the sources of our historical and conceptual understanding of Africa. Who, the students ask, writes African history? What are the sources —archival? oral? written? Western? African? When did *Africa* in its continental and diaspora consciousness emerge?

Here Africanists stand on shaky ground, for all the reasons elaborated above on the character and legacy of the institutional and global construction of the knowledge-base of the social sciences and Africa. A reading of the footnotes of academic articles suggests that little work has been undertaken by scholars outside Euro–North American locations. To send a student to the library serves only to confirm this. Even in my university's library—the third-largest university library in the country—we receive only a handful of daily newspapers from the whole of Africa, whereas we receive at least this many from each major European country. Africana and Afro-American studies share one room in the library, in sharp contrast to large, lending, departmental libraries for other disciplines and areas. The search for African sources (as when I send students into the library to contrast African and North American constructions of African and North American events) is thus exceedingly difficult. Even for more formally academic materials, there are institutionalized obstacles. Send students to research materials on Africa in the largest social science data base, the *Social Sciences Citation Index*, and they will find, from among the thousand or so indexed journals, only two from Africa—and these from South Africa (*Social Dynamics* and *The South African Journal of Economics*). No sign here of leading African social science journals such as *Africa Development*, or interdisciplinary journals from independent African research centers such as *Estudos Moçambicanos* from the Centro de Estudos Africanos, Universidade Eduardo Mondlane. As for U.S. journals and disciplines, sociology is undoubtedly typical: fewer than 6 percent of the articles in what are commonly accepted in the United States as the major journals in the discipline address one or more cases from the whole of the Third World.[17] Obviously, the percentage is much lower for Africa taken alone.

The popular images of Africa thus share far more with academic knowledge than we would care to admit, for in both instances we confront the well-entrenched foundations and forces behind the creation of knowledge regarding Africa. As all these examples attest, Western scholarly institutions and academic practice have themselves been based upon the centralization of resources within core areas of the world economy—and a continuing process of unequal exchange with peripheral areas. Indeed, if current conditions continue, increased polarization along these lines may well take place, as African universities and scholars bear the brunt of continuing global stagnation and structural adjustment. Might we not here stop talking of a book famine and fraternal assistance and recognize that book famines, like food famines, are socially-determined events—and stop blaming the victim; and at least begin to look northward?

To do so would of course raise serious issues regarding the nature of the relation between the United States and Africa, just as, in the classroom, the abandonment of an encapsulated set of African societies and states opens the door to novel explorations. From almost day one, I and my students find ourselves moving backward and forward across not just the whole of the continent but the diaspora and globe as well (obviously, extending Africa beyond sub-Saharan Africa is but a beginning step). Gone are the notions of national developmentalism, isolated paths of history (at least from the Atlantic trades onward), and following in the footsteps of the West. Indeed, students, particularly those engaged in the several, undergraduate-initiated, Afrocentrist reading groups on campus, will raise these issues if I fail to do so. I can always expect questions on the possible Arab origins of the enslavement process; serious and opposed interpretations regarding the impact of Islam and Christianity; and, most consistently, the definition of *Africa/n.* In every one of these areas the extension of subject matter from Africa to the United States is direct and immediate. Discussion of inequality, class formation, and reform in and through the education system in Africa, for example, leads directly to the United States (where inequalities between rich and poor schools in many states are greater than the per capita gap in spending on black and white students in South Africa). To take another example: talk about the creation of a colonial racial order turns into a discussion of the diaspora—and then this very modern creation in our lives and communities, and its legacy, becomes ever more obvious.

To follow this road leads not, as it is often claimed, to the better understanding of our own national culture through the study of a foreign one, but to an understanding of an increasingly shared and unequal history. It is a task no less challenging for the instructor than for the student, and one that constantly underlines a summary theme that runs through all the above discussion: we need a far more world-relational and world-historical perspective as we engage with the reconstruction of our concepts, theories, disciplines, and curricula. To become multicultural by adding sections on Africa, feminism, contemporary globalization, or even racist images and beliefs is simply a stopgap.

REPRISE: THE CUTTING EDGE

Such observations suggest, as Samoff argues, that we must abandon in all our work the notion of *we and them.* For teachers who wax long about foreign/African cultures but can never discern cultural differences in the language, position, and perspectives of their students, this means a serious readjustment. Much more in the way of change is involved, however, for African studies and the teaching of Africa in general. As I have sketched briefly above, we have little reason to suspect that African studies can continue as it is currently constituted. Nor can it be presented as a solution to educational crises or cultural conflicts that bedevil the U.S. academy and nation. Indeed, African studies as constructed during the post–World War II period is part of the problem, with Africanists themselves now confronting new global realities and the shaking pillars of their field. To proceed in any positive manner will require nothing less than abandoning past concepts, theories, and methodological orientations. For a variety of well-known reasons, African and other area studies may be particularly well-suited to begin the reconstruction of the historical and social "sciences." The opportunities to be on the cutting edge of the reconstruction of knowledge are quite substantial.

For Africanists to proceed down this road would be a difficult and painful process. It would, most likely, mean abandoning the prospect of funding predicated on the U.S. role in world affairs, at least in the enduring definitions of "national interest," and listening to those insurgent communities who are both insisting upon new definitions of Africa and demanding the teaching of African materials. It would certainly entail relinquishing the role of Africanist as secular missionary and liberal mediator,[18] whereby highly specialized scholars provide a bridge between a compartmentalized United States and Africa—and devolve upon students, Africans, and African scholars the largesse of extended stays on the continent. Difficult as it may be to choose such a road, the alternative future is, really, a much brighter and more fulfilling one for Africanists. It involves the potential forging of new, more equitable, and stimulating relationships with students and colleagues—and among the latter, particularly those in Africa.

NOTES

1. See, for example, Giovanni Arrighi, "The Developmentalist Illusion," in *Semiperipheral States in the World-Economy,* ed. William G. Martin (Westport, Conn.: Greenwood Press, 1989): 11–42; or, from even a world development agency, UNDP, *Human Development Report 1992* (New York: UNDP, 1992), especially chapter three: 34–47.

2. One may now find even basic introductory texts in sociology making this argument. See, for example, Stephen K. Sanderson, *Macrosociology,* chap. 20 (New York: Harper Collins, 1991): 480–487. This selection remains, of course, the exception, but still stands in stark contrast to the developmentalist models (either of left or right versions) that have dominated until quite recently.

3. This is a long argument we cannot pursue here. But clearly the results are not what either the Western powers or the peoples and politicians of Russia and Eastern Europe expected. Having led, or ridden, popular demands, leaders in these states (and the West) now confront increasingly hungry and rebellious populations. The situation is compounded by the illusive promise of rapid capitalist development and aid from the West. As Poland's president, Lech Walesa, recently noted, "The full victory of Lenin has been achieved by us. In the moment when the proletariat finally feel they are the proletariat, we propose to them capitalism. . . . This causes the absurdity we are in today, that the factory workers are strong. They protest and we will not shoot. . . . We made a revolution, and it was the West that made profit on this, pushing on us all this nicely wrapped scrap" (*New York Times,* 14 January 1992, A2). Or, in tone with comments from Africa, the statement by Georgy Arbatov, director of the Institute of the USA and Canada Studies of the Russian Academy of Sciences and a member of President Boris Yeltsin's consultative council: "The IMF bureaucracy and its Moscow buddies . . . resemble neo-Bolsheviks who love expropriating other people's money, imposing undemocratic and alien rules of economic and political conduct and stifling freedom" (*New York Times,* 7 May 1992, A17).

4. Even the stereotypes are now challenged far more extensively than ever before. Witness the debates over how to celebrate the five-hundredth anniversary of Columbus's arrival in the Americas; the use by conservatives of the rhetoric of "political correctness" in response to challenges to a unicultural, bourgeois civilization; and the rise within academia of postmodernism and (as Samoff details) studies of the "invention of Africa" and the construction of "the native other."

5. I have developed these arguments as they relate to the conceptual tools of world-historical studies at greater length in "Fifteen Years of World-Systems Analysis: Assessing the Attempt to Move Beyond Euro–North American Conceptions," forthcoming *Review,* XVII, 2 (1994).

6. History and the humanities have been ridden with similar tendencies, but that cannot be traced here.

7. See Neil Smelser's statement on the declining prospects for funding research in the introduction to Smelser, ed., *Handbook of Sociology* (Newbury Park: Sage, 1988): 9–19.

8. This is not to say that the discipline is not still the "model social science" to those who pursue an epistemology that even natural scientists no longer find adequate to describe their world. In the world of development advisors (most notably that of the World Bank), claims along these lines may still be rigorously held; but within the academy and the study and teaching of Africa, by contrast, there seems to be little place for Africa or area studies in the discipline of economics.

9. For examples of exchanges on this topic see the *CODESRIA Bulletin:* Mahmood Mamdani, "A Glimpse at African Studies, Made in the USA," (Dakar:

CODESRIA, 1990): 7–11, and responses in nos. 3 & 4, 1990; the special issue of *Africa Development* on "democratization" (XV, 3/4, 1990); and debates in the Carter Center newsletter, *Demos*.

10. A simple indicator of this is that there are very few scholars of Africa in the discipline of sociology. Only 4 percent of the faculty members, and less than 2 percent of student members of the African Studies Association are sociologists— Edna Bay, "African Studies" in National Council of Area Studies Associations, *Prospects for Faculty in Area Studies,* (Stanford, Calif.: American Association for the Advancement of Slavic Studies, 1991): 1–18; data from 8–13. But it is necessary carefully to note the coverage of this source, which is one of the few (and thus most often cited) sources of such information. Membership in the African Studies Association does not cover all students of things African, or even professional scholars of Africa; and the data excludes members the African Heritage Studies Association.

11. In this regard, note that postmodernism has as yet shed little light on how we might understand and study Africa, Latin America, and Asia. The reason is simple: the foundational statements and the literature as a whole are profoundly limited to the study of postindustrial, northern states. As François Lyotard states in the opening paragraph of his *The Postmodern Condition: A Report on Knowledge*, "The object of this study is the condition of knowledge in the most highly developed societies. I have decided to use the word *postmodern* to describe that condition" (Minneapolis: Univ. of Minneapolis Press, 1989): xxiii. Fredric Jameson is no less open and blunt in the opening pages of his *Postmodernism, or the Cultural Logic of Late Capitalism* (Durham: Duke University Press, 1991): x. "Postmodernism is what you have when the modernization process is complete." The danger here is that *modern/tradition* may easily be replaced by *postmodern/modern*. In this vein, it is no surprise that the most enlightening writings about "nonmodernized/highly developed societies" are focused on the creation of Western visions or discourses of the colonized (e.g., Mudimbe, Miller); whether writings by, about, or from noncore cultures can overcome these weaknesses remains to be seen (see e.g., the work of Spivak, Guha, Kane, Cheikh Hamidou, Trinh Minh-ha, and the *Subaltern* group).

12. See Edna Bay, "African Studies," in National Council of Area Studies Associations, *Prospects for Faculty in Area Studies* (Stanford, Calif.: American Association for the Advancement of Slavic Studies, 1991): 1–18.

13. See, for example, Michael Crowder, "'Us' and 'Them': The International African Institute and the Current Crisis of Identity in African Studies," *Africa* 57, 1 (1987): 109–122.

14. As to the Soviet Union, this was most likely the case there also. I simply have never seen any assessment. We may be sure, however, the collapse of Cold War justifications will see the demise of the importance of Africa for the Russian academy and most likely its demise as an area receiving substantial state support. Whether and to what extent this will occur in China—given the contradictory importance of the Third World to China and the continuation of centralized educational planning and funding—remains to be seen.

15. There are a number of ways to foster discussion of racism as an ongoing social construction. The organization and rhetoric of some introductory sociology texts present contemporary examples (see note 2); or assign chapters 3 and 4 of Immanuel Wallerstein's *Historical Capitalism* (London: Verso, 1983): 75–111. Other possibilities are to reread Fanon (and, for Euro–North Americans, Sartre's preface to *The Wretched of the Earth*), and there are numerous examples of the "invention" of Africa. I send students to analyze the presentation of human history

(and especially Africa) in campus and municipal museums. In every case, it is critical not simply to illustrate the creation of stereotypes about Africa but also to show the historical and relational creation of Euro–North Americans' consciousness of their place in the capitalist world economy—including the intellectual creation of an evolutionary hierarchy of civilizations, national societies, and the methods of their analysis.

16. See, for example, essays published over twenty years ago by such scholars as Ben Magubane ("A Critical Look at Indices of Social Change," *Current Anthropology* 12, [October 1971]: 419–445), or Archie Mafeje ("Ideology of Tribalism," *Journal of Modern African Studies*, 9, 2 [1971]: 353–361).

17. Gary Gereffi and Stephanie Fonda, "Regional Paths of Development," *Annual Review of Sociology* 18 (1992): 419–448; data from 421.

18. The terms *secular missionary* and *liberal mediator* are Immanuel Wallerstein's. See his "The Evolving Role of the Africa Scholar in African Studies," reprinted in his *Africa and the Modern World* (Trenton, N.J.: Africa World Press, 1986): 3–10.

PART TWO

REASSESSMENTS AND NEW DIRECTIONS

4

Transnational Cultural Studies and the U.S. University

Neil Lazarus

I would like to discuss a few of the debates that have been playing themselves out within left-wing circles recently, concerning the status of Third World or postcolonial literatures and their place in the U.S. university curriculum. Of course, these are minoritarian debates. We live in deeply reactionary times, such that the most widely publicized discussions of late have not been over where best to situate transnational cultural studies courses in the curriculum, but over whether they warrant a place there at all. I do not plan to devote attention to this latter question in this chapter. Intellectually, it is not a subject that much interests me, since I tend to view as specious the representations of "cultural pluralism" typically encountered in the writings of the neoconservative scholars who oppose it. One enters the fray over multiculturalism not for philosophical but for institutional reasons.

Within radical scholarship, however, recent work has raised interesting and challenging questions for those of us who teach literature in U.S. colleges and universities, and who are committed to offering courses in so-called postcolonial, emergent, or Third World literatures. (I should note in passing that although I intend to keep using these labels in this chapter, they have, themselves, been the subject of searching criticism: in his emphatic critique of Fredric Jameson's influential theorization of Third World literature under the homogenizing rubric of *national allegory*, Aijaz Ahmad asserts that the term *Third World* can be deployed only polemically; it has "no theoretical status whatsoever."[1] Similarly, in an article just published, Ella Shohat argues that the term *postcolonial* obscures the reality of neocolonialism and tends to be ahistorical, falsely universalizing, and depoliticizing in its contemporary scholarly usage.[2]

One of the most profound of these critical questions has been that concerning language. Aijaz Ahmad notes that very few U.S. scholars of so-called postcolonial literatures have "ever bothered with an Asian or African language." Because of this, he explains, "major literary traditions—

105

such as those of Bengali, Hindi, Tamil, Telegu, and half a dozen others from India alone—remain, beyond a few [translated] texts here and there, virtually unknown to the American literary theorist."[3] This, in turn, has as its consequence the fact that the few texts that, having been translated, are known in the West tend to be lionized—celebrated simultaneously for their cultural representativeness and their difference, not to say, marginality, from the canonical texts of Western culture. Occasionally, as Ahmad points out (not in the same essay), this produces almost comic effects; as, for instance, when a Rabindranath Tagore novel, "patently canonical and hegemonizing inside the Indian cultural context," is positioned "in the syllabi of 'Third World Literature' as a marginal, non-canonical text, counterposed against 'Europe.'"[4] More typically, however, it is not translated texts but anglophonic texts—those written in English—that tend to receive all the attention. As Ahmad puts it,

> The few writers who happen to write in English are valorized beyond measure. Witness, for example, the characterization of Salman Rushdie's *Midnight's Children* in the *New York Times* as "a Continent finding its voice"—as if one has no voice if one does not speak in English. Or Richard Poirier's praise for Edward Said in *Raritan* which now adorns the back cover of a recent book of Said's: "It is Said's great accomplishment that thanks to his book, Palestinians will never be lost to history." The retribution visited upon the head of an Asian, an African, an Arab intellectual who is of any consequence and writes in English is that he or she is immediately elevated to the lonely splendor of a representative— of a race, a continent, a civilization, even the "Third World."[5]

Plainly, the monolinguisticality of U.S. scholars and students where non-Western cultures are concerned poses a very real problem. Nor, of course, is it only of language, narrowly conceived, that we are speaking here. When Chinua Achebe observed in a famous statement that no person could understand another whose language he or she did not know, he was referring, beyond "language," to culture in the widest, anthropological sense; that is, to a whole way of life, to a set of socially structured practices, ways of seeing, thinking, and acting. It is obviously difficult (I say *difficult*, not *impossible*) for U.S. or U.S.–based scholars to write with authority about African or Asian cultural traditions and practices if they cannot speak or read the requisite languages. Moreover, inasmuch as the only exposure to the cultures of Africa or Asia that U.S. students of postcolonial discourse are typically afforded is to the work of such elite (although not necessarily elitist: the distinction is crucial, yet it is often elided), cosmopolitan, and internationally renowned anglophonic figures as Salman Rushdie, Edward Said, Nuruddin Farah, and Derek Walcott, it is scarcely to be wondered at that, in their writing and thinking, these students should tend to overestimate the representativeness of these cosmopolitan voices;

to misconstrue their registers and concerns as definitive of the registers and concerns of Third World literatures in general. It is for reasons such as these, perhaps, that, in a recent essay entitled "The Making of Americans, the Teaching of English, and the Future of Culture Studies," Gayatri Chakravorty Spivak should have been led to offer a caution about the dangers of a "new orientalism," and to propose that literature departments no longer permit themselves to serve in any instances as the sole sponsors of courses and research into the discourses of colonialism and postcolonialism.

Spivak argues that "a cursory acquaintaince with world literature outside of Euramerica should be part of the general undergraduate requirement."[6] But she feels that a survey course of this nature has no place in a literature major, above all in a major that retains a traditional commitment to single-author courses.[7] In Spivak's view, it would be "an insult to world literature" to install a survey course in a curriculum that required students to devote a whole semester to, say, Milton or Austen or Lawrence. Instead, she proposes that a strictly interdisciplinary, optional senior seminar be instituted, "utilizing the resources of Asian, Latin American, Pacific, and African studies, in conjunction with the creative writing programs," in which students would be "made to share the difficulties and triumphs of translation."[8]

With respect to world literatures at the undergraduate level, this is the only recommendation that Spivak makes. She seems to believe that no sustained research into literatures "outside of Euramerica" is possible at this level; at least, it is not possible from within the confines of a literature department.[9] For Spivak, evidently, teachers of literature cannot hope to accomplish anything more at the undergraduate level than to destabilize, somewhat, the taken-for-grantedness of English Literature or French Literature as ideological terrains. The task is to begin to defamiliarize the disciplinary formation of *English* or *French*. But only to begin: for Spivak, a more serious encounter with world literatures can be undertaken only at the graduate level; and even there, it is imperative that such work take place outside of, or "beyond," the English or French department. She writes that

> The doctoral study of colonial and postcolonial discourse and the critique of imperialism as a substantive undertaking cannot be contained within English. In my thinking, this study should yoke itself with other disciplines, including the social sciences, so that we have degrees in English *and* history, English *and* Asian studies, English *and* anthropology, English *and* African studies. . . . I think this specialty should carry a rigorous language requirement in at least one colonized vernacular. What I am describing is the core of a transnational study of culture, a revision of the old vision of Comparative Literature. . . . If this study is contained within English (or other metropolitan literatures), without expansion into fully developed transnational culture studies, colonial and postcolonial discourse studies can also construct a canon of "Third World Literature (in

translation)" that may lead to a "new orientalism. . . ." It can fix Eurocentric paradigms, taking "magical realism" to be the trademark of Third
World literary production, for example. It can begin to define "the rest of
the world" simply by checking out if it is feeling sufficiently "marginal"
with regard to the West or not.[10]

Obviously, the warning that Spivak gives us about a "new orientalism" should be taken seriously. Elsewhere, she has linked this warning
more generally to an argument as to the indispensability of deconstructive
critical procedures, suggesting that unless we as teachers and researchers
ceaselessly raise the question of the positionality of theory, our work will
be "sustained" by the "assumption and construction of a consciousness or
subject," and this assumption/construction will "in the long run" assure
that our work "cohere[s] with the work of imperialist subject-constitution,
mingling epistemic violence with the advancement of learning and civilization."[11] I was made to reflect upon this formulation a couple of years
ago in the context of a course that I was teaching on "postcolonial" literatures: quite near the beginning of the semester, the class was discussing
Hanan al-Shaykh's novel *Women of Sand and Myrrh* (Quartet Books 1989)
when a student was moved to object to the inclusion of this text in the
course, arguing that, inasmuch as its standpoint was not actively anti-
imperialist, it could not be considered "postcolonial." *Postcoloniality,* in
this student's vocabulary, consisted in a particular political outlook; one
that was deemed appropriate. This outlook was exemplified not in al-
Shaykh's novel but in the work of other writers such as Fanon, Ngugi, Ma-
hasweta Devi, and Ghassan Kanafani, with which we had begun the semester. For all its intended radicalism, the prescriptiveness of my student's
assessment was of precisely the kind that Spivak had described: a consciousness was constructed and then ascribed, in an epistemological ges-
ture decidedly reminiscent of "imperialist subject-constitution." The fact
that the student who objected was from the Indian subcontinent, not the
United States, complicated the issue.

For all this, I must confess that some of Spivak's emphases in the passage I have just cited strike me as being questionable. I would like here to
consider two of these: first, the suggestion that the study of postcolonial
literatures should be undertaken only on the basis of an interdisciplinary
curriculum that couples a literature specialty with a specialty in an area
studies program or in a field such as history or sociology; second, and related to the first, the proposition that (doctoral) research into colonial or
postcolonial discourse should "carry a rigorous language requirement in at
least one colonized vernacular." I hope to make clear that I do not agree
with either of these suggestions. However, before turning to discuss them,
it might be helpful for me to say something briefly about my own training
and intellectual formation, not only by way of taking myself as an example and declaring an interest, but also with Pierre Bourdieu's caution in

mind that, whenever intellectuals are moved to "speak with aspirations toward the universal, they are always liable to be nothing more than the unconscious spokesmen of an historical unconscious that is linked to the peculiarities of a specific history of the intellectual field."[12]

I do not speak a "colonized vernacular." The only non-European language that I can read and write is Afrikaans. The emblematic language of
apartheid, Afrikaans scarcely qualifies as a colonized language, even
though it is spoken by more blacks than whites in South Africa (the only
country—if one exempts a residual presence in Zimbabwe and Namibia—
in which it is spoken); and even though its origins are precisely as a creole
language quite similar in its structure to that spoken by the Creoles of the
Dutch Antilles and the Moluccas islands of Indonesia. My undergraduate
training, in South Africa, was in English literature and the history of
drama; my graduate work, completed in Britain, was undertaken first in an
interdisciplinary program in the sociology of literature, and subsequently
in a sociology department. Since moving to the United States in 1981, I
have been based successively in a department of sociology, a center for the
humanities, and an English department; and, since 1986, I have held a
joint appointment in English and Modern Culture and Media at Brown
University. Methodologically, my interests have always turned on the articulation of culture with wider social processes; substantively, my area of
focus has always been cultural production in the contemporary Third
World, with a particular emphasis upon anglophone African literature. In
summary form, then: *cultural studies*, on the one hand; *transnationalism*,
or the *world-system*, on the other. My first book, *Resistance in Postcolonial African Fiction* (Yale University Press 1990), which centered on the
figure of the Ghanaian novelist, Ayi Kwei Armah, was about anticolonial
nationalism, radical African intellectualism, and the forms of African fiction in the postcolonial era. The project upon which I am currently engaged, tentatively entitled *Hating Tradition Properly*, attempts to theorize
the transformations undergone by (elite and popular) cultural forms in
their diffusion across and between the social spaces brought into being by
the globalization of capitalism in the specific contexts of colonialism and
postcolonialism. Its particular project is to identify and offer an assessment
of various counterhegemonic cultural practices situated neither exclusively
in the universe of socialized capital—the First World—nor exclusively in
the Third World, but between them, so to speak. Ranged in diverse ways
across or athwart the international division of labor, the cultural practices
that I have chosen to examine are African pop music, West Indian cricket,
and "emergent" English literatures. These are cultural forms, I argue, that
can be understood only in terms of a systemic analysis that insists on the
global dimensions of contemporary social existence.

Even on the basis of this skeletal outline, it is perhaps obvious why I
cannot universally affirm Spivak's insistence that students wishing to
do research into postcolonial cultures should have to study a "colonized

vernacular." I shall leave aside the specificity of the Caribbean and Latin American contexts, which Spivak fails to mention but with respect to which she would presumably allow that questions of whether the languages are "colonized vernacular" are often moot. In general, however, it seems to me that just as one would demand of graduate students hoping to write extensively about Proust that they would have mastered French, so one would demand of graduate students hoping to write extensively about Thomas Mofolo that they would have studied Sesotho, or about Naguib Mahfouz that they would have studied Arabic. But the situation is already somewhat different in the case of such writers as, say, Solomon T. Plaatje, —a contemporary of Mofolo—who wrote as much in English as in his native Setswana; or Abdelkebir Khatibi, still active today, who writes as often in French as in Arabic. And it is emphatically different in the case of a vast array of contemporary writers—emigrants, as Rushdie puts it in *Shame*, from their countries of birth, and sojourners in other countries (often more than one), and who write principally if not solely in English or another metropolitan language. Rushdie himself is one such *mohajir;* so also are many other well-known contemporary writers, among them Ama Ata Aidoo, Anita Desai, Amitav Ghosh, Kazuo Ishiguro, Timothy Mo, Ben Okri, Ninotchka Rosca, and Moyez Vassanji. For precise, historical reasons, there are few parallels in the past, either in metropolitan or in colonized cultures, to the situation of these contemporary diasporic, migrant writers. If the figure of Joseph Conrad comes closest, this is perhaps because, as Rosemary George has recently argued, Conrad stands (facing the wrong way, it might be introjected, but even so . . .) at the gateway of the distinctively twentieth-century and colonial problematic of "globality" and "English as a world language."[13]

One would not, I think, require of Conrad students that they be able to read Polish. By the same token, I do not believe that knowledge of a "colonized vernacular" is always indispensable for research into such writers as Vassanji or Rosca. Sometimes, it is an understanding of subcontracting, transnational labor flows and the new international division of labor, or of the contemporary politics of identity and "imagined community,"[14] that is essential. This is conceivably true even in certain cases where language competence *is* indispensable. I am thinking, for instance, of the relationship within the Arabic novel between the established discourse of Naguib Mahfouz and that of such experimental contemporary writers as Elias Khoury and Emile Habiby, as Edward Said represents it in his Foreword to a recent English translation of Khoury's *Little Mountain*. Of course, it is necessary to know Arabic both to be able to read the work of these writers and to be able to place their different stylistic and formal registers (despite his Nobel prize, not even Mahfouz's fiction is widely available in translation). But to know Arabic is not enough: for on Said's account it is what these different formal registers betoken *in social terms* that matters.

Mahfouz, for example has an almost organic connection to the historical events depicted in his novels, produced over half a century, and Said reads the extraordinarily cumulative thrust of Mahfouz's career in terms of his specific location as an Egyptian (and indeed Cairene) intellectual:

> The thing about Mahfouz is that he can and has always been able to depend on the vital integrity and even, cultural compactness of Egypt. For all its tremendous age, the variety of its components and the influences on it . . . the country has a stability and identity that in this century have not disappeared. Put differently, this is to say that the Arabic novel has flourished especially well in twentieth-century Egypt because throughout all the turbulence of the country's wars, revolutions, and social upheavals, civil society was never eclipsed, its existence was never in doubt, was never completely absorbed into the State. Novelists like Mahfouz had it always *there* for them, and accordingly developed an abiding institutional connection with the society through their fiction.[15]

Mahfouz's discourse is then contrasted with that of the contemporary Palestinian or Lebanese writer, for whom civil society is *not* there. Where Mahfouz's fiction stems palpably from a "fundamentally settled and integral" society, Habiby's *The Secret Life of Saeed, the Ill-Fated Pessoptimist* and Khoury's *Little Mountain* derive equally palpably from "fractured, decentered, and openly insurrectionary" locales.[16] In these fictions, therefore, "form is an adventure, narrative both uncertain and meandering, character less a stable collection of traits than a linguistic device, as self-conscious as it is provisional and ironic."[17]

I will now turn to the second of Spivak's recommendations; namely, that the study of colonial and postcolonial discourse ought not to be conducted under the sole auspices of a literature department, but ought instead to be a matter of interdisciplinary sponsorship. On the face of it, this seems to be an incontrovertibly reasonable suggestion. Just as I believe that graduate students wishing to do extensive research on authors who do not write in English should have to acquire a mastery of the appropriate languages, so too it seems self-evident that students planning to write on Tsitsi Dangarembga or Dambudzo Marechera, say, should have to acquire a knowledge of modern Zimbabwean and African history, politics, and culture. But there is something unselfcritical about Spivak's proposal: this kind of knowledge, surely, is indispensable for *any* literary scholarship, and not merely for research into so-called world literature? One could scarcely claim to be a good Shelley scholar unless one had read widely in the history and sociology of England and Europe in the so-called Age of Revolution— the late-eighteenth and early-nineteenth centuries. And this is true not only because Shelley was a particularly "political" poet. To write with authority about any cultural producer, it is necessary to know a great deal about his or her world. Hence, I find rather unconvincing the proposition that the study of *postcolonial discourse* cannot be contained within a literature department. If by this Spivak means to indicate that a *formalist* approach to world literatures will lead to the imposition of the dominant culturalist and Eurocentric paradigms, this is true, but it is not true with respect only to so-called world literatures; rather, it is true across the board, with respect to Shelley or Shakespeare or Duras as much as to Dangarembga—and in this case Spivak ought to have called for the discontinuation of doctoral programs in literature as such, and for their wholesale replacement by genuinely interdisciplinary programs.

However, if by her proposition Spivak means that what might be appropriate to the study of such novelists as, say, Thomas Hardy or Herman Melville is not appropriate to the study of such anglophone writers as George Lamming or Witi Ihimaera, I am not sure that I can agree. We must concede that what Rey Chow has called "the politics of reading from West to East" are particularly fraught and complex[18] (with my particular interests, I would have wanted to say: from North to South); but if, in order to study Lamming, for example, it is seen to be necessary to step outside of English into History or "the Caribbean," I do not see how a case can plausibly be made for not following a similar general procedure in the case of Melville. Perhaps Spivak feels that, with regard to such writers as Hardy and Melville, held fast within the romanticizing embrace of Literature as an institutionalized ideology, the battle is already won and lost.[19] In my view, however, it remains both necessary and possible for radical scholars within literature departments in the United States to produce the kinds of work to which they are committed—historicized, politicized, materialist, alert to questions of representation and subalternity, and so on—and to do this with respect not only to texts and bodies of work deemed marginal, but equally to canonical writings.

I have, in a sense, been defending literature departments in the United States against Spivak's insistence upon their severe limitations. At the graduate level, I have taught only within English departments (at Brown and, before that, at Louisiana State University), and, where courses in colonial or postcolonial discourse are concerned, I have simply *required* my students to undertake research of a sociohistorical and political nature. Nor, as far as I know, has this ever seemed to them implausible or inappropriate. However, I recognize that one consequence of my particular experience is that I find it very difficult to specify the kind of relationship that ought to obtain between the literature department (in my case, English) and the area studies program (African studies, for instance). In practical terms, this is not a problem that I have had to deal with: at Brown, for instance, there is an African-American program but not one in African studies; and courses on African literature are not automatically or even routinely offered under the rubric of African-American studies. Sometimes, indeed, they are not even cross-listed with African-American studies.

The area studies program is not, of course, a disciplinary field, but, as its name indicates, a field demarcated by its object domain. The faculty who make up an African studies program will, by definition, be African-ists; but they will also have disciplinary specializations, as anthropologists, political scientists, musicologists, art historians, and so forth. I have tried to argue above that students of postcolonial *literatures* based in literature departments do not need to undertake formal (i.e., institutionally endorsed) cross-disciplinary training in order to equip them to write about postcolonial discourse. The same is true of students in other disciplinary fields: history, sociology, anthropology, and so on. The area studies program, on the other hand, needs to link itself as actively as possible with all research ventures that bear in any way upon its terrain. As area studies programs, African or Asian studies cannot afford to adopt essentialist definitions as to their field of sponsorship.

Consider once again, for example, the vexed question of language. It might seem commonsensical to distinguish between the terrain of African studies and the terrain of English on the basis of language, such that literature written in Yoruba, say, or Zulu, would fall under the purview of African studies (and not of English); and work composed in English would fall under the purview of the English department (and not of African studies). In my view, however, such a procedure would be seriously in error. First, it would have the effect of ghettoizing literatures not written in metropolitan languages, and of reinforcing their wider cultural inscription as marginal, not-quite-literatures. Second, and conversely, it would have the effect of de-Africanizing English-language African literatures, since the works of such writers as Achebe, Armah, Soyinka, and Nwapa would be positioned as English rather than as African. This would be to replicate in a slightly different context the standpoint most decisively associated with the name of Ngugi wa Thiong'o, and which, despite Ngugi's reputation and his brilliance in other respects, I regard as being both theoretically and empirically unsustainable.

In his enormously influential book *Decolonising the Mind*,[20] Ngugi argues that the literature produced by African writers in English or French or Portuguese cannot truly be considered African, but must be regarded instead as Afro-European. He is perfectly willing to concede both that this "hybrid tradition" has produced writers of genuine talent, and that the work of many of these writers—he mentions specifically Ousmane Sembene, Ayi Kwei Armah, and Agostinho Neto, among others—has played an important cultural role in the struggle against imperialism. But, as he puts it,

> We cannot have our cake and eat it! Their work belongs to an Afro-European literary tradition which is likely to last for as long as Africa is under this rule of European capital in a neo-colonial set-up. So Afro-

European literature can be defined as literature written by Africans in European languages in the era of imperialism.

But some are coming round to the inescapable conclusion articulated by Obi Wali with such polemical vigour twenty years ago: African liter-ature can only be written in African languages, that is, the languages of the African peasantry and working class, the major alliance of classes in each of our nationalities and the agency for the coming inevitable revo-lutionary break with neo-colonialism.[21]

This is not the place to develop a full critique of Ngugi's position, but in passing I will observe that his general argument about language and African literature is susceptible to criticism on several grounds: it is Manichean in structure and therefore falsely homogenizing in its social thrust; it attributes to the classes of the African peasantry and proletariat a privileged political awareness that is merely asserted, and never demon-strated, to be in place; it takes for granted that "the languages of the African peasantry and working class"—for instance Gikuyu or Luo or Luhya or Kamba—are Kenyan languages not merely by (colonial) defin-ition but also by inclination and political will; and so on. Above all, though, Ngugi's formulation is insistently unhistorical and essentialist—like that, incidentally, of such purists in the field of ethnomusicology as Hugh and Andrew Tracey. It is true that English, French, and Portuguese were imposed on Africa as alien languages, and as languages of domina-tion. It is also true that their distribution in Africa continues to follow the logic of class division. As languages, they are widely spoken among the urban middle classes, less widely among the urban working classes, and hardly at all among the rural peasantry. None of this, however, sanctions Ngugi in his blanket representation of these languages as foreign to Africa today or as uniformly elitist upon African soil: "The question is this," he states, "we as African writers have always complained about the neo-colonial economic and political relationship to Euro-America. Right. But by our continuing to write in foreign languages, paying homage to them, are we not on the cultural level continuing that neo-colonial slavish and cringing spirit?"[22] The correct answer to this intendedly rhetorical question is not "yes" but "no." Ngugi is too reductionistic here, and he fails to grapple with the relative autonomy of language and culture from their socioeconomic conditions of existence. The fact that English was not native to Africa does not mean that African writers cannot make themselves at home in it without losing their souls. Similarly, the sugges-tion that to write in English is inevitably to perpetuate a cringing neo-colonialism is not only undialectical, it is also crude and dogmatic. Con-sider for instance Wole Soyinka's witty poem "Telephone Conversation," which, set in England, uses English against the English in a manner that seems to me clearly neither cravenly apologetic nor remotely neocolonial in substance:

The price seemed reasonable, location
Indifferent. The landlady swore she lived
Off premises. Nothing remained
But self-confession. "Madam," I warned,
"I hate a wasted journey—I am African."
Silence. Silenced transmission of
Pressurized good-breeding. Voice, when it came,
Lipstick coated, long gold-rolled
Cigarette-holder pipped. Caught I was, foully.
"HOW DARK?" . . . I had not misheard . . . "ARE YOU LIGHT
OR VERY DARK?" Button B. Button A. Stench
Of rancid breath of public hide-and-speak.
Red booth. Red pillar-box. Red double-tiered
Omnibus squelching tar. It *was* real! Shamed
By ill-mannered silence, surrender
Pushed dumbfoundment to beg simplification.
Considerate she was, varying the emphasis—
"ARE YOU DARK? OR VERY LIGHT?" Revelation came.
"You mean—like plain or milk chocolate?"
Her assent was clinical, crushing in its light
Impersonality. Rapidly, wave-length adjusted,
I chose. "West African sepia"—and as afterthought,
"Down in my passport." Silence for spectroscopic
Flight of fancy, till truthfulness clanged her accent
Hard on the mouthpiece. "WHAT'S THAT?" conceding
"DON'T KNOW WHAT THAT IS." "Like brunette."
"THAT'S DARK, ISN'T IT?" "Not altogether.
Facially, I am brunette, but madam, you should see
The rest of me. Palm of my hand, soles of my feet
Are a peroxide blonde. Friction, caused—
Foolishly madam—by sitting down, has turned
My bottom raven black—One moment madam!"—sensing
Her receiver rearing on the thunderclap
About my ears—"Madam," I pleaded, "wouldn't you rather
See for yourself?"[23]

In the face of this kind of writing, it seems to me that Chinua Achebe's pragmatic standpoint, expressed as long ago as 1964 in his essay "The African Writer and the English Language," is altogether more compelling than that of Ngugi. Responding explicitly to Obi Wali, the Nigerian critic whose conclusions we have seen Ngugi describe as "inescapable," Achebe wrote that "I have been given this language [English] and I intend to use it," and—crucially—that "I feel that the English language will be able to carry the weight of my African experience. But it will have to be a new English, still in full communion with its ancestral home but altered to suit its new African surroundings.[24] It is not, of course, that African writers should ever feel obliged to choose English over their native tongues as their language of literary expression, or that their decision to do so would ever be innocent or without significant ideological implications. But for those writers who do, for whatever reason, take the decision to write in English, the task in Achebe's view is precisely to transform the European language of empire into an African language; and Achebe differs sharply from Ngugi in believing that the indigenization or Africanization of English is not only possible but, indeed, inevitable, and already well under way. It may be true that what is produced on the basis of this decision is, with very rare exceptions, not a working-class literature. But this is scarcely to render it un-African. It is in this connection that the distinction between *elite* and *elitist* discourse becomes critical.

Against Ngugi's line of argument, therefore, and with a view to recommending that scholars of African culture and society do not, in seeking to oppose the logic of imperialism, fall back upon the assertion of a nativist essentialism, I would like, in closing, to insist upon the paradoxes of imperialism in its ideological dimensions. With regard to the imperialized regions themselves, it might be helpful to reflect, for instance, as C.L.R. James has done, on the social history of cricket in the West Indies in the years leading up to and immediately following decolonization in the mid-1960s. It needs to be remembered that the social space of the West Indies during these years was initially marked out as a colonial space. Cricket had not been introduced to the West Indies, as it had in Australia, New Zealand, and South Africa, under the bourgeois rubric of moral education—"character building." On the contrary, it had been imposed upon a subject people from without, and it had had a quite specific and explicitly thematized role to play in the maintenance of colonial authority. The extraordinary feature of cricket, as James describes it, is that even in the face of these unpromising originary circumstances, it proved possible to transform the sport into "a means of [West Indian] national expression."[25] West Indians contrived, over the course of this century, to pull cricket across the Manichean divide of colonialism. They were able to force it to carry the weight of *their* social desires and to speak *their* language—whether of emergent anticolonialism, of nationalist affirmation, or, after independence, of international self-presence. This continuing ability of politically and economically subject peoples at the peripheries of the world system to indigenize—to refunction and appropriate—imposed cultural forms, bespeaks their continuing autonomy, however relative, from imperialist ideology. Throughout the (post)colonial world, the effectivity of imperialism as a cultural force is limited by its lack of hegemony.

Nor is it only at the peripheries of the world-system that the paradoxes of imperialism reveal themselves. On the contrary, it seems to me that one consequence of the strictly contemporary forms of capitalism's globalization is to put the formal separability of First and Third worlds into jeopardy. In a critical discussion of theories of "post-Fordism" as a regime of accumulation, Michael Rustin has argued that "without a grasp of th[e] larger integration of capitalism," it is not only the contemporary status of Third World populations that cannot be understood: in addition, "[n]ot even the position of the subordinate classes in the First World can be correctly theorized."[26] Raymond Rocco provides further evidence for this view when he suggests, in a recent essay, that in order to examine the political economy of Los Angeles, it is necessary to grapple with the "internationalization of production," and, more specifically, with the interpenetration of the city's economy with the Southeast Asian, Caribbean Basin, and larger American economies.[27]

Under these circumstances, it becomes possible to insist that, if the culture of postcolonialism often presents itself preeminently as hybridic in nature, the space of this postcolonialism is global, and no longer refers only to the non-West. In the era of transnational capitalism, social identity has become world-historical in its constitution, being secured neither exclusively at the level of the nation nor even at that of multinationalism, but very specifically, and of course unevenly and differentially, in terms of global processes. Salman Rushdie has his narrator, Saleem Sinai, observe in *Midnight's Children*: "To understand just one life, you have to swallow the world." This formulation is today valid, I believe, not just for Third World subjects like Saleem Sinai, but for all subjects everywhere. And this means that, even for subjects on the Western side of the imperial divide, our students and ourselves—and however we came to be here—the ideological implications of taking up the latent challenge posed by the hybridity of postcolonial cultures are potentially considerable. For in their hybridity, postcolonial cultures might be conceived not as supplements to Euro-American culture but as forms capable of subverting the ideological parochialism of imperialism. To respond to postcolonial cultures in dialogical rather than monological terms—as more and more Western-based subjects are today belatedly equipped to do—might be to allow oneself to take seriously the suggestion of a world free of imperial domination. The proposal is not that we who are based in the West embrace postcolonial cultures for what they can tell us about life across the international division of labor, "over there," but that we embrace them for what they can suggest to us about radically different ways of living "over here," ways of living that are unimaginable under prevailing social conditions.

NOTES

1. Aijaz Ahmad, "Jameson's Rhetoric of Otherness and the 'National Allegory'" in *Theory: Classes, Nations, Literatures* (London: Verso, 1992): 96. Subsequent note references to this essay are given under the short title "Jameson's Rhetoric."

2. Ella Shohat, "Notes on the 'Post-Colonial'" *Social Text* 31–32 (1992): 99–113.

3. Ahmad, "Jameson's Rhetoric," 97.

4. Aijaz Ahmad, "Orientalism and After: Ambivalence and Metropolitan Location in the Work of Edward Said," in *Theory*, 197.

5. Ahmad, "Jameson's Rhetoric," 98.

6. Gayatri Chakravorty Spivak, "The Making of Americans, the Teaching of English, and the Future of Culture Studies," *New Literary History* 21 (1990): 790. Subsequent note references to this essay will be given under the short title "Making Americans."

7. Spivak is not by any means arguing in favor of single-author courses. On the contary, she feels that they cannot be justified today, when it is essential to "make room for the coordinated teaching of [a whole series of] new entries into the canon" ("Making Americans," 785).

8. "Making Americans," 790.

9. Since Spivak's article is devoted to an investigation of the English department and its curriculum, it does not address the question of the adequacy or otherwise of "postcolonial" literature courses in area studies programs.

10. "Making Americans," 791.

11. Gayatri Chakravorty Spivak, "Can the Subaltern Speak?" in *Marxism and the Interpretation of Cultures*, ed. Cary Nelson and Lawrence Grossberg (Urbana and Chicago: University of Illinois Press, 1988): 295.

12. Pierre Bourdieu, "Universal Corporatism: The Role of Intellectuals in the Modern World," trans. from the French by Gisele Sapiro in *Poetics Today* 12.4 (Winter 1991): 660.

13. Rosemary George, "Home-Countries and the Politics of Location" (Ph.D. dissertation, Brown University), 1992: 121–180.

14. The reference is to Benedict Anderson's now-classic study, *Imagined Communities: Reflections on the Origin and Spread of Nationalism* (London: Verso, 1983).

15. Edward W. Said, foreword to Elias Khoury, *Little Mountain*, trans. from the Arabic by Maia Tabet (Minneapolis: University of Minnesota Press, 1989): xii. Subsequent note references to this foreword will be given under the name Said.

16. Said, foreword, xiv.

17. Said, foreword, xv.

18. I refer here to the subtitle of Rey Chow's book, *Women and Chinese Modernity: The Politics of Reading Between West and East* (Minneapolis: University of Minnesota Press, 1991).

19. This would be surprising, however, since Spivak's disciplinary training was in romanticism, to which—as a Marxist, feminist, and deconstructionist—she retains a strong commitment.

20. Ngugi wa Thiong'o, *Decolonising the Mind. The Politics of Language in African Literature* (London: James Currey; Portsmouth, N.H.: Heinemann, 1987). Subsequent note references to this book will be given the short title *Decolonizing.*

21. Ngugi, *Decolonising,* 27.

22. Ibid., 26.

23. Wole Soyinka, "Telephone Conversation," in *The Penguin Book of Modern African Poetry,* ed. Gerald Moore (Harmondsworth: Penguin Books, 1984): 187.

24. Chinua Achebe, *Morning Yet on Creation Day: Essays* (London: Heinemann, 1977): 62.

25. C.L.R. James, *Cricket,* ed. Anna Grimshaw (London: Allison and Busby, 1986): 171.

26. Michael Rustin, "The Politics of Post-Fordism: or, The Trouble with 'New Times,'" *New Left Review* 175 (May-June 1989): 69.

27. Raymond Rocco, "The Theoretical Construction of the 'Other' in Postmodernist Thought: Latinos in the New Urban Political Economy," in *Cultural Studies* 4.3 (October 1990): 323.

5

I Think You Should Hear Voices When You Look at African Art

Patrick McNaughton

I very much appreciate Neil Lazarus's positions on the teaching and study of African literature in U.S. universities. He is prudent and pragmatic in the development of his ideas on issues of language, lionization, marginality, urbanism, neocolonialism, ideologies, global processes, and interdisciplinary dispositions. In addition, his views on African literature in metropolitan languages are valuable because they expand and enrich our notion of voices and experience, situation and action. Lazarus sees that people think, feel, and act in complex ways; that the consequences of vested interests can cut in many directions; and that African literature in any language offers readers in Africa and everywhere else the chance to explore themselves as well as others and gain perspectives on the nature of personhood, society, and culture.

The same is true of the visual arts, which have never been just for entertainment or detached encounters with the sublime. People and institutions use art to contemplate and to negotiate their lives, promote their positions, garner critical resources, and acquire or maintain important forms of cultural or social authority. Thus, teaching about art can be teaching about thinking and maneuvering in complex social worlds, and it can encourage students to be more perceptive, analytical, critical, and self-aware. Teaching about African art offers all of this, and the opportunity for students to see the ways in which other societies and other individuals have faced the situations that patinate their lives. Because the social, political, economic, spiritual, and aesthetic landscapes in African societies are intricate and enigmatic, just as they are here, but different in a variety of ways, the experience of exploring them is vitally important to U.S. college students, who have much to gain from examining both the similarities and the differences.

I teach and study African art, in an art history department at a university that has a very large and active African studies program. While many scholars would assert that the arts I teach are traditional, I insist that

119

traditional is a complex idea too frequently simplified and misconstrued, and the arts I teach have always been in a perpetual state of emergence. I will return to that, because the idea of emergence presents issues that college students need to examine.

In this chapter, I will move some of Professor Lazarus's discussion into the realm of the visual arts; and, as he did, go beyond the arts and into the practice of people's lives. The issue of terminology is my point of departure for arguing the importance of African humanities courses. I like Professor Lazarus's use of the term *postcolonial* to identify a historically explicit body of literature that addresses specific issues of domination and oppression. In Lazarus's usage, the term signals a political consciousness and mobilization that has played important roles in this century's cultural critique. But in my undergraduate classes, I find it important to consider at some length the ongoing consequences that were initiated by colonial processes—the underbelly of postcolonialism.

In that vein I think the label *postcolonial* can be illusory and we must be careful how we use it. It can be a kind of subterfuge that works in tandem with many others, such as *Africa's unfortunate legacy of tribalism,* which of course purports to explain much of today's violence, even to the sophisticated people in the United States who listen to National Public Radio or watch public television. Such subterfuge, intentional or naive, helps make Westerners think that it is only natural for African peoples and nations to be persistently in dire straits. After all, so the logic of this popular representation goes, colonialism is a thing of the past, and if Africans still have enormous problems it might be because they were never really ready for independence anyway. Such a mentality of course ignores both the brutal practices of colonialism and the enterprise of African societies to adapt and survive. It also denies the domination and exploitation that characterize the asymmetrical systems of power and authority with which the West still engages African peoples and nations.

Two critical features of a colonial mentality are particularly relevant to the study and teaching of African arts. First, the popular and sometimes even scholarly imagery that a great many Westerners use to contemplate African societies still bear more than a full load of simplistic and sharply biased misconceptions. The so-called legacy of tribalism is just one of them. In upper-level undergraduate classes, I spend four to five weeks introducing African people and societies, and I learn a lot about what students think. Two years ago, a very bright student said she thought that in Africa thieves had their hands cut off. Africa, for her, was just one place: monolithic, extremely conservative, backward, and barbaric in the area of handling crime. For many if not most undergraduates, Africans live simple, dreary lives. The oldest guy in town is automatically the leader; magic and fear characterize spiritual orientations; and economic, political, and social formations are surely just plain basic. And it is not just the kids in

Indiana who hold such notions. I encountered them in Milwaukee and Santa Cruz, too.

With these kinds of impressions, it is impossible to understand the sophisticated workings of art in African societies, since in a great many ways African arts are both grounded in and influential on complex economic, political, social, and spiritual formations. But beyond art, these impressions make it impossible to imagine that African people, societies, or nations could be serious players in international domains. Thus, African people are marginalized, distanced, and devalued, and that becomes a rationale for ignoring how Africans are treated by the rest of the world. During colonialism, such rationalizations made it easier for Westerners to accept the European domination and manipulation of Africa's natural resources. Today, those rationalizations make it easier to accept a Western domination and manipulation of Africa's cultural resources.

That is the second critical feature of a colonial mentality that affects most directly my work in the classroom. Western institutions do dominate and manipulate African cultural resources, the cultural productions of African individuals and societies. This manipulation is not always intentional. In literature, I imagine it results from the intended and unintended consequences of business acumen and self-interest in the world of publishing, and the complex academic and institutional processes by which scholarly disciplines validate their expertise, authority, and self perpetuation.

In art history, the situation is similar, with the history of collecting and publicly displaying African visual arts in museums (and of course galleries) as an added dimension. One result of these processes is the fact that a great many historians of Western art do not have the slightest inkling of what the African arts are about, and a shocking percentage of them believe that what I teach is not art at all, and not very sophisticated, either. That, by itself, is a powerful argument for keeping our teaching centered in disciplines.

Other results of these processes include the fact that certain kinds of African art have been favored while other types have been ignored or neglected; and all types, until recently, have been explored with research methodologies and perspectives that could not possibly generate reasonable notions of what the visual arts in Africa can mean or do.

Here is one example of how information on artworks was reduced and channelled to fit the asymmetries of power in a colonial mentality. For the longest time, artworks full of visceral protuberances and coated with apparently unsavory substances such as the power sculptures used in many areas of Zaire, were viewed by Westerners as unsightly, ungainly, and certainly unaesthetic. They occupied a kind of blood-and-guts category in Western thinking that served to affirm many erroneous notions about African modes of thought, spiritual practices, and art. Works such as the highly abstract, forcefully composed masks used in West African initiation

associations were represented as fetishes, or objects believed to be magical and deadly by their makers, who used them to combat witches and
maybe even hurt a few innocent bystanders.

My understanding of such works, however, is different. The helmet
masks with large mouths in front and large horns in back, named *Komo*,
are an example. In a superficial nutshell, I see such masks as complicated
and subtly composed instruments of social, spiritual, and political action,
created through processes that combine science and ritual. They are judged
by some local users to be scary as hell, by other local users to be ab-
solutely beautiful, and by still others as awesome but refined embodiments
of many of their society's deepest ideological components. My understanding is simply an interpretation based on many, patched together experiences and conversations while I was doing research, but it comes
closer to the representations that local users make than does the simple-
minded assertion that these are murderous, magical devices that fight
witches.

Simple-minded Western assertions are fostered and empowered by the
two features of colonial mentality that I have mentioned. And they are numerous. The notion that African art is anonymous, that it is mindlessly reproduced, that it just reflects and supports preestablished beliefs and practices, that it has no history, that it is frequently simple and not subject to
local aesthetic contemplation, that it is strictly functional, that it is fragile
in the face of Islamization or Westernization—all of these assertions and
many more are made believable by neocolonial thinking. Once made, of
course, these assertions justify the colonial mentality that engendered
them.

I will present one more, blatant example. When Western artists embarked upon the path of modernism, they appropriated and transformed
many elements of the African arts. They allowed African art to inspire new
interpretations in processes of profound change and reinvigoration. Such
borrowing and adapting is an essence of creativity, and from the vantage
point of the Western art world, it was just fine. But what happens when
African artists do the same thing? All too frequently, Westerners degrade
it as borrowed, or derivative, thereby casting it into a marginal status which
devalues it on the art market and makes it harder for many people to take
seriously. Thus, the West controls an important African cultural production
and absorbs it into an ideology of misrepresentation and manipulation.

Terminology veils insidious attitudes and foster onerous misrepresentation. It can enhance the chances that students will think reductionistically
and it can create almost tacit barriers to understandings that are richer and
more reasonable. I find it important to make clear to students that neo-
colonialism is still a powerful force that infects their impressions and even
directs aspects of their behaviors toward the peoples and artworks we

explore in class. Doing that in the context of African humanities courses helps to predispose students to be sensitive to the processes by which social formations and people interact.

Many U.S. campuses, including my own, continue to experience a rise in racial incidents. This suggests that efforts to expose neocolonial mentality are all the more important because of its galvanizing relationship to U.S. racism. Perhaps we can hope that the harder we work at it now, the better the chances of future generations coming to college with healthier representations of their fellow human beings. I think that is one of the important reasons for teaching African art and African literature in the first place.

Professor Lazarus's interest in African literature in the English language might seem to suggest the asymmetrical control typical of colonial and neocolonial practices. He certainly notes its dangers. He cites several kinds of distorted images that literature in European languages can produce about African situations; and he presents Ngugi's assertions that authors writing in European languages are not producing African literature, but rather a "hybrid tradition." Lazarus argues convincingly, however, for the importance and validity of anglophone literature, and furthermore that it should be viewed as African, not as hybrid or imperial-era. Soyinka argues as convincingly with his English-language poem, "Telephone Conversation"; and Achebe drives the point home with his powerful conviction that he can create a new English, "altered to suit its new African surroundings."

This is important, and it involves the idea of emergence. English is not just a European language. It is a vehicle that intelligent, capable individuals can use to construct their own expressions. Certainly it is a system of communication that is joined in many ways to a multitude of other cultural formations. But it is not so rigid or constraining, and it is not so stuck to preconfigured cultural formations, that it cannot be adapted and transformed, so that it will, as Achebe notes, "carry the weight of my African experience." Certainly European languages were once alien to Africa. So was Islam.

To Achebe, Soyenka, and Lazarus I would add this. It is just as creative, just as intellectually demanding, just as self-reflexive, and just as African to convert the vehicle of a European language into an African medium of cultural exchange as it is to adapt aspects of Western art to African needs, desires, and circumstance. New styles, new basic forms, new conceptualizations, new goals, new functional environments, new thoughts—these are the sorts of developments that people encounter and people create in the practice of making all forms of art. Art is never static—always emergent. In both large and small ways, art hovers at the edge of becoming something new, because, while it is on the one hand a tangible entity resolved by people into a collection of meanings and significances, it is on the other hand a resource of aesthetics and imagery that can be solved and resolved as individuals or situations change. In that way, every artwork is both actual and virtual simultaneously. It does not matter if a particular kind of art does not appear to change much over time, because the point is that it changes, or does not change, at the hands and in the minds of people who continually recreate or reconfigure it, as they bring it afresh into their consciousness and the changing situations of their lives.

In literature, Robert Coles has shown how powerful and instrumental this reshaping can be. Trained to do psychiatric work, Coles also has a deep interest in literature. He has taught in a number of contexts, including a seminar called "literature and medicine" for Harvard medical students. In his book *The Call of Stories: Teaching and the Moral Imagination*,[1] Coles presents instance after instance of students reading classics of Western literature, and dramatically internalizing and realigning the themes and images to make them profoundly relevant to important situations in the students' lives. Those students use the literature to explore problems, test solutions, and make changes in their lives. Such behavior constitutes the recreation of perpetually emergent texts, and similar transformations occur in works of visual art. Thus, artworks become instruments for people who are becoming capable, knowing agents in the complicated human processes by which individuals and culture constantly reinvent each other. This is one of the finest things the arts can help people do, and few things could be more important to teach about. That is especially true in the United States, where most people are taught to consider the visual arts as decoration or elitist esoterica. What better area to focus on than Africa, where so many people are taught to use art to think and to act?

Because art is so complex and so potentially relevant, it is important to teach students that simplistic dichotomies, such as traditional oral literature vs. modern written literature, or traditional sculpture vs. contemporary sculpture, must not be allowed to stand unchallenged. Instead, such alleged categories should be explored to see what sorts of ideas, institutions, and individuals are at work within them. Art may not be life in the direct linear sense of that old cliché, but it is so enmeshed in life's rich mental, emotional, and social practices that to remove it for study as a text risks missing far too much of what really counts.

The title of this chapter is "I Think You Should Hear Voices When You Look at African Art." What are these voices? They are all the perspectives, all the vested interests, all the heartfelt revelations, all the aspirations of the people involved with a work of art—be it literature, sculpture, or a multimedia, high-impact, dramatically spectacular West African masquerade performance. Because works of art both expand in social space and extend through social time, there are lots of voices to listen to; and even under the best research and teaching circumstances, lots of voices will have been missed. While many of these voices will hail from the local users of artworks, an ample number will represent the interests and perspectives of researchers and teachers, and those voices must also be focused upon and examined. Perhaps most important, whenever we can, we should embody at least some of those voices in actual people—such as the people I talked to and lived with in Mali, and the people Robert Coles talked to and taught in his courses—so that we can hear them present the images they have fashioned of themselves, their situations, and the artworks they experience and employ.

That brings me to my last point. Professor Lazarus argues that African literature can be studied in English departments. We should consider this seriously. Some prominent scholars think area studies should be more strongly emphasized. In a highly politicized discussion that shares various points of view with Lazarus, Janet Wolf, for example, has recently discussed the idea that art studies could be housed in cultural studies centers.[2] She notes that, on the whole, social scientists have failed to explore representation; and art historians seem, generally, not to comprehend the depth and significance of relations between representations and social processes. Lazarus notes that to study cultural products we must know the cultural, social, and historical atmospheres from which the products emerge. But he believes that, from within departments, we can do scholarship that is "historicized, politicized, materialist, alert to questions of representation and subalternity." I, too, think it can be done. But, like Janet Wolf, I am convinced it is a demanding and difficult task.

The essence of an argument against discipline-centered teaching and research is that the tacit dispositions that come from years of practical experience in a discipline, coupled with the incredible wealth of detailed information that disciplines manage and manipulate, can make it very difficult for individual teachers and scholars to work between or among them. For my work to be good, for example, I must read and understand a great deal of thinking that comes out of anthropology. Yet constantly, persistently, the realization descends upon me that I know very little about that, my neighbor discipline, and it is a wonder that anthropologists have the patience to talk to me.

So I take Lazarus's position to be an ideal. Perhaps we can do good work from within our disciplines. But our work must include frequent dialogue with colleagues in other disciplines, and, in the best of all possible worlds, that dialogue should be enhanced and amplified by the presence of an active African studies program. In this way, more of the voices, which are never-ending, will have a chance to be heard.

NOTES

1. Robert Cole, *The Call of Stories: Teaching and Moral Imagination* (Boston: Houghton Mifflin, 1989).

2. Janet Wolf, "Excess and Exhibition: Interdisciplinarity in the Study of Art," in *Cultural Studies,* eds. Laurence Grossberg, Cary Nelson, and Paula A. Treichler (New York: Routledge, 1992): 706–717.

6

Beyond Boundaries in the Humanities: A Response to Neil Lazarus

Paul Stoller

With so much discussion of language and literature in Neil Lazarus's thoughtful chapter, I will invoke a Songhay proverb to begin my comments:

Boro si molo kar farkey se
(One doesn't play the lute to a donkey)

Well, yes, this is an immediately comprehensible proverb. The lute player is an artist of sophisticated musical and cultural sensibilities. By contrast, in Songhay villages the donkey is kicked, spat on, and abused. The lute player is smart; the donkey is slow-witted. In Songhay, some human beings are called donkeys; they are the socially abused beings of Songhay society. The proverb is completely understandable. What is more difficult to understand is why—after twenty-three years of fieldwork—Songhay elders continue to recite this proverb to me!

One reason for the persistence of the Songhay elders devolves from typical scholarly practice. Anthropologists frequently remark that they "work" on a particular ethnic group. Early in my fieldwork, I used to say that "I work on the Songhay." But now I realize that it is better to say that "Songhay people work on me." For the past twenty-three years the Songhay people have been working on me—with much patience—in the western regions of the Republic of Niger. There is still much to learn and more to understand. My travels to Niger are hardly surprising. Africanist scholars, after all, would expect someone like me to travel to the Sahel to learn about a Sahelian people. But today we live in a topsy-turvy world in which expectations are reversed, sometimes delightfully so.

In July 1992 Songhay people continued to work on me, but in New York City rather than the dusty byways of western Niger. How will I ever forget getting off a bus at 125th and Lennox Avenue in Harlem on a hot afternoon? I was looking for the People's Market. At the corner of 125th and Lennox, I asked a bead merchant in French where I might find the

127

people from Niger. *"Nigeriens?"* "Oh yes," he said nonchalantly pointing his forefinger toward 6th Avenue. "You take that sidewalk and you'll find them." I walked one hundred meters down the sidewalk and came upon a man with a oval face. "Where might I find people from Niger?" I asked him in French. "We are here," he responded in Songhay.

His response unleashed a torrent of greetings, and, before I knew it, I was surrounded by Songhay merchants, greeting me in Songhay. I had stumbled upon a scene that before that day I would have found to be unimaginable: a group of Songhay men, many of whom came from small rural villages, selling shirts, jackets, strawhats, and, most remarkably, Malcolm X T-shirts and baseball caps, trademarked goods that were part of the packaging of Spike Lee's forthcoming motion picture, *Malcolm.* Most of the men spoke little English and all of them lived in a single tenement building in Harlem—a vertical village. The best cook of the group prepared food for everyone. In this way, said one of the men, "We have no trouble." During their long days at the market, the men buy cooked foods from a Senegalese woman who strolls by periodically with a supermarket cart loaded with styrofoam boxes containing *yassa, mafé,* and *riz au gras.* At 2:00 p.m. the men, all of whom are Muslims, pray in shifts so they can monitor their goods. "How do you wash before praying?" I asked one of them. "Watch," he said. He walked to the street corner and opened a fire hydrant. Following the remarkable Songhay scene in Harlem, I've come to realize that there are always creative solutions to problems along the ethnoscapes of the transnational world.

The meaning of this, of course, is that the study of Songhay can no longer hermetically be sealed in Songhay country, with a similar truth for the study of other peoples. The meaning is also that the categorical assumptions of the Western academy are, to be blunt, painfully out of synch with the speed-of-light change that occurs in the hyperspace of the global economy. Scholars can no longer "do" Songhay history or Songhay kinship or Songhay ritual in a state of insulated bliss. To understand Songhay people in Songhay or in New York City one must now learn a great deal about informal economies and the intellectual property issues germane to the trademarking of goods and to the copyrighting of cultural materials.[1] To comprehend sociocultural situations such as that of Songhay traders in New York City, scholars must also focus upon what I like to call social life *from below.* How do people confront the quotidian in a transnational arena marked by the postmodern condition? My guess is that they confront situations of mind-boggling change through creative and pragmatic cultural production. They colonize a vertical village; they prosper in the Malcolm X T-shirt market; they open the valves of fire hydrants to wash before they recite afternoon prayers between market tables on 125th Street. This social life from below sparks cultural production from below. The culture of the transnational traders—Songhay or other—is expressed in new sayings, new social practices, new social configurations, and new rituals, all of which are ever changing.

Which brings me to Neil Lazarus's stimulating and provocative essay. Lazarus presents a sobering and careful assessment of the impact of postcolonial literatures on the teaching of literature in the U.S. university. Using his own experience, he warns us about the dangers of a "new orientalism" in a transnational age. The crux of Lazarus's essay considers the rich complexities of the relation of language to literature. Must one have studied a "colonized language," following Gayatri Spivak's prescriptions, to grasp a postcolonial novel? Must a program in postcolonial literatures construct an institutionalized interdisciplinary program? Lazarus demonstrates powerfully why the answer to these seemingly reasonable questions is not an unqualified "yes." The language of literature is a complicated affair. Should we dismiss the writings of Achebe because they are in English and not in Igbo? It is to his credit that Lazarus says "no." I share Lazarus's anxiety about the ever increasing reductionism and essentialism found in cultural studies. In short, Lazarus's contentions about postcolonial literatures engage the full complexity of the contemporary.

However, as an ethnographer of the Sahelian Songhay who now contemplates years of fieldwork in Harlem, Lazarus's discussions of the putative autonomy of departments of English or Comparative Literature and his analysis of whether African literature should be written in English, French, Swahili, or Yoruba seems to miss at least some of the message of the postmodern critique. In the social sciences, many scholars have dismissed attempts at a postmodern anthropology or a postmodern sociology. Scott Lash correctly asserts that the notion of postmodern sociology is oxymoronic,[2] but the sociology of postmodernity is quite another matter. The condition of postmodernity in late global capitalism cannot be dismissed. As Kenneth Gergen admits with regret, postmodernity is here to stay.[3] It certainly has had an intellectual and artistic impact: it has also affected the nature of our social relations.

The question of transnationalism in cultural studies, then, transgresses the neat and tidy boundaries of academe. It is a question that forces us to confront the issue of what and how we teach. My question to Neil Lazarus is this: Does literature, in and of itself, really matter in Africa? Should it be isolated for study?

Neil Lazarus's paper reminds me in some ways of Christopher Miller's noteworthy achievement in literary criticism, *Theories of Africans*.[4] One of the great strengths of Miller's book is that he invokes new developments in cultural anthropology and feminist theory to analyze several novels written in French by authors from the Sahel. That said, I must add that Miller's book suffers from a chronic ailment found in many works of cultural studies: they are not cultural enough. Limiting himself to the study of African literature—albeit, some of it oral—Miller bypasses other forms of African cultural expression: ritual, local folk theater, and radio theater—all of which are performed in African languages.

The most powerful form of African cultural expression is not the much discussed novel, but the cinema. Filmmakers from the West African Sahel constitute the vanguard of the African cinema. Such films as Sembene's *Xala* and *Ceddo,* Cissé's *Yeleen,* and Ouedraogo's *Yabba* have been internationally acclaimed. The African cinema projects cultural themes to a wide range of audiences in Africa, Europe, and North America. Most of these films present localized portraits of social and political reality in Africa.

Is it enough to present theories of Africans, to borrow the title of Miller's book, through textual encounters? These ideally insulated encounters seem far removed from the energetic debates between deities and mortals at a spirit-possession ceremony, or the lively conversations between audience and image(s) on the silver screens of outdoor theaters, or the creative responses of Songhay traders to the gritty life of the street economy of Harlem. These interactions are not textual or literary theories of Africans: they are quotidian sites of Africans theorizing through a wide range of expressive media, through a wide range of cultural production *from below.* The challenge of postmodernity is not to abandon our quest for knowledge and understanding; it is rather to confront the inadequacy of our longstanding categorical assumptions. Until we do, the cultural expression of artists, filmmakers, ritual specialists, and transnational traders will continue to articulate what our categorical assumptions prevent us from understanding; namely, that the sky is lower than we think, to paraphrase Antonin Artaud.[5] Who knows when it will crash down on our heads?

NOTES

1. See Rosemary J. Coombe, "Objects of Property and Subjects of Politics: Intellectual Property Laws and Democractic Politics," *Texas Law Review* 69 (1991): 1853–1883.

2. Scott Lash, "Discourse or Figure" in *Postmodernism,* Mike Featherstone, ed. (Menlo Park, Calif.: Sage, 1988): 187–206.

3. Kenneth Gergen, *The Divided Self* (New York: Basic Books, 1990).

4. Christopher Miller, *Theories of Africans: Francophone Literature and Anthropology in Africa* (Chicago: University of Chicago Press, 1990).

5. In Antonin Artaud, *The Theatre and Its Double,* trans. Mary Caroline Richards (New York: Grove Press, 1958).

7

New Directions: Teaching Economics to Undergraduates in African Studies

Ann Seidman

Africanists from the United States have always understood Africa's close historical ties to the United States and valued its rich contributions to our cultural and artistic heritage. Over the last four decades, we have made major efforts in the universities to expand African studies programs to increase undergraduate students' awareness and comprehension of those contributions. African studies has helped U.S. students gain new insights into their own lives and subcultures. My comments aim simply to urge that we adopt bold new ways to exploit the potentials in African studies for helping our students to deal more effectively with the changing global system.

The post–World War II technological revolution shrank the globe. We all recognize that what happens in remote corners of the world—whether it be the oil fields of Kazakhstan, the ancient forests of the Amazon, or the shifting Saharan deserts—inevitably affects everyone living in the United States. The increasing ease of communication with our global neighbors has facilitated our access to their many, excitingly different cultures. However, the otherwise welcome demise of the Cold War has brought a shift of public attention—and funds—away from Africa. This is particularly unfortunate in the face of the deepening economic, social, and political crises that today permeate almost all aspects of African life. It underscores the challenge we face now, more than ever before, of finding new ways to help U.S. undergraduates to comprehend and appreciate Africa's many-faceted realities, and their implications for our own lives.

Drawing primarily on my own field, economics, I would like to center my remarks on ideas for strengthening our teaching along three lines:

1. Overcoming the constraints imposed by disciplinary boundaries and methodologies
2. Developing participatory, problem-solving learning processes to enable our students and their African colleagues to grapple more effectively with today's global realities

3. Helping to improve development theory and practice by facilitating systematic comparisons of regional experiences

I will elaborate each of these briefly.

STRENGTHENING PARTICIPATORY PROBLEM-SOLVING METHODOLOGIES

I suggest that, within the increasingly interdisciplinary framework of African studies programs, we should help our students to adopt and improve a participatory, problem-solving methodology. There are, in many U.S. university curricula, two characteristics that hinder formulation of methodologies appropriate for discovering rational solutions to the pressing problems that now confront Africa and other Third World countries: the limits imposed by disciplinary boundaries; and the positivism that, within those limits, too often permeates scholarship.

Africanists have long recognized that development problems—in Africa as throughout the world—never come packaged in boxes neatly labelled *economics, history, law, engineering,* or *sociology*.[1] To address the causes of the deeply rooted obstacles to development requires formulation of theories and methodologies that cut across disciplinary lines. Some people argue that dangers lurk in jettisoning disciplinary boundaries. To the contrary, I would underscore the dangers if we fail to encourage our students to look beyond the boundaries imposed by the academic disciplines.

My own discipline, economics, for example, tends to center researchers' attention on markets. Some economists may admit that technologically determined economies of scale hinder realization of the perfect market conditions that their models assume. Nevertheless, their toolbox does not contain instruments for analyzing the technical conditions in which those scale economies arise. For that, they ought to call in engineers, but they seldom do. Again, economists often inveigh against state intervention, which, they insist, hampers the operation of the perfectly competitive markets that their models assume. Without tools capable of explaining institutional behaviors, however, they cannot explain why existing Third World circumstances block realization of the goods their models promise. Likewise, to explain why the present African crises impose special burdens on women requires anthropological or sociological understandings of historically shaped attitudes and cultures—but the focus of economists on market forces typically excludes these insights.[2] However, anybody who studies development problems realizes that resources do not allocate themselves. Markets do not function in a vacuum. Society, the state, and law shape the particular institutions that comprise the "forces" of particular markets. We might ask why more sociologists, psychologists, and historians do not take part in African studies programs. All three disciplines, it seems to me, have much to contribute to, and perhaps much to learn from, a deeper engagement with the issues that African studies raise.

Recognizing the limits imposed by academic disciplines, we Africanists, along with teachers in other regional studies programs, increasingly have designed courses along interdisciplinary lines. In these, we have long sought to encourage our students to appreciate the necessity of formulating theories and methodologies that everywhere facilitate exploration of the interrelated aspects of development problems. At the same time, our studies have led many of us to realize that the positivist ends-means methodology so pervasive in many academic disciplines hinders effective, policy-oriented research and analysis. To say that policymakers determine ends, leaving researchers only the task of attaining them, inhibits rather than assists Africans and other Third World peoples from discovering the causes of their poverty.

I will turn again to my own discipline: many economists treat theory as metaphor.[3] They assume as the goal of development the attainment of their ideal model of perfect competition. Tucking their prepackaged models into their briefcases before leaving home, they commonly prescribe similar means to attain that end—regardless of the fact that countries differ in their circumstances. Ignoring the structures and institutions (shaped by different histories) that impose monopolistic tendencies throughout the Third World, they urge governments everywhere to adopt measures presumed necessary to submit their economies to the market's (assumedly benevolent) "invisible hand." They would eliminate price controls and minimum wages; lower taxes on high-income groups and raise across-the-board taxes on sales; devalue national currencies and scrap foreign exchange controls and import licencing; privatize state enterprises; and introduce fees for public services. In this respect, the economist seems to behave much like the moonstruck lover who declared, "My love is like a red, red rose." Then, assuming his floral metaphor represents reality, he woos her with a shower of water and well-rotted fertilizer.[4]

In contrast to this ends-means approach, African experience teaches the advantage of using a problem-solving methodology. Ben Wisner emphasizes this in the case of hard science, but it holds equally true for the social sciences. It calls for research—the gathering of evidence to test hypotheses drawn from theories—at every stage of an ongoing learning process:[5]

1. To identify, in its country-specific setting, the nature and scope of the particular problem that apparently blocks the development process
2. To review, critically, all available, alternative theories in order to tease out and warrant[6] a hypothesis that (if proven consistent with

the available evidence) may adequately explain the problem's causes

3. To assess evidence relating to the constraints and resources inherent in the country-specific circumstances to determine which of the range of solutions, logically suggested by the hypothesis, seems most likely to succeed in overcoming the causes identified

4. To implement the solution thus selected, monitoring it in light of the new evidence generated to identify, explain, and solve the new problems that must (inevitably) arise. (To paraphrase one student, "The development process seems to be just one damn problem after another.")

Furthermore, work in Africa has convinced many of us that it is advantageous wherever possible to involve the people affected by the problem in every stage of analyzing it. Obviously, they have the most intimate, personal knowledge of the problem's impact. Moreover, their participation in the learning process of testing explanations against evidence, attempting to design solutions to overcome the causes, and evaluating the results will help to empower them to tackle future difficulties more effectively.[7]

I would like to underscore one point: this approach does not require a prepackaged static definition of *development*. Rather, it emphasizes that, in their efforts to explain and overcome the obstacles that block their progress, people can and will evolve their own development process.

In sum, in contrast with compartmentalized, positivist disciplines, increasing numbers of Africanists encourage undergraduate students to adopt interdisciplinary problem-solving approaches. That approach offers a framework for rational, critical thinking. Its premise holds that we cannot come up with proposals for solution unless we find evidence to warrant the explanations that underpin them. That emphasizes the importance of insisting that our students explicitly state and test their explanations. Only if they have rigorously tried to falsify their explanations and failed, (i.e., only if they cannot prove them inconsistent with the available evidence) can they claim to have a rational foundation for their position.

Students might, of course, disagree with my conclusions: obviously, I do have a position on the issues we discuss in classes. But I try hard to persuade students to consider all the possible positions suggested by alternative available theories. To give them practice, I find it helpful to organize students into teams to debate central issues, each taking a contrary theoretical stand, and backing it up by evidence. I often promise any student who disagrees with me, and who provides adequate evidence to support his or her argument, an A.

Some academics, today, seem to reject any attempt to develop a rational approach to resolving social problems. Some ask whether Africans might encourage students to prefer other approaches to arrive at community consensus. The justified criticism of Western positivism, it seems to me, far from warranting rejection of a problem-solving approach, points to the necessity of adopting just such an approach. Africans who trained in the ancient African system of apprenticeship (I understand) used to engage in a kind of participatory education process, learning to ask the right questions in the framework of set rules. In a sense, in adopting a problem-solving approach, are we not really seeking to engage in a process of improving the rules for structuring the discourse, the gathering and presentation of relevant evidence, to arrive at consensus? In engaging our students, African and non-African, in this process, are we not proposing that they assess the problem-solving approach in terms of evidence accumulated through their own experience?

In this connection, of course, we must recognize that different people looking at the same evidence may interpret that evidence differently. This emphasizes the necessity for our students to evaluate alternative ways of gathering and interpreting evidence, continually devising better ways of doing it. But is that not part of the challenge we confront? To find ways to assist undergraduates to compare and contrast and in the process continually to improve their methodologies for arriving at better solutions to the problems that threaten to disrupt our increasingly interlinked realities?

BUILDING THE LEARNING PROCESS INTO UNDERGRADUATE AFRICAN STUDIES PROGRAMS

This leads to what I view as a second element necessary to strengthen the contribution of African studies to U.S. undergraduates' comprehension of our rapidly changing world: continued rethinking and the devising of new methods of teaching. Many Third World educationists, including increasing numbers of those teaching in Africa, have long criticized the traditional lecture/examination system. In particular, it relies too heavily on rote memorization and destroys the creative initiative required to assess alternative explanations of the causes of problems—the essential step in solving them.

African studies programs offer exciting possibilities for encouraging undergraduates to learn by working together with African students in a participatory problem-solving search for mutually beneficial answers to development problems. Only if we engage undergraduates in research will we really help them to engage fully in a creative learning process.

Problem-solving research is a learning process, a way of developing independent, critical thinking about how to gather facts about the causes of problems in order to solve them. To illustrate the potentials of participatory research as a means of engaging our students in learning-by-doing, I would like to discuss some concrete ideas related to exploring the causes and consequences of Africa's political and economic crises. We all accept the notion that laboratories provide science students essential opportunities to learn by doing. In reality, the global community comprises a laboratory for the social sciences, one that is readily available and not that expensive. Ben Wisner gives some insightful examples of using the community even for hard sciences research in this volume. Here, however, I will confine my comments to my own area of knowledge, the social sciences. The book *21st Century Africa: Towards a New Vision of Self-Sustainable Development*, prepared by the Task Force for Sustainable Development in Africa, provides useful background materials, including relevant bibliographies.[8]

The economic features of Africa's crisis are well known: worsening terms of trade, growing national and international debt, devaluation and austerity programs. All of these have undermined Africans' real incomes. Over the last decade, nine more African countries slid into the poverty category, raising the number to thirty-two. Africa has three-fourths of the world's poorest nations. Many of us have helped to document the social impact, especially on women and children, of drastic reductions in programs for education, health, and environment. Not only families but whole societies find themselves tragically ill-equipped to deal with the deadly new disease, AIDS. And from southern Africa to the Horn, national and ethnic military conflicts have disrupted development efforts, leaving in their wake perhaps the world's largest numbers of refugees. As the UN Economic Commission for Africa has pointed out,[9] Africa's crisis has put the very fabric of the continent's societies at risk.

Almost daily, television screens bring into the homes of middle America new pictures of human tragedies in Africa. Yet few people in the United States realize the extent of the U.S. involvement there. With control of over one-fifth of the votes in the IMF and the World Bank, the U.S. government exercises a predominant influence in shaping the lending policies of those agencies. Moreover, although the U.S. government spends barely one-fourth of 1 percent of our national product on giving aid—a smaller fraction than that for any other leading industrial power—it still constitutes a leading source of bilateral funds for Africa. Unfortunately, in the past too large a share of those funds went to financing sophisticated weapons like shoulder-held rocket launchers and antipersonnel mines, instead of literacy campaigns and rural clinics. The United States long supported Mobutu's corrupt military rule in Zaire. The U.S. government gave Samuel Doe's military government in Liberia more aid per capita than any other country in sub-Saharan Africa. For years, the United States spent more than $50 million annually to fund UNITA, which, initially with South African support, disrupted SADCC transport lines and the lives of millions of Angolan peasant families[10]—a mindless civil war that still continues. In the Horn, U.S. bases—first in Ethiopia, then in Somalia—contributed massively to building up the region's military capacity. Today,

Ethiopia's new government is struggling to build peace, though on fragile foundations; Somalia remains a center of violence. As Ben Wisner points out, we need to help our students to learn the perverse effects of that kind of use of hard science.

True, for better or worse, U.S. policymakers and the U.S. media have recently shifted their mercurial attention to Eastern Europe and the Middle East. This partly explains why African studies programs experience dwindling funds and the loss of faculty posts. Using relatively few resources along with a considerable amount of ingenuity, we need to devise new ways to help our undergraduates to understand why and how, in today's shrinking world, events in Africa affect and are affected by what happens in the United States. At the same time, as part of our students' learning experience, we should encourage them to take part in the task, identified by Adebayo Adediji at the 1990 African Studies Association meeting, of blending "cold-blooded economic rationality with the invigorating humanist virtues of ethically guided international development."[11]

On the one hand, while studying African history and culture our students could begin to evaluate the evidence relating to core debates over U.S. economic policies in Africa.[12] They could begin to assess the impact of the International Monetary Fund and the World Bank Structural Adjustment Programs (SAPs) on African countries. They could sift through the critics' claims that, not only do SAPs require deep social-welfare cuts and the privatization of public enterprises, but by pressuring African and other Third World governments to devote more and more resources to expanding exports of raw materials and labor-intensive manufactures, they also aggravate the underlying factors that led to Africa's crises.

Students could research other questions still subject to debate. For example: Did inherited colonial institutions gear African and other Third World countries' economies primarily to the competitive export of crude agricultural produce and minerals? Did post–World War II expansion of agricultural export crops spread over the best, most well-watered soils, reducing the availability of land for domestically consumed foodstuffs? Did newly imported technologies limit the numbers of new jobs generated by expanded, export-oriented mines, farms, and factories? To what extent did the developed countries' introduction of synthetic substitutes narrow demand for the Third World's raw materials? Did all these factors, as some scholars insist, inevitably push down Africa's terms of trade until, a decade later, they hovered at "virtually half their 1979–1981 averages"?[13] Does this help to explain why hundreds of thousands of rural people have crowded into urban squatter compounds, desperately seeking any kind of work at almost any wage?

Our students could also begin to explore a topic that touches the interests of working people in both Africa and the United States—a view of the ongoing global restructuring process that is gaining increasingly wide credence. On one side of this coin is Africa's socioeconomic crisis; on the other, a deepening dichotomy to be seen in the people of the United States.[14]

Students can evaluate for themselves the claim that the postwar technological revolution, especially in shipping, communications, and finance, has put U.S. wages and working conditions into competition with those of the world's most impoverished Third World populations, including those in Africa.[15] Our students should, of course, conduct a library search to document the changing economic trends of production, income, and employment in their home communities in the context of changing global trends. But we should encourage them to do more than that. They could also interview community leaders to assess whether and to what extent the process of global change has cost growing numbers of U.S. blue-collar workers the high-paying jobs and fringe benefits they won in earlier decades. Students might try to find out why as many as one out of five workers, particularly women and minorities, have had to take low-paid, part-time employment without fringe benefits. They could ask about conditions in the inner cities, like the ones in Los Angeles, to find out why as many as half of all young Afro-American and Hispanic workers cannot find work.[16]

Some of our students might want to investigate the effect of the U.S. military buildup, including arms sales to impoverished Third World areas like those in Africa. They could judge for themselves whether it furnished more than a limited additional market for U.S. industrial output; more than a relatively few, well-paid jobs. They could review the argument that financial mergers within and across national boundaries created huge, world-encircling conglomerates, each scouring the world for the lowest-wage areas for labor-intensive production to beat their global competitors—and pushing down real incomes in Third World countries.[17]

Working with U.S. community groups, our students could seek the answers to these and many more questions. They could work on understanding the nature of community problems as community members see them. They could examine the evidence related to the community members' explanations, as well as those available in books. Together with community participants, they could seek to assess the costs and benefits of possible solutions. In short, we might engage our undergraduate students in exploring whether and to what extent the post–World War II global restructuring process intensified a downward-spiralling competition that inevitably aggravated global inequality and contributed to worsening economic conditions within the United States.

Obviously, the task in engaging U.S. undergraduates in this kind of research varies from one university or college to another, depending on its location, its student body, and its resources. Some might ask, given the scarce resources and very large undergraduate classes at big state universities, how can anyone involve their students in this kind of research?

Certainly, we will need to employ all our ingenuity. We can use lectures to structure the discourse, to explain the problem-solving methodology, and to provide essential information. We might organize teams of students to debate before the class the pros and cons of critical issues like the consequences of global competition for U.S. as well as African living standards; and require them to provide evidence to support their explanations. We could encourage teams of students, not only to study library materials but also to gather evidence by undertaking community surveys.

In Tanzania, I assigned each of three hundred students in a first-year lecture class to undertake a survey of the consumption patterns of five low-income households. Some of the students, working as a group, computerized the results as an exercise in the statistics class; then all the students analyzed the results. These gave them valuable insights into the market implications of Tanzania's skewed income distribution. In Zambia, another first-year class of 150 students undertook a similar survey of prices in their home provinces.

In smaller institutions, getting students out into the larger community should be easier. The experience will give them a useful opportunity to break out of their limited, sometimes homogeneous, surroundings. In so doing, they should learn a lot about the way their circumscribed reality relates to the problems that pervade the lives of their neighbors—the beginnings of a greater understanding of factors at work in our global society. To facilitate our students' task, we need to provide them with community contacts: local government officials or leaders of church social action groups, women's and young peoples' organizations, and trade unions. We should talk with the leaders in advance, helping them to understand the students' concerns. In some instances, we might find leaders with an interest in involving the students in obtaining information that will help the leaders in their own work.

Engaging undergraduates in this kind of research in the United States could help to sensitize them to some of the issues involved in working together with African students and faculty members. The spread of more student exchanges would facilitate this kind of collaborative learning process. Working with African students who come to the United States, our students could gain a new perspective on life here as well as in Africa. In this context of exchange programs, we should bring more African teachers to the United States as visiting scholars. Not only would this help them to extend their own opportunities to write and conduct research, it would also give students an opportunity to learn from them in classes in this country. Together with our African colleagues, we could encourage senior undergraduates to join with African students to undertake research projects during the term here in the United States, and during long vacations in Africa. This would allow students to participate with Africans, comparing experiences as well as discovering the underlying causes of obstacles to self-sustaining development.

Undergraduates could learn a great deal by working with African students. Often, they are somewhat older than U.S. undergraduates. In my eleven years of teaching and conducting problem-solving research in Africa, I have worked with teams of African students in many kinds of projects, ranging from analyzing Zimbabwe's financial institutions to participatory evaluation of nongovernmental organization aid programs in Tanzania, Zimbabwe, and Zambia. As teachers, we helped them to structure the learning process along problem-solving lines,[18] not only to improve their own work, but also—where relevant—to facilitate the learning process among those with whom they worked. In the process, the African students, too, discovered they learned a great deal that they could not find in books. Summing up her experience in working to help peasants discover why aid projects so often failed to help them achieve self-reliance, one Zambian woman declared she had learned more in the four weeks she lived with them than she had in any class in the university.

Political and economic crises still constitute the biggest obstacles to the development process. But, as I have tried to emphasize, that crisis is global. We all need to work on it together and share what we are learning so we can do a better job. As we take part, too, we can critique the educational systems in which we work and find new ways to teach and conduct research together.

Our undergraduates could also cooperate with African students to make videotapes and recordings about their respective communities. These could not only document their involvement together in participatory learning activities, but also produce valuable records of music, art, and dramatic performances. Back home, the students might use university television and radio channels to share what they have learned with student and community groups.

Beyond acquiring a better understanding of their respective communities, U.S. undergraduates and their African colleagues might explore the possibilities of greater international cooperation. They might study, for example, the greater potential for trade if Africans were to succeed in building more regional cooperation through SADCC, ECOWAS and perhaps some new form in the Horn. With increased trade, African governments could redirect the billions of dollars now wasted by war and destabilization to people-oriented development. They could invest in more productive farms and factories as well as schools, hospitals, and roads, to meet peoples' basic needs.[19]

By conducting cooperative research with their African counterparts, our students might assess these possibilities. As U.S. and African citizens and future teachers, entrepreneurs, or government employees, they might bring their knowledge to bear on problems of expanding new kinds of global production and trade. Over time, attainment of sustainable development in Africa could create a large and growing market for goods made by

U.S. workers; and the United States might sell about ten times more goods, per capita, than we sell today to the half billion inhabitants of Africa.[20] In return, in the context of constantly reshaped patterns of comparative advantage, our country could buy Africa's increasingly manufactured mineral and agriculture produce. The resulting expansion of trade could contribute to improved productive employment opportunities and rising living standards on both continents.

In their research, our students would have an opportunity to evaluate the mounting claims that, in contrast to IMF and World Bank prescriptions, this potential cannot be achieved by national or international "market forces."[21] Far from matching the conditions of the ideal competitive model proposed by mainstream economists, this view asserts that a century of colonial rule deliberately shaped those markets to deprive Africans of access to their continent's resources. Left to themselves, the markets' "invisible hands" (or not-so-invisible hands) serve primarily to replicate and exacerbate existing African inequality and poverty. Within Africa, only firm government measures can redirect investable surpluses to expanded productive employment opportunities and an improved quality of life in the context of increasingly integrated domestic and regional development.[22] On a global scale, only governmental cooperation to establish stable export prices of the kind urged by proponents of the New International Economic Order can facilitate more successful national and regional development.

To assess this debate, however, our students would have to come to grips with a harsh reality: independent African governments have seldom proved willing, far less capable, of playing the role that the opponents of the IMF–World Bank approach seem to propose for them. If market forces cannot do the job, if the state remains society's primary instrument for implementing the required transformation, what measures might ensure that governments do respond to their peoples' needs? That they strive to combine their resources to attain democratic sustainable development?

This puts the spotlight on another all-important issue that U.S. undergraduates, together with African students, could investigate. In the process, they might share with and learn from the efforts of people, both in the United States and in Africa, to build more democratic, participatory, state and nongovernment institutions. Exploring the evidence as to the contradictory factors brought into play by the global restructuring process, they might help to identify and exchange information about new ways of achieving this task. Again, by way of illustration: the evidence shows that South Africa's emergence as a regional industrial and financial subcenter simultaneously created the largest industrial working class on the continent. In the 1980s, South African workers, organized in industrial unions built around shop-floor democracy, played a leading role in the mass democratic movement.[23] In their struggle to end apartheid, the unions, together with community organizations—in South African these are called civics—created their own forms of democratic peoples' participation.

In 1991, I took part in a fascinating three-week workshop with twenty-five leaders of South African community organizations and trade unions. These leaders fully recognized the dismal performance of many Third World governments, including many in Africa. In an effort to avoid a similar outcome, they met in the workshop to reevaluate not only other countries' experiences but the lessons of their own decades-long struggle for liberation. They sought new ways to ensure that a democratically elected, post-apartheid government would respond to their people's concerns. Among other strategies, they proposed national democratic fora to provide an ongoing framework for peoples' organizations to input government decisionmaking. Of particular interest to teachers, the workshop participants specifically discussed the possibilities of involving university (and even high-school) students in analyzing and documenting the role of inherited institutions in the perpetuation of undemocratic procedures and poverty.[24] They recognized this kind of information as essential before restructuring those institutions, or creating new ones. Might not our students, working with Africans in such projects, learn a great deal about building democratic, participatory institutions?

Perhaps, too, African students coming to this country could join our students in gathering information relating to the experiences of church and community groups tackling similar tasks here. During the African Peace Tour in Alabama, for example, we met members of a federation of rural cooperatives, mainly blacks.[25] Although the right to vote was already won, they had learned the hard way that they still had to press for government support to overcome the causes of poverty. "You can't eat votes," they said bitterly. They worked to elect candidates who would promote people-oriented development strategies—strategies in many ways similar to those South Africans had discussed at the 1991 workshop. Joining groups, like these in the United States, and sharing experiences with African university and community groups, our students might learn a great deal about building more democratic institutions.

EMPHASIS ON COMPARATIVE STUDIES

Finally, as a third approach to strengthening African studies programs, we should encourage undergraduates to undertake more comparative studies, not only of different African countries but also other Third World regions. In a global perspective, these could help them to gain insight into difficulties likely to thwart efforts to restructure regional economies and institutions.[26] Together with faculty in other area studies programs, Africanists need to think through ways to enable students to review and compare evidence relating to all the currently evolving theories and methodologies for analyzing the global development process. Given historical, geographical, and social differences, no one country's experience can provide a model or blueprint for success for another.[27] Nevertheless, with students from many different regions, African studies students could begin to reassess the evidence relating to the many factors causing poverty and powerlessness throughout the Third World, and the reasons for a given alternative strategy's success or failure.

As teachers, we might explore the possibilities for extending cooperative U.S.–African teaching and research methods into the undertaking of comparative interregional studies. Although there is no universal blueprint for successful development, comparative studies at least suggest what mistakes to avoid, and participants might gain useful ideas. Some immediate steps seem possible. We could organize more of the seminars and conferences of the kind we have already occasionally held to consider comparative issues. Where possible, we should try to arrange these, not only in the United States but also in Third World regions. On our own campuses, we should explore the possibilities of closer cooperation between area programs in designing and conducting comparative research.[28] We might expand this kind of cooperation into obtaining and sharing resources for research, as well as planning joint introductory courses that focus on common theoretical and methodological issues. Perhaps, too, we could arrange joint senior research seminars in which students could compare and contrast the results of their regionally focused investigations.

In sum, approaching the twenty-first century, as American Africanist teachers and students we face a new challenge. Changing global relationships require that we continually improve our theories and methodologies. The creation of African studies programs has already begun to help break down the disciplinary boundaries that for so long hindered adequate analysis of complex development problems. Now we need to think through ways of engaging our students in gathering evidence to review alternative theories as potential guides for explaining and finding solutions to those problems. In today's shrinking globe, we should seek new channels for our students to participate in problem-solving learning processes to discover how, and why, poverty and underdevelopment plague not only inhabitants of the Third World but also increasing numbers of those living in the First.

Many possibilities exist. We could encourage our students to work together with community organizations to explore the implications of U.S.–African relations, past and present, not only for Africans but also for U.S. citizens. We could explore new opportunities for enabling them to work more closely with African students to conduct participatory, multidisciplinary investigations as to the impact and causes of Africa's crisis and possible strategies for sustainable development. We could also find ways in which our students could cooperate with other regional studies programs to learn from comparative analyses.

In this kind of learning process, we could help our students to acquire, not only a greater appreciation of Africa's past and present contributions to world culture but also a deeper understanding of the full implications of today's global restructuring process. In addition, our students could help to accumulate, debate, and disseminate the information that citizens and policymakers need to work for sustainable democratic development, laying the essential foundation for peace, jobs, and steady improvements in the quality of life throughout the world.

NOTES

1. Peter Dorner, *Latin American Land Reforms in Theory and Practice: A Retrospective Analysis* (Madison, Wis.: University of Wisconsin Press, 1992).

2. Brooke Grundfest Schoepf, "Gender Relations and Development: Political Economy and Culture," in *Twenty-first Century Africa: Towards a New Vision of Self-Sustainable Development*, ed. Ann Seidman and Frederick Anang (Trenton, N.J.: Africa World Press, 1992): 203–241.

3. Arjo Klamer, Donald N. McCloskey, and Robert M. Solow, *The Consequences of Economic Rhetoric* (New York: Cambridge University Press, 1988).

4. Neva Seidman Makgetla, "A Note on Gary Becker's Use of Metaphor," *Journal of Economic Issues* 26 (1991): 900.

5. Seidman and Anang, *Twenty-first Century*; Ann Seidman and Robert B. Seidman, *The Long Rocky Road to Development* (forthcoming).

6. In Popper's sense of making every effort to falsify it in light of all available evidence. Karl R. Popper, *The Logic of Scientific Discovery* (London: Hutchinson, 1968).

7. Denny Kalyalya et al., *Aid and Development in Southern Africa: Evaluating a Participatory Learning Process* (Trenton, N.J.: Africa World Press, 1988).

8. Seidman and Anang, *Twenty-first Century*.

9. United Nations Economic Commission for Africa, *African Alternative Framework to Structural Adjustment Programmes for Socio-Economic Recovery and Transformation* (Addis Ababa: Economic Commission for Africa, 1989).

10. Ann Seidman, *Apartheid, Militarism and the U.S. Southeast* (Trenton, N.J.: Africa World Press, 1990).

11. Adebayo Adedeji, "Development and Ethics: Putting Africa on the Road to Self-Reliant and Self-Sustaining Process of Development" (keynote address delivered at the first plenary session of the Thirty-third Annual Meeting of the African Studies Association, Baltimore, 1 November 1990).

12. Seidman and Anang, *Twenty-first Century*, chap. 2.

13. Almost three-quarters of all African exports, more than any other Third World region, comprise unprocessed primary commodities. Although their prices may fluctuate, even optimistic predictions expect them to reach only two-thirds of 1979–1981 levels in real terms. Roy Laishley, "Commodity Prices Deal Blow to Africa," *Africa Recovery* 6, (April 1992).

14. Barry Bluestone and Bennett Harrison, *The Deindustrialization of America* (New York: Basic Books, 1982); Peter Dicken, *Global Shift: Industrial Change*

in a Turbulent World (London: Harper and Row, 1986); Folker Frobel, Jurgen Heinrichs, and Otto Kreye, *The New International Division of Labor: Structural Unemployment in Industrialized Countries and Industrialization in Developing Countries* (Cambridge: Cambridge University Press, 1980); Phil O'Keefe, ed., *Regional Restructuring Under Advanced Capitalism* (London: Croom-Helm, 1984); Andrew Glyn and Robert Sutcliffe, *British Capitalism, Workers and the Profit Squeeze* (London: Penguin, 1972); David Gordon, Richard Edwards and Michael Reich, *Segmented Work, Divided Workers: The Historical Transformation of Labor in the United States* (Cambridge: Cambridge University Press, 1982); Joseph Grunwald and Kenneth Flamm, *The Global Factor: Foreign Assembly in International Trade* (Washington, D.C.: The Brookings Institution, 1985); Richard Peet, ed., *International Capitalism and Industrial Restructuring: A Critical Analysis* (Boston: George Allen and Unwin, 1987); Jacqueline Jones, "Forgotten Americans," *New York Times*, 5 May 1992.

15. See, for example, Michael Tanzer and Stephen Zorn, *Energy Update: Oil in the Late Twentieth Century* (New York: Monthly Review Press, 1985); Frederick Clairmonte and John Cavenagh, *The World is Their Web—Dynamics of Textile Multinationals* (London: Zed Press, 1981); Folker Frobel, Jurgen Heinrichs and Otto Kreye, *The New International Division of Labor: Structural Unemployment in Industrialized Countries and Industrialization in Developing Countries* (Cambridge: Cambridge University Press, 1980).

16. Lawrence Mishel and David Frankel, *The State of Working America* (Washington, D.C.: Economic Policy Institute, 1990).

17. For data relating to transnational corporate market control in specific sectors, see *Ward's Business Directory, Major International Companies,* vol. 3 (Belmont, Calif.: Information Access, 1986).

18. See, for example, Kalyalya et al., *Aid and Development.*

19. For a review of alternative economic theories as guides to this process, see Makgetla, "A Note."

20. Ann Seidman, *Apartheid, Militarism and the U.S. Southeast* (Trenton, N.J.: Africa World Press, 1990).

21. United Nations Economic Commission for Africa, *African Alternative*; Seidman and Anang, *Twenty-first Century*, chaps. 2 and 8.

22. See, for example, the debates in Seidman and Anang, *Twenty-first Century.*

23. G. Seidman, *Labor Movements in Newly-Industrialized Countries: South Africa and Brazil, 1960–1985* (Berkeley: University of California Press, forthcoming).

24. Initially, based on pilot research in independent southern African states (see Kalyalya et al., *Aid and Development*), the proposal aimed to include only university students. However, Ms. Mujeja, a high-school principal from the Transkei, recalled the vital role South African high-school students had played in the liberation movement.

25. Ann Seidman, *Apartheid, Militarism and the U.S. Southeast* (Trenton, N.J.: Africa World Press, 1990).

26. See, for example, Peter Evans, Dietrich Rueschemeyer, and Theda Skocpol, *Bringing the State Back In* (New York: Cambridge University Press, 1985), chap. 11.

27. See, for example, Robert B. Seidman, *State, Law and Development,* (New York: Croom-Helm, 1976); Seidman and Seidman, *Long Rocky Road.*

28. The International Development Program at Clark University benefits from this kind of cooperation.

8

Learning by Disagreeing: Comments on Ann Seidman

Sara Berry

As Ann Seidman points out in Chapter 7, "New Directions: Teaching Economics to Undergraduates in African Studies," teaching about Africa to undergraduates in U.S. universities invites and challenges faculty to develop innovative conceptual and pedagogical approaches to their subject. As a field of study defined in terms that are geographical and cultural, rather than conceptual, African studies has traditionally cut across academic disciplines. Whether engaged in recovering the past or elucidating contemporary practices and problems, scholars working on Africa face particular methodological challenges that have pushed them actively to pursue interdisciplinary modes of enquiry.

For example, the paucity of documentary sources from which to study African history—together with the fact that, for many areas and periods of time, most available documents were written by non-Africans—has led historians to explore alternative sources of evidence. Efforts to collect and interpret archaeological, linguistic, ethnographic, or climatological evidence has in turn obliged Africanist historians to learn something about the academic disciplines that produce them and to incorporate some of their concepts and paradigms into historical research. Historians of Africa have also worked extensively with oral traditions and played a leading role in debates over the methodological issues involved in doing so.

Similarly, the difficulties encountered by many professionals—such as doctors, agronomists, and engineers—in applying the results of Western science to improving systems of health care, agricultural production, or infrastructure in contemporary Africa have stimulated efforts to reexamine boundaries between the natural sciences, on the one hand, and humanities and social sciences, on the other. Developing improved crop varieties or cultivation practices that enable African farmers to increase their incomes has turned out to require, for example, effective collaboration between anthropologists and botanists. Similarly, to adapt Western methods of treating illness, both physical and mental, to African conditions it is often

147

necessary to have an understanding of African cosmologies and social relations, as well as Western medical science. Interdisciplinary research on
the development of "appropriate technologies" has, in turn, led Western-
trained scholars to a new understanding and appreciation of African systems of knowledge. In general, introducing undergraduates to the results
and challenges of interdisciplinary research does more than enrich their
understanding of Africa; it can also offer them new perspectives on the intellectual architecture and cultural foundations of their courses in other
fields.

In addition to stressing interdisciplinary approaches, Seidman urges
students of contemporary African economic problems to place them in
comparative perspective by examining similarities and differences between Africa and other regions of the Third World (Asia, Latin America),
and by studying the effects of recent global economic restructuring on
women, workers, and ethnic minorities in the United States. Teaching
African studies in the United States offers opportunities for other kinds of
comparative analysis as well. As several participants in this conference
have emphasized, African studies have a direct bearing on the United
States: many U.S. citizens are of African origin, and African influences
are widespread in U.S. society and culture. While there is historical prece-
dent (and sometimes compelling institutional reasons) for treating African
and African-American studies as separate fields, there are equally strong
intellectual and institutional reasons for recognizing and exploring their interconnections, both as historical realities in their own right and as a
basis for addressing issues of race and racism in U.S. culture and U.S.
classrooms.

Comparative approaches to African studies can lead to conceptual as
well as practical and historical insights. Cultural and social boundaries—
within Africa, among peoples of African origin, and between Africans and
non-Africans—are often multifaceted, ambiguous, and historically fluid.
By exploring multiple inventions of the concepts *Africa* and *Africans,* and
examining particular issues of African experience from comparative perspectives, teachers and students are likely to find themselves reexamining
the nature of cultural and political boundaries in general. By situating such
comparisons in global and historical perspective, African studies can shed
light on relations between micro and macro processes in a variety of
disciplines.

In discussing strategies for teaching undergraduates about economic
development and democratization in Africa, Ann Seidman makes a particular appeal for participatory learning. Specifically, she suggests that students should be actively engaged in collecting and analyzing evidence on
economic and political problems that beset Africa and Africans; that they
should do so in collaboration with African students; and that their studies
should be directed toward solving such problems as well as analyzing

them. Her case is an appealing one. I would argue that it merits both elaboration and some qualification.

Participatory strategies of learning can be applied to intellectual inquiry in general, as well as to research directed toward solving practical problems. Students need never be left to absorb received knowledge passively. They should continually be engaged in questioning established precepts and evidence, framing new questions, and learning to evaluate both evidence and arguments for themselves. Such engagement may, of course, be achieved by the assignment of research projects; but participatory learning can also be built into the structure of classroom instruction. By foregoing the convenience (and security) of textbooks, by allowing students to address divergent or conflicting representations of any given topic (or even insisting that they do), by framing exam questions (as well as paper assignments) to elicit informed debate rather than predetermined responses —in all these ways teachers can instruct by having students engage in intellectual inquiry.

Such an approach is likely to prove fruitful in teaching almost any subject; in teaching about Africa—a subject on which undergraduates in U.S. universities are likely to start out with many different perspectives— it is essential. Clearly, too, the degree of participation and the potential for learning from others' perceptions will be greater the greater the cultural, national, and racial diversity of participants. By strengthening programs for recruiting African and minority-group students and faculty, colleges and universities in the United States stand to enhance the quality of higher education as well as its relevance to society.

Participatory learning is not, however, without risk. If participatory learning is itself democratically organized, students will be empowered to pose questions as well as to answer them, to define problems as well as to solve them, and to make independent as well as informed judgments about the quality of evidence and the validity of interpretations. In her essay, Seidman advocates "encouraging undergraduates to learn by working together with African students in a participatory problem-solving search for mutually beneficial answers to development problems." But independent inquiry does not necessarily lead to consensus. Indeed, the more diverse the backgrounds of students and/or faculty in a given classroom, the greater the chances will be that they will not arrive at "mutually beneficial answers" to pressing economic and political problems, or even agree on mutually acceptable definitions or diagnoses of the problems to be addressed. Faculty members who invite active student participation may find themselves confronted with deep divisions—divisions that imperil constructive dialogue among students or challenge teachers' ability to evaluate students' work fairly.

Such divisions are, in my view, part of the reality of scholarly inquiry as well as social interaction and should, therefore, be addressed in the classroom. Ultimately, we all need to confront the question of how to advance intellectual inquiry or frame social action in the face of such divisions; to learn (and to teach) the difference between respecting others' conclusions and accepting them, between criticism and contempt. Field research, study abroad, and extracurricular activities are all effective sites of participatory, experiential learning. But students learn by experience in the classroom, too—whether or not we take account of the fact. Because of its deep resonances with sometimes unrecognized and/or uncomfortable aspects of U.S. society and culture, the study of Africa offers both a rich and a daunting field in which to explore the possibilities of participatory learning. Taken seriously, teaching about Africa is itself a continuing education.

9

From Periphery to Center: African History in the Undergraduate Curriculum

Thomas Spear

Most of what I know about teaching African history and African studies at the undergraduate level has been learned during twenty years of teaching and developing African studies programs in two undergraduate institutions, and I want to use this opportunity to reflect on that experience: to explore what I have learned over that period rather than to adopt a theoretical, programmatic approach.[1] Not that the latter is less relevant: certainly, in this day of reactionary assaults on the curriculum we must continue to argue forcibly on theoretical and programmatic grounds for the necessary inclusion of Africa in the curriculum. But we now have enough practical experience to expand our arguments beyond merely advocating inclusion of a hitherto neglected area in the curriculum. We now can demonstrate the degree to which Africa has so transformed our thought that a classic liberal arts curriculum that does not include Africa is an impoverished curriculum.[2]

My experience has been gained in two very different institutions. La Trobe University in Melbourne, Australia, was new, growing rapidly, and progressive in its approaches to teaching and scholarship; Williams College was old, established, and still largely empiricist. Many La Trobe students were working-class adults seizing an opportunity for education that had largely been denied them in their youth; Williams students were young, predominantly upper-middle-class whites, with an increasing number of minorities. The role of African studies in both schools has been quite similar, however. La Trobe sought to develop a comprehensive curriculum from the beginning, and we quickly developed a small African studies program allied with Pacific studies that rapidly gained a reputation among students for innovative and challenging approaches to thinking about and reconstructing non-Western history. Williams, too, was supportive, but it had an established curriculum and faculty that took longer to nudge in new directions. Soon, however, we were able to develop an African and Middle Eastern studies program that embraced eight different disciplines and offered some twenty courses together with a parallel Afro-American studies program.

Few students in either school entered with an interest in Africa, but many developed strong interests after discovering the challenges of viewing the world afresh through the eyes of others. Africa provided cultural affirmation for many African-American students, and it challenged the received wisdom of all. Both U.S. and Australian students brought preconceived notions to the study of Africa to be sure, but they generally recognized that they knew little and were open to new approaches. Africa offered the opportunity to encounter new cultural worlds, and in the process it challenged their conventional understandings of themselves. Thus, they developed critical thought.

It is not only the cultural strangeness of Africa that promotes such critical awareness, however; it is also the way we approach it—interdisciplinarily, explicitly analyzing basic social organization, historical processes, and cultural values that most historians assume or only sketch in lightly as background. Students learn much about their own cultures and societies in the process, much as the process of learning another language illuminates the grammar of one's own. The study of Africa in general, and African history in particular, thus has much to teach us and our students about our disciplines as well as our selves—in addition to filling a vast void in most peoples' historical consciousness. In the comments that follow, I will first sketch in some of the contributions African history has made to the wider discipline of history, and, by extension, to our students, as well as discussing its relation with the contemporary phenomena of deconstructionism and Afrocentricity. I will then discuss some of the reasons why I feel African studies has become such a critical component of the undergraduate curriculum. Finally, I will deal with some of the more practical, institutional issues regarding implementing African studies in the curriculum.

AFRICAN HISTORY AND THE WIDER DISCIPLINE

African history has moved, over the past two decades, from the periphery to the center of historical studies, though this is often not recognized, either by our colleagues or ourselves.[3] Twenty-five years ago, African historians were struggling to develop appropriate methods and theoretical models for the study of preliterate societies, while simultaneously defending the new field against widespread skepticism in the discipline as a whole. Today, African history is accepted; and our methods and theory have been widely adopted to expand our overall understandings of Early Modern European history, British history, Colonial American history, African-American history, and Women's history, among other branches of the field.

Our own recognition of African history's impact has often lagged behind the reality, however, as we continue to maintain the familiar, beleaguered postures adopted early in our careers—postures that are periodically reinforced by reactionary attacks to restore outmoded elitist and empiricist approaches. While such attacks can easily dominate our concerns, they are little more than a sideshow to the more important movements transforming history today. We must learn to ignore the Trevor-Ropers and their modern equivalents (as much as we enjoy perversely evoking their smug, ignorant phrases) and to recognize the significance of our own historical role within the discipline in order to capitalize on it.

While we are constantly reminded of earlier colonial views of Africa itself in the sources we consult, it is easy to overlook how far history in general has moved from empiricist political history to more methodologically and theoretically sophisticated socioeconomic history, a shift in which African history has played an important part. In developing African history we were among the first to *deconstruct* official discourse to reveal the implicit biases in our sources and the ways in which they masked power, and to *decenter* our studies to shift our perspective from that of European to African historical forces and actors. We did so long before such terms became academically fashionable. We devoted considerable energy to developing new historical methodologies to validate and analyze oral traditions, and we integrated anthropology, archaeology, and historical linguistics into normal historical practice. Lacking written documents that emphasized individual agency, we focused our analyses, perforce, on institutions and on the social and cultural process that made them, in the course of which we fundamentally expanded the scope of political economy to encompass precapitalist and transitional modes of production as well as capitalist ones.[4]

All of these have become common historical practice today as other historians seek to recover similarly "hidden" histories of ordinary people and their institutions to trace deep-seated, fundamental structural changes in society. African historians were in the forefront of this development. There have been, of course, the subsequent claims of deconstructionists who, like Columbus, have belatedly discovered a world that was already there, well-known to its inhabitants, and sought to relate it to their European and U.S. contemporaries in familiar terms. Deconstructionism has certainly sharpened our general critical awareness, but there is much for Africanists to be wary of in the attempt to deconstruct older historical discourses so as to recenter them on familiar European terrain. While Africanists have sought to move beyond colonial discourses to try to understand African historical realities on their own terms, deconstructionists return the focus to colonial discourse itself. Africanists have often decentered to the point where the former center becomes a remote periphery, while deconstructionists seek to recapture the center for their own analyses rooted in European intellectual traditions. Deconstructionists correctly note the problematic nature of all texts, but they then tend to invalidate them. Africanists, on the other hand, appreciate that our texts are both partial and incomplete. Often we recognize that certain texts may testify to colonial attitudes (in the case of colonial documents) or to particular reconstructions of the past (in the case of oral traditions) in the course of describing African historical realities. But we must struggle with them if we are to gain any understanding of those realities, however imperfect. Moreover, in their concern for *the other,* deconstructionists tend to reify complex, endogenous realities in simplistic exogenous terms.

While deconstructionists' interests have largely been focused elsewhere and their impact on African history has been correspondingly minor, Afrocentricity focuses directly on Africa and calls for an African perspective to recover and understand African historical experience throughout the diaspora. I could not agree more on the critical importance of seeking to understand African social realities from an African perspective, as African historians from Africa, Europe, and North America have been trying to do since the early 1960s, and we should all welcome the opportunity critically to reassess our efforts in this regard. A problem, however, is that Afrocentric historical concerns and interpretations do not always accord with those of African historians. An excellent example of this concerns the role of Egypt in state formation throughout Africa. In responding to E.G. Seligman's "Hamitic hypothesis" concerning the founding of African states by wandering (white) Hamites, Cheikh Anta Diop retained Seligman's diffusionism and racial definition of culture—but redefined Hamites as black.[5] These common emphases on diffusionism and a racially determinist definition of culture contrast markedly with the current emphasis in African history, which is generally on the endogenous development of states and the historical basis of culture, as reflected in such African texts as *History of West Africa*, edited by Ajayi and Crowder.[6]

Such differences stem from the fact that, while emphasizing an African perspective, Afrocentricity's political and intellectual foundations and scholarship are rooted in North America and deeply reflect African-American experiences and political concerns. Africa has long played critical roles in African-American intellectual history and politics—roles that reflected blacks' changing experiences and responses.[7] It is important to recognize these roles if we are to understand and assess the distinctive interpretations of African history made by Afrocentric scholars and avoid a further round of mythmaking about Africa that has less to do with Africa than with the roles it plays in the thought of others.[8]

It is also important to recognize that Afrocentricity represents only one among many of the intellectual responses African-Americans have made to their experiences in the Americas. Many black Americans feel that Afrocentricity devalues those experiences and diverts attention from critical historical and political issues regarding slavery, its aftermath, and the intricate dialectic between Africa and America that has shaped black and white cultures throughout the Americas. Racial definitions of culture allow little room for creative historical action, while the burgeoning studies of how Africans in the diaspora drew on their cultural heritages to come to terms with oppressive slavery and its aftermath convey the vitality of African-American agency as people continued to make their own histories.[9] It thus remains as critical as ever to explore *perspective and bias* together with *intellectual and political contexts* and in this way carefully to establish firm foundations for exploring and understanding the African and American pasts.[10]

African history thus continues to contribute much to the overall discipline of history, even as it continues to be enmeshed in European and North American political and intellectual contexts. Within the field itself there needs to be a swing back to the importance of African perspectives if we are to understand the complexities of African politics in terms other than postcolonial, neocolonial, or underdeveloped (i.e., Eurocentric).[11] Recent histories of Tanzania have reinforced this point for understanding nineteenth century and colonial-era history as well, as they seek to focus on African agency within the wider context of the world economy.[12]

EDUCATIONAL AND PEDAGOGICAL PERSPECTIVES

It goes without saying that Africa represents a great void in most of our students' learning, a void marked only by the stereotypes of popular culture, as Joel Samoff reminds us in Chapter 2. It is also obvious that, in a global economy where issues of economic distribution, environmental destruction, and political freedom increasingly affect everyone, we can no longer ignore a vast number of people who have so often been exploited for others' gains. Finally, it is self-evident that past mistruths, stereotypes, and prejudices regarding Africa and Africans continue to affect adversely large numbers of our own people in addition to those still living in Africa, portraying their heritages and abilities often in negative and derogatory terms.

These are important arguments for the need to include accurate representations of Africa in the curriculum. They have been made in numerous national reports and proposals for educational reform, and in this book I take them as given. What is less frequently argued, however, is that learning about Africa is crucial to our students' intellectual development, an argument that puts Africa firmly within the bounds of educational issues as well as social or political ones.

The critical importance of trying to understand Africa from an African perspective, one of the contributions of African history to the discipline, is also one of its main contributions to the undergraduate curriculum. For students to try to look at Africa through African eyes necessitates major shifts in the ways they look at the world and, ultimately, themselves. As they are forced to think in African terms about social organization, economic practices, or cultural values, they begin to see their own, "natural" beliefs about social relationships, political action, economic goals, and even the environment for the cultural constructs they are. Once one has experienced another culture, one becomes more aware of one's own cultural values and practices. Students slowly discover that they, too, have ideologies (a word they defined heretofore as false beliefs akin to propaganda held by others); that, they too, are historical products, created by and creators of culture; and the ultimate U.S. heresy, that socioeconomic structures and cultural values constrict and channel their individual action.

These are all revolutionary intellectual discoveries for U.S. students with their implicit belief in unrestrained rationality, individuality, and freedom.[13] In a seminar for school teachers sponsored by NEH, I noted similar reactions. These mature, concerned, and intellectually aware adults responded to relatively simple concepts, such as the ways farming practices (and, by extension, social and economic relations) are related to the environment, with comments to the effect that they had never thought of that before—in spite of the fact that one can easily demonstrate similar relationships in our own society. Then again, whenever I return from Africa I am struck anew by the degree to which we are ourselves the cultural aliens that need explaining. Thus, as we close our critical distance from Africa, we become more critically distant from, and aware of, ourselves.

Providing critical distance from ourselves is only one of the ways Africa helps us to understand ourselves better, however. African history also provides explicit conceptual frameworks for understanding and analyzing social and economic organization, values and beliefs, ecology, and processes of change. Kinship, exchange, legitimacy, patron-clientage, modes of production, and spirit possession are only a few of the many concepts we deploy to assist our thinking. While such frameworks have often been adapted from anthropology or political economy, African historians use them far more consciously than most historians, providing students with an array of analytical tools to understand their roles and those of others in culture and society. Indeed, how many historians even discuss the concept of culture, an essential concept to our understanding of ourselves as human beings?

But African history is more than merely another social language useful for dissecting the cultural grammar of our own. It also embraces a myriad of human worlds—each a world unto itself—a vast historical panorama displaying an extraordinary range of human diversity. Each people, each historical event, each social process is a lesson in human experience and ingenuity worthy of exploration in its own right. The very elegance of

African societies teaches us much about fundamental human values, patterns of behavior, and institutions, as the NEH seminar participants discovered. Nor is there any shortage of great historical themes, ranging from the impact of culture on the development of humankind to the relationship between the development of farming or herding and social organization. The study of African history offers the development of states and their relationship with local social organization, the impact of commercialization on politics and society, and the ways in which forms of dependency changed with different modes of production. In particular I will mention the impact of the world's greatest intercontinental migration of its time—the slave trade—on the migrants, the societies they left, and those they joined.

Issues of perspective and bias also loom large in normal intellectual development as adolescents progress from absolutist (teacher/book as authority) to relativist (choice made among equally valid alternatives) and finally to critical (judgment based on analysis) modes of thought.[14] Historians frequently talk about bias, but we must also distinguish between bias and perspective: perspective as point of view and bias as moral judgment, often along predetermined lines. One can, for example, see the colonial encounter from the point of view of the colonizers or from that of the colonized, while, in a separate, independent process assessing its effects as either good or bad. Thus—to pursue the example further—while colonial history usually took an imperial point of view and saw the impact of colonization positively, dependency theory often shares the imperial perspective but judges the impact of colonialization more harshly. Nationalist history takes an African point of view and emphasizes colonialism's negative impact; others have taken an African perspective while approving of colonialism.

As undergraduate students are disabused of absolutism, usually as a result of repeatedly encountering dissonance among competing authorities, they become prone to see everyone and everything as equally biased, and hence, equally right or wrong. Historical judgment then becomes merely a matter of moral preference among equally valid (or invalid) competing interpretations. Identifying perspective at this stage provides students with initial grounds for discriminating critically among competing views. While they may, for example, prefer an African participant's account of an act of resistance, they can begin to appreciate that a colonial officer's account of the same event, while dramatically different, may be equally valid from his point of view. Thus they have two takes on the same event. The ability to identify and see multiple perspectives is an important one in developing powers of thought, and once attained it moves students to assess competing accounts not merely on their point of view (which they have seen as bias up to this stage), but on their relative accuracy. This is the start of critical thinking, and eventually students learn to read context into varying accounts, interpreting them in terms of their language, biases, and perspectives to move beyond their factual content to their wider meaning and significance. An appreciation of bias and perspective is thus critical to developing critical thought, and African history, because of the wide array of biases and perspectives revealed in its materials, is an excellent vehicle for developing it.

I have mentioned an array of goals for teaching African history: from historical content to conceptual frameworks and intellectual development, from cultural contexts to narrative detail, from the family and stateless so-cieties to vast states—and all these have to be covered in twelve weeks or less! The array is such that I feel I must suggest some of the strategies that I use for accomplishing these goals. Africa is too vast, and our knowledge too sparse, to pretend to cover the continent in detail. Therefore, I am highly selective in my approach. I focus on structure and process, my most important goal being that students develop a basic understanding of and ways of thinking about a diverse selection of African societies and some of the ways they have changed through time. For a precolonial course, I or-ganize the material into a few select themes—stateless societies, state for-mation, the spread of Islam, and slavery and the slave trade—and explore a few representative case studies for each theme to focus on the particular structures and processes revealed there. The process is cumulative, with each case and theme building on previous work to develop a sophisticated understanding of social process in Africa, so that, by the end of the se-mester, students have an empathetic appreciation of African societies and are beginning to be able to interpret and think creatively about them.

For the section on stateless societies, for example, I might start with Achebe's *Things Fall Apart* and Uchendu's *The Igbo of Southeastern Nigeria* to develop a basic understanding of African societies and social process. We then discuss various analytical frameworks and historical methodologies for understanding African societies, exploring the nature of our sources and what they can, and cannot, tell us. By the time we get to the section on state formation, we have a considerable analytical and methodological repertoire for examining how states incorporated stateless societies, how African empires differed structurally from Western states, and the impact of economic development and trade on political develop-ment. By the time students get to colonialism in the second semester, they are readily able to analyze the interaction between Africans, with their val-ues and goals, and Europeans, with theirs, in terms of complex dialectical models of social, economic, and cultural change.

How does this measure up against my above list of goals? Clearly, I circumscribe narrative, and the areas I focus on I cover in great detail. But vast areas of Africa do not get covered. This is a problem, but in my de-fense I note the relative lack of effective literature for teaching; the ever present danger of students becoming lost in a profusion of narrative detail, as they do even in my sharply circumscribed African world; and the degree to which they learn to think for themselves, capably tackling detailed research papers on areas we have not covered in the course. Cultural contexts and conceptual frameworks are the substance of my course and are well covered. Students learn not only about patrilineal kinship systems and patron-client relations but also modes of production and charismatic authority, and put them all together to understand processes of state formation. Finally, what about critical thinking, on which I have laid so much stress? This is, I find, largely a fortuitous by-product. I do, it is true, discuss issues like perspective and bias explicitly, but most of the benefits of critical distancing and critical thought flow naturally from the material, with cross-cultural comparisons being made frequently as we go along. It is for precisely this reason that I see Africa as such a crucial component of the undergraduate curriculum, especially after talking with colleagues in U.S. and European history about the difficulties they have in getting students to think critically because the students feel that they already "know" those areas. Rural France in the seventeenth century is, after all, simply a minor variation on suburban U.S.A. in the late twentieth, or so students often think.

INSTITUTIONAL INFIGHTING
AND TEACHING AFRICAN HISTORY

If I am right, African history should already occupy a crucial place in any undergraduate curriculum for sound intellectual, educational, and social reasons, but as we all know theoretically, institutions are less than rational and tend to stasis, the sum total of the vested interests of those in them. That African history does not presently occupy a crucial place in most curriculums is due to a number of institutional factors, not the least of which is that African historians are rarely present before the fact to argue for its inclusion. Thus, few of the above arguments are put forward in the typical institutional struggle between people in established traditional fields and those advocating new ones. Arguments for including Africa in the curriculum are more often made on political and social grounds than on intellectual ones, leaving the field open to attack by the self-appointed guardians of the academy and Western civilization (i.e., Western civilization as they know it).

The politics of African studies are also usually intertwined with issues regarding the recruitment and inclusion of minorities in the student body and faculty. In the best of all possible worlds, an inclusionary curriculum is developed prior to, or simultaneously with, the expansion of the faculty and student body as part of an overall policy to expand institutional horizons to better serve the needs of its students and society at large. In the worst, curriculum is developed and faculty are appointed ad hoc in response to student demands. The first approach bodes well for the overall success of the transition, and the resultant curriculum is likely to embrace many of the broader goals enumerated above. The second usually lacks coherence and is often viewed, by supporters and detractors alike, as merely a sop thrown to students with little intrinsic educational value, thus initiating endless disputes with students and among faculty over course offerings and hiring and promotion of faculty. While the two approaches appear to be opposed, they may in fact be pursued simultaneously as institutions get caught up in the flow of events. In my experience, Williams College made a concerted effort to develop area studies programs at the same time that it was seeking to diversify its faculty and student body (to include women as well as minorities), both goals adopted for sound intellectual and educational reasons. A number of new faculty were hired with explicit mandates to develop Afro-American, African, and Asian studies, and were given broad institutional support to do so. Such transitions are rarely smooth, however, given the often glacial pace of academic change, and when students demonstrated periodically to speed the pace, the administration often made ill-considered promises to still the unrest, such as hiring temporary faculty to offer courses sporadically, while avoiding commitments to long-term institutional change.

An ironic incident stands out in my mind. Neglecting normal consultation with affected faculty, departments, and programs, the administration presented a "cultural diversity" requirement to the full faculty with little notice. The requirement mandated that all students take at least one course in non-Western studies, which was broadly defined to include African and Middle Eastern, Asian, Latin American, Native American, Afro-American, Latino, or Asian-American studies. It was intended to meet a student demand for more courses specifically on U.S. minorities, but the administration deemed expansion of minority studies would be too costly and cause too great a shift in student enrollments from less popular departments. The administration therefore added the more established African, Asian, and Latin American studies programs to those focusing on U.S. minorities, which meant that 85 percent of students already met the proposed requirement. This necessitated little need to hire new faculty, develop new courses, or change student enrollments. The requirement was, in short, largely symbolic, but it was precisely on symbolic grounds that it ran into trouble. Faculty in the nominated areas were virtually unanimous in opposing the requirement, while others, including a number of well-known conservatives, supported it. Why was there such a complete turnaround of support, so different from what might have been expected? The affected faculty felt that they had done an excellent job in developing challenging programs that already attracted a large majority of students, and they did not welcome the prospect of a small number of students being resentfully force-marched into their programs. Given administrative support, they would have preferred to develop additional courses on U.S. minorities—courses which, while in the process of being mandated for students, had not, up to that time, been offered.

A number of conservatives were bewildered by the opposition. They remarked that, ten years earlier, the opponents would have supported the requirement. They were probably correct, but in the intervening years the opponents felt that they had learned the dangers of lumping people together into a single, indistinguishable category of *other* that promoted people's sense of a monolithic mass of *them* opposed to *us*. Such lumping together merely reinforced prevalent stereotypes, they felt; whereas their goal was to undermine stereotypes by showing what was distinctive about each culture or group. The opponents thus felt that the requirement undermined the integrity and successes of their programs as well as what they were trying to achieve educationally and intellectually. In short, a requirement based on political and symbolic grounds would operate to the ultimate detriment of intellectual and educational ones.

The issues raised by the non-Western requirement raises the broader issue of the appropriate role of African studies within broader movements for African-American studies, area studies, and multiculturalism generally. The relation between African studies and Afro-American studies at Williams College was never a problem, with each area feeling that its interests were best served by the existence of strong parallel programs, with African history included in both. The relationship elsewhere, however, has often been more conflictual, embroiled in political as well as intellectual issues over interpretation, turf, and responsibility for teaching, such that programs have become politicized, fragmented, or moribund. There are, it seems to me, no easy answers. We are all caught up in the fraught issues surrounding race in our society, the United States' original sin. But we should be able to agree on the critical intellectual and educational relationship between African and African-American studies and offer complementary, if not coordinate programs.

My own preference for separate area studies programs follows the position of the opponents to the "cultural diversity" requirement noted above. It is important for students to learn about other cultures generally, for all the reasons I have given; but it is also important that they learn to understand and appreciate each culture for its own cultural distinctiveness and historical contributions. The same applies to the relationship between African and African-American studies. The two are obviously intertwined in such crucial ways that it is impossible to teach one without the other, but each area and people are also distinct and deserve to be portrayed with due respect.

Similarly, the wave of multiculturalism now sweeping the United States is certainly to be welcomed for expanding our historical vision and raising critical issues, but we must be careful to develop coherent programs lest ethnic studies merely becomes an exercise of adding more subjects to a re-defined, albeit spicier, melting pot. Gregson Davis makes a significant contribution to this debate in Chapter 1 in his argument for *inter*cultural studies, emphasizing the degree to which comparative approaches can transform the way we all think, and his ideas should be in the forefront of all our discussions of multiculturalism.

Developing an undergraduate African studies program in a new or expanding institution, where there are few confrontations with established areas over resources, is certainly the fastest way to develop a new program; but most of us are presently confronted with shrinking resources and increasingly bitter competition over access to them, and so we have to develop our programs slowly, capitalizing on what we have and on opportunities as they arise. Williams College first initiated a generic area studies program to serve as an umbrella for recruiting new faculty and establishing new areas. As a coherent program it was a shambles, but it did serve its intended purpose of encouraging departments to shift appointments and recruit faculty in new areas, as well as providing a focus for existing faculty who had interests in them. In the end, only a few of the participants in any of the areas were new faculty hired specifically to teach it. Most were existing faculty who were interested in developing an area-focused course in their discipline, but their contributions allowed us to expand our coverage to include such often neglected areas as art, music, and theater.

The one key element for a successful program, we discovered, was the need for a full-time historian for each area to provide the solid core of courses around which a variety of others could be offered. There were two reasons for this. First, only the history department, in spite of its generally conservative reputation, was sufficiently large, foresighted, and generous enough to make full-time appointments in what were initially feared as minor areas. The second reason was that history tends to be the most comprehensive and interdisciplinary of the disciplines normally included in area studies programs, and thus comfortably serves as the core discipline for the entire area. The development of our area programs was thus highly dependent on the goodwill of one department, but the new areas proved so popular that the department grew by leaps and bounds as a result of its commitments. As each area expanded and reached a critical mass of faculty and courses, it left the (combined) area studies program; and eventually, separate programs were established in African and Middle Eastern studies, Asian studies, Russian studies, and Latin American studies. Faced with declining enrollments, several of the foreign language departments have since followed suit to establish their own interdisciplinary area studies programs.

The first step in establishing African studies, then, is to gather whatever resources one can to establish a presence on campus, and, once established, to use that presence to compete actively for available resources.

Frequently this has to be done through a series of tactical alliances within departments or with other programs. Within the History Department, we frequently traded off a new Americanist or Europeanist for an additional non-Westernist until we were able to cover most of the major world areas. Similarly, all the area studies programs formed an alliance to support each other's needs in turn.

Once established, however, the problems of teaching African history or African studies do not end. Too often a program is primarily a one-man or one-woman show, with a number of cooperating colleagues, leading to profound loneliness among full-time professionals in the area. Other colleagues in one's discipline rarely understand what an Africanist does sufficiently to share research; while area colleagues in other disciplines are often focused on their disciplines. Only twice at Williams College did I have colleagues with whom I could really share my work, and each was there only for a short time. Obligations to students, one's department, and the college are also frequently so time consuming that one has little time to make connections with others, much less do one's own research. Finally, undergraduate programs or institutions rarely provide the institutional support required to remain active in one's field, and they are often less than sympathetic to frequent requests for long and expensive trips to the field (a situation that is different for Africanists as compared with U.S. historians, who can, after all, take Amtrack to Washington for a long weekend).

While such loneliness often encourages us to continue to see ourselves as occupying the margins of our discipline and the curriculum, we have come to occupy a far more central role in both than we think. Our failure to recognize this fact and to capitalize on it has allowed others to see us in similarly marginal terms. Recognizing our own potential is thus essential if we are to play the central role in the undergraduate curriculum of which we are capable.

NOTES

1. I am grateful to Rowan Ireland, Sheila Spear, and Richard Waller for their helpful suggestions, to Lidwien Kapteijns for her thoughtful and thought-provoking commentary, and to a number of the participants at the conference for their suggestions.

2. A task Gregson Davis has accomplished marvelously in Chapter 1.

3. I take Kapteijns' point here. She questions (in Chapter 10) whether other historians, much less some of our colleagues in African studies, were listening, but notes that British and U.S. social historians such as Keith Thomas, E.P. Thompson, and Rhys Isaac have explicitly made reference to important insights they gained from reading African materials, and I have often traded books and ideas with colleagues in U.S., Asian, European, and Latin American history.

4. For an introduction to African historical methodology, see, e.g., my *Kenya's Past: An Introduction to Historical Method in Africa* (Burnt Hill, UK:

Longman, 1981). For oral traditions, see Jan Vansina, *Oral Tradition as History* (Madison: University of Wisconsin Press, 1985) and Joseph Miller, ed., *The African Past Speaks: Essays on Oral Tradition and History* (Hamden, Conn.: Archon, 1980). For political economy, see Claude Meillassoux, *Maidens, Meal, and Money: Capitalism and the Domestic Community* (New York: Cambridge University Press, 1981), among others.

5. E.G. Seligman, *Egypt and Negro Africa: A Study in Divine Kingship* (London: Routledge, 1934); Cheikh Anta Diop, *The African Origins of Civilization: Myth or Reality?* (New York: L. Hilla, 1974).

6. J. F. A. Ajayi and M. Crowder, eds., *History of West Africa* (New York: Columbia University Press, 1972).

7. The importance of Africa in African-American thought is a topic desperately in search of an author, but changes in that thought are reflected in changing terms of self-reference from *African* in the sixteenth to eighteenth centuries to *Negro* or *Colored* in the nineteenth and *Black, Afro-American,* and *African-American* in the twentieth, as noted by Joseph E. Holloway, in the introduction to his *Africanisms in American Culture* (Bloomington: Indiana University Press, 1991).

8. As we have been recently reminded by Valentine Mudimbe, *The Invention of Africa: Philosophy and the Order of Knowledge* (Bloomington: Indiana University Press, 1988) and Kwame Anthony Appiah, *In My Father's House: Africa in the Philosophy of Culture* (New York: Oxford University Press, 1992).

9. See, for example, Lawrence Levine, *Black Culture and Black Consciousness* (New York: Oxford University Press, 1977) or Charles Joyner, *Down by the Riverside: A South Carolina Slave Community* (Urbana: University of Illinois Press, 1984). For an important theoretical approach, see Sidney Mintz and Richard Price, *The Birth of African-American Culture* (Boston: Beacon Press, 1992).

10. Lest my comments be wrongly interpreted as dismissive of Afrocentricity's contribution to the study of Africa, however, let me reiterate that I feel that Afrocentricity is a valid mode of discourse for studying Africa and the diaspora, that it offers a critical corrective to Eurocentric interpretations, and that it presents an important critique of African historiography. It remains as important, however, critically to assess Afrocentric perspectives and interpretations as it is for any other approaches to the African past.

11. As Joel Samoff reminds us in an incisive review of several modern Tanzanian studies in the *International Journal of African Historical Studies* 2 (1991): 432–441.

12. See, for example, Steven Feierman, *Peasant Intellectuals: Anthropology and History in Tanzania* (Madison: University of Wisconsin Press, 1990); Isaria N. Kimambo, *Penetration and Protest in Tanzania: The Impact of the World Economy on the Pare, 1860–1960* (London: James Currey, 1991); Abdul Sheriff, *Slaves, Spices, and Ivory in Zanzibar: An Integration of an East African Commercial Empire into the World Economy, 1770–1873* (London: James Currey, 1987); and James Giblin, *The Politics of Environmental Control in Northeastern Tanzania* (Philadelphia: University of Pennsylvania Press, 1992). The dominant perspective in African historiography has swung between imperial and local foci, shifting from colonial to nationalist in the 1960s, the world economy and dependency in the 1970s, and back to local politics within an expanding international arena in the 1980s.

13. They can be equally revolutionary for Third World students, as Gregson Davis relates from his own experience in Chapter 1.

14. For bias and perspective, see John Smail, *Journal of Southeast Asian Studies;* for intellectual development, William G. Perry, Jr., in *The Modern American College,* ed. Arthur W. Chickering (San Francisco: Jossey-Bass, 1981): 76–116.

10

Teaching African History
in U.S. Colleges:
A Discussion of Thomas Spear

Lidwien Kapteijns

There is a Somali proverb that says: In the presence of a king, one must watch one's hand; in the presence of a scholar, one must watch one's tongue; and in the presence of a saint, one must watch one's intent.[1] Our audience, as African historians, includes all three types of authority; as we reflect on our teaching of African history in U.S. colleges, we must therefore watch hand, tongue, and heart, for our actions as teachers and administrators, our knowledge and wisdom, and our moral and political values are all under scrutiny. In Chapter 9, "From Periphery to Center: African History in the Undergraduate Curriculum," Thomas Spear sketches the contours of this vast subject matter. In this chapter I will engage and add to some of the issues raised by him.

Spear examines three important dimensions of teaching African history to U.S. undergraduates. First, he analyses the most significant intellectual and historiographical developments in the field of African history since 1960; in a second section he explains the educational benefits U.S. undergraduates derive from a thorough exposure to African history; and in a third section he locates the teaching of African history in its contemporary U.S. context of social, political, and intellectual power struggles. Spear deals, less explicitly and extensively, with two other themes: what African historians in the United States teach about Africa; and (here expressing his opinions) what African historians, as scholars and teachers, should and should not do. I will address each of these five themes in turn.

AFRICAN HISTORIOGRAPHY SINCE 1960

In his concise and insightful survey of historiographical developments, Spear notes how historical research "decentered itself": historians of Africa moved away from a concern with European actions in Africa and shifted their focus to how Africans, in dynamic interaction with each other

165

and outsiders, shaped and experienced their own history. Historians of Africa also moved away from an empiricist political history of great men and great events toward the history of longer-term processes of change as they affected groups of people. Thus, they came to see African societies not as monolithic but as themselves socially stratified along the axes of age, gender, ethnicity, and class, or otherwise. Historians of Africa developed a theoretically more complex reasoning about causality, context, and meaning, and a more inclusive view of reality, including ecological, economic, social, and cultural realities. Thus, historians of Africa have, over the last thirty years, offered important new insights both into the diverse historical experiences and modes of social organization of precapitalist African societies and into the diverse ways in which these societies chose (or were forced) to reforge their material and cultural realities in the crucible of the colonial encounter.

When thinking about cultural studies, one may argue that the historiography of Africa "decentered," or shifted focus, twice; first, from the superficial level of political events to underlying processes of socioeconomic and ecological change; then, from an analysis and reconstruction of socioeconomic changes to that of the interface between material reality and culture. Of those who have worked on culture, not all were elitist, idealist (in the sense of assigning causality to ideas alone), and deconstructionist, as Spear might seem to imply. One should note that these historians did much work to remedy both earlier idealism and materialist reductionism.[2]

African historians have been innovative both in their use of a wide array of interdisciplinary research techniques and methodologies and in their adoption of innovative theoretical foci (on gender, agriculture, consciousness, the invention of "tradition," and so forth). Spear's claim that African historians have influenced the wider discipline of history, however, needs further elaboration and documentation. Many of the insights we applied to Africa derive ultimately from progressive European social history (the Annales school in France, labor studies in Britain, and so forth). It seems to me that we Africanists read at least some historical studies about Early Europe, Native Americans, and Latin America, but I still have to meet a European or U.S. historian who reads our works. We may all breathe the same paradigmatical air and catch the same paradigmatical viruses, but while we read their stuff, they don't read ours. We may have been, in some ways, at the forefront of the discipline, but I wonder who noticed. Even our bridges to Africanist colleagues with a more contemporary focus such as development issues are rickety at best. Their insufficient attention to the power inequalities within African communities and their tardy realization that development aid often benefited some at the expense of others is evidence of their blindness to history and their deafness to what we had to say about it.

With regard to our teaching, we have not succeeded (and maybe not seriously attempted) to theorize (that is to say, to give a coherent and systematic interpretation of) the historical experiences of all of Africa. North Africa is generally not included and is left to Middle Easternists or European historians. If this point seems nonpolitical, it really is not, for it rests upon and conceals old and pernicious value judgements. In perpetuating it, we fail to deal explicitly with old racist stereotypes and thus fail to engage an educational need of many of our students. The topic of the slave trade is an even clearer example. In historical analyses of the 1960s and 1970s—as was widely perceived—the topic became a plaything in the hands of conservative historians who, hiding behind complicated but highly imperfect quantitative methods, pushed a specific political agenda: that of playing down the trade's significance. Newer studies, doing full justice to the complex and deep impact of the slave trade, have come into existence but have not yet been made accessible to a wider audience. We must address the needs of all our students, including those of African descent who wish to analyze and determine their own relationship to the subject matter of African history.

THE EDUCATIONAL BENEFITS
OF STUDYING AFRICAN HISTORY

Spear gives an excellent analysis of the benefits that undergraduate students might derive from studying African history. Apart from filling a void in their historical knowledge, apart from correcting stereotypical views and prejudices that negatively affect their views of Africans and people of African descent, African history can teach students how to think. It can teach students how to think analytically by encouraging students to adopt a toolkit of analytical concepts of their own and by enhancing their awareness of the complex ways in which social institutions and socioeconomic processes constrain individual choices and in which material realities shape and are shaped by cultural ones. African history can teach students to think critically by confronting them with a variety of historical perspectives and asking them to develop their own coherent moral, political, and intellectual understanding of the world. The richness and diversity of social organization and cultural expression in African history, as we have come to teach it, constitute a valid and valuable educational experience in their own right. When used to stimulate analytical and critical thinking, these courses deserve an important place in our curriculum. Spear's analysis of the educational value of African history is insightful and eloquent and will be quoted by anyone in need of advocating or defending the significance of the field. However, Spear is not fully persuasive in arguing why and how African history is more valuable to undergraduates than, for example, Chinese or Latin American history. This is a point that can only be properly examined in the context of how we teach African history at U.S. colleges. Spear gives us the general principles of his approach to socioeconomic history as well as some specific examples from his syllabus on precolonial African history, but this is not enough. In a discussion of African history in the undergraduate curriculum, the contents must— sooner or later—be a crucial focus of reflection. I will address this issue further below, after an examination of the political and social context of teaching African history in this country.

LOCATING THE TEACHING
OF AFRICAN HISTORY IN ITS U.S. CONTEXT

Spear examines several dimensions of the contemporary U.S. context of the teaching of African history. In this context, one power struggle focuses on resources. Spear's argument presents the Africanist historian as an ally of other advocates of broadening and diversifying canon and curriculum through the inclusion of cultures and peoples formerly excluded and de- spised as culturally, politically, economically, and socially less successful. Spear defines three schools of thought as the enemy: (1) the conservatives, who resent any politicization of the curriculum and defend their own, tra- ditionally accepted subjects as representative of true, worthwhile culture and civilization; (2) the deconstructionists, who are maybe rather casually and harshly characterized by Spear; and (3) the Afrocentrists, who are characterized as believers in the racial determination of culture. The prac- tical dimension of the struggle for resources must remain undiscussed here; however, the competing claims for truth, and the wider social, polit- ical, and intellectual struggles for power deserve further analysis.

Within the scope of this chapter it is impossible to do justice to the de- bate on either deconstructionism or Afrocentrism. However, the latter can not just be pushed aside by defining it as an important episode in the an- nals of African-American thought. In institutions less privileged and less educationally sound than Williams or Wellesley Colleges, Afrocentrism interferes with the teaching of African history (and with the educational and intellectual benefits) in the ways specified by Spear. We must address the needs of Africanists at beleaguered educational institutions and the power struggles going on in academe and quasi academe.

Furthermore, while resisting Afrocentrist theories proposing the racial determination of culture, we must constructively engage those elements of the Afrocentrist program that rightly challenge or indirectly reveal (1) real shortcomings in African history as we have taught it and are currently teaching it; and (2) real injustices in the ways in which field and profes- sion institutionally fit into the wider U.S. education system.

With regard to institutional inequalities, the last thirty years have wit- nessed an increased participation of Africans in the discourse about African history that had long been dominated and monopolized by outsiders. Serious imbalances still exist, and their context and causality are highly complex and are certainly not reducible to discrimination against black people by whites. The existence of the imbalance, however, in the context of wider disparities between black and white people in the United States and the world, invites a struggle for power, a struggle between competing truths in which some are victims and others are powermongers. In one of its aspects, Afrocentrism represents such a struggle. Thus, while we must prevent African history from being intellectually brutalized in the service of any political agenda, we must make the African history that we teach be a tool in analyzing and addressing those inequalities. In this way, Afrocentrism is relevant to all historians of Africa in this country; and to the extent that its political appeal already reaches into Nigeria and other parts of Africa, it is part of the annals of African history as well.

THE CONTENT OF TEACHING AFRICAN HISTORY

Spear does not explicitly address what historians of Africa at U.S. colleges teach or should teach. He himself is a social historian who, in his teaching, emphasizes basic social organization—types of society and differences in social stratification within African societies. He pays attention to the wider cultural and socioeconomic contexts of historical events and phenomena, to the relationships between structure/process and individual action, and to the ways in which cultural values are socially and historically constructed. He is in favor of explicit conceptual frameworks and coherent programs. He is against hard-core deconstructionisms and Afrocentrism and calls for an Africa-centeredness that does not sacrifice the centrality of Africans as agents of history to analytical attention to outside contexts and actors. Spear conveys the analytical methods, approaches, and toolkit of this educational package to his students by focusing in each course on a limited number of case studies with a limited amount of historical narrative. It seems to me that most students would learn a great deal from taking such a course and might well learn about critical and analytical thinking as described by Spear under "educational and pedagogical perspectives."

However, Spear smooths over some serious shortcomings in our teaching of African history. If we can take the state of our textbooks as a symptom of the weakness of African history teaching in the United States, then that teaching is very weak indeed. With the exception of the field of South African history, we have no proper texts, partly perhaps because African history is not yet a widely taught or highly valued part of the undergraduate curriculum, but also because historians of Africa have not found (or looked for) answers indispensable to any comprehensive, theoretically rigorous, and coherent African history text. The most crucial issues center on periodization and geographical focus. If one examines the old standard texts by Davidson, Oliver and Fage, Hallett, July, Gailey, or the last, and probably best, collectively authored *African History* (Curtin, Feierman, and Thompson), one may find oneself in agreement with the judgement of two historians writing about "The Periodization of Precolonial African History":

> What these works have in common is a failure or refusal to address the logic of the historical process that brought Africa from Pithecanthropus to the eve of the colonial age. All agree that the colonial era was indeed a period in African history, but what came before can only be discussed within the Procrustian framework of an arbitrary three-dimensional conceptual grid, which partitions the continent into a half-dozen peculiar geographical regions, within each of which the flow of time is chopped into convenient blocks of centuries for no apparent reason. The reader is dragged around the continent from region to region during Block of Centuries One, then taken on a second tour for Block of Centuries Two, and so forth. Within each cubicle of their geochronological grid, the authors stuff little capsule summaries of whatever specialized monographs happen to exist for the time and place under consideration. The effect produced by a book so organized is one of extreme empirical complexity and analytical chaos.[3]

Those who avoid analytical chaos give up on attempting a comprehensive examination of the historical experiences of all of Africa. South Africa has, due to its political relevance and to increased student interest, taken up some of the space it deserves in the undergraduate curriculum. Northeast Africa, however, crucial to an understanding of the African experience (among other things) because of the lateness of its incorporation into the world economy and the demise of its precapitalist forms of social organization, is always left out. Thus, Ralph Austen's recent *African Economic History* gives up on this area from the very start of his analysis: "Some regions not easily incorporated into general patterns (particularly the Nilotic Sudan and the adjoining Horn of Africa) receive little attention."[4] There are other areas whose historiography is somehow not considered relevant to "real" African history. North Africa as a whole is a case in point.

I am not interested in imposing on anyone a periodization of precolonial social history that seems compelling to me. Periodizations must vary with the specific set of historical processes we study. However, the negative impact of our failure as African history teachers to arrive at sound, theoretically rigorous periodizations and our failure to focus on the historical experiences of all of Africa affect the quality and significance of African history in the undergraduate curriculum.

There is one other problematic issue in our discipline that I must briefly raise. It concerns the use of theory and its application to the correct level of social analysis. Thus, Jack Goody, in his *Technology, Tradition and the State in Africa* (London: Oxford University Press, 1971) gets away with treating "a handful of low-level technological variables . . . as major determinants of African social structure and historical process."[5] Most African historians have overcome the old "fear of theory." Theory is embedded in both our writing and our teaching but is rarely an explicit part of our African history curriculum. Yet being explicit about theoretical perspective and examining how alternative theories reflect and derive from different moral and political values and objectives is indispensable to our mission of teaching critical and analytical thinking. I believe that every course in African history represents one historian shining a torch back into the African past. I do not believe that there should be only one kind of torch, lighting up only one kind of historical experience. But I do believe that African history teachers individually and together should throw light upon a subject matter that has internal cohesion and is inclusive of the historical experience of all of Africa.

NOTES

1. The Somali text reads: *Meel boqor joogo gacantaadaa la ilaashadaa, meel caalin joogana carrabkaaga, meel weli joogana niyaddaada.*

2. Leroy Vail, ed., *The Creation of Tribalism in Southern Africa* (Berkeley: University of California Press, 1989) and Martin Chanock, *Law, Custom and Social Order: The Colonial Experience in Malawi and Zambia* (New York: Cambridge University Press, 1985) are but two examples. The topic was pioneered by anthropologists.

3. Jay Spaulding and Lidwien Kapteijns, "The Periodization of Precolonial African History," working paper, African Studies No. 125 (Boston: Boston University African Studies Center, 1987): 1.

4. Ralph Austen, *African Economic History: Internal Development and External Dependency* (Portsmouth, New Hampshire: Heineman, 1987): 7.

5. Jack Goody, *Technology, Tradition and the State in Africa* (London: Books Demand, 1971). This is further discussed in Jay Spaulding and Lidwien Kapteijns, "The Conceptualization of Land Tenure in the Precolonial Sudan: Evidence and Interpretation" (presented at the twentieth annual spring symposium entitled "State, Land and Society in Africa," held at the University of Illinois in April 1993).

11

Teaching African Science: Notes on "Common Sense," "Tribal War," and the "End of History"

Ben Wisner

This chapter is principally concerned with teaching undergraduates about Africa. It is, as the title suggests, about a great deal more as well, but these other themes emerge either as preconditions for successful teaching or reflections on the broader goals of undergraduate education. I will begin by suggesting that the educational goals one should strive for in teaching African science should be to enable students (1) to learn something about Africa and Africans, (2) to learn something about science, and (3) to learn something about themselves.

This chapter argues that these three goals may not be mutually compatible, or at least that their simultaneous pursuit is not as easy as it seems. The difficulty arises because of multiple ambiguities: there is science *in*, *about*, and *from* Africa. Western scientists and Western-trained African scientists can do science *in* Africa on questions of physiology, astronomy, or geophysics that could as well be done elsewhere and have no role in attempts to understand Africa or in Africa's attempt to understand itself. An extreme example might be the siting in Zaire of the commercial satellite launching facilities by OTRAG.[1] These same scientists (irrespective of their national origin) can also study questions that bear uniquely or significantly on African realities: sickle-cell anemia, the Great Rift Valley, or tsetse flies, for instance. I call this science *about* (or sometimes with a slightly different connotation, *for*) Africa. Methods and thought paradigms remain Western. Finally, there is a popular or vernacular science in Africa. This is science *from* Africa. It is not strictly non-Western, especially since much of the vernacular practice of agriculture, healing, fishing, and so forth has been interacting for years with Western influences. Yet the basis of this practice is often traditional understanding of the world (ontology), of the social production of knowledge (epistemology), and the use of language (taxonomy). The use of the preposition *from* is meant to signify that this body of knowledge constitutes a potential contribution to global human culture. Usually it is not recognized as such; at times "ethnoscience" is used as a wedge by outsiders to obtain the confidence of the farmers, foresters, and blacksmiths that they want to convert, improve, or modernize. Graduate students have been used to learn the vernacular language and understanding of soil processes, and so on, only to have this knowledge used in the packaging and marketing of Western agronomic advice. This functionalist appreciation of ethnoscience fits nicely into the world view of Euro-American triumphalism. After the End of History there is nothing left to do but to engage in small, postcolonial wars (e.g., Iraq) and to conduct "social marketing"[2] in order to convince *the other* to join the New World Order in body and mind. *To convince* can mean "to coerce," "to win over by argument or example," and a host of other things. Resistance to "dominating knowledge" is very strong and subtle.[3] To this extent, not much has changed since Father Placide Tempels[4] attempted to understand the worldview of the colonized African (who at the time of his book was still very resistant) sufficiently to make the European civilizing mission acceptable.[5] These three ways of interpreting the phrase *African science* are not the same, and while they all have some value in themselves and for teaching, a confusion among them leads to poor results in the classroom.

Human beings in Africa are "agents" or "persons" in moral and historical terms like everybody else.[6] However, in academia they are often treated as "populations," "cultures," or "systems," depending on the epistemological stance adopted. Likewise, these human beings inhabit "places" that are objectified and abstracted as "field sites," "museums," or "reserves," depending on the kind of teaching or research.

Person and place are often closely identified in Africa, which partially explains why expulsion and refugee status is so traumatic for Africans[7] and also explains the often remarkable depth of local ecological knowledge. For instance, Cohen and Odhiambo[8] describe the relationship of person and place as follows:

> For the person of Siaya [Western Kenya], "landscape" is not a reference to the physiognomy of the terrain. Rather it evokes the possibilities and limitations of space: encompassing the physical land, the people on it, and the culture through which people work out the possibilities of the land.

Local residents are aware of a wide variety of microenvironments to which the outsider may be culturally blind. Chambers[9] lists the following examples:

- Home gardens
- Vegetable and horticultural patches
- River banks and riverine strips
- Levees and natural terraces

- Valley bottoms
- Wet and dry water courses
- Alluvial pans
- Artificial terraces
- Silt trap fields
- Raised fields
- Water harvesting in its many forms
- Hedges and windbreaks
- Clumps, groves, or lines of trees or bushes
- Pockets of fertile soil (termitaria, former livestock pens, etc.)
- Sheltered corners or strips, by aspect of slope, configuration, etc.
- Plots protected from livestock
- Flood recessional zones
- Small flood plains
- Springs and patches of high ground water and seepage
- Strips and pockets of impeded drainage
- Lake basins
- Ponds, including fishponds
- Animal wallows

Diane Rocheleau[10] points out that, with commercialization, rural women in Africa have often lost formal access to land and grow food for their children in many such niches between and among spaces that are officially recognized as "productive" and controlled by men.

Recent attempts to introduce North American students to such realities (that is, to Africans as persons and to Africa as places), even through experiential learning, fail. In the classroom, existential agency or personhood and place are forced into functionalist models of adaptive systems: "livelihood systems," "drought-coping systems," or "therapy management groups." This is a weakness of some of the best of the literature recommended to students: works such as *The Greening of Africa, Famine That Kills*, or *Camping with the Prince*.[11] Although these books go well beyond the doom-and-gloom approach to Africa, they remain functionalist. However, they also portray Africans as caring, active, and intelligent in pursuit of their well-being. This is a good start.

There are many severe impediments to the understanding of Africa and its contribution to the world. It does not diminish the significance of ethnocentrism and racism as obstacles to point out that there is another, related, problem: Euro-Americans are often imprisoned by a series of myths about progress, development, technology, and science. In the United States and Europe, most of us grow up accepting, uncritically, a worldview in which Western rationality, scientific method, and technical problemsolving are seen as the ultimate evolutionary products of history. The common story is that Europe and the United States achieved "development" and "progress" through correct thinking and hard work—and maybe a favorable climate;[12] and that the rest of the world, including Africa, is underdeveloped and must develop (modernize)—must become like "us."

U.S. and European undergraduates share these attitudes with their African counterparts. Many African leaders and intellectuals see modernization as "the application of the results of modern science for the improvement of the conditions of human life."[13] In his book *Africa Tomorrow*, former Organization of African Unity (OAU) Secretary-General Edem Kodjo envisions an Africa highly industrialized, mining all its mineral wealth, pulsating with the energy of many nuclear power stations.[14] Philosopher Peter Bodunrin[15] takes a whole series of assumptions for granted in asserting: "No one laments the lack of African physics. African mathematicians have, as far as I know, not been asked to produce African mathematics. No one has asked that our increasing number of expressways be built the African way."

Another African philosopher, Oyeka Owomoyela[16] puts his finger on the issue by noting that a number of his colleagues propose (or assume) a cascade of logical dependency: development depends on science, science depends on philosophy. I do not disagree; however, the important thing is to look carefully at what one means by *development*. A critique of the myth of "modernizing development" and the remaking of the planet in the image of Los Angeles County, complete with expressways—a nonsustainable, life-threatening, energy-and-waste-intensive human ecosystem—demands careful consideration of what science from Africa has to offer. This, in turn, nourishes the vigorous debate concerning the existence and contours of African philosophy and its place in the world.

No one denies that there is indigenous science in Africa. Most agree that African cultures have science defined as the accumulation of experience of the physical and biological world, discussion and symbolic manipulation of that world, and the passing on of accumulated knowledge.[17] Even more broadly, science can be defined as "ways of observing, describing, explaining, predicting and controlling events in the natural world."[18] In this sense, it is not controversial to assert that African science exists.

Even more rigorous institutional definitions of science can be defended. From the early fourteenth century, the Islamic mosque of Sankore in Timbuktu (in ancient Mali) was a center of research and teaching in astronomy, geography, history, law, and surgery.[19] Diop provides details of the institutionalized study and accumulation of knowledge in such fields as geometry, algebra, astronomy, medicine, and chemistry.[20] The modern equivalent may be the International Center for Insect Physiology and Ecology in Nairobi, where director Thomas Odhiambo has pulled together a diverse group that includes people from many scientific disciplines and also social scientists. Elsewhere, in such technology development centers as

Kanje, in Botswana,[21] and in farmer-training centers in Uyole, Tanzania,[22] ordinary citizens, indigenous experts, and Western-trained scientists collaborate in solving problems. These are the new institutional locations on the pioneering edge of science.

The resistance to accepting the everyday practice of Africans as science is more subtle. African knowledge of the natural world is often considered to be second-class knowledge. It is not theorized abstractly (at least not in the way it is in the West) and it is not professionalized (again, not in a Western manner). Just as the wisdom of elders (*sagacity* in Oruka's terms[23]) and collective beliefs are not given the status of philosophy by some African philosophers,[24] the discussion of weather, seed varieties, or the behavior of insects by rural people, or the practice of healing by local experts, is not seen as real science.

I will take the position in this chapter that science *from* Africa, vernacular or popular science, is definitely science. Furthermore, in combination with Western science it can help Africans to break out of the impasse created by three "disappointing decades of development."[25] More than this: I believe that the emergence of such combined or hybrid science, bred of mutual respect, in participatory action-research situations, can point the way to a new science for all people. This would be a problem-focused science—very concrete but also reflective. Moreover, it would be a committed science. The children whose lives we are trying to save, the land we are trying to restore, are *our* children, *our* land.[26] We feel connected to them. There is an emotional component to our commitment to using our knowledge and skill in their behalf: it involves emotions like compassion and empathy. There is also anger, that the children and the land have been so abused. Inspired by a feminist philosophy of science, this new science in Africa would be one of the pioneering locales where "hand, brain, and heart" are combined.[27] Harding sees the overcoming of the separation of intellectual and manual labor in the late feudal era in Europe as the event that marked the birth of Western science.[28] She speculates that the next major breakthrough may be the integration of emotional labor, conventionally termed *women's work.* There is no reason why it should remain exclusively a woman's domain.

The problem-focused science discussed below under the subheading Key Areas has already taken on this character in some cases. The playful exchange of rice seed and maintenance of experimental plots in Sierra Leone described by Richards,[29] or the deeply felt gender conflicts over the choice of tree species for family woodlots in western Kenya described by Bradley,[30] include the emotional with the intellectual or manual labor. Project workers in these cases accepted and entered into these cases of geographically located and humanly situated praxis. What emerges from such scientific work is something quite different from that which takes place exclusively in a laboratory or field station. Difference is celebrated—the different standpoints determined by gender, class, age, culture—but it is still intelligible. The result is not chaotic relativism. What makes understanding and communication possible is the problem-focus and mutual respect for the dignity of common struggle. African and non-African scientific approaches meet in mutual respect in an "innovative dialogue."[31] There is theoretical underpinning for such shared action-research; namely, "structuration theory,"[32] "situated inter-subjectivity,"[33] and "thoughtful practice."[34]

It is nearly thirty years since agronomist René Dumont wrote of Africa's "false start."[35] The oil-price shocks of the 1970s, civil wars, growing mountains of public debt incurred in order to finance war and pay for oil imports, luxury consumption by the elite, and prestige projects have brought on economic collapse. Dumont's earliest warnings concerned the importation of inappropriate technology and models of development. The internationally negotiated Structural Adjustment Programs (SAPs) signed by country after country in the 1980s have reinforced those external influences and models, leading to an even tighter stranglehold over Africa.[36] The burden of the SAPs has been felt most heavily by the poor, especially women and children.[37] Subsidies on staple foods and agricultural inputs such as fertilizer have been reduced or phased out. Public services such as education and health have been slashed. Nutrition is deteriorating. Infant and child mortality is increasing.

Under these circumstances, the priority for ordinary Africans today is survival.[38] If science is to have any relevance to their lives, it will have to move into the back streets and cattle *bomas*, sit alongside the inventors of improved charcoal-burning cooking stoves in their open-air workshops, and walk alongside rice farmers as they visit a neighbor to see the result of a varietal trial. At the community and national scale, the survival struggle takes the form of programs for, in the most favorable cases, environmental restoration—the reclamation of soil, vegetation, and water resources and the protection of endangered plant and animal species. In the war-torn, least favorable cases, there is, in addition, the challenge of national reconstruction. In Somalia, for instance, besides the cost in human lives, the war has decimated livestock and wild animal herds, encouraged regrowth of tsetse fly habitat, spilled toxic substances (often caused in the shelling of cities), accelerated deforestation, and has caused many other ecological effects. War has destroyed all trace of maps, reports, and rainfall and river-flow data. A great effort at recovery will be required.[39]

War, Science, Tribe, Nation, Planet: The Need for a New Science

Because one has to be clear about the great obstacles to understanding posed by "the development story," I will take a few pages to explore some of this territory—real and surreal, historical and mythic. I will, as Wolf-

gang Sachs puts it, dig a bit into the ruins of twentieth-century development, although I cannot claim to make original contributions to an emerging "archaeology of the development idea."[40]

Reflect on the relationship between science and war.[41] On a superficial level, it seems that science has contributed toward improving the machines of war for a very long time. Catapults and smart bombs would both
seem to be children of science in the service of war. Galileo calculated
cannon ballistics for his prince; scientists at Bell Labs or General Electric
do the equivalent for their prince. In a manner—a simplified manner—this
is true. However, in the late twentieth century two important differences
take one deeper into the issue. First, the so-called civilian application of
science has given rise to a technostructure that depends on a vast array of
raw materials, many of them from overseas: uranium, tin, chrome, oil, and
so on. These imports also include biologicals—in the fundamental form,
increasingly, of wild genes and other genetic material.[42] The machines of
war in the late twentieth century are engineered in large part for defense of
the supply lines of the technostructure. This reveals a very close connection between bellicose and peaceful applications of modern science;
closer, in fact, than the so-called spin-offs of war in the form of atoms-for-
peace, the commercial aerospace industry, telecommunications, imaging,
and computing.

Even the most sympathetic reader might object at this point that there
is "another" science—a science concerned with understanding the cosmos,
our planet, nature, and with improving human life. This is also certainly
true, up to a point; yet at a deeper level, even this aspect of science is "at
war." It is war for the hearts and minds of the masses of human beings in
"underdeveloped" countries who will only progress when they become like
us; when they think like we do.

Such progress is problematic. There are two very troubling ideas at the
root of Western thinking about progress that have to be considered before
one can address African science. The first is a close connection between
progress and control. The purpose of science in the West has been thought
of as increasing control. Vandana Shiva, herself a Western-trained theoretical physicist, cites Renaissance sources to show how science was con-
ceptualized as forcing nature's secrets from her: not merely reading the so-
called book of nature but ravishing and controlling nature.[43] The Western
ideal is still to control such natural forces as rivers, insects, and wild fires,
to eliminate risk and uncertainty.[44] These imperatives have given rise (literally) to some 35,000 high dams that commonly flood useful land, dis-
place people, breed disease, and disrupt downstream ecology and human affairs. Many of these dams are silting up very quickly because of upstream
soil erosion and will provide their benefits for only a fraction of their
planned lifetimes. The drive to control has created the pesticide treadmill.
In the United States each year, billions of dollars' worth of agrochemicals

are sprayed on crops, and yet the level of crop-loss to pests is as it was in the 1950s. Attempts to control wildfire culminated in the great fire in Yellowstone, described in Chase's detailed narrative, *Playing God in Yellowstone*.[45] *Playing God* is not an exaggerated phrase. In its extreme form, the compulsion to control becomes what Ed Regis[46] calls "hubric science" in his wonderful book *Great Mambo Chicken and the Transhuman Condition*. At the extreme, it is assumed that science should be capable of conquering death (through molecule-sized robots that "heal" by reconstructing the brain and body atom by atom, for instance). From this point of view, everything in the universe is raw material to be used. The goal of human existence is to "go everywhere and do everything." Regis describes preparations by members of a Last Proton Club for a party at which members (by then rendered immortal by downloading themselves into computers) will converge to watch the last piece of nuclear matter decay. A charter member of the club, Keith Henson, says: "If the party got big enough, the bean dip alone would form a black hole. . . . Where do you park fifty billion starships? . . . Where are you going to find a big enough party hotel? . . . I expect to convert a whole galaxy into beer cans."[47] This may be a joke (although it's hard to tell from the text), and is, of course, an extreme statement to say the least. But I would argue that the tendency to emphasize control of nature leads in precisely this direction.

Related to the drive toward control is the somber realization that, to create and to build, one must first destroy. Goethe's Faust must first cause two old people who live in a fishing cottage to die before he can realize a master plan for the development of a utopian seaside complex with the help of Mephisto. He is the prototypical regional planner. According to the dominant Western position, to "modernize" people, old ways of thought, old patterns of relating with nature and with each other must be destroyed. Colonial science in Africa set out to control nature and to modernize what it interpreted as childlike, primitive practices of African farmers, pastoralists, and healers. Colonial authorities in the shape of the *Gesundheitspolizei* (nineteenth-century health police) applied public health regulations with the force of an occupying army (which, in fact, they were). Forced cultivation of export crops such as cotton was required, and, when hunger resulted, scientifically planned cultivation of famine crops such as cassava was recommended by nutrition experts of the League of Nations.[48] Wildlife and livestock were assigned to scientifically designed spatial compartments and not allowed to mix as they had done before.[49] When the system inevitably broke down, the director of the Frankfurt zoo called on the United Nations to take over a large portion of northern Tanganyika and manage it on behalf of the animals—otherwise, he said, *die Schwartzen* (Blacks) would destroy the wildlife.[50]

The writings of Grzimek, that former director of the Frankfurt Zoological Society, reveal a great deal about the misapprehension of African person and place that still distorts Western understanding. *Places* in Africa have been celebrated as exotic landscapes, filled with great beauty[51] or great danger and nastiness,[52] but have not been recognized as homes, known and loved in their mundane, everyday specificity. Certain features like Ngorongoro Crater are abstracted and idealized as dramatic backdrops against which Wagnerian heroes fly around in light aircraft saving animals. The people, too, are abstracted. Their specific qualities and gifts and weaknesses disappear behind the names they are given: "the poachers," whom the professor's pilot-son Michael would have liked to machine-gun; the "negro botanist" who is pictured with Michael.[53] We may believe that we are living in another age from Faust, from Grzimek, and from the colonialists and developers responsible for such great economic and environmental disasters as the Office Niger, the Groundnut Scheme, the Aswan High Dam, or the disastrous introduction of Nile perch into Lake Victoria. Today, we mostly agree that Small Is Beautiful and that one should build on the basis of indigenous knowledge. (The latter has even been granted the status of an abbreviation in the literature, IK, as a sign of conventional acceptance.) But what has really changed?

As noted earlier, functionalist *use* of African popular science does not imply its acceptance as "real" science. At best, many development workers think of African solutions to problems of pests, water supply, irrigation, or childhood diarrhea as "second best" (low-cost solutions). At worst, the linguistic categories and modes of thought and communication about the natural world are co-opted for purposes of "social marketing."[54] The same type of consultancy firm that helped Nestlé to sell breast-milk substitute is now helping UNICEF to sell the breast! Something is wrong.

Whereas the colonial scientist and administrator thought of Africans as irrational, is it an improvement, or even a change, that the neocolonial expert terms them rational? The naming is still externally applied in reference to a system ("Western rationality," "market behavior") whose universal value is unquestioned by the one who names. For Lévi-Strauss to call African and other non-Western thought and technology "concrete science" was both a concession to the humanity of the other and an assertion that they remain *other*. *Bricolage*[55] is not, for Lévi-Strauss, the same as "engineering."[56]

What I am beginning to recognize in the field in Africa, in the few rare cases where Western-trained scientists and local people collaborate in equal partnership, is a new bricolage. These solutions, far from being second best, may well be better than high-tech solutions. Given the enormous environmental challenges to be faced by Europe, North America, Japan, the Asian NICs,[57] and the industrial enclaves and megacities of the rest of the world, such a new science is necessary. A citizen-based, problem-focused approach to such problems returns science to the community, rescues it from the factory-like industrial science production, and returns it to the realm of craft,[58] where democratic control is possible. This new, or re-vived, science would liberate us all from the deskilling "shadow work" documented for so many years by Ivan Illich.[59]

However, to allow the possibility of such a new science, one has to give up the illusion that Western science is fundamentally already as highly evolved as it can be (in a way similar to that in which Western mar-ket economies are supposed to have triumphed over communism and are, therefore, evolved and superior—hence the so-called "end of history"). That is, one has to reject the assumption that while empirical details may still accumulate, and while models, techniques, and theories may change, the *method*, the fundamental metaphysical and epistemological basis of Western science is unchanging and needs no change. Westerners need to admit that their science is a tribal story. Science and myth are not that far apart. Our Big Bang theory of creation, for instance, is no different from creation myths of the Kikuyu or Zulu. Does one prefer the Big Bang be-cause it is supported by an elaborate system of mathematics? Is it prefer-able because these mathematics are understood and discussed by a tiny elite in Western society? Do we disparage the African stories and call them myths because they are understood and discussed by the masses?[60]

It is hard for Westerners to give up the uniqueness and superiority of their cultural system; no harder, however, than facing the true magnitude of the threat to human and many other kinds of life on this planet produced by the industrial revolution and its aftermath.[61] What is possibly hardest is to see Euro-Americans not only as one of many tribes, but as a particularly vicious and dangerous tribe. The explosion of military conquest and mer-cantile exploitation that erupted from a tiny edge of Europe some five hun-dred years ago was unprecedented.[62] The tight connection between war and science that made this expansion possible (the white diaspora and con-quest) marked and distorted science down to the present moment. I rather suspect that the vicious circle connecting an overextended, resource-hungry technostructure to the military system necessary to protect over-extended supply lines (and to a science establishment required to provide the military technology) has trapped the West (certainly the United States) into a terminal loss of flexibility. I hope not! It may be that our last best hope is Africa, where we might learn humility and the new science neces-sary to muddle through the twenty-first century.

KEY AREAS OF STUDY

The foregoing introduction provides a justification for, or at least an ex-planation of, a particular view of key areas for teaching. These areas would focus on science *from* Africa and science about, or, more precisely, *for* Africa. These Africa-related sciences are unlike colonial science in

Africa, which was concerned to control African land and African people, to make them malleable and useful for the purposes of the colonizer, and unlike "modernizing" science that has sought to remake African places into close approximations of European towns and mid-Western farms, and Africans into "black men with white masks." The alternative is an applied science that grapples with problems directly concerned with human needs.

Environmental Science

Soil and vegetation studies. A combination of "development" policies, economic crisis, war, and frequent droughts has left the soil of large areas of sub-Saharan Africa eroded, vegetation degraded, reservoirs filled with silt, wildlife depleted. A great deal of ecological restoration is required. However, restoration without knowledge is not possible. Research is therefore required, and, given the urgency of the situation, often this takes the form of "action research"—work that attempts to be self-critical and self-correcting even as steps are taken simultaneously to reverse environmental degradation and extend the knowledge base. Some of this work already combines indigenous knowledge and Western methods.

A good example is various soil treatments used to induce regeneration of vegetation for fodder and fuel in semiarid Kenya.[63] A team from the African Centre for Technology Studies, Commonwealth Science Council, and King's College, London, experimented with a variety of techniques for constructing microcatchments in the flat lowlands of the semiarid Baringo district and "ripping" the bare hardpan in the rocky foothills. This, combined with fencing and trials of over fifty potential tree species for use in afforestation, provided the basis for greatly enhanced grazing and provision of woodfuel and grass for thatching roofs. The Turkana Rural Development Programme further to the north in Kenya has similar elements.[64]

Comparable approaches, especially the use of microcatchments, have been used in many parts of Africa, including the Sahelian West African countries, as well as in the countries of the Horn,[65] although not always in a citizen-based, participatory manner. Many African farmers and pastoralists have considerable experience with indigenous soil and water conservation technologies,[66] but this experience is not often tapped in projects.

Likewise, a controversial project in central Tanzania excluded all livestock from a highly degraded, hilly, mixed herding and farming area measuring 11,300 hectares. Some 85,000 animals were moved to lower-lying areas in 1979. By 1986 much of the natural vegetation had regrown, fuel wood was available to farming families, and the locally occurring depressions, *mbuga*, formerly used for dry-season cropping but covered with sand before destocking, were moist and used for farming again.[67] From an ecological point of view, these results are not surprising. A number of experimental plots in various parts of Africa have shown remarkable recovery in a few years.[68] As Alan Berg has recently observed concerning nutrition research, what is often missing is not knowledge of why something happens or does not happen, but the *how* of practically applying the answers to the *why* question.[69] In the case cited above, how does one approach the destocking question in situations where animals may be the only security people have?

A great deal of work on revegetation and soil conservation work is underway in Africa today. Overviews are available in both Kerkof and Grainger.[70] Rocheleau et al. and Harrison review approaches involving more community participation.[71]

Water-resource studies. Water is a limiting factor in many aspects of life in Africa, especially affecting agriculture and health. Given disappointing results from large-scale dams and irrigation projects—high cost, poor maintenance, limited benefits for a small number of tenants and workers, and severe health impacts, including increased malaria and bilharzia—as well as a shortage of funds for investing in such megaprojects—there has been more interest in indigenous methods of water management. These include water harvesting[72] and traditional floodwater regression farming. The latter includes a wide variety of systems in many parts of Africa that take advantage of seasonal river-flooding to plant crops in the moist soil as the flood retreats.[73]

Domestic water supply has received a great deal of attention because of the United Nations Decade for Water Supply and Sanitation (1981–1990). While some of the Water Decade activities involved community participation in building and maintaining water systems,[74] there have been fewer attempts to integrate local knowledge of water supply into the design phase. For instance, women in groups with a history of mutual labor exchange and democratic control in the Laikipia District of Kenya were able to construct a large number of roof rainwater catchment systems for one another.[75] These systems included 500-gallon ferroconcrete tanks (thin-walled tanks made of concrete reinforced with chicken wire) that the women became expert in constructing. As successful as this Swiss-financed project seems to have been, the women did not contribute to the design of the water systems.

Exceptions include fascinating reports from Mali and Sudan. In Mali, Guggenheim and Fanale[76] based a water supply program on traditional Dogon water-siting knowledge and improvements in well design developed with the local participants. In Sudan, herbal products traditionally gathered and used to clarify domestic water were systematically tested and a system was designed to increase their effectiveness together with local women.[77]

Farm Studies

As noted above, from the early 1960s it became fashionable to recognize the order contained in the apparent chaos of African polycultures. Meanwhile, agricultural economists continued to try to simplify these systems, introducing export crops and using linear programming techniques to work out the "optimal" land use to maximize farm income. When it came to "development," traditional systems such as shifting cultivation were seen as stagnant, having perhaps an internal logic but potential to produce no more than what Allan called "normal surplus."[78] To reiterate a theme already struck, it is one thing to appreciate the logic and complexity of traditional agriculture as a completed cultural product (like a nicely woven basket or ebony carving) and quite another to see the traditional as a contemporary system with its own research and development mechanism built in. Paul Richards was possibly one of the first to fully appreciate that African farmers conduct experiments and that they share and criticize the results of their experiments and those of neighbors.[79]

Beginning with the stunning failure of modernization to protect the majority of small farmers and pastoralists from the ravages of drought in the late 1960s, a number of attempts were made to integrate indigenous, drought-coping strategies and government actions. For instance, Wisner and Mbithi found a very large repertoire of potential coping mechanisms among farmers in eastern Kenya.[80]

Many others have written on the necessity of understanding the small farmer's and pastoralist's ways of coping with the environment and using this as the starting point for designing improvements. Much of this recent work has centered around the limited objective of improving early-warning systems to predict famine, improving famine relief, or better fitting national government food and agricultural policies to the realities of ordinary farmers and pastoralists.[81]

Increasingly, however, the need to involve farmers in all aspects of agricultural research—crop breeding, work on tillage, pest control, and so on—is becoming recognized. Also missing from normal science applied to African agriculture has been a concern with crops and animals that were seen as unimportant economically. These tended to be crops of nutritional importance to women (who in the main are those responsible for feeding their families), and animals such as camels, goats, and sheep that are not as important as beef in export markets. Recently there has been more attention paid to such food crops as roots and tubers of importance in many African diets, and date palms; and to animals such as the camel. Horowitz and Jowkar have reviewed the literature of the role of women in pastoral production, an aspect very much neglected in development projects.[82]

Juma studied the cycle in which farmers in the Bungoma district of Kenya sought possibly useful plants in the forest zone of Mt. Elgon, returned home, grew them experimentally at home, shared the results with neighbors—some receiving great praise and prestige—and later symbolically returned them to the wild forest, in order to perpetuate them.[83] To my knowledge, very few Western scientific workers concerned with the preservation of African germplasm have grasped the excitement and open-endedness of such truly African science.

Applied Zoological Studies

Thomas Odhiambo is one African scientist who believes strongly both in the potential for science to lead an African recovery and that indigenous knowledge must be integrated into science in Africa.[84] The International Centre for Insect Physiology and Ecology (ICIPE) that he directs works in this spirit. Its research on tsetse flies, for instance, has been very effective.[85] This work is based on experiments with a variety of flytraps using color, reflectivity, and sexual attractants. Local residents were included in the research teams.

By contrast, research and programs to understand and to control river blindness in West Africa have proceeded in a more conventional manner.[86] This has involved spraying vast areas of seven West African countries repeatedly with insecticides in order to kill the black fly that vectors the parasites that cause the disease. While large areas have been declared free of the fly and open again to agriculture, whether this ecological situation can be sustained is open to question, as are the long-run consequences of such massive use of insecticide. In most countries, there is little integration of local knowledge of wildlife into biological research or into programs for conservation. The situation remains much as that described by Gerald Durrell in *The Zoo in My Luggage*.[87] In the late 1940s, Durrell hunted animals in Cameroon for his private zoo. According to his account, friendly, simple, somewhat bemused "natives" helped him to find the animals, and he toasted his successes in whiskey that he shared with the local chief—the Fon of Bafut, who had organized the labor required to seek this "fine beef," to use the chief's patois as reported by Durrell. An exception to this state of affairs is Operation Campfire in Zimbabwe under which local residents are economic beneficiaries of wildlife tourism and are involved in animal census-taking and the study of wildlife.

Fish, both freshwater and marine, are a highly underutilized food resource in Africa. Data for one FAO map produced in the early 1980s suggested that the average fish consumption in most African countries was only a few pounds per capita. Little is known about freshwater fishing resources. In retrospect, some disastrous consequences of so-called development projects such as the creation of artificial lakes or the introduction of species into natural lakes are coming to light. For instance, the Nile perch was introduced into Lake Victoria in East Africa as a large, commercial species. It fed on the small fish (haplochromines) that had been the staple product of small-scale fishing and which also kept algae growth under control. Now that the smaller fish are nearly eliminated from the lake, algae has bloomed, and oxygen levels in this great body of water—on which some 30 million people in Kenya, Tanzania, and Uganda depend economically—have fallen to nearly zero, which adds to the demise of fish.[88] Research on the biology of African lakes and rivers is accelerating,[89] but this is an area where there has not yet been much attempt to involve fishermen and their fund of knowledge in research.

Engineering Studies

No doubt there are differences between Super Collider and Star Wars technology on the one hand and grain drying and storage structures built with local materials in Africa. The former are more expensive, and the engineering calculations required are more complex. But is the engineering and physics performed by Big Science better in any way? If the satisfaction of human needs is taken as a criterion, it might be argued that the grain-silo project is, in fact, better science. Some might object that smashing atoms reveals a deeper level of physical reality than one has access to in daily experience. Here, however, we return to the issue of *myth*. If one feels more secure in one's world, more satisfied aesthetically perhaps, in a reality composed of quarks and gluons, who can object? But we must recall that a reality composed of angels and demons felt right to our European ancestors. Also, we should entertain the possibility that work on the grain-silo problem reveals a deeper level of human and social reality. Certainly this seemed to be the case to a mixed team of researchers who worked in a Tanzanian village in 1976, as a brief account of this work will reveal.[90]

The losses of food to pests (up to 30 percent) had been identified by villagers in the western, central district of Morogoro, in the Uluguru mountains. The villagers were responding to a survey by a national development NGO (nongovernmental organization), the Community Development Trust Fund of Tanzania (CDTF). Dutch government funding was obtained by the CDTF for an exercise in designing, together with these villagers, improved storage systems. A team was formed: as a Swahili-speaker with experience in community nutrition and food systems I was leader; we also had a Mexican food technologist with experience of small-scale storage, two Tanzanian experts in adult education (one of them a gifted artist), an expatriate administrator of the CDTF with experience in credit, marketing, and institutional development. The team shared a common methodological starting point based on the writings of the Brazilian adult educator Paulo Freire,[91] who by chance was in Tanzania shortly before we began our work and who kindly reviewed our plans. This team worked with counterparts chosen by the village. The enlarged team worked for three months.

First, a house-to-house survey was conducted to ascertain the variety of ways in which people were storing grain. Physical measurements of temperature and humidity in the storage structures were taken as well as a census of pests and estimates of damage to stored crops. During this first phase, group discussions of storage problems and previous attempts to deal with them were held in four residential zones of the village. The social infrastructure for these groups were preexisting adult literacy study groups.

Phase two involved designing an improved system of storage. Again discussion groups were the "workshop." Physical data was discussed. The artist in the team produced a series of graphics, and the designs were criticized in the groups. Prototypes from other countries (e.g., Mexico and Nigeria) were introduced, criticized in terms of local knowledge, and elements of them incorporated or rejected. The range of local knowledge ran from animal behavior—for example, rats were reported to jump higher than the level of the rat-guards on silo stilts—to local meteorological conditions—for example, it was pointed out that storms would blow rain horizontally under the roofs of one proposed design. Other input was of the order of materials science, regarding the strength and resistance to termite attack of local tree species useful as supports and beams.

Phase three involved building several of these new systems with villagers at the homes of volunteers. In the course of the work, a great deal of contextual knowledge was produced—relevant to both the "how" of improving storage and the "why" of storage loss. For instance, it became known that poorer villagers suffered seasonal hunger and had to sell their labor to richer neighbors in return for food. This occurred just as the fields were being prepared for the major maize planting. The poorer villagers cultivated the fields of the richer, as well as their own fields. As a result, the rich were able to plant both earlier and in greater quantity. The poor harvested less maize and—a very relevant fact—had to harvest it later. When the team studied rainfall records for this area, they found that the poor were forced by this circumstance to harvest their maize during the rainiest month of the year! Wet grain is notoriously difficult to store, being more subject to insect attack and to mildew. The poor, in addition to harvesting less, had greater storage losses and thereby suffered seasonal hunger. This was a vicious circle. The engineering and food-science challenge of designing improved systems was therefore given a broader context. What could be done to address the different storage needs of rich and poor? This question was discussed in village meetings, and a system of subsidies was worked out that made it possible for the poor to afford the modest cost of the improved system.

Work on a wide variety of engineering problems at neighborhood and village level in Africa provides a wealth of entry points for thinking about a new hybrid science that incorporates citizens' knowledge and is controlled by them. Marilyn Carr describes a number of design-solutions used by women's groups in Africa in her book, *Baker, Blacksmith, Roofing-sheet Maker. . . .*[92] Women's participation in the design phase is not universal in the cases she cites, but as women gain experience with low-cost technology there is no reason why they should not become coinvestigators in the process of further elaboration and innovation.

Calestous Juma, director of the African Centre for Technology Studies in Nairobi, similarly has a high opinion of the metalsmiths and other inventors in the so-called informal sector in Kenya (the "open air sector," from *jua kali*, literally "[under] the very hot sun" sector). These inventors are self-taught or are graduates of training schools or "village polytechnics." Among their designs is an energy-efficient, charcoal-burning cooking stove with a ceramic insert that has become both famous and popular with users and experts alike.[93]

Energy Studies

Most energy consumed in Africa comes from biomass. Wood (and wood converted to charcoal), together with crop residues and, occasionally, dried animal manure constitute as much as 70–90 percent of the national energy balance of many countries.[94] The commercial energy sector is usually dominated by transport and depends on imported petroleum (except in a few oil-producing countries such as Nigeria and Angola). Coal, hydropower, and imported diesel fuel are used to generate electricity that is fed into tiny grids, mostly providing a few large towns and industrial enclaves (e.g., mining) with intermittent power. Some rural hospitals and district headquarters have small, diesel generators.

The gap between the levels of per capita energy consumption in most of Africa and those of industrial countries is enormous. However, before such observation leads to despair, it is important to note two things. First, energy consumption in industrial countries is unsustainably high, wasteful, and not necessary for the maintenance of human welfare. Second, the satisfaction of basic human needs, as measured, for instance, by the Physical Quality of Life Index (PQLI), may require as little energy as one kilowatt per capita if it is used efficiently.[95]

Science *about* Africa, conducted with no contribution from indigenous knowledge, includes numerous surveys using geological, petrological, and other earth and atmospheric sciences to find fossil fuel deposits or sources of geothermal, wind, and hydro power. Certainly, some increase in the consumption of these energy sources is needed in Africa. The problem-focused, citizen-based kind of scientific inquiry that I am proposing does not deny the importance of these energy sources. On the other hand, from the point of view of meeting human needs in the crisis that faces Africa today, future research should help to design more efficient end-use devices (stoves, grain driers and mills, forms of local bulk transportation, plows, lighting devices, and cooling-sterilization-refrigeration devices that are essential for rural health centers, for instance). In addition, research is required on the more efficient transformation of locally available energy sources (solar, wind, mini- and small-scale hydropower, more efficient kilns for converting bulky wood to charcoal, and so on).

Biomass energy consumption by rural people in Africa, and by urban dwellers who use charcoal produced in ever-more-distant rural zones surrounding the cities, is causing deforestation, erosion, and the silting up of rivers. Hence, programs focused on wood fuel and multipurpose tree production are one of the highest priorities.[96] Another key area for research is the question of how farm byproducts can become energy sources and how the byproducts of energy transformation (e.g., slurry from methane generation) can become inputs into farming (e.g., biofertilizer). Much research into such interconnections exists in Latin America and Asia, but work on the so-called food-energy nexus has just begun in Africa.[97]

Some, but not enough, of the research in these key areas has been conducted with citizen participation. Some improved stove design has been credited to rural women.[98] An ingenious hot-box that used dried banana leaves for insulation was designed in Rwanda by a team that included local women. The area in which the hot-box originated is very densely populated, and cooking fuel is scarce; however, a major staple crop is beans, a food that requires a long cooking-time. (Other research[99] had shown that such foods tend to be replaced by lower-quality food as wood fuel and women's time become scarce.) In the Rwanda situation, the proposed system was to begin to cook the beans over the conventional three-stone (improved) stove, but then to transfer the pot to the insulated box before going out to the fields to work. On her return the woman finds the pot of beans nicely cooked. This same team studied the wide range of traditional varieties of beans that women planted, selected those with shorter cooking time, and bred a bean that required 40 percent less cooking fuel.[100]

Not all priorities are worked on at the grassroots level, however. An important energy question at the macro level involves the planetary energy budget, global warming, and climate change. A group of Kenyan scholars is presently trying to forecast the consequences of climate change in Kenya.[101] Such exercises will eventually need to be put alongside work at the level of household coping mechanisms (see the earlier discussion of drought, for instance).

Health Studies

As with agriculture, indigenous knowledge of health and disease has often met with scant respect from outsiders. Just as traditional farming systems were seen as static, cultural products with little or no developmental potential, so African herbalism, bonesetting, midwifery, and mental health practice have been seen as limited. True, one group—midwives—have been professionally recognized, and although this was part of a process of selecting them for retraining it can result in a useful blending of practices. Aseptic technique was a valuable addition to the traditional birth attendant's repertoire. Its acquisition did not, by good fortune, cost the African midwife the renunciation of her entire worldview and approach to interpersonal caring as it might have in colonial days. (By asserting the essentially scientific nature of African practice in relation to the natural world, I should not be taken as implying that these systems are perfect. Such romanticism would be mistaken. All systems have their strengths, weaknesses, limits, gaps in knowledge, and confusions.)

Health and health care are in crisis in Africa.[102] Health-care financing has collapsed. Immunization campaigns focused on childhood diseases such as measles that interact synergistically with malnutrition are faltering. Chronic malnutrition is rampant. Food security is tenuous. Childhood diarrhea is a major killer. Environmental disruption due to war has caused the resurgence of tsetse-vectored sleeping sickness; and the creation of artificial lakes for hydropower and irrigation has caused more malaria. The dams have also brought more bilharzia.[103]

In addition, there are many health problems faced by millions of Africans that do not even rank mention among the top priorities listed by outside agencies, mostly because they are not objects of biomedical research or are costly to address in economic or political terms. Among these are disability (including the social and psychological rehabilitation of youth forced to fight or otherwise caught up in Africa's wars as child soldiers). Among disabilities at least one cause of blindness is being addressed, vitamin A deficiency, but others, such as trachoma, are not. The former can be treated with a "magic bullet" (a megadose of vitamin A), while the latter requires investments in water supply and sanitation.

Other hidden health priorities are a variety of concerns shared by women—for instance, infertility, domestic violence, and rape.[104] Occupational and industrial health is rarely considered important in Africa, where the assumption is that industry is relatively unimportant. However, mines, plantations, ports, and the transport and construction industries are all very dangerous and often unregulated. In addition, recent attempts to export toxic waste in large quantities from European industries for disposal in Africa are bound to continue, and if they succeed, a new generation of health hazards will arrive.[105] This is not an exaggerated fear. In the midst of the civil war in Somalia, the warlord controlling the former capital city, Mogadishu, has agreed to allow a Swiss firm, Achair Partners, to store and burn 500,000 tonnes of waste a year near the city. There are also allegations that, under the cover of chaos, Italian companies are dumping toxic waste off Somalia's coast.[106]

The widespread commitment in African countries to primary health care (PHC) and community-based health care (uneven and underfunded as it may be) provides the basis for rapid increase in popular participation in health research in these priority areas.[107] The most virulent African viruses must remain the subject of specialized and highly technical research;[108] however, it is well-established that community health workers can be trained to do basic epidemiological research on malnutrition, diarrhea, tuberculosis, and so forth, and that this work can serve as the basis of community health programs.[109] Indigenous methods of controlling and arranging protection from mosquitos has sometimes been integrated into malaria-control programs.[110] Increasingly, there is a call for, and experiments with, involvement of local women in research on the epidemiology and control of HIV infection.[111]

TEACHING METHODS AND RESOURCES

I mentioned a number of valuable published resources in the previous section; however, a manageable selection for use in a one-semester undergraduate course might include the works listed below.[112] A suggested syllabus follows the list.

Resources

Texts

- Thomas Bass, *Camping with the Prince*. [TB]
- Fantu Cheru, *The Silent Revolution in Africa*. [FC]
- Paul Harrison, *The Greening of Africa*. [PH]
- Calestous Juma, *The Gene Hunters*. [CJ]
- Bill Rau, *From Feast to Famine*. [BR]
- Else Skjønsberg, *Change in an African Village* [Optional: see Methods below]
- Ben Wisner, *Power and Need in Africa*. [BW]

Reserve Resource: Chapters and Papers

- W. Beinhart (1984), "Soil Erosion, Conservationism, and Ideas about Development: A Southern African Exploration, 1900-1960." [WB]

- Jorge H. Hardoy and David Satterthwaite, *Squatter Citizen*, chapters 3–5. [HS]
- Bernard and Michael Grzimek, *Serengetti Shall Not Die*, chapters 1, 2, 8, 16. [BMG]
- Calestous Juma (1989a), "Intellectual Property Rights for *Jua Kali* Innovations." [CJ-2]
- Thomas Odhiambo (1967), "East Africa: Science for Development." [TO]
- Randall Packard (1989), chapter 7, "Segregation and Racial Susceptibility: The Ideological Foundations of Tuberculosis Control, 1913–1938." [RP]
- Tsenay Serequeberhan (1991), "African Philosophy: The Point in Question." [TS]
- Vandana Shiva (1989), chapter 1, "Development, Ecology, and Women." [VS-1]
- Vandana Shiva (1989), chapter 2, "Science, Nature, and Gender." [VS-2]
- Megan Vaughan (1991), chapter 2, "Rats' Tails and Trypanosomes: Nature and Culture in Early Colonial Medicine." [MV]
- Rodger Yeager (1986), "Land Use and Wildlife in Modern Tanzania." [RY]

Video

- "Man-Made Famine" [MMF]

Syllabus

Week	Topic	Resources
	Part I: Overview	
1	The African Crisis	BR1; FC1; PH2, 3; BW pp. 13–23
2	The Meaning of "Development"	BR2, 3; BW1; VS–1
3	"Science" and "Development"	VS–2; TO
4	Is There an African Science?	BR10; CJ1; TS
	Part II: Case Studies	
5	Restoring the Land	PH7, 8, 10; WB
6	Managing Water	BW3; TB pp. 87–116; PH9
7	Conserving Wild Genes	RY; TB pp. 51–86; CJ4, 6; BMG
8	Securing the Food Supply	BW5; BR8, 9; TB pp. 117–186; MMF

9	Providing Shelter	BW3; HS
10	Transforming Energy	BW7; PH11, 12
11	Healing the Sick	BW; TB pp. 227–276;
		MV; RP

Part III: Policy Issues

12	Roles of Government and	CJ-2; FC3–6;
	Business	BR5, 6
13	Role of International Aid	CJ3, 6; FC2; BR7
14	Democratic Control of	BW8; BR11, 12;
	Science & "Development"	FC7; CJ7

Methods

Class discussion is vital. The connection between science and daily life should be continually brought back to the experience of the students. The topics involving case studies, such as land restoration, water management, food security, energy, and health, should be opened up by inquiring about the students' homes and experience. Has their land been restored or is it in need of restoration? A Superfund site, perhaps? Where does the water they drink come from? How safe is it? Will there always be enough? Where in the United States might there be water shortages? Where does our food come from? How is it produced? Have students ever experienced an "energy crisis"? Have they heard of one? What is a childhood disease? Who has had one? Was it serious? Why or why not? (Measles killed more children in the Sahel during the famine years 1967–1973 than did hunger.)

Teams of two to four students should choose topics from Part II and research a particular technology or scientific question using primary literature. What is the relevance of this scientific paper to the crisis in Africa? Groups, in turn, report to the class. In large research universities or metropolitan settings, it should be possible to locate African graduate students willing to make guest appearances in the class at appropriate times.

I have also found that team-teaching is valuable. At Hampshire College, I have for five years been teaching a course (more general than that outlined above, but similar) entitled "The World Food Crisis." I always teach with one of my colleagues trained in biological sciences. This provides the in-depth background needed to field students' questions and gives support for one-on-one sessions with students whose project options are more strongly oriented toward the natural science end of the social science/natural science continuum.

In an advanced class, or one with highly motivated students, the text listed as optional, *Change in an African Village*, should be read in its entirety alongside the other weekly readings during the first four weeks. During Part II of the course, each major topic should be related in class discussion to material in the village of Kefa, portrayed in the book. Conversely, discussion can start with concrete topics in the book (e.g., economic activities such as raising pigs or healing stomach pains), and then students can be asked what "science" is applicable.

A valuable source of supplementary material for class discussion is a collection of case studies of Nordic development projects dealing with environmental problems available from the Panos Institute.[113] Ten of the fourteen case studies documented are in Africa, and the accounts give background information as well as independent critiques of the projects' strengths and weaknesses.

Versions of this course taught as a senior seminar or other advanced learning activity could include the requirement that each participant follow and interact with a computer conference on the international network, ECONET. This system has numerous conferences on forestry, water resources, energy, agriculture, wildlife, and health at any given time.

I noted early in this chapter that undergraduate field visits to Africa often, fail. Students may enjoy them, but *failure* in the context of this chapter means that they have not learned what they could about science, about Africa, and about themselves. The reason for this is that very few overseas programs place students in citizen-based, problem-focused, action-research situations. Contact with science and African communities tends to be compartmentalized. Typically, students participate in something like counting giraffes or elands in a commercial game-ranching operation (this is the "science" bit) and later visit an African family for a "home stay." The latter constitutes contact with the community. The two parts of the visit are not connected. The ideal situation would be placement with a family that is engaged in a community self-help project that involves citizens themselves as coinvestigators in areas such as child health, food science, water treatment, agroforestry, or renewable energy.

But more than this is required to take maximum advantage of the learning possible while visiting Africa. I would suggest that, before and after such a journey, students work in similar citizen-based, problem-focused situations at home. There are a wide variety of community groups at work on air and water pollution, waste disposal, recycling, urban gardening, food access through food banks and prepared-food salvage programs, child health issues such as removal of lead paint, AIDS education, and so on. At first glance there may seem to be a world of difference between women building ferro-cement water storage tanks for roof-rainwater catchment in Kenya and parents researching and protesting lead poisoning of their children in New Jersey. There are, however, many similarities that concern the role of science, the role of the citizen, power, communication, and control over one's life. There are groups such as Global Exchange and IRED (International Network for Educational Development)[114] that specialize in connecting grassroots groups in this country with counterparts in Africa. Kevin Danaher, of Global Exchange, has written a very useful resource guide to building people-to-people ties with Africa, *Beyond Safaris*.[115]

DIFFICULTIES AND OPPORTUNITIES

One of the most obvious difficulties of this approach to African science is its interdisciplinary nature. A problem-focus, especially one that involves local people and respects their knowledge and participation, tends to cut across academic disciplinary boundaries. This is apparent in the model syllabus, where readings also often cut across historical time in their treatment of colonial science, developmentalist or modernizing science, and contemporary problem-focused science. Interdisciplinarity is also evident in the way that key areas are identified (see the second section of this chapter). For instance, climate is not discussed under Environmental Science but under Energy Studies. In these and most other key areas, work at a wide range of scales is recognized: studies that attempt to model climate change or water balance at a continental scale at one extreme; others that deal with specific cultural responses to drought or vernacular techniques for well-digging at the other.

None of this fits nicely in academic niches labelled *geophysics* or *biochemistry*. There may, consequently, be a feeling on the part of some science faculty that such a course is not doing justice to "science." Moreover, in order to provide the socioeconomic, cultural, and political context within which science has meaning in Africa today, the books I have cited contain much material from the social sciences and humanities. This might provoke an even more extreme reaction from some colleagues, to the effect that the wolf of radical social criticism is masquerading in the clothing of innocent, sheeplike science. Administratively, efforts to overcome the above objections with a team approach that involves a natural scientist and social scientist may be stymied if full teaching credit toward their required load is not given to both teachers. This is a general problem, faced by those attempting innovative team approaches, especially in interdisciplinary areas such as African studies, women's studies, and environmental studies.

At a deeper level, the weight of uncriticized assumptions about the unity of science, its value-neutrality, the transcultural validity of its methods, and so forth, are very hard to counterbalance. This problem was discussed early in the chapter. Also discussed at the outset was the assumption that development and progress are real and positive. Some of the literature cited under each of the key areas listed above discusses a number of negative effects of so-called development on African lives, livelihoods, and landscapes. Each of these negative social or ecological consequences, and the entire series for that matter, could be dismissed as costs that are outweighed by greater benefits. Certainly one hears this reaction. It is hard to find common ground in such an argument. No one has yet drawn up a definitive balance sheet of this kind for any African nation, much less for the continent. Costs tend to accumulate on the side of the poor, the less vocal, and less visible. They also tend to accrue to future generations in unpredictable ways. Elsewhere, I have shown that even on as basic a criterion as infant mortality, Africa had begun to lose the alleged benefits of so-called development by the mid-1980s.[116]

Apart from this, some would reject a "balance sheet" approach to African development out of hand. Historian Walter Rodney made this argument, for instance, on the basis that the African masses need to determine what *development* is in the first place.[117] Balance sheets are usually based on someone else's definition of "development."

Opportunities

On the other hand, the time is ripe for a radical rethinking of Western academic understanding and approaches to both Africa and to science. Both Africans and students are tired of the doom-and-gloom view. African voices are calling for respect and autonomy. Even the most well-meaning systems-analysis of African crisis imposes an alien structure on Africans' lived reality. Real people do not inhabit graphs and diagrams, the boxes connected by arrows that many of us, including myself, are fond of drawing. To move forward, beyond the myths of development, all of us need to learn from each other. We need to listen to Africa.[118] In the case of science, this means we need to move out of laboratories into urban neighborhoods and villages. We need to adopt a radically participatory mode of research in which local knowledge plays a key role.[119] Such a problem-focused approach offers the opportunity to empower our students to deal creatively, in a similarly participatory manner, with people in this country as they confront the massive challenges posed by pollution, poverty, and homelessness.

This is a time of considerable restlessness among scientists. Women in science are often uncomfortable, and they have sought to understand their dis-ease in a feminist critique of male science.[120] Both female and male scientists welcome the talk of a peace dividend and of economic conversion from war to peace applications of science and technology. However, they are becoming impatient as time goes by with little follow-through in budgetary terms. Big Science remains king despite setbacks for the super-collider and space programs. This restive atmosphere among many scientists and science students presents the opportunity for courses that provide not only a critical perspective on "normal" science but also discuss applications to people's basic problems and the democratic control of science priorities.

CONCLUSION: IKEM'S CHILD

By way of conclusion, I will return to the three goals of teaching African science mentioned at the beginning. If one were to think about African science in the ways I have suggested, what would students learn about science? What would they learn about themselves? What would they learn about Africa? About "normal" science, students might learn that it is not what they think it is and that it is not all that it could be. Certainly, it is possible to appreciate the fact that the Western story is only one of many when one looks at the history and contemporary activities of science in, about, and from Africa. Called into question can be both the standard Popperian notions (strict, rule-based methods of observation, hypothesis formation, and falsification) and Kuhn's reinterpretation.[121] But this should not plunge the student into a bottomless morass of relativism. Students can also learn that "hybrid" sciences are constantly being created in the fields, workshops, villages, refugee camps, *favelas*, *barrios*, and other squatter settlements in the megacities of the late twentieth century. Students can also learn that *myth* and *science* are not opposites; that both seek to unify and systematize experience. The possibility of a much more open science in the twenty-first century parallels discussions of the possibility of a major revolution in grassroots democracy and the emergence of a new civic culture.[122] A glimpse of the possibility is visible in the Chinese program for integrating the efforts of Western biomedical and traditional Chinese medical research. Both benefited, and new, surprising things were discovered.[123]

About themselves, students can also learn a good deal. If only through print and electronic media, in meetings with Africans who confront their problems and struggle with them, it is possible for students to imagine themselves also in a problem-solving role. The problems Africans are confronting may appear extreme, but they are not qualitatively different from the ones North Americans and Europeans confront. Learning to perceive the unity, or interrelatedness, of person and place in Africa, students can learn to see themselves, as persons, in such relations with their homes, and places. I agree strongly with David Orr when he writes of the importance of *place* in pedagogy. The advantages he notes are that place-based study integrates experience and intellect, counters the widespread tendency toward overspecialization, and provides the basis for "an applied ethical sense toward habitat."[124] By this, I think Orr means the same thing as the "connectedness" to people-in-places I referred to earlier while discussing the integration of mental, manual, and emotional labor.

About Africa, the student can learn that it is not all dust and cattle bones, lions, mosquitos, dictators, wild-eyed, teenaged soldiers, and starving babies.[125] It is possible to learn that Africa is composed of places where people live; that it is not merely a place of exotic ecosystems characterized by torrid inhospitability ("the White Man's Grave") or unimaginable riches ("King Solomon's Mines"). Like all other places, Africa's places have environmental strengths and limitations in relation to the satisfaction of human needs. Ordinary people have a great deal of knowledge of these strengths and limitations. For the most part, Western science has ignored this local knowledge and has worked as handmaiden to the external interests or elite local interests that were concerned less with meeting human needs than with extracting minerals, hydropower, fossil fuels, cash crops, livestock, and forest products from Africa. It is also possible to learn that African scientists, intellectuals, and other leaders are working hard to understand Africa's crisis and to map out a coherent vision of the future.[126]

It is also possible to frame this new awareness of the potential of African places and of a more humanistic role for science in the context of a greater understanding of African people and their potential. I will close on this note with a highly evocative passage from the end of Achebe's novel *Anthills of the Savannah*.[127] A group of women are mourning the death of a man who tried to fight against corruption, arbitrary use of political power, and the arrogant distance of government officials from the needs of ordinary people.[128] The man, Ikem, was finally shot down by a drunken soldier when he tried to save a young girl the soldier was abducting. The women, as they mourn, dedicate themselves to the same struggle for justice and sustainability that Ikem fought. Ikem's child has just been born. They name her Amaechina: *May-the-path-never-close*. Someone objects:

> "But that's a boy's name."
> "No matter."
> "Girl fit . . . also."
> "It's a beautiful name. The Path of Ikem."
> "That's right. May it never close, never overgrow."
> "Das right!"
> "May it always shine! The Shining Path of Ikem."
> "Dat na wonderful name."
> "Na fine name so."

The women continue to discuss:

> "In our traditional society . . . the father named the child. . . . What does a man know about a child anyway that he should presume to give it a name. . . ."
> "Na true my brother. . . . Na woman de come tell man say na him born the child. Then the man begin make *inyanga* and begin answer father. Na *yéyé* father we be."
> "Exactly. So I think our tradition is faulty there. It is really safest to ask the mother what her child is or means or should be called."

Later an old man comes in and is visibly shocked that the women have named the child.

> "Who gave her the name?"
> "All of us here."
> "All of you here . . . all of you are her father?"
> "Yes, and mother."

These women are asserting themselves in a way that heals themselves and can heal Africa. In speaking about the "path" they are discussing more than an infant's name. They are referring to the future, to Africa's future. In giving the infant girl a boy's name, by pronouncing themselves all both mother and father—women *organized*, not alone—they, and the living women of Africa like them, declare that the construction of Africa's future is also their right. This chapter is dedicated to these women and to the street children, dry-land farmers, miners, stevedores, cattle and goat herders, excombatants of the liberation movements, who, through their struggles, are giving birth to a new science for all humankind.

NOTES

1. Orbital Transport-und Raketen-Aktiengesellschaft, based in Munich, is a commercial satellite launching corporation that leased a 39,000-square-mile territory within Zaire. This is an area about the size of the state of Virginia. The lease expires in 2001. E. Regis, *Great Mambo Chicken and the Transhuman Condition* (Reading, MA: Addison Wesley, 1990).

2. R. Manoff, *Social Marketing: New Imperative for Public Health* (New York: Praeger, 1985).

3. J. Scott, *Weapons of the Weak: Everyday Forms of Peasant Resistance* (New Haven: Yale, 1985); F. Marglin and S. Marglin, eds., *Dominating Knowledge: Development, Culture, and Resistance* (Oxford: Clarendon, 1990).

4. P. Tempels, *Bantu Philosophy* (Paris: Présence Africaine, 1959).

5. E. Wamba-Dia-Wamba, "Philosophy in Africa: Challenges of the African Philosopher," in *African Philosophy: The Essential Readings,* ed. T. Serequeberhan (New York: Paragon House, 1991): 211–246.

6. V. Mudimbe, *The Invention of Africa* (Bloomington: University of Indiana Press, 1988); T. Serequeberhan, "African Philosophy: The Point in Question," in *African Philosophy: The Essential Readings*, ed. T. Serequeberhan (New York: Paragon House, 1991): 3–28.

7. B. Harrell-Bond, *Imposing Aid: Emergency Assistance to Refugees* (New York: Oxford University Press, 1986).

8. D. Cohen and E. Odhiambo, *Siaya: The Historical Anthropology of an African Landscape* (London: James Currey, 1989): 9.

9. R. Chambers, "Microenvironments Unobserved," Gatekeeper Series no. 22. (London: International Institute for Environment and Development, 1990): 6–7.

10. D. Rocheleau (panel contribution at Annual Meeting of the Association of American Geographers, San Diego, April 1992, in session organized by L. Yapa and B. Wisner on the theme "'Development' as Destruction").

11. P. Harrison, *The Greening of Africa: Breaking Through in the Battle for Land and Food* (New York: Penguin, 1987); A. De Wall, *Famine that Kills* (Oxford: Clarendon, 1989); T. Bass, *Camping with the Prince and Other Tales of Science in Africa* (New York: Penguin, 1990).

12. E. Jones, *The European Miracle* (New York: Cambridge University Press, 1981). See J. Blaut, *Diffusionism: The Colonizer's Model of the World* (New York: Guilford, 1992) and J. Blaut et al., *1492: The Debate on Colonialism, Eurocentrism, and History* (Trenton, N.J.: Africa World Press, 1992) for a brilliant critique of what Blaut calls "cultural racism," the position that it is the superior rationality of Western thinking and institutions that accounts for economic and material accumulation.

13. K. Wiredu, "How Not to Compare African Thought with Western Thought," in *African Philosophy: An Introduction,* ed. R. Wright (Lanham, MD: University Press of America, 1984): 153–154; O. Owomoyela, "Africa and the Imperative of Philosophy: A Skeptical Consideration," in *African Philosophy: The Essential, Readings,* ed. T. Serequeberhan (New York: Paragon House, 1991).

14. E. Kodjo, *Africa Tomorrow* (New York: Marrow, 1988).

15. P. Bodunrin, "The Question of African Philosophy," in *African Philosophy: The Essential Readings,* ed. T. Serequeberhan, (New York: Paragon House, 1991): 68.

16. Owomoyela, "Africa and the Imperative," 162.

17. B. Wisner, "Introduction: Science and Technology in Africa," in *Science Across Cultures: An Annotated Bibliography of Books in Non-Western Science, Technology, and Medicine,* ed. H. Selin (New York: Garland, 1992).

18. K. Dugan, "Introduction: Science and Technology in Asia," in *Science Across Cultures: An Annotated Bibliography of Books on Non-Western Science, Technology, and Medicine,* ed. H. Selin (New York: Garland, 1992).

19. T. Odhiambo et al., *Hope Born Out of Despair: Managing the African Crisis* (Nairobi: Heinemann Kenya, 1988): 66.

20. C. A. Diop, *Civilization or Barbarism* (Brooklyn: Lawrence Hill Books, 1981): 231–308.

21. B. Wisner, "Botswana," in *Energy and Development in Southern Africa: SADCC Country Studies, Part I,* ed. P. O'Keefe and B. Munslow (Uppsala: Scandinavian Institute of African Studies and the Beijer Institute, 1984).

22. E. Marealle, "Research for Peasant Farmers" (in Panos Institute, dossier no. 5, 1987).

23. H. Oruka, "Sagacity in African Philosophy," in *African Philosphy: The Essential Readings,* ed. T. Serequeberhan (New York: Paragon House, 1991): 47–62.

24. See the debate in Serequeberhan, *African Philosophy,* especially contributions by Serequeberhan and Wamba-Dia-Wamba that emphasize the importance of the political and survival struggles of the masses as a source of ideas that philosophers can (and should) systematize; and Oruka, *Sagacity* and Owomoyela, *Africa and the Imperative,* who, in different ways, defend the so-called illiterate culture of the masses as philosophy.

25. B. Wisner, *Power and Need in Africa: Basic Human Needs and Development Policy* (London: Earthscan Publications, 1988): 13–23.

26. The *we* in this section is intentionally ambiguous. It certainly refers to teams—research and action teams, to be sure—but it also refers to the fact that all knowledge and action are social, not individual. *We* can be a team composed of local people and Western-trained African scientists, students on vacation from the university, "barefoot" scientists of many kinds with just a few months' formal training as dynamizers of locally based action-research in some area like sanitation,

malaria control, crop protection, or grain storage. *We* could be extended to include expatriate, Western-trained scientists, volunteers, or students doing field-work. In a more general way, in regard to local survival issues in the United States and Europe, *we* generally means citizens; but again, not just the formally trained, because the approach of the new science should be participatory here as well. Such U.S. teams could also include visiting African scientists.

27. H. Rose, "Hand, Brain, and Heart: A Feminist Epistemology for the Natural Sciences," in *Signs: Journal of Women in Culture and Society* 9, no. 1 (1983).

28. S. Harding, *The Science Question in Feminism* (Ithaca, NY: Cornell University Press, 1986).

29. P. Richards, *Coping with Hunger: Hazard and Experiment in an African Rice-Farming System* (London: Allen and Unwin, 1986).

30. P. Bradley, *Woodfuel, Women and Woodlots.* (London: Macmillan, 1991).

31. A. Pacey, *The Culture of Technology* (Cambridge: MIT Press, 1983): 149–159.

32. A. Giddens, *The Constitution of Society* (Berkeley: University of California Press, 1984).

33. S. Kruks, *Situation and Human Existence* (London: Unwin Hyman, 1990).

34. D. Curtin and L. Heldke, eds., *Cooking, Eating, Thinking: Transformative Philosophies of Food* (Bloomington: University of Indiana Press, 1992).

35. R. Dumont, *False Start in Africa* (New York: Praeger, 1966).

36. R. Dumont and M.-F. Mottin, *Stranglehold on Africa* (London: André Deutsch, 1983).

37. On the impacts of structural adjustment in Africa, see G. Cornia, G. R. Jolly, and F. Stewart, eds., *Adjustment with a Human Face*, 2 vols. (New York: Oxford University Press, 1987); D. Bell and M. Reich, eds., *Health, Nutrition and Economic Crises: Approaches to Policy in the Third World* (Dover, MA: Auburn House Publishing, 1988); Wisner, *Power and Need*; B. Onimode, ed., *The IMF, the World Bank, and the African Debt*, 2 vols. (London: Zed Press, 1989): 198; D. Elson, "How is Structural Adjustment Affecting Women?" *Development* 1 (1989): 67–74; W. Weissman, "Structural Adjustment in Africa: Insights from the Experience of Ghana and Senegal," *World Development* 18, no. 12 (1990): 1621–34; B. Rau, *From Feast to Famine* (London: Zed Press, 1991).

38. D. Taylor and F. Mackenzie, eds., *Development from Within: Survival in Rural Africa* (London: Routledge, 1992).

39. B. Wisner, "Jilaal, Gu, Hagaa, and Der: Living with the Somali Land, and Living Well" (paper commissioned for the conference "The Somali Challenge," Centre for Applied International Negotiations, Geneva, under the sponsorship of St. Lawrence University, the Ford Foundation, and the U.S. Institute of Peace, 1992).

40. W. Sachs, introduction to *The Development Dictionary*, ed. W. Sachs (London: Zed, 1992): 1–5.

41. J.D. Bernal, *Science in History* (New York: Macmillan, 1954).

42. C. Juma, *The Gene Hunters: Biotechnology and the Scramble for Seeds* (London and Princeton: Zed and Princeton University Press, 1989).

43. V. Shiva, *Staying Alive: Women, Ecology, and Development* (London: Zed, 1989), Chap. 2. See also D. Haraway, *Simians, Cyborgs, and Woman: The Reinvention of Nature* (New York: Routledge, 1991); C. Merchant, *The Death of Nature: Women, Ecology and the Scientific Revolution* (San Francisco: Harper and Row, 1980).

44. K. Hewitt, *Interpretations of Calamity* (London: Allen & Unwin, 1983); A. Kirby, ed., *Nothing to Fear: Risks and Hazards in American Society* (Tucson: Arizona University Press, 1990).

45. A. Chase, *Playing God in Yellowstone* (San Diego: Harcourt, Brace, Jovanovich, 1987).

46. Regis, *Great Mambo Chicken.*

47. Regis, *Great Mambo Chicken,* 279.

48. M. Little, "Imperialism, Colonialism and the New Science of Nutrition: The Tanganyika Experience, 1925–45," *Social Science and Medicine* 32, 1 (1991): 11–14.

49. W. Muiruri, "Bio-Economic Conflicts in Resource Use and Management: A Kenyan Case Study," *Geo-Journal* 2 (1978): 321–330; M. Parkipuny, "Some Critical Aspects of the Maasai Predicament," in *African Socialism in Practice,* ed. A. Coulson (London: Spokesman, 1979): 136–157; C. Odegi-Awvondo, "Wildlife Conservation and the Decline of Pastoralism in Kenya," *African Journal of Sociology* 2 (1982): 74–83.

50. M. Parkipuny, "The Ngorongoro Crater Issue: The Point of View of the Indigenous Maasai Community of Ngorongoro," (paper for the International Congress on Nature Management and Sustainable Development, University of Groningen, 1988, 4 citing B. Rensberger, *The Cult of the Wilds* [New York: Anchor, 1973]): 4.

51. B. Grzimek and M. Grzimek, *Serengeti Shall Not Die* (New York: E.P. Dutton, 1960).

52. P. Gourou, *The Tropical World* (Longmans: Green, 1953).

53. Grzimek and Grzimek, *Serengeti,* 160, 294.

54. B. Wisner, "Doubts about 'Social Marketing,'" *Health Policy and Planning* 2, no. 2 (1987): 178–179.

55. The term "bricolage" implies tinkering, jury-rigging, making do in an unsystematic way.

56. C. Lévi-Strauss, *The Savage Mind* (Chicago: University of Chicago Press, 1966); Mudimbe, *Invention of Africa.*

57. In newly industrializing countries, such as Taiwan, Singapore, and South Korea, pollution and resource degradation have reached very high levels.

58. Harding, *Science Question.*

59. I. Illich, *Tools for Conviviality* (London: Calder and Boyars, 1973) and *Shadow Work* (Boston: Marion Boyars, 1981).

60. On the similarities between science and myth, see Feyerabend, *Against Method* (London: Verso, 1975); and R. Horton, "African Traditional Thought and Western Science," *Africa* 37(1967): 87–155.

61. Despite scientific disagreement over details, there is little doubt that the last 150 years of industrial activity (in manufacturing, agriculture, fishing, and forestry) has resulted in global warming, upper atmospheric ozone depletion, marine pollution, overfishing, acid precipitation, water and air pollution, soil contamination, salinization, erosion, decrease in wetland ecosystems, deforestation, and loss of genetic diversity.

62. J. Blaut, *Diffusionism;* and Blaut et al., *1492.*

63. P. De Groot, A. Field-Juma, and D. Hall, *Taking Root: Revegetation in Semi-Arid Kenya* (Nairobi: African Centre for Technology Studies Press, 1992).

64. P. Ngunjiri, "In a Dry Land" (in Panos Institute, dossier no. 8, 1987).

65. Harrison, *Greening of Africa.*

66. J. Beyer, "Africa," in *World Systems of Traditional Resource Management,* ed. G. Klee (New York: Halsted, 1954): 5–37; B. Wamalwa, "Indigenous Knowledge and Natural Resources," in *Gaining Ground: Institutional Innovations in Land-use Management in Kenya,* ed. A. Kiriro and C. Juma (Nairobi: African Centre for Technology Studies Press, 1989): 45–66; C. Reij, "Indigenous Soil and

Water Conservation in Africa" (Gatekeeper Series no. 27, London: International Institute for Environheit and Development, 1991).

67. G. Leach and R. Mearns, *Beyond the Woodfuel Crisis: People, Land and Trees in Africa* (London: Earthscan Publications, 1988): 156–159.

68. For example, see H. Pereira et al., "Hydrological Effects of Changes in Land-use in Some East African Catchment Areas," *East African Agriculture and Forestry Journal* 27 (1962): 42–75.

69. A. Berg, "Sliding Toward Nutrition Malpractice" (Martin Forman Memorial Lecture, mimeo, 1991).

70. P. Kerkof, *Agroforestry in Africa* (London and Washington: Panos Institute, 1990); A. Grainger, *The Threatening Desert: Controlling Desertification* (London: Earthscan Publications, 1990).

71. D. Rocheleau, F. Weber, and A. Field-Juma, *Agroforestry in Dryland Africa* (Nairobi: International Council for Research in Agroforestry, 1988); Harrison, *Greening of Africa*.

72. A. Pacey and A. Cullis, *Rainwater Harvesting: The Collection of Rainfall and Runoff in Rural Areas* (London: Intermediate Technology Publications, 1986); C. Barrow, *Water Management in Developing Countries* (London: Longman, 1985).

73. J. Beyer, "Africa." in *World Systems of Traditional Resource Management*, ed. G. Klee, (New York: Halsted, 1954): 5–37.

74. J. Mukela, "Piped Water by the People" (in Panos Institute, dossier no. 11, 1987); B. Omoro, "Marginal Soil, Marginal Farms" (in Panos Institute, dossier no. 1, 1987); C. Kerr, ed., *Community Health and Sanitation* (London: Intermediate Technology Publications, 1989.

75. C. Wacker, "Participatory Development Planning for Sustainable Development with Women's Groups in Kenya," in *Women and the Environment*, ed. A. Rodda, (London: Zed, 1991): 141–146.

76. H. Guggenheim and R. Fanale, "Water Storage Through Shared Technology: Four Projects Among the Dogon in Mali," *Assignment Children* 45/46 (1975): 151–166.

77. S. Al Azharia Jahn, *Proper Use of African Natural Coagulants for Rural Water Supplies* (Eschborn: GTZ, 1986).

78. W. Allan, *The African Husbandman* (Edinburgh: Oliver and Boyd, 1965).

79. P. Richards, *Indigenous Agricultural Revolution* (London: Hutchinson, 1985) and *Coping with Hunger*.

80. B. Wisner and P. Mbithi, "Drought in Eastern Kenya: Nutritional Status and Farmer Activity," in *Natural Hazards*, ed. G. White (New York: Oxford University Press, 1974): 87–97.

81. P. Walker, *Famine Early Warning Systems* (London: Earthscan Publications, 1989); A. De Wall, *Famine that Kills*, (Oxford: Clarendon, 1989); J. Oguntoyinbo and P. Richards, "Drought and the Nigerian Farmer," *Journal of Arid Environments* 1, (1978): 165–194; M. Watts, *Silent Violence: Food, Famine and Peasants in Northern Nigeria* (Berkeley: University of California Press, 1983); T. Downing, K. Gitu, and C. Kamau, eds., *Coping with Drought in Kenya* (Boulder: Lynne Rienner, 1989); M. Glantz, ed., *Drought and Hunger in Africa* (Cambridge: Cambridge University Press, 1987); M. Mortimore, *Adapting to Drought: Farmers, Famines and Desertification in West Africa* (Cambridge: Cambridge University Press, 1989); B. Wisner, "Too Little To Live On, Too Much to Die From: Lesotho's Agrarian Options in the Year 2000," in *Transforming Southern African Agriculture*, ed. A. Seidman, K. Mwanza, N. Simelane, and D. Weiner (Trenton, NJ: Africa World Press, 1992): 87–104.

82. J. Guyer, "Women's Work and Production Systems: A Review of Two Reports on the Agricultural Crisis," *Review of African Political Economy* 27/28 (1984): 186–192; T. Gammell, *Date Palms in Kenya: An Economic Resource for*

Arid and Semi-arid Areas (Nairobi: African Centre for Technology Studies Press, 1989); A. Hjort af Ornäs, ed., *Camels in Development: Sustainable Production in African Drylands* (Uppsala: Scandinavian Institute of African Studies, 1988); M. Horowitz and F. Jowkar, *Pastoral Women and Change* (Binghamton, NY: Institute for Development Anthropology, 1992).

83. C. Juma, *Biological Diversity and Innovation: Conserving and Utilizing Genetic Resources in Kenya* (Nairobi: African Centre for Technology Studies Press, 1989).

84. T. Odhiambo, "East Africa: Science for Development," *Science* 158 (1967): 876–881; T. Odhiambo, "Designing a New Science-led Development in Tropical Africa" (paper presented at the Summer Institute for African Agricultural Research, Madison, WI, 1990); Odhiambo et al., *Hope Born Out of Despair*.

85. T. Bass, *Camping with the Prince and Other Tales of Science in Africa* (New York: Penguin, 1990).

86. J. Hunter, "Progress and Concerns of the World Health Organization Onchoceroiasis Programme in West Africa," *Social Science and Medicine* 15D, (1981): 261–275.

87. G. Durrell, *The Zoo in my Luggage* (New York: Viking, 1960).

88. S. Okie, "Lake Victoria Faces Death by Asphyxia," *Guardian* (London), 8 July 1992, p. 10.

89. Bass, *Camping,* 90–115.

90. B. Wisner et al., "Designing Storage Systems with Villagers," *African Environment* 3 (1979): 85–95; E. Mduma, "Appropriate Technology for Grain Storage at Bwakira Chini Village," in *Participatory Research: An Emerging Alternative Methodology,* ed. Y. Kassam and K. Mustafa (New Delhi: Society for Participatory Research in Asia, 1982): 198–213; B. Wisner, D. Stea, and S. Kruks, "Participatory and Action Research Methods," in *Advances in Environment, Behavior, and Design,* ed. E. Zube and G. Moore, vol. 3, (New York: Plenum Press, 1991): 271–296.

91. P. Freire, *Education for Critical Consciousness* (New York: Continuum, 1992).

92. M. Carr, *Blacksmith, Baker, Roofing-sheet Maker . . .* (London: Intermediate Technology Publications, 1984).

93. C. Juma, "Intellectual Property Rights for *Jua Kali* Innovations," in *Innovation and Sovereignty,* ed. C. Juma and J. Ojwang (Nairobi: African Centre for Technology Studies, 1989): 123–144; R. Clarke, ed., *Wood-stove Dissemination* (London: Intermediate Technology Publications, 1985).

94. To give four examples, in the early 1980s the contribution of biomass (wood, charcoal, and crop residues) in the total energy budget of Kenya was 74 percent; for Somalia it was 89 percent; for Mozambique, 89 percent; and for Tanzania 91 percent. However, there are exceptions, such as Botswana, where coal is important even for domestic use, and biomass accounts for only 44 percent. B. Munslow et al., "Energy and Development on the African East Coast: Somalia, Kenya, Tanzania and Mozambique," *Ambio* 12, 6 (1983): 335; and Wisner, "Botswana," 92.

95. For discussions of basic human needs and how (and how not) to measure their satisfaction, see M. D. Morris (inventor of the PQLI), *Measuring the Condition of the World's Poor* (Oxford: Pergamon Press, 1979); Wisner, *Power and Need*; and L. Doyal and I. Gough, *A Theory of Human Need* (New York: Guilford, 1991). The PQLI is an index made up from statistics on life expectancy, infant mortality, and adult literacy. Morris found that, when combined, these statistics serve as a good surrogate for a wide range of other welfare measures. J. Goldemberg et al., "Basic Needs and Much More with One Kilowatt Per Capita," *Ambio* 14, 4–5 (1985): 190–200.

96. B. Wisner et al., "A Matrix-Flow Approach to Rural Domestic Energy: A Kenyan Case Study," in *Demands on Rural Lands,* ed. C. Cocklin, B. Smit, and T. Johnston, (Boulder: Westview Press, 1987): 211–238; Leach and Mearns, *Beyond the Woodfuel Crisis.*

97. B. Wisner, "Report on the Second International Symposium," in *Food-Energy Nexus and Ecosystem,* ed. T. Moulik (New Delhi: Oxford University Press, 1988): 9–52.

98. Clarke, *Wood-stove Dissemination*; Wisner, *Power and Need.*

99. E. Cecelski, *Linking Energy with Survival* (Geneva: ILO, 1987).

100. K. Shellie-Dessert and G. Hosfield, "Implications of Genetic Variability for Dry Bean Cooking Time of Tropical Dry Bean Cultivars: Screening Method and Relevance to Firewood Use in Central Africa," *Ecology of Food and Nutrition,* 1990.

101. W. Ottichilo et al.,*Weathering the Storm: Climate Change and Investment in Kenya* (Nairobi: African Centre for Technology Studies, 1992).

102. B. Wisner, "Health of the Future/The Future of Health," in *Twenty-first Century Africa: Towards a New Vision of Self-Sustainable Development,* ed. A. Seidman and F. Anan (Trenton, N.J.: Africa World Press, 1992): 149–181.

103. Malaria resurgence is a particularly troubling problem. The Western medical community does not have an answer except to wait for a vaccine! Bradley (D. Bradley, "Malaria—Whence and Whither?" in *Malaria: Waiting for the Vaccine,* ed. G. Targett [New York: Wiley, 1991]: 18–22) has referred to the 1980s as a period of chaos from the point of view of malaria control. On the impact of development policies and of environmental disruption on health, see Lee (J. Lee, *The Environment, Public Health, and Human Ecology: Considerations for Economic Development* [Baltimore: Johns Hopkins University Press, 1985]), and Cooper Weil (D. Cooper Weil et al. *The Impact of Development Policies on Health: A Review of the Literature* [Geneva: WHO, 1990]). The negative impacts of development projects in AFrica, especially the hazards of large-scale water developments, have been documented for a long time (C. Hughes, and J. Hunter, "Disease and 'Development' in Tropical Africa." *Social Science and Medicine* 3 [1970]: 443–493; B. Wisner, "Health and the Geography of Wholeness," in *Geography of Contemporary Africa,* ed. G. Knight and J. Newman [Englewood Cliffs, N.J.: Prentice-Hall, 1976]). It is a scandal and great shame that in light of very clear, agreed-upon models for anticipating health problems (M. Birley, *Guidelines for Forecasting the Vector-Borne Disease Implications of Water Resource Development* (PEEM Guideline Series 2, Geneva: Joint WHO/FAO/UNEP/UNCHS Panel of Experts on Environmental Management for Vector Control [PEEM] 1989) and guidelines for provision of health safeguards (M. Tiffen, *Guidelines for the Incorporation of Health Safeguards into Irrigation Projects through Intersectoral Cooperation* (PEEM Guideline Series 1, Geneva: Joint WHO/FAO/UNEP/UNCHS Panel of Experts on Environmental Management for Vector Control, 1989) that dams are still built *without* safeguards and are *celebrated as successes* even when the surrounding population is sick with malaria and bilharzia (A. Ngaiza, "Mtera Dam" [in Panos Institute, dossier no. 13, 1987]).

104. A. Raikes, "Women's Health in East Africa," *Social Science and Medicine* 28, 5 (1989): 447–460; M. Turshen, "Gender and Health in Africa," in *Women and Health in Africa,* ed. M. Turshen (Trenton, N.J.: Africa World Press, 1991): 107–124.

105. P. O'Keefe, "Toxic Terrorism" *Review of African Political Economy* 42 (1988): 84–90.

106. A. Hartley, "U.N., Italy Probe Toxic Waste Dumping in Somalia," *Reuter News Reports,* 1992; United Nations Environment Program (UNEP) "Disposal of Hazardous Wastes in Somalia: Statement by UNEP Executive Director Dr.

Mostafa K. Tolba," UNEP Press Release, 9 September 1992 (Nairobi: UNEP).

107. Wisner, *Power and Need*, chap. 2.

108. Bass, *Camping*, 227–282.

109. D. Werner, and B. Bower, *Helping Health Workers Learn* (Palo Alto: The Hesperian Foundation, 1982).

110. C. MacCormack, "Human Ecology and Behaviour in Malaria Control in Tropical Africa," in *Applied Field Research in Malaria in Africa*, ed. World Health Organization (Geneva: WHO, 1984): 81–88.

111. B. Grundfest Schoepf et al., "Gender, Power, and Risk of AIDS in Zaire," in *Women and Health in Africa*, ed. M. Turshen (Trenton, N.J.: Africa World Press, 1991): 187–204.

112. The initials following titles are used in the subsequent suggested syllabus.

113. The Panos Institute may be contacted at 1405 King Street, Alexandria, VA, 22314.

114. Contacts in the United States are: Global Exchange, 2141 Mission Street, Rm. 202, San Francisco, CA, 94110; and IRED—North, 8319 Haddon Drive, Tokoma Park, Md., 20912.

115. K. Danaher, *Beyond Safaris: A Guide to Building People-to-People Ties with Africa* (Trenton, N.J.: Africa World Press, 1991).

116. Wisner, *Power and Need*, chap. 2. See also Cornia et al., *Adjustment with a Human Face*; B. Onimode, ed., *The IMF, the World Bank, and the African Debt*, 2 vols. (London: Zed, 1989); Wisner, "Health of the Future."

117. W. Rodney, *How Europe Underdeveloped Africa* (London: Bogle L'Ouverture Press, 1972).

118. P. Pradervand, *Listening to Africa: Developing Africa from the Grassroots* (New York: Praeger, 1989).

119. B. Wisner, D. Stea, and S. Kruks, "Participatory and Action Research Methods"; R. Chambers, A. Pacey, and L. Thrupp, eds., *Farmer First: Farmer Innovation and Agricultural Research* (London: Intermediate Technology Publications, 1989); D. Kalyalya et al. *Aid and Development in Southern Africa: A Participatory Learning Process* (Trenton, N.J.: Africa World Press, 1988).

120. H. Longino and E. Hammonds, "Conflicts and Tensions in the Feminist Study of Gender and Science," in *Conflicts in Feminism*, ed. M. Hirsch and E. Keller (New York: Routledge, 1990): 164–183; Harding, *Science Question*.

121. T. Kuhn, *The Structure of Scientific Revolutions*, 2nd ed. (Chicago: University of Chicago, 1970).

122. E. Boulding, *Building a Global Civic Culture* (Syracuse, N.Y.: Syracuse University Press, 1988).

123. P. Feyerabend, *Against Metho* (London: Verso, 1975).

124. D. Orr, *Ecological Literacy: Education and the Transition to a Postmodern World* (Albany: State University of New York Press, 1992): 131.

125. If these stereotypes seem exaggerated, consider French geographer Pierre Gourou's negative assessment:

> We who live in temperate lands find it difficult to realize how baleful Nature can be to man or to understand that in unreclaimed regions water may swarm with dangerous germs, myriads of blood-sucking insects may inject deadly microbes into the human body and the very soil may be harmful to the touch.

126. A. Mabogunje, *The Development Process: A Spatial Perspective* (New York: Holmes and Meier, 1981); Odhiambo, et al. *Hope Born Out of Despair*; C. Achebe et al. *Beyond Hunger in Africa: Conventional Wisdom and an African*

Vision (Nairobi and London: Heinemann Kenya and James Currey, 1990); F. Cheru, *The Silent Revolution in Africa* (London: Zed, 1989).

127. C. Achebe, *Anthills of the Savannah* (New York: Anchor, 1987).

128. Achebe, *Anthills*, 206–209.

12

Science from Africa and Science About Africa: Comments on Ben Wisner

Celia Nyamweru

In commenting on Ben Wisner's detailed and stimulating chapter, it is necessary to bear in mind our central objective: to contribute to the teaching of African studies at the undergraduate level in North American universities. After his initial differentiation between science *in, about,* and *from* Africa, Wisner stresses the importance we should give to the last of these three, vernacular or popular science *from* Africa, in our teaching of North American college students. I am far from rejecting this point of view. I would, however, like to point out the need to preserve a more balanced picture of African science in our teaching. We need to make our North American students aware that Western science *is present in Africa,* as part of the intellectual apparatus of many Africans. We should make our students aware of the element of contrast that is so much a part of all African society: within one family and generation, there may be individuals who have lived out their lives in an essentially traditional, indigenous context and others who have become fully incorporated into the global intellectual community.

It is too easy, in undergraduate teaching about Africa, to overconcentrate on the so-called primitive and the exotic, especially in view of the many films about Africa that focus on the "disappearing worlds" of pastoral and hunter-gatherer groups. We do not easily find films about the daily life of a young African who works as a laboratory technician or a land-surveyor—or indeed as a university physics professor. In the introductory slide presentations to a course I teach on Kenya, I show several slides of village life (cultivators and pastoralists, women collecting water and firewood); but I also show a slide of a weather-station observer (who, incidentally, is a woman) photographed as she takes a temperature reading, and one of a land-surveyor at work with a transit. I believe it is necessary for our students to recognize that Africa—for better or for worse—has access to a very wide range of modern science and technology, and that the expertise and control of this science and technology is to a considerable extent in the hands of indigenous Africans. Given the cultural baggage that many of our students bring to class, it is perhaps salutory for them to learn that there are Africans living and working in Africa who have higher scientific qualifications and technical skills than they (our students) may ever achieve.

Wisner also gives little attention to science *about* or *for* Africa. Here, again, I would like to raise a mild caveat. North American students need to understand the physical realities of the African continent, and these physical realities must be expressed in scientific terms—through geology, soil-science, ecology, hydrology, climatology, and the like. Unfortunately, in most U.S. universities these subjects tend to be separated (in terms of department and program structure) from the social sciences and humanities, which provide African studies programs with the majority of their students and courses. Trained as a physical geographer, I believe that any consideration of a region, a nation, or an ethnic group must begin with an evaluation of natural resources and environmental constraints. I have learned over the years, however, that such a "scientific" explanation of the physical realities underlying African life is not much appreciated by the majority of my students, who heave an audible sigh of relief when we move away from the boring stuff to "the real people" of Africa. Yet, unless they have some understanding of the physical realities of the African environment, how can we expect our students to appreciate the challenges facing the continent's inhabitants? To teach regional case studies of, say, a water conservation project is a superficial exercise unless the students appreciate the physical as well as socioeconomic realities underlying the degradation of ecosystems. We need to continue to teach science *about* Africa, and we should not be unduly concerned that, of necessity, we must do this according to Western methods and paradigms.

This, indeed, will provide the foundation for what, according to Wisner, is the core of teaching African science: the teaching of science *from* Africa. I agree that we need to convey to our students an understanding of and respect for indigenous knowledge-systems. We must show these knowledge-systems as science and not as folklore, countering the prevalent mindset under which, as Wisner points out, "the discussion of weather, seed varieties, or the behavior of insects by rural people . . . is not seen as real science." But let us have our students set the indigenous African perceptions side by side with the perceptions of Western science; which returns me to the point made above—that of the need for our students to understand the Western interpretation of the African environment, which will provide the necessary comparison with the indigenous knowledge-systems.

Although we should show the richness and relevance of indigenous knowledge-systems, we must not exaggerate their importance, especially to current development strategies in much of Africa. Indigenous knowledge-systems have provided a rich and rewarding research frontier for generations of expatriate graduate students, but they have not generally received adequate respect in Africa itself. I remember visiting a highly respected and successful traditional herbalist in Meru District, Kenya. He told me that during the colonial era he and his colleagues had been called to attend patients at the King George VI Hospital for Africans: this had not continued after independence, when the hospital became the Kenyatta National Hospital. Aklilu Lemma, the Ethiopian scientist responsible for drawing the attention of the world scientific community to the molluscicidal properties of the endod plant (*Phytolacca dodecandra*), had this to say in an American Association for the Advancement of Science publication: "Even our own government officials, who rely on foreign assistance and external advice, may be unduly influenced concerning local research."[1] Lemma goes on to recommend the training of African scientists through the integrated application of traditional and modern technologies.

Wisner rightly stresses that the main problem for ordinary Africans is survival, and that science in Africa must address itself to the daily problems of African lives in "the back streets and cattle *bomas*." But I do not think we as teachers should present an image of Africa that is exclusively focused on the struggle for survival; nor should we limit all African scientific research to the application of basic principles originally derived elsewhere. Here I think it is appropriate to quote from the words of two distinguished African scholars: Bede Okigbo, director of the United Nations University Programme on Natural Resources in Africa, draws attention to "the disappointing fact that African universities conduct mostly applied research, and very little basic research";[2] and Thomas Odhiambo, director of the International Center of Insect Physiology and Ecology in Nairobi, points out that

> We scientists are supposed to have a keen sense of awe and wonder at the rich phenomenological heritage of nature. How to have a true understanding of natural phenomena, and to explain their causal relationships, is a matter that concerns all scientists of whatever persuasion and from whatever geographical zone.[3]

Odhiambo stresses the overwhelming richness of Africa's plant and animal life and the need for more work on these topics, especially in view of the increasing rate of extinctions brought about by human disruption of the environment. North American students show strong interest in studies relating to animal behavior, extinctions, and human evolution, and these topics are likely to be an important part of African studies courses for many years to come. In these areas, basic research and fieldwork of global significance continue to be carried out in Africa. I do not think that anyone would limit such research to non-African scholars, nor restrict African researchers to applied topics. On the contrary, many of us have been concerned that the great names in African ecology, animal behavior, and paleoanthropology have for too long been those of non-Africans, and it is satisfying now to see that an increasing number of young African scientists are entering these fields. For example, recently Kadzo Kangwana, a Kenyan woman, has been doing research on elephant behavior in Amboseli National Reserve; and other young Kenyan scholars are looking into the interaction of humans and wild animals, and the involvement of local communities in decision-making about wild-animal resources.

This brings me to my final point. I would venture to submit that many North American college courses about Africa may still rely on reading lists containing a very small proportion of works by African authors. I would go further and say that, in the social sciences and humanities, this imbalance may be less than it is in the biological and earth sciences. I would be far from suggesting that only Africans can produce valuable writings about Africa, but reading lists heavily loaded with non-African names must surely send a not-so-subliminal message to our North American students. Ben Wisner's chapter is exceptional: he identifies a wide range of sources by African scholars. Let us hope that the financial stresses facing many African universities and research institutions do not unduly slow the progress of research by African scholars, in all fields, and that the results of this research continue to be made available to the academic community in all parts of the world.

NOTES

1. Quoted in *Science in Africa; Achievements and Prospects* (Washington, D.C.: AAAS, 1991): 33–34.
2. Ibid.: 87.
3. Ibid.: 7.

13

Information Dynamics for African Studies: Resources in Libraries and Beyond

Gretchen Walsh

The library resources available to students and faculty for curriculum and research are as important a factor in the success of an undergraduate program in African studies as they are in the success of a graduate program. When the undergraduate program is an adjunct of a graduate program and shares access to a research-level library collection, the main concern of faculty and library staff is that students learn to use these resources to the best advantage. When the library available to students taking courses related to Africa is basically an undergraduate collection, the primary concern is one of selection. What materials are essential to support class assignments? What materials will capture students' imaginations and make Africa a reality for them?

The interplay of several factors affects the strength and utility of a library collection supporting the study of Africa: the budget allocation; the people who make decisions concerning the development of the collection; the materials that can be acquired; and access to materials and information outside the library. The dynamics of this interplay and the strategies that can be employed to assure information for the study of Africa is the focus of this chapter.

Libraries are clearly an essential part of the education process. One is likely to find some laudatory description of the library in college or university brochures, and all academic libraries describe their mission as supporting the curriculum and the research of students and faculty. Despite their value, however, because it is hard to quantify the benefit they give for money spent, libraries often suffer more deeply than other units of the university when budgets are cut. Most academic libraries have experienced severe financial constraints for the past five years. A combination of factors—the demographic trough following the baby boom, the small pool of traditional college-age students, and the overall recession—has reduced both tuition revenues and income from endowments and grants. For libraries, this situation is exacerbated by continuing high rates of inflation for books and journals, combined with the effect of a weak dollar causing foreign publications to cost even more. Also driving up library costs are automation of library functions and the need to supply information in new electronic formats.

In this situation, there is considerable competition for allocation of the library budget among different subjects. The sciences must cope with publication costs far higher than those of the social sciences and humanities. By and large, however, the science departments bring in more grants than the social sciences and humanities, and are thus usually more favored in the budget division.

In times of budget constraints, library staff must try to get the greatest benefit from each purchase. This can result in more concentration on the generalist, mainstream materials—those likely to be used by large numbers of students. Fields with low enrollments, and very specialized or exotic materials likely to be used by only a few students, tend to be given shorter shrift.

An African studies program of whatever stature, whether it is well-established or fledgling, whether it has established a broad range of courses or offers only a few each year, can find it difficult in this environment to persuade the library to acquire the materials that the faculty deem necessary for meaningful teaching and student research. The current budget situation means that faculty cannot assume that the library will automatically acquire key publications, or even that faculty suggestions can always be acted upon favorably. However, as gloomy as the situation is, African studies programs can work successfully with library staff to develop a collection that supports curriculum and student research.

The partnership of an academic program and the library can take many forms, but the essential element is the idea of partnership itself. Emphasizing this point may be preaching to the converted, since in my experience Africanists are virtually universally cooperative with librarians and library programs. Nevertheless, strategies for effective partnership can always benefit from review.

An adversarial relationship in the matter of fund allocation is counterproductive, but the African studies program can and should communicate clearly to the library administration the needs of its students in terms of library resources. The program should also make a concerted effort to include provision for additional library resources in grant proposals, particularly if those proposals are for new branches of curriculum or research projects in areas for which the library has not been collecting. By and large, resources for the collection of materials should go to the library and not go into the development of departmental reading rooms. The vision of a student lounge stocked with key journals and essential, "core" readings is beguiling; however, although a student lounge provides the setting for fruitful discussion, departmental libraries established in them are seldom cost-effective. It is better, in the long run, to build the collection in the main library.

It is important to establish a rapport with the library staff responsible for selecting materials for the program. This may include some involvement in the design of that process. Because African studies is interdisciplinary, responsibility for collection development may be shared by several librarians, each selecting materials for an academic discipline. This is not the optimal arrangement. Better coverage and more coherent collection strategies are possible if one selector oversees development and management for the African studies collection. One selector implies one budget fund, which can present difficulties when the arrangement is first introduced. The money may have to come from other subject funds, such as anthropology, political science, history, economics, and/or other disciplines forming the core of the African studies curriculum. Setting this initial budget figure can be crucial, since it is the baseline for all future budget negotiations.

The Budget

What is a reasonable figure? That depends on the purpose of the collection; primarily, on whether the emphasis is on curriculum or research, and what level of research is to be supported. Among the major Africana research collections, budgets range from around $70,000 to $200,000 per year. The lower the budget, the more tailored the collection has to be to current needs. Only the few libraries with high budgets can continue to pursue the ideal, mythical as it is, of collecting "everything." Let us assume library support of an undergraduate program of African studies to be between $5,000 and $10,000. At this level, a respectable undergraduate collection can be built and maintained, particularly if certain basics are already in the collection and the subject disciplines included in the African studies program are also relatively strong and well maintained in the library collection.

If the person responsible for building and maintaining the African studies collection has a strong background in African studies, selection of materials presents few problems. This serendipitous situation is unlikely, so the faculty should be ready to work collegially with the librarian to build the collection. This should include not only lists of books to buy, but participation of the librarian in departmental meetings, particularly those planning curriculum or projects in new areas where the library may not have resources to meet new demands. Library staff should be sent notices of lectures and events, and included in social occasions. In other words, the librarian should be welcomed as part of the African studies campus community and given every opportunity to see the program in action, the better to understand its library resource needs.

Africana Librarian Council

The African Studies Association's Africana Librarians Council (ALC) can be useful to the librarian. The ALC meets during the fall African Studies Association (ASA) meeting and also has a spring meeting of its own, usually at the campus of one of the member librarians. They discuss and act on concerns of acquisitions, bibliography, cataloging, and other issues affecting Africana librarianship. While the spring meetings provide more time for formal and informal discussion, the book exhibits at the fall meeting are particularly useful for librarians and there may be panels of interest as well. If feasible, departmental funding for travel to an ASA meeting can be money well spent. The librarian may or may not want to add ASA membership to her other professional organizations, but an institutional membership in ASA will bring the *ASA News*, which carries considerable bibliographic and other useful information. The *Africana Libraries Newsletter* (ALN) published by the Africana Librarians Council is free of charge. It provides bibliographic information and other news focused on libraries.

The membership of ALC is comprised mainly of librarians from research libraries and meetings, and articles in ALN tend to focus on matters and concerns of research libraries. This may be tangential to the concerns of undergraduate libraries. The agenda of the ALC is shaped by its members, so increased attendance of librarians from nonspecialist libraries and communication of their interests to the membership could broaden the focus of ALC discussions and the content of ALN. Another group within ASA might be able to offer useful advice and materials. The Outreach Council is a group that concentrates on the need to bring awareness of Africa to the community at large. Emphasis has tended to be on school levels K through 12, but the council's work in reviewing and evaluating text and trade books, films, and other audiovisual materials, as well as developing curricula and doing workshops with teachers, librarians, journalists, and others make them a good group to contact.

For Africana librarians, in addition to attending ASA meetings, it can be fruitful to take part in regional African studies organizations, or symposia and conferences. Undergraduate libraries have particular concerns, and a panel or working group on libraries and library resources in a local or regional African studies organization may be particularly effective in helping librarians formulate strategies for building the collection and meeting the needs of students and faculty. If the African studies program is formally or informally part of networks of other undergraduate African studies programs, librarians can use those networks for information sharing.

Librarians are likely to be members of the American Library Association (ALA). However, the ALA has no group that focuses on African studies, or area studies in general, for undergraduate collections. The Asian and African section of the Association of College and Research Librarians (a subgroup of ALA) concentrates on material from, rather than about, Asia and Africa, but that would be the group to contact for possible panels or roundtables on collection development for those areas in undergraduate libraries.

Information on Africa

Let us assume the campus partnership is established: the African studies faculty and librarian, working as a team, have established a reasonable budget and know what the information needs of students and faculty will be, from the syllabi of the courses offered, term paper assignments, and so on. The questions now are: What is out there for the library to acquire? How can the librarian become aware of it? How can that material be evaluated; that is, will it fit the need of students and faculty that have been defined?

There is no lack of information published about Africa.[1] The Library of Congress's *U.S. Imprints on Sub-Saharan Africa: A Guide to Publications Cataloged at the Library of Congress*, volume 6/7, 1990/91, lists 1,648 monograph titles published between 1988 and 1991, mostly 1990 or 1991. (The 1988–1989 entries comprise those left out of the volumes for those previous years.) This is not a complete list of everything published on Africa in the United States, but it is a good indication of the volume and variety of publications on Africa.

It is beyond the scope of this chapter to explore the political economy of publishing, but it is important to note that the choices publishers make can cause difficulties for librarians trying to tailor a collection to specific curriculum needs. Publishers—university presses as well as trade houses—want sales at least big enough to break even. Thus, they tend to publish titles with potentially broad appeal. This has meant, for instance, more books on South Africa, or very broad reviews of popular topics such as women's or environmental issues, and fewer intensive studies of less well-known areas or issues. Some information can be hard to find in published form.

No African studies collection, even a modestly sized undergraduate collection, should be limited to U.S. imprints on Africa. It is essential that students realize, not just from lectures but subliminally from example, that Africa is not just a continent to be studied, that it has citizens who study both themselves and the rest of the world. African publications—scholarship, fiction, news analysis—should share shelf space with U.S. or European books. There are book shortages in Africa, and the publishing industry there suffers from severe problems. Nevertheless, there is a vigorous and exciting publishing scene, particularly in Nigeria, Kenya, and Senegal, and many other countries produce publications worthy of note. The important thing is to give students a substantial taste of information published in Africa by Africans, and to incorporate African publications into the working collection for undergraduates.

With so many publications, both U.S. and African, available, some criteria for selection are essential. Development of the collection will be based largely on the topics needed by the students, but assessment of the quality of information and scholarship is also needed. The periodical *Choice* offers reviews of a considerable number of books about Africa, most of them U.S. imprints but not all: it includes books published in Africa if they are distributed in the United States. This publication is favored by libraries because of the currency of its reviews. Most of the academic journals for African studies carry significant numbers of book reviews, although these often appear months or years after the book has been published.

For books published in Africa, the reviews in *African Book Publishing Record (ABPR)* provide a good basis for selection. It also provides a printout of recent publications. Other sources of lists with description and some subject information include *Joint Acquisitions List of Africana*, published by Northwestern University's Africana library, and *Accessions List Eastern Africa*, published by the Library of Congress Nairobi Field Office. The winners of the Noma award, presented each year for books of excellence published in Africa on any topic, are listed in *ABPR*. Winners of this award, or recipients of honorable mentions, should be considered "musts" if their subjects are appropriate to the collection.

Obtaining books from Africa can be difficult, but several firms make it possible for any library, specialist or general, to add African publications to their collections. The African Books Collective (ABC), a cooperative of Anglophone African publishers, has a high-quality line of scholarly works, fiction, and children's books. They provide excellent service from their office in Oxford, England. A good source for those publications not supplied by ABC is African Imprint Library Services (AILS), a U.S. importer of books from Africa and the Caribbean. AILS also offers an approval service that can be tailored to fit specific needs, as well as filling firm orders from their lists. Some African publishers have co-publishing or distribution arrangements with U.S. or British publishers, from whose catalogues African books can be ordered.

The purpose of this chapter is to explore strategies rather than to recommend books, but it will be useful to look at some specific titles to build a hypothetical model collection based on the budget range of $5,000 to $10,000. The cornerstone of any collection is its reference works. I have often said—only partially in jest—that I could run a successful African studies library with a few key reference works, a telephone, and a photocopy machine. Having become more technologically aware, I would change that now to a PC with a modem and printer. The reference works I consider essential are:

Africa South of the Sahara. (London: Europa). Annual. About $350 per year. This work contains essays for each country on geography, recent history, and economic conditions. It provides, for each country, a directory, a compilation of statistics, and a select bibliography. Introductory chapters cover earlier history and regional organizations. The statistical information is included in the *Europa Yearbook*, but the essays justify a separate purchase. North African countries appear in the same publisher's annual *Middle East and North Africa.*

Africa Contemporary Record. (New York: Africana). Annual. $375 per year. Since 1968, Colin Legum and staff have compiled essays for each country of Africa, describing events of the reporting year—political, economic, cultural/social. One section provides commentaries on contemporary issues and foreign relations, another reprints key documents. The series is currently behind schedule—1988–1989 appeared in 1992. Legum has retired and Marion Doro is now the editor. It now appears that the series will continue. If it does, it is invaluable, especially if it gets back up to date. Acquiring the back run would be worthwhile, although expensive.

Encyclopedia of the Third World. (New York: Facts on File). Fourth edition, 1992, $225. Good country maps and general information. Combines well with *Africa South of the Sahara* for most preliminary work and students' short papers.

Atlas of Africa. (New York: Free Press, 1973). The front section contains continental maps illustrating climate, vegetation, geological formations, and political history, among other topics. Two maps are provided for each country—physical features on one; natural resources, industries, and other information on the other. This splendid work has not been revised for over twenty years, so country and place names are dated, as are some boundaries and colonial relationships. Despite this, it is an essential atlas. However, although still in print recently, it is not in the current *Books in Print.* Two historical atlases complement *Atlas of Africa*, and each other. These are *Historical Atlas of Africa*, edited by J. F. Ade Ajayi and Michael Crowder (Cambridge, New York: Cambridge University Press, 1985), $95; and J. D. Fage, *An Atlas of African History* (New York: Africana Publishing, 1978), $45.

These are the basics. There are also several monographic series that are useful for either the reference collection or the bookstacks. The *Country Study* series, formerly called *Area Handbooks*, were originally written by the Department of Defense and are now done by the Library of

Congress. They provide an excellent array of information, and are relatively inexpensive, in the $15–$25 range. Not all countries are covered. The *Historical Dictionary* series published by Scarecrow Press combines historical information in a useful dictionary format with extensive bibliographies. Again, not all countries are covered, and some volumes are outdated. Revised editions are available or planned, in the $25-$30 range. A third series worth having is the *World Bibliographical Series* published by ABC Clio. Not all countries are covered. Prices vary widely, in the $40-$80 range.

Bibliographies. Bibliographies should be a major part of any reference collection. Guides for selection beyond the standard guides, such as Sheehy's *Guide to Reference Books* and Balay's 1992 update, include Scheven's *Bibliography of Bibliographies for African Studies* and the annual list of Africana reference works which appears in *African Book Publishing Record*. There has been considerable, well-deserved concern on the part of Africana librarians over the declining quality of reference books, particularly bibliographies. Partly because libraries are consistent markets for bibliographies and partly because bibliographies are the stepchildren of scholarly writing, there are few established standards. Those that exist are often ignored. Bad reference books will sometimes be recommended because they are the only ones available, or because the reviewer does not look beyond what the author says the book provides. For instance, in Balay's 1992 supplement to Sheehy, I found two titles recommended that I had reviewed very critically because of their inaccuracy and general poor quality, and another that had been used as a prime example of bad bibliography in David Henige's articles critiquing current standards of bibliography writing.

Looking at the budget, it is important to note that two of these key reference works are annuals and that together they cost more than $700 per year. That is 15 to 20 percent of our hypothesized Africana budget, for just two volumes. The others I mentioned add up to nearly $500, not counting a selection of titles from the several series cited.

Journals. The rest of the budget could be quickly spent on a few journals. Selection of journals and other serials should precede consideration of monographic series since the serial commitment is ongoing and will continue year after year. In the past, the nature of serials gave them an inertial weight in libraries—they were continued because they had been started, and because the collection already had *x* number of volumes in the collection. The rising costs of serials have necessitated cutting serial titles—indeed, without reduction of serials there might not be any money at all for monographs. Thus, the inertia these days is against the addition of new serial titles. The African section of Katz's *Magazines for Libraries* includes sixty-five titles, selected for their general utility. The number of journals dealing with Africa is much larger: major African studies libraries have between five hundred and a thousand or more journal subscriptions.

The shape of the journals collection will depend a great deal on how it is to be used. It is best to have a balance of several types. One group would cover current events, news, and raw data, both general and geographically specific. This group would include titles such as *Africa Report*, $34; *New African*, $70; and *Africa News*, $48. Economist Intelligence Unit *Country Reports* and *Country Profiles* are very expensive (for Africa the costs are over $4,000 even with an educational institution discount), but these are nevertheless excellent sources of economic and political information. The reports are quarterly and the profiles annual. A subscription to the reports includes the annual profiles. The profiles also seem to be sold separately. Also in the raw-data grouping are *AED/African Economic Digest*, $330; and *Africa Research Bulletin*, both the economic, financial, and technical series; and the political, social, and cultural series —$410 for both (also available separately).

A second area to cover is the scholarly—general and specific to either discipline or geographic area. Some titles include: *Africa*, $120; *Journal of African History*, $91; *International Journal of African Historical Studies*, $65; *Journal of Modern African Studies*, $113; *African Affairs*, $90; and *Journal of Southern African Studies*, $94.

Another grouping is special interest and activist journals. These would be selected to tailor the collection to the specialities of the program. Titles in this category might include any of the many anti-apartheid journals and newsletters, dissident newsletters, and journals produced by immigrant and refugee groups. Special interest is not limited to politics, of course. Many UN publications, such as *Desertification Control, Ceres,* and *Prospects,* offer low-cost information of considerable interest in the fields of environment, agriculture, and education.

Among the journals in the collection should be at least some representative titles published in Africa. The task of obtaining serials from Africa has the reputation of being extremely difficult, but in many cases, particularly for those titles most appropriate for undergraduate collections, subscriptions can be quite straightforward. In Boston University's experience, the major serials agent, Faxon, can supply many titles. These include *Weekly Review*, $160, a Kenyan newsmagazine; and *Afrique Developpement/African Development*, $35, published by CODESRIA. Among publications that have proved reliable on direct subscription are *Newswatch*, $104, a Nigerian newsmagazine; and *Work in Progress*, approximately $50, a news source from South Africa. Of particular interest to college students would be *Wits Student*, a student paper from the University of the Witswatersrand, $49.

Subscriptions to African newspapers should be considered, particularly for countries where Study Abroad programs exist. The costs of subscriptions vary enormously, from over $900 for the *Daily Times* of Nigeria, through $400 for the *Daily News* from Tanzania, to $18 for *Voz di Povo* from Cape Verde. Subscriptions can be handled in a number of ways. Of Boston University's fifteen subscriptions, Faxon handles most; a local agent supplies the *Daily Times*, and the Library of Congress' Nairobi Field Office supplies two papers from Kenya; AILS supplies a paper from Uganda and has in the past supplied two from Zaire; and a few other subscriptions are arranged directly with the publishers.

More About the Budget

Even these few titles, offered only as examples and not as a core collection of essential journals, would consume a large portion of the budget; in fact, they would wipe it out if the EIU *Country Reports* and *Profiles* are included. There are far more good journals than most libraries can acquire. No single selection strategy can be recommended: this is a matter for faculty and library to work out, including what percentage of the budget to spend on serials. Taking the arbitrary, but not uncommon, level of 50 percent for serials, and assuming that the two annual reference works are purchased, our hypothetical collection has from $2,100 to $4,600 to spend on journals and the same amount for books. This means perhaps twenty to forty journal titles in the $50 to $100 range, and fifty to a hundred books per year. If the library is starting from scratch, with no material on Africa already in the collection, a grant or other special funding may be in order to amass the core collection.

Building a Collection

Beginning an African studies collection can be difficult. There are few guides for core collections. One is *Africa South of the Sahara: A Bibliography for Undergraduate Libraries*, which was published in 1971 and is quite outdated. Many of the titles recommended are likely to be out of print. The African titles in *Books for College Libraries* provide some guidance. More to the point is Nancy Schmidt's "Checklist for Updating Holdings on Africa in Community College Libraries, 1988 update," *ASA News* vol. 22, no. 1 (January/March 1989): 45–49. Schmidt's guide is especially useful since it is designed specifically for those libraries selecting only a few African titles per year, rather than those that are striving to cover all of Africa at a research level. Even these guides are dated: a lot has been published since 1988. *African Book Publishing Record* carries each year a checklist of reference works and bibliographies, compiled by members of the African Studies Association's Africana Librarians Council. As noted earlier, more information on library materials on and from Africa appears in *Africana Libraries Newsletter* and *ASA News*.

All guides for building library collections are subjective, and for African studies the possibilities for idiosyncrasy seem especially pronounced. To build a successful collection, selection is always going to be a series of decisions based on the specific needs of students within the program, the courses offered, and the term papers and other research assigned. The way to judge if the selection is on the right track is to measure how much the collection is used and how many research questions can and cannot be answered by the sources within the collection. There are a number of ways of measuring use and utility of a collection, but the results from the standard approaches are not always valid for African studies. The kinds of survey techniques described in library literature are usually time-consuming, and most libraries depend on the subjective, day-to-day observations of library staff to assess library use and user satisfaction.

Indexes. Assessing use of African studies materials is a challenging task because of the way library research has changed and developed in the last few decades. Access to information has become increasingly automated. Only a few decades ago, paper indexes were the state of the art, making research easier by compiling references from hundreds of journals to articles on broad subject areas such as biology, psychology, and so forth, and providing access through a controlled vocabulary of index terms. Over the past two decades, these paper indexes were put into electronic databases accessible through major vendors, reaching researchers for the most part through searches conducted by librarians. More recently, the trend has been to put these databases on CD ROM, which is still available mainly through libraries, but searchable by the researchers themselves. CD ROM technology also makes full text accessible and searchable. Another recent approach is the Table of Contents index services. These computerized databases are often mounted as a choice on online catalogs and can be searched for keywords in the titles of articles. While not as fully indexed as other databases, which provide access to words in the abstract as well as the descriptors, this system gives wide access to a large number of journals. Undergraduates come to college increasingly computer literate, having learned in high school how to use the electronic databases available to them, and they expect these services to be available for all college research.

While these developments make research much faster and easier (it remains to be determined if the results of research show a similar improvement in quality), it also sets the stage for the mistaken assumption that the electronic databases cover everything there is to know, or that what is available electronically is somehow better than what might be found through more traditional strategies. These assumptions bode ill for African studies research projects.

Africa has never been well served in indexes. There are a few indexes or serial bibliographies that cover Africa: *Africa Bibliography*, *International*

African Bibliography, Current Bibliography on African Affairs, and *Current Contents Africa* (a compilation of tables of contents of journals rather than an index). These tend to cover mostly Africanist journals, rather than combing more general journals for the occasional African article, and are by no means complete, even for the specialized literature. Recent studies have shown that there is surprisingly little overlap among them. None of these is available electronically. Of the major, subject-based databases, none covers Africa adequately for research. Although such databases as ERIC, Psych Abstracts, PAIS, and so on do yield material on Africa, one can never assume that one has found all there is to be found simply by using those indexes because the number of Africanist journals included is always relatively small. The increasingly popular Table of Contents services cover only the most widely used journals. While this number may be large (UnCover, for instance, includes 10,000 titles), there are seldom more than a dozen African titles.

The real problem is that many of the best journals that should be in the collection are not indexed reliably and often not indexed at all. In particular, few African journals are indexed. An exception is the service offered by the Library of Congress Nairobi Office, *Quarterly Index to Periodical Literature, Eastern and Southern Africa.* For the rest of Africa, indexing is sparse indeed. A journal indexing Nigerian periodicals produced one volume, then ceased. This means that, in order to research Nigerian political events using the Nigerian newsmagazine *Newswatch,* the student must plow through volume after volume of the original paper copies to find articles pertaining to his topic, and this can proceed only after he has identified that journal as the most likely source for the information sought.

Collection development for African studies is, then, quite intimately bound with bibliographic instruction. As much as can be afforded, the specialized indexes and indexes should be part of the collection, even though this inevitably means reducing the number of journals that contain the articles cited. The choice must be made as to whether to have resources themselves in the collection, or tools that provide information about resources that might then be borrowed or copied elsewhere. To some extent materials, particularly journal titles, should be selected because they are indexed, but important journal titles that are not indexed should not be left out. Students must be taught to depend less on electronic aids for African studies research and to learn to wade through the material. In-house guides and bibliographies are very important tools. The creation of these might even be set as a class exercise so that successive generations of students would both contribute to the expanding facilities and have the use of them.

Shelf Room for Conflicting Views

My own philosophy of collecting Africana is to put into the collection examples of many approaches to the important issues in African nations. The most obvious example is apartheid in South Africa. In the worst days, the South African government was particularly generous to college and school libraries in the United States in terms of books and magazines. These handsome, well-executed items of course portrayed South Africa as the most reasonable and happy of countries. Since these materials were free and apparently of high quality, it was a matter of concern to many Africanists that these might be the only books on Africa in some libraries. Some activists advocated outright rejection. A better course would have been also to acquire material from the African National Congress and as many of the other anti-apartheid groups as possible. Some publications of extreme right-wing white groups should also have a place on the shelves.

South Africa is not the only area with conflicting ideologies and agendas in Africa. There is considerable heat between the Kenyan government and dissidents, civil war in Liberia, and political strife in Cameroon, to name only a few areas. If publications of the various sides can be obtained—either through merchants or faculty/students traveling in the area, they should be added to the collection. (I would not, however, advise asking anyone, ahead of time, to pick up such materials. In some countries, possession of controversial literature can have serious consequences.) Often, organizations of Africans living in the United States will produce newsletters or broadsides on issues back home. This kind of material can really get students excited about doing research. It is also the kind of material that requires that students are grounded in critical reading. Teaching about this may be done in the classroom, but it should also be part of the bibliographic instruction process.

Remote Access

When the collection has been built as wisely as possible to the extent of the budget, when all feasible indexes and aids to access have been purchased or developed, when the students (and faculty) know how to use the collection and extract the last drop of information from it, how can one deal with the inevitability that some research projects cannot be completed satisfactorily with the resources available in the library? Interlibrary loan has always made materials from other libraries available; and many of the Table of Contents services provide fee-based document delivery. There is also the Cooperative Africana Microforms Project, located at the Center for Research Libraries in Chicago—a large collection of primary research materials on microfilm that can be borrowed by members.

Increasingly, library catalogs (both nationwide and internationally) are computerized and can be accessed from remote locations. This can be done from a PC with a modem, but access to an Internet connection lowers the cost considerably. The Internet is a network of computer networks with, as backbone, the federally funded NSFnet. Through standardized protocols of computer communication, an Internet connection allows the user to telnet to a distant computer, such as a library's online catalog, login, and use it as if at its keyboard. Many libraries have set up gateways so that this is possible from the terminals of the library catalog. Directories of Internet addresses for library catalogs have been compiled by Billy Barron and Art St. George and are available electronically. Accessing the library catalog directly enables the student to locate specific books and get the necessary identifying information for interlibrary loan. Some libraries have additional aids to access mounted on the catalog, and some have files of uncataloged materials.

An example of the utility of this kind of long-distance access is provided by a visiting researcher we had at Boston University last year. A professor called from Kent State University in Ohio to determine our library hours. He had used the Boston University catalog from a terminal at Kent State, printing out items he wanted to look at. He arrived the next morning, having driven through the night, armed with a thick printout and accompanied by several family members. They fanned out through the library, gathering books and journals from the stacks. The professor skimmed through them, tagging pages for copying. By 5 P.M. they were packing up reams of photocopies, having used their eight hours in our library to the maximum advantage.

Other resources available on the Internet include databases, discussion groups, and news services. Internet connections are possible to many countries in Africa, although they are not as widespread as they are here and are much more expensive on the African side. The kind of carefree and sometimes frivolous use of electronic communication enjoyed in the United States could cost African colleagues a great deal of money.

The information available on Internet is vast, but it is also confusingly arranged. Some technologies provide tools for exploring. One is Gopher, which searches directories of files; another is Wide Area Information Server (WAIS), which finds keywords in the files themselves. It is not a user-friendly system, largely because it is rapidly growing and completely idiosyncratic. The availability of all this information electronically—while it is a very interesting world of information to be explored—raises questions of copyright and ownership, as well as very serious questions of credibility and validity.

The dynamics of information for African studies are complex. Considerable effort must go into providing the environment in which students can learn about Africa. Faculty and librarians working together can overcome the vicissitudes of budgets, the problems of acquisitions, and the inadequacy of indexes to create an educational environment in which Africa will become real for students.

NOTES

1. For the convenience of readers, this note gives a consolidated list of the books and journals mentioned in this chapter. There is also a list of addresses that will be of use in obtaining materials on Africa.

Accessions List, Eastern Africa. Nairobi, Kenya: Library of Congress Office, 1971–.

Africa Bibliography. Manchester, Eng.; Dover, N.H.: Manchester University Press, 1984-1989 (annual). Edinburgh, Scotland: University of Edinburgh Press, 1990–.

Africa South of the Sahara: a Bibliography for Undergraduate Libraries by Peter Duignan and others. Williamsport, Pa.: Bro-Dart, 1971. Foreign Area Materials Center (University of the State of New York), Occasional Publication no. 12.

African Book Publishing Record. Oxford, Eng.: Hans Zell, 1975–

Books for College Libraries: A Core Collection of 50,000 Titles. 3rd ed. Chicago: American Library Association, 1988.

Choice. Middletown, Conn.: Association of College and Research Libraries, 1964–.

Current Bibliography on African Affairs. Farmingdale, N.Y.: Baywood Pub. 1962–.

Current Contents Africa. Oxford, Eng.: Hans Zell, 1978–.

Guide to Reference Books, 10th edition. Edited by Eugene P. Sheehy. Chicago: American Library Association, 1986.

Guide to Reference Books, covering materials from 1985 to 1990. Supplement to the 10th edition, ed. Robert Balay. Chicago: American Library Association, 1992.

International African Bibliography. London: Mansell, 1971–.

Joint Acquisitions List of Africana. Evanston, Ill.: Melville J. Herskovits Library of African Studies, 1962–.

Magazines for College Libraries, 7th edition. Bill Katz and Linda Sternberg Katz, eds. New Providence, N.J.: Bowker, 1992.

Nigerian Periodicals Index. Jos, Nigeria: Committee of University Librarians of Nigerian Universities, 1986–.

Quarterly Index to Periodical Literature, Eastern and Southern Africa. Nairobi, Kenya: Library of Congress Office, 1991–.

Scheven, Yvette. *Bibliographies for African Studies 1970-1986.* London: Hans Zell, 1988; *U.S. Imprints on Sub-Saharan Africa: A Guide to Publications Cataloged at the Library of Congress.* Volume 6/7, 1990/1991. Washington, D.C.: Library of Congress, 1992.

Books and Guides for Internet Resources

Barron, Billy. *UNT's Accessing On-Line Bibliographic Databases.* ftp from: ftp.unt.edu (anonymous) in directory: /pub/library, file name: libraries.ps (postscript version).

Krol, Ed. *The Whole Internet User's Guide and Catalog.* Sebastopol, CA: O'Reilly and Associates, 1992.

La Quey, Tracey. *The Internet Companion: A Beginner's Guide to Global Networking.* Reading, MA: Addison-Wesley, 1993.

Rittner, Don. *Ecolinking: Everyone's Guide to Online Environmental Information.* Berkeley, CA: Peachpit Press, 1992.

St. George, Art. *Internet-accessible Library Catalogs and Databases.* ftp from ariel.unm.edu (anonymous) in directory: /library, filename: library.ps (post-script version).

Addresses

African Books Collective
The Jam Factory
27 Park End Street
Oxford XO1 1HU
England

African Imprint Library Services
236 Main Street
Falmouth, MA 02540
(508) 540-5378

African Studies Association
Credit Union Building
Emory University
Atlanta, GA 30322
(404) 329-6410

Africana Libraries Newsletter
Joseph Lauer, Editor
Africana Library
Michigan State University Libraries
East Lansing, MI 58823
(517) 255-2397

Cooperative Africana Microforms Project
Center For Research Libraries
6050 South Kenwood Avenue
Chicago, IL 60637
(312) 955-4545

Library of Congress Field Office
P.O. Box 30598
Nairobi, Kenya

PART THREE

Programs Abroad

14

Developing an Approach to Integrated Study in a Non-Western Context: The St. Lawrence University Kenya Semester Program

Paul W. Robinson & W. Howard Brown

St. Lawrence University in New York State has, during the past two decades, developed one of the finest long-standing undergraduate Study Abroad programs in Africa. The Kenya Semester Program was founded in 1974 and has since introduced some one thousand university students to the study and experience of Africa. This chapter describes and discusses our approach to developing an integrated study of culture and development within the context of East Africa.

The fundamental goals of the St. Lawrence program are twofold: to integrate the variety of formal and informal learning experiences offered in the program in order to achieve a coherent, comprehensive academic program; and to integrate the semester in Kenya with the broader curriculum at St. Lawrence University in New York. The academic and experiential structure of the program has evolved with invaluable input by the Kenyan faculty, home-stay hosts, student participants, and the faculty and administration at St. Lawrence University. This self-evaluative, developmental process is ongoing: East Africa continues to change, and new issues emerge.

St. Lawrence, seeking to achieve the goals of liberal education in contemporary circumstances, has, since 1964, developed numerous off-campus, academic programs outside the United States—in Austria, Canada, Denmark, England, France, Japan, Spain, India, and Costa Rica, as well as in Kenya. These serve to broaden the perspective of U.S. students and to increase their awareness of other societies and of the interdependence of the modern world. Presently, approximately one-third of the student body participates in one or more of these programs while at the university.

THE PROGRAM'S STRUCTURE AND GOALS

The general educational aim of the Kenya Semester Program is to introduce U.S. university students to different values and cultural traditions, promoting cross-cultural understanding through the disciplined study of African history, anthropology, language, politics, geography, literature, and ecology. Students are challenged to broaden their view of the world, and themselves, through critical examination of and personal reflection on their experience in East Africa. They take part in both experiential and academic learning situations. This integrated structure is intended to present students with an African perspective on a range of issues.

Students actively participate in Kenya's rich cultural diversity, through rural and urban homestays, field study courses, internships, free and directed travel, and through an integrated academic program in which both field and classroom learning are stressed. Kenya faces a wide variety of social, economic, political, environmental, and cultural issues, and these must be confronted by students. Cultural integration and understanding remain among the primary educational objectives of the program.

The theme of the semester program (and indeed the organizing focus for the African studies minor at St. Lawrence) is "Development and Cultural Change in Africa." Courses in Kenya supplement the curriculum on the home campus, with a particular focus on East Africa. These have included the following: an anthropology course on the prehistorical background to East Africa; a geography course examining the nature and development of the physical environments of Kenya and their human occupation; a history course on social, economic, and political development, from the precolonial period to the end of British rule in Kenya; a second history course on ecological disasters and survival strategies, particularly among pastoralist groups; and a third on the history and culture of the Swahili coast; one government course comparing the postindependence development strategies in Tanzania and Kenya; and another examining postindependence civil society in Kenya; a course on women, environment, and development; and biology courses in tropical ecology and African grassland ecosystems. Instruction in Kiswahili is an important aspect of the curriculum: students are encouraged to begin their study at least one semester before they arrive in Kenya and are required to take Kiswahili (unless already fluent) when there. They may also continue taking Kiswahili when they return to the main campus. Rigorous language instruction combined with immersion experience means that many students are conversant in basic Kiswahili within eight weeks of arrival in Kenya.[1]

Home-Stays

The Kenya Semester begins, after a three-day orientation, with a rural home-stay, an experience of total immersion designed to provide students with an immediate context for developing empathy between them and their hosts. For eight days, students live with Kenyan families, sharing in the full range of their lifestyles in both traditional and modern contexts. Host families are selected from the rural middle class. Average family holdings tend to be five acres or less. Occupations of hosts include farming, primary and secondary teaching, veterinary services, medicine, local administration, and public and private service.

The Kenya program has arranged home-stays for three or more consecutive years in the same communities. Sustained involvement has proven to be a strong asset. Hosts are increasingly familiar with our goals and at ease in having U.S. students in their homes; hence, students are able to ask questions freely, and the level of learning has dramatically increased. The program is popular in the communities, and large numbers of people apply to be hosts. Following each semester's home-stays, a seminar evaluates the students' experience and learning. Student Peter Demerath reported:

> I learned a lot about Kenya and myself. Often the former helped with the latter. [The rural home-stay] was the most incredible week of my life. I was [very moved] by the relation-based society; it gave me new faith in man's needs for connections—a need often sublimated by our society . . . coming here was the best thing I've done in my life.

A second, urban, home-stay, of longer duration, takes place in the following weeks as students take up their academic classes in Nairobi. This four-week period allows students to understand the processes of modernization and urbanization in Kenya and facilitates the development of close, long-term relationships with Kenyans. Hosts are selected from all ethnic groups that make up Kenyan society, including Asians and Europeans.

Field Study

In addition to participating in academic courses and home-stays, all students do two two-week field-study courses among pastoralists in Tanzania and Kenya. The courses are designed to facilitate a direct confrontation with the dynamics of society, social change, land use and development.

The fourteen-day Tanzania field-study course provides students with an integrated perspective on issues of ecology, wildlife conservation, and development in Kenya's neighbor. Tanzania has, since independence, pursued policies based on *ujamaa* socialism, and only within the past several years has begun to shift toward a more capitalist, market economy. Traveling through several distinct environments, including regions continuously inhabited by humans for more than three million years, students examine processes of development and change. Topics covered include archaeology, human evolution, Maasai pastoralist ecology, geology, geography and plant ecology, and wildlife ecology and conservation. The focus is on resource utilization, development priorities, and local participation in decision-making. Students have contact with the pastoral Maasai. They have discussions with both traditionally based communities and local management (previously *ujamaa*) committees. During this time students begin to compare the fundamentally different strategies for political and economic development pursued by Kenya and Tanzania. The field course takes students through the highland environs of Mt. Meru to the southern Maasai steppe and the Ol Donyo Sambu and Tarangiire area; to the Ngorongoro Conservation Area and Olduvai Gorge; and to the Serengeti and the regions south of Lake Natron, including the active volcano, Ol Donyo Lengai.

A second field-study course explores facets of the complex physical, biotic, and social environments in which the Samburu cattle pastoralists live. The course is an intimate field study hosted and largely taught by members of the highly traditional, pastoralist Samburu of Kenya. In this field-learning situation, students study the complex dynamics of traditional social organization and pastoralist ecology, together with contemporary social, political, and environmental development issues. Students have extended contact with the highland and lowland pastoralist Samburu. The course includes discussions with elders and home-stay hosts and formal teaching.

During the first week, students are guided on foot through three Samburu lowland habitats—montaine, riverine, and dry thorn bushland. They see the pastoral environment and its resultant lifestyle and are expected to use the information gained in subsequent study of the highland Samburu. This is during the second week, when students share settlement and herding life and explore highland forests with Samburu warriors as guides. Interpretive lectures are given by the field course leaders. These include such topics as Samburu survival strategies, pastoralist strategies, life-cycles, philosophy and cosmology, and development and modernization. Commenting on her time in this region, student Julie Convisser said:

> During my too-short two-week stay with the pastoralist Samburu peoples, I faced so many challenges: challenges to my ideas about the relationship of love and sex; about romantic love and marriage; about ownership; about the essence of time. [I learned] of an entirely new set of relationships for which the "give" is a commitment to the happiness and welfare of [others] and satisfaction gained from being a secure member of a stable and cohesive larger social group. [I] began to understand their words about the qualitative difference between the kind of self-centered love of youth and the highly rewarding love that grows out of and is the basis for a family.

Both field courses are intellectually, experientially, and physically challenging. They demand that students gather and process information from disparate and unconventional sources. Students begin to realize that knowledge and understanding demand interdisciplinary competence.

The Final Month

In the final month of the semester, students elect either an internship or independent study—the style arranged to suit a student's academic field of specialty and interest. The timing and format allow students to have time in and away from Nairobi. Projects are assigned throughout the country. By this time, students have sufficient language and cultural skills to be productive interns. Where possible, students live with Kenyan families during their internships, which maximizes interaction with and sensitivity to local issues. Internships/independent study may have a preprofessional focus, but this is not mandated. This period of study and service offers students opportunities for professional growth, personal challenge, and self-discovery perhaps unparalleled in their undergraduate careers. Students can apply academic learning to practical experience. They can meaningfully contribute intellectual and physical skills, albeit in a small way, directly to Kenya.

Internships have been consistently highly evaluated by students; indeed, many students are drawn to the program because of this aspect of the curriculum. Student Lauren Abrams said:

> "It is important that [we] students get a chance to give something back to a country from which [we] have gotten so much. I am really glad that I got the chance to do that."

In many internships, students are challenged to the limits of their formal training and abilities. This is our experience. In very many cases, they have been able to make a real contribution to their hosts and to Kenya. In most instances, students put a lot of effort into the internships, and the program has established considerable credibility among international organizations, government ministries and parastatals, nongovernmental organizations, financial and business institutions, and individuals. Few other institutions can duplicate this record.

For students who want an alternative to formal, individually arranged internships or independent study, field courses may be offered that develop issues explored during the semester. Those with a background in history and/or development studies can do a four-week field course in African development. These students do background reading in development and visit projects that range from those organized by the World Bank to small-scale operations initiated by nongovernment organizations. Students are often involved either in the writing of project proposals or in project assessment. These field courses have focused on development initiatives in dryland regions and on continuing problems of hunger, refugees, and ecological crises.

Students with background in cultural history and/or archaeology have the option of doing a four-week field course on Kenya's coast. This course visits many of Kenya's important archaeological sites as well as Mombasa, Lamu, and Paté. The focus is on the development of Swahili culture and the Indian Ocean trade.

Not all of the students' time is structured. Independent travel and time for contemplation enhance and deepen the experience. Julie Convisser, a student already quoted above, said of her "free" time:

> I did much of my learning by sitting and observing what was going on around me. I have come to realize that doing, moving, and even questioning are not necessarily the most fruitful ways to spend an hour learning; that just being a silent observer can be the best means to gain the most from an experience. After hours of sitting in the shade of an acacia tree with my Samburu brother as he contemplates his grazing cattle; after hours spent quietly shelling groundnuts with my Western Province mother and sisters; after hours spent waiting in bank queues in Nairobi while the teller catches up on his colleague's social calendar—I have come to know that time is not yours to waste or save or spend; it isn't what you *have,* it is what you live in. Life is not measured by what you *get done.* Life *is doing.*

St. Lawrence University maintains a study center in Nairobi where the program's office, directors' and staff's residences, and student housing are situated. We have seminar rooms and a small but comprehensive library of 1,200 volumes. Students can live at the study center during examination week and in emergencies. St. Lawrence courses are held at the YMCA, close to the University of Nairobi, and students have reading privileges at the university library as well as access, for particular courses, to special collections and laboratory facilities. Students are encouraged to meet and interact with Kenyan university students. Adjunct teaching faculty are drawn from the University of Nairobi, Kenyatta University, and from other international organizations operating in Kenya. All courses are offered through the auspices of and accredited by St. Lawrence University. Student N. Bodurtha said of the academic aspect of the semester:

> Although sitting in a Nairobi classroom was never quite as exciting as milking a goat outside a *manyatta* . . . it was more satisfying than a similar class [in the United States]. Suddenly we could challenge each other and our professors with real experiences and observations rather than something someone saw in the last issue of *Newsweek* and reshaped to fit their argument. . . . Often what we had seen or done was so intriguing that assigned readings and lectures [became much more] relevant.

SELECTION OF STUDENTS, ORIENTATION, AND EVALUATION

Review and selection of students for the Kenyan Semester is based on a combination of academic records, letters of recommendation, application essays, and personal interviews. Application is open to students from any college or university, and during recent years over one-half of the participants in the program have been drawn from institutions other than St. Lawrence University. The program directors have continued to see an increasingly strong intellectual commitment and deepening of training in African studies on the part of students. We believe this is due both to a continually improving selection process and to a stronger program.

In recent years, the number of women in the approximately thirty students accepted each semester has steadily increased. The current female-male ratio is two-to-one. The greater participation of women may be attributed to a number of factors: a greater tendency on the part of men toward preprofessional courses of study that generally have less flexibility for study abroad; greater participation by men in athletics, which again reduces the time they can spend abroad; and positive choices by women toward innovation in their curriculum choices.

Participation in the program by minorities, including African-American students, rarely has exceeded ten percent of the total. Several important factors may be significant in explaining the degree of participation by minorities. First, the percentage of minority students attending most of the colleges and universities from which students have traditionally been selected closely parallels the percentage of students participating in the Kenya program. Second, financial constraints may be a deciding issue for students who would like to apply but do not. Third, and perhaps most importantly, there may be a perception by minority students that the program, in its design, methodology, and student composition, does not address their needs; that it is primarily for white, upper-middle-class students. These are significant concerns and the program is addressing them. The nature of each group, including the ethnic, economic, and racial diversity represented, has presented significant challenges to the program's approach and methodology. Our commitment continues to be to present students with an African approach, maintaining this as a baseline against which each aspect of the program is measured. All student participants have to put aside their individual biases and prejudices and work, both individually and corporately, to understand issues from an African perspective. In many cases where problems of interpretation, context, and methodology have arisen, these can be traced directly to the inability or unwillingness of the students involved to step outside the limitations and bounds of their own experience.

Orientation

Students are prepared for the Kenya Semester Program in two phases: in the United States, during the semester prior to their departure for Kenya; and in Kenya, immediately upon arrival. Their first three days at the study center in Nairobi include intensive Kiswahili study; exercises designed to familiarize students with cross-cultural interaction, situations and ethics; health and health care; Kenyan laws and regulations; and the program's design and schedule. The sessions stress practical application of both classroom and field learning, and students emerge prepared for their rural home-stays, which immediately follow, and for the remainder of the program.

The program attempts to anticipate problems relating to culture shock and social convention, giving students access to take care of individual needs. In addition, a series of formal seminars (held periodically throughout the semester) gives students the opportunity to review, reflect upon, contextualize, and integrate the various components of the program. These seminars, which offer group support, are invaluable.

Students are actively encouraged throughout the semester to discuss academic and personal matters with program staff. The faculty-administrators and coordinator have had extensive experience in East Africa. A rewarding aspect of program administration has been the close and extended contact with students and Kenyans. It affords opportunities to participate with them in situations that lead to a great deal of personal and intellectual growth. Much of the directors' time is spent with students and Kenyans, either as individuals or on a group basis. Learning can be slow, and in many cases difficult, and it is necessary for staff to be both open and flexible.

Evaluation

Evaluation of the program is done in a number of ways and is a process in which all those who participate in the program (directors, faculty, students, home-stay hosts, and students, among others) have a part. Input from all perspectives is solicited. It is part of a continuous effort to improve the program. Two students contributed the following:

> The first thing that comes to mind when I consider what I've gained from this semester is independence and confidence in my ability to handle myself in any situation. These feelings grew continuously over the semester—Lauren Abrams.
>
> It is hard to define what I've learned this semester. I've learned about a Third World country in general; I've learned about life and my own ideas—I've been able to shed misconceptions. I have a stronger, more real idea of who I am, what is important in life and what isn't. I know that I'll be able to use these few months as a solid base for the rest of my life. It is a positive feeling—a good one to have, facing [the future]—Alexandra Kammerer.

Evaluation is an ongoing process throughout each semester. The directors assess each segment of each semester's curriculum as it occurs. This is done formally through participation in field components, through attendance at classroom lectures, and through assessment of student reaction to the program. We also attempt, each semester, through discussion and correspondence, to secure evaluations and suggestions for improvement from faculty, home-stay hosts, and others.

Students are encouraged to discuss all aspects of the program with faculty and administrators, and this feedback is later used in compiling written evaluations. Seminars also help in assessing student reactions to the program. Through this process, it is possible to identify both student reactions and potential problems and to incorporate these into student counseling and planning for the future.

Following the completion of classes and examinations, evaluation of individual instructors/courses is done by students and administrators. These evaluations follow the format used in the university in New York. The results are discussed individually with faculty and then sent to the Kenya Semester committee in New York. Faculty are expected to consider the evaluations in assessing their courses for content, presentation, and examination. The program director uses the evaluations in assessing future course offerings and in suggesting improvements. Students also complete a comprehensive program evaluation form, which focuses on the role of the directors, the center, logistics, home-stays, internships, and other noncurricular matters.

Mindful that the program has an impact on Kenyans, the directors give formal attention to assessing the effects of the cross-cultural learning upon Kenyan participants in the program—particularly those families that are involved in the rural, urban, and Samburu home-stays. Meetings are held with each group to discuss the program and its involvement in these communities and to discuss any problems that might have emerged.

These discussions have deeply confirmed our belief that cross-cultural learning is a two-way process. However, it also appears that the effects upon students may be much more profound than they are on the Kenyan hosts. Notwithstanding this, Kenyans involved with the program evidenced a very good understanding of their roles as instructors who demonstrate their lifestyles and values to the students. In each instance, and within each community in which we have been involved, there has resulted an increased personal, cultural, and national pride. There has also been an increasing commitment and interest in the program, and we have long waiting lists of people wanting to participate.

RECIPROCITY: SCHOLARSHIP AND TRAINING

St. Lawrence University has for a number of years recognized the importance of reciprocity of opportunity and has thus regularly made available training opportunities for Kenyan students. At present, St. Lawrence University offers two full, four-year undergraduate scholarships to Kenyan students annually and one graduate scholarship. In effect, this provides for nine fully sponsored students on campus in 1994.

This program has grown out of the St. Lawrence University Kenya Scholarship Program that was implemented in 1981–1982. In those years, the university made the commitment to admit one promising Kenyan student per year on full scholarship, to a maximum of four students present at the university. The scholarship provided all university fees. In 1984, in recognition of the outstanding academic achievements of the Kenya Scholarship recipients, of the role of the Kenya Semester Program in educating U.S. students in African studies, and of the pressing needs of Kenyans for opportunities to pursue university degrees, the university doubled the annual intake of Kenyan students on full scholarship. The program of graduate masters' scholarships, for two-year courses of study, was added in 1990, and one Kenyan graduate student is in residence at all times. These scholarship recipients are expected to teach Kiswahili at introductory and advanced levels.

In addition, a number of Kenyan students have studied at St. Lawrence University on a private basis. Many of these students have received scholarship funding in addition to the formal Kenya Scholarship described above.

There are also other forms of training for Kenyans. Kenyan adjunct faculty teach in the Kenya Semester Program, and they find this valuable professionally, intellectually, and personally. Several Kenyan adjunct faculty have been offered visiting professorships at the university campus in New York during their sabbaticals. It is proposed that funding for this kind of faculty exchange be continued, and we hope to institutionalize such an exchange within the next two to three years.

A number of Kenyans have been offered training opportunities during the program's field courses. Scholarships have been provided for Kenyans to participate in the biology field course, and participants were taught field research methodologies in censusing. The scholars were drawn from the Kenya Wildlife Service, staff from the International Union for the Conservation of Nature, and behavioral research staff.[2] Scholarships have also been offered to Kenyans on the history and development field course, in which the instruction included field methodologies in project design and assessment.

In 1994, the St. Lawrence University Kenya Semester Program has successfully completed its twentieth year of continuous operation in Kenya. More than one thousand university students have been introduced to African studies in a practical and sensitive manner. It has developed into one of the finest, most rigorous programs of its kind in the Third World. The Kenya Semester Program is in the forefront of undergraduate, non-Western area studies curriculum development. It is on the cutting edge of multidisciplinary, cross-cultural educational philosophy. Students consistently demonstrate considerable personal, intellectual, and spiritual growth during their semester in Kenya, which in and of itself is a demonstration of the program's success. Well in excess of 10 percent of program alumni are estimated to have continued to pursue studies or careers with African and/or international content.

The program is committed to the comprehensive integration of classroom and experiential learning, and to a multidisciplinary perspective to learning. In the field, students must confront many relationships between widely varied areas of interest and study, and they must learn the methodologies for critical examination of primary data. Such learning is predicated on the immediacy and reality of the observed—and this way of learning is fundamentally exciting. The immediacy of the real world often presents intellectual dilemmas of interpretation and understanding to which students must respond. For true learning to take place, an attitude of openness must be discovered and cultivated.

The methodological tools that students learn to use in a program such as this are applicable to processing and understanding the issues—cultural, political, and economic—that divide the world. These students confront seminal issues of development and cultural change that face East African societies. They begin to acquire the intellectual and personal resources needed to deal with those issues—both for Africa and for the world.

NOTES

1. For full descriptions of current course offerings in Kenya, contact St. Lawrence University's Office of International Education.

2. When the Kenya Semester Program was initiated, and periodically since, St. Lawrence University has inquired of the University of Nairobi regarding formal affiliation. The University of Nairobi administration recommended that formal affiliation on an institutional basis was inappropriate, due to the size and nature of the Kenya Semester Program. The University of Nairobi has neither the staff nor the facilities to be directly involved with the program. The program is reviewed and authorized by the Office of the President of Kenya and has been granted "standing approval" by the government to operate in Kenya—support that St. Lawrence University has greatly appreciated.

15

Nowhere to Hide: Perspectives on an African Foreign-Study Program

Sandra E. Greene

Study Abroad programs in the United States have traditionally been categorized according to their organizational characteristics.[1] Among the groups so defined are the university-integrated programs, in which U.S. students enroll directly into one of the institutions of the host country, where they take courses from the established curricular offerings, live and eat with local families or their fellow students, and participate in the social life of the campus and the community in which the university is located. Kalamazoo College's African foreign-study program is such a program.

THE KALAMAZOO PROGRAM

Pedagogical Foundations

In 1962, when Kalamazoo College launched its foreign-study program, the most widely accepted approach to college learning was classroom oriented. The core component was highly structured, in-classroom contact with a professor who imparted information. Most often, this was done through lectures, demonstrations, and carefully designed assignments. Foreign study, on the other hand, at least in the minds of many in the Midwest, was associated with sightseeing, guided-tours, and a superficial exposure to a different culture. Partly in response to the educational norms of the time, and the wish to avoid any hint of frivolous overseas adventures, Kalamazoo College opted to establish a foreign-study program in which the student was placed in the position of having to approach learning largely according to the pattern established at Kalamazoo College. There was, of course, the added component of experiencing constant interaction with individuals and groups from the host country. The primary emphasis was on Europe, but, in what was considered quite a daring move at the time, the college also opted to open a center in Africa—in Sierra Leone.

Enthusiasm about Africa grew thereafter among U.S. students as many countries during the mid-1960s discarded the yoke of colonialism. In response, Kalamazoo expanded the number of African sites, and by the mid-1970s, the college had established six more centers, one each in Senegal, Liberia, Ghana, Nigeria, and Kenya, and in Sierra Leone a second center, at Njala, upcountry.

Whereas emphasis in the European programs was on language development,[2] Kalamazoo College defined the value of the Africa program more broadly as the exposure of the students to a culture much different from that found in the United States. Thus, while the administrators of the program acknowledged the need for foreign-language training and for students to master information about Africa in the classroom, whether at the college or in Africa, they also designed the program to facilitate cross-cultural learning through cultural immersion. Students were not just placed in African university classrooms with their African peers: they were housed in residence halls with African roommates, a situation that forced them to confront on a daily basis for their entire stay of six to twelve months the cultural similarities and differences that existed between themselves and their peers. This pedagogical approach is based on an understanding of intercultural education that distinguishes between cognitive, intellectual, affective, and emotional learning—and values all four modes.

As described by Sikkema and Niyekawa, in this approach the essential difference between passive and active understanding lies in intellectual and rational understanding on the one hand and affective or emotional understanding on the other.

> Passive understanding can be . . . achieved to a significant extent by studying the literature, philosophy, religion, history or art of a particular culture. At a time when international cooperation is essential for survival, learning to see people of other cultures as . . . similar [and] different is essential. [But] it is much easier to understand and accept cultural differences at the rational level than at the emotional level where reactions are not usually under conscious control.
>
> Active understanding requires the development at gut level of an attitude of acceptance, respect, and tolerance of cultural differences. This can hardly be accomplished through traditional classroom methods, because learning in the classroom takes place primarily at the intellectual level. Descriptions and analyses of other cultures and peoples may be presented, but the student does not experience the embarrassment of making mistakes or the joy of successfully functioning in another culture.[3]

In the Kalamazoo College African Studies Program, these kinds of emphasis on both cognitive and affective learning have been the principle shaping factors. They shape both the structure and content of the pre-departure orientation session, the in-country experience, and the program admissions process. In the following overview of the Kalamazoo African

Studies Program, I will briefly review these three aspects of the program, their impact on the students, the host country, and the home campus. I will then discuss the continuing challenges that face the program as it strives to enhance the quality of intercultural education.

PREDEPARTURE ORIENTATION

Throughout the thirty years that the college has operated the Africa program, preparations for the visit to Africa have taken place during the summer quarter, a regular term in the year-round Kalamazoo academic calendar. During this quarter, students are required to enroll in at least one introductory course in African studies. The list of courses offered usually includes at least five courses from the disciplines of history, politics, sociology and anthropology, literature, biology, and art and music. The college supplements these courses with a required-attendance, nine-week, film-and-lecture series that combines both specific and general information about the issues and concerns, both historical and contemporary, that exist in Africa. Always included in the series are presentations on the South African situation; on country-specific or region-specific concerns about ecology and political economy; on developments in contemporary art and music; and on health issues. Students also attend a general foreign-study orientation, as well as continent-specific and country-specific orientations, led by administrators, faculty, student alumni of the Africa foreign-study program, and citizens of the host country. All are designed to prepare the students intellectually for the cultural experience of living overseas and the specific conditions they will face.

In the 1980s, the African Studies Program added to the orientation a program that encourages students to develop intercultural social skills. Students are divided into groups for a number of "culture simulations." In one such cross-cultural game, BaFa-BaFa, the students have to learn how to operate in a society in which they cannot understand the language, where their inherited social skills prove ineffective, and where there are few aids to assist them in their efforts to interact with the culture.[4] The games are followed by discussions about how much of the culture the students perceived and understood, how much was lost to them, how they handled the situations in which they were personally involved, and what alternatives they might consider in the future.[5]

The In-Country Experience

The universities into which the students are placed in Africa constitute a superficially familiar environment in which they can continue the educational experience they have had in the United States. But it is also the site of intense culture contact. For example, the program director makes sure that the U.S. students are assigned roommates from the host country, and that every effort is made to scatter the students throughout the residence halls in order to discourage the natural tendency for students to cling together. Each student has a local professor as academic advisor, but usually the level of contact is minimal. Students are expected to take principal responsibility for getting themselves through the course registration process, enrolling in courses that build on their foundation in African studies or their major field of study. Science students, for example, are advised to enroll in field courses that cannot be duplicated at home, but it is up to the student to find out what those courses are, where they are offered, and when. In recent years, the program has arranged for there to be offered credit-bearing educational field trips and internships with local artists, agriculturalists, and schools and hospitals. Even if students confine their principle activities to the university, they soon learn that the perspectives of the professor and the students, the content of the course, and the extent of faculty supervision of student work can be jarringly different from that which they are used to.

However, the most challenging experiences for U.S. students occur in the residence halls and in their interaction with the community outside the university. On a regular basis, hour after hour, day after day, month after month, students must learn to handle common but unfamiliar social situations such as:

1. Having to be much more conscious of their behavior, in a situation in which they are not sure what proper behavior is, but where the imperative to find out is great because of negative reactions by fellow students
2. Managing a city transportation and marketing system in which the novice can be taken advantage of within the flexible pricing system
3. Coping with more traditional attitudes and social interactive styles among host country students in the context of male/female and female/female relations
4. Handling the long hours in which there is no ready-made, fast-paced entertainment system into which they can easily insert themselves
5. Learning when they stay in villages (as many students do during school vacations), the rural (as distinct from urban) etiquette that obtains
6. Facing the discomfort of power outages and water shortages (especially during exam periods and on particularly hot days)
7. Coping—if they are white-skinned—with their conspicuousness, without becoming paranoid, and interacting with blacks as both their peers and their superiors, perhaps for the first time in their lives

8. Dealing—if they are black U.S. students—with their expectations and the reality of their relationship with the host culture

Locally based U.S. citizens, who have expressed a willingness to do so, serve as a resource with whom the students can discuss more personal questions and concerns during their adjustment period. Most often, however, this person does not reside on the campus. It is, therefore, up to students to adjust to their situations—at the same time as they are struggling with the desire (purposely instilled during the predeparture orientation) to do well in their courses; not to associate so much with compatriots; and not to appear as tourists, uninterested in the people except for what they can see from a distance, buying souvenirs, taking photographs, and then departing.

Success Indicators

As noted above, this structure exists for both cultural and economic reasons. It is consistent with the philosophy behind a cultural immersion program in which students are forced to devise for themselves strategies that will facilitate their own learning within an unfamiliar university environment in Africa;[6] and the minimal staffing overseas makes it financially and structurally possible to maintain a strong, on-campus program that exposes students to Africa while avoiding expenditures that simply duplicate the staffing at Kalamazoo.

The saved revenue is used by Kalamazoo College to finance an exchange program. Students from the universities in Africa that our students have attended may spend an academic year at Kalamazoo, most often as a transition year before entering a U.S. graduate school. Other arrangements have the college deposit the overseas tuition and room and board fees in a fund that supports graduate students being sponsored by the government of the host country. In this way, both the college and the overseas university have a vested interest in maintaining the program.

The success of this approach is attested to by a number of indicators. (1) The program has been in continued existence for thirty years. (2) The number of students who have subsequently continued their education in graduate school by specializing in African studies (or in a field concerned with another Third World area) is relatively high. Current information on Kalamazoo College alumni of the Africa program indicates, for example, that in the thirty-year history of the program, at least one student on average every year completed graduate work in the areas mentioned above. Of the thirty-six known instances, sixteen obtained masters' degrees; twenty received the doctorate. (3) The program is also recognized among the faculty, staff, and students at the college as the one which has the most profound effect on the participants, providing them with an understanding of the world and themselves unmatched by other programs. (4) Very few students exit the program before its scheduled end. (5) Many former participants (and still others who have experienced Africa only through the recollections of their friends and/or the Africa on-campus activities) opt to return (or go for the first time) to Africa immediately after graduation as Peace Corps volunteers and as researchers working on senior theses or post-B.A. projects.

THE SELECTION PROCESS

Cultural immersion in Africa, even in a setting as superficially familiar as a university, is not for every student. For one thing, these are universities in which support services are limited. Students must be able to handle all of the situations mentioned above, and more; they must want to be challenged and at the same time be open-minded enough to withstand the inclination to fall back on the common cultural distancing techniques of stereotyping, paternalism, and ethnocentrism.

In light of these demands and the limited financial commitment for significant in-country personal support structures, Kalamazoo College has developed a rigorous screening process in an attempt to limit the program to those who have the personal, intellectual, and physical ability to manage the experience successfully. Students interested in Africa principally as an exotic tourist adventure are automatically eliminated. Applicants with a fuller interest in Africa, whether enrolled at Kalamazoo College or another institution, must indicate why they are interested in participating and submit a biographical statement, transcripts, and letters of recommendation. At the interview (in person or by telephone) students must demonstrate some knowledge about the country in which they wish to study and indicate that they have considered the challenges, personal and physical, that they will encounter. After acceptance, students must continually demonstrate their ability to take responsibility for themselves—meeting deadlines for the submission of passport applications, following inoculation schedules, and taking seriously the predeparture orientation sessions.

CONTINUING CHALLENGES

In the more than thirty years that Kalamazoo College has been sending students to study in Africa, much has changed—in Africa, in the United States, and in U.S. student culture. The period between the early 1960s, when the college initiated the program, and the late 1970s, when there was the first world oil-shock, saw African economies suffer terribly. Rising fuel costs led to declines in prices for African goods on the world market.

Student protests led to temporary government closures of universities to which the college had been sending students. In the early 1980s through the early 1990s, economic difficulties, and the marginal political position of Africa in world affairs, made Africa seem to be, in the minds of many U.S. students, a place that was irrelevant to their lives. Media coverage focused almost exclusively on spectacular disasters, ignoring other African issues, thus reinforcing stereotypic images of the continent. Students who, nevertheless, participated in the program faced far greater difficulties than had their predecessors. Food, water, and electricity shortages, and limited health care and transportation caused by the local economic difficulties, made the experience of studying in Africa additionally challenging. This affected enrollments in the Kalamazoo program. The most significant drop occurred among Kalamazoo College's own students, who had easy access to information about the difficulties in Africa. But the number of students from other institutions also declined.

Table 14.1   **Student Participation in the Kalamazoo Africa Program, 1962–1992**

	1962–1972	1973–1982	1983–1992
Kalamazoo students	167	306	82
Students from other schools	28	105	88
Total	195	411	170

In the decade of the late 1970s through the late 1980s, significant changes were also occurring in U.S. student culture that made students less prepared for the Africa experience. One example is in the area of use of "free" time. Both families and U.S. educational institutions have come to provide so much ready-made entertainment for students in the United States that many undergraduates are unequipped to handle the large amounts of unstructured time they have in Africa. Similarly, the highly structured nature of U.S. education—some say students are spoon-fed—makes it difficult for students to benefit from the European-based university systems in Africa. Students are expected to take more responsibility for educating themselves, both inside and outside the classroom. A third factor is the impact that the feminist movement has had in the United States on students' understanding of appropriate behavior between men and women. Many, and perhaps most, of the women who in recent years have participated in the Kalamazoo College Africa program view themselves as socially progressive on gender issues, and they tend to associate with male students who hold similar views. When these women arrive in African universities, they are often unprepared for the persistent attention that frequently is directed their way by some of the male students. The social interaction clashes with their notions, both cultural and political, of how men and women do and should communicate with one another. Their limited experience with such situations provides them with few models from which to derive coping strategies. These difficulties are not new, but over the years I have noticed that U.S. women students, particularly those who have consciously embraced the feminist movement, have been having greater and greater difficulty dealing with this attention. I attribute this to the changes occurring in U.S. culture—changes that do not coincide with those occurring in Africa.

These developments present new challenges to the structure of the Kalamazoo program. Perhaps the most worrisome are in the areas of gender and race relations. Both are difficult subjects in which to engage students, whether in-country or in the orientation period, without having students resort to fearful, silent withdrawal, defensiveness, or hostility. Experiences overseas can heighten the tensions that surround these issues; and these tensions, in turn, can affect the relations both between the students and the hosts and among the U.S. students themselves. If, for example, a white female student participates in the Africa program because of a genuine interest in Africa, but has failed to confront and deal with images received from U.S. culture that instill an unconscious fear of black men, her inability to cope with the different patterns of male/female relations can have serious consequences for the entire group. In a worst-case scenario, it will ruin her experience, reinforce in her own mind the negative stereotypes she has received from the United States, prompt her white, male colleagues to adopt the same attitude and to take on the role of protector against black males, and at the same time seriously alienate black U.S. students—at a time when they are having their own adjustment difficulties. The difficulty is compounded if, because of housing constraints, the administrators of the program have to place all the U.S. students in the same residential site. The tensions then begin to reinforce one another and for some participants can lead to early exit from the program or a sense of dissatisfaction. Often, neither the staff overseas nor the administrators at home are trained or emotionally prepared to handle these difficulties; yet to ignore these issues can lead only to additional problems for the students and the program. Training programs are available, however. Staff interested in being trained should explore the possibilities well before the students depart for Africa.[7]

A second challenge stems from the fact that, while experiential, predeparture orientation sessions can play an important role in preparing students, differences still exist between the simulation and the educational setting in which students will be placed. In many ways, the format of both the experiential and the intellectual components of the program, with their predetermined assignments and structured experiential exercises, works against encouraging students to learn how to define their own projects, how to work more independently. The principle efforts so far made to address this situation have involved encouraging students to define a project during their stay and to carry it out under the supervision of a local advisor. For this to happen on a more systematic basis, and for the in-country staff to be better able to handle gender and race issues, changes are needed in the way the college has defined the relationship between the local advisors and the students. Training must be made available, along with more support staff. This will require the college to reevaluate the financial structure of the program. In the past, much more support has been given to the development of on-campus personnel than to the development of the overseas component. Both are critical to a self-sustaining program.

A third area of challenge involves language instruction. Kalamazoo College has experimented with a number of formats to enable students to become quickly integrated into local cultures through their use of local language. Summer courses in Krio, Swahili, Seswati, and Wolof have been offered at the college, and arrangements are frequently made for continued study in-country. Ideally, however, African languages should be included as an integral part of the preparation for an African foreign-study experience—just as European-language training has always been an integral part of the European foreign-study program. For the Europe program, student eligibility is contingent upon the successful completion of at least two quarters of instruction in the relevant language. Neither the college administration, nor the European language faculty, have been enthusiastic about such a move with regard to Africa, however. This is due, in part, to numbers. There has never been a sufficient number of students to sustain the permanent addition of African languages to the curriculum.[8] In addition, the university-based nature of the program makes it particularly vulnerable to problems within the host country. A year of language training in Swahili, for example, could be seen by students as a year of wasted effort if they do not have the opportunity to go to Kenya because the University of Nairobi is closed. However, the African Studies Program must remain committed to providing some language training, if only in limited form, and to exploring other options.

A fourth area continues to challenge the Africa program: its relationship with African universities. Most Study Abroad programs advertise themselves as exchange programs: theoretically, both the home and the host institutions benefit from an exchange of students (and sometimes faculty). More commonly, however, this exchange is one-way. U.S. students enroll in a foreign university, but few foreign students from the host institution affiliate with the U.S. college or university; similarly with faculty. This problem is particularly acute in Africa programs like that at Kalamazoo College. Several explanations are offered to account for this situation: (1) the savings obtained (from the difference in the amount paid by the students to the U.S. college to participate in the overseas program and the amount paid by the U.S. college to the African institution for enrolling the U.S. student) do not cover the costs that the U.S. institution must absorb in order to enroll significant numbers of African students—because the financial needs of these students are so great; (2) funds to support having an African faculty member at the U.S. university are limited; (3) administrators are reluctant to alter the structure of a program that they view as being successful even though those structures conflict with the theoretical goals of the program by giving unequal advantage to the U.S. institution. These factors should not preempt attempts to meet the stated goals of an exchange program, however.

There is another concern in this matter of U.S.–African university relations. It involves the way in which foreign-study programs (including the Kalamazoo program) manage relations with people in host countries who are employed to carry out administrative and educational services. If these relations are managed by the program staff rather than the administrative offices of the U.S. college, it can lead to significant disparities between the pay offered to part-time employees of the college who are based in the United States and those employed in the host country. The existence of this disparity will inevitably become known, given the ease of modern communication. This can lead to significant tensions between U.S. program administrators and African employees. These tensions are heightened by the differences in culture, race, and economic position of the two groups. Through care in the structuring of the relationship, these disparities should be minimized or eliminated.

There is a fifth challenge—involving student readjustment to the home culture. Anyone who spends significant amounts of time overseas experiences difficulties "reentering." As part of its traditional, cognitive approach to the experience, the Foreign Study Office at Kalamazoo College (which handles the European program and oversees the one in Africa) used to organize a reentry session in which students were encouraged to discuss their overseas experiences in terms of what they had learned about their country as a field of study. No structured forum existed to help them to examine how the overseas experience affected their perceptions of themselves and their own culture. Most students found it difficult to discuss this with friends and family because of a gap in understanding about the depth to which they had been affected. More recently, some effort has been made to modify this situation. Returning students break into small groups and speak about their personal reactions, but this occurs only once, and in my opinion does not adequately address the needs of the students to sort out the experience.[9] There are limits to what any program can do, of course, and students must do some of this on their own, over time; nevertheless, I believe it would be valuable to gather the students (perhaps six months after their return, and prior to their involvement as previous-participant resources for a new, predeparture set of students) so that they can again review how the experience has affected them. This would help them to assess what they saw in themselves and in their culture that they had not seen before, and what, with greater hindsight, they saw as the positive and negative aspects of the experience. For the College to do this, an increased number of African studies faculty and administrative staff would have to serve as facilitators, but several positive objectives would be accomplished: students would have a forum in which to share their experiences; the faculty and staff would become more involved in the overseas experience (it would be more than something that takes the students away from them for six to nine months)—and they would, hopefully, come to value the personal changes and intellectual growth that had occurred in the students. Faculty could then take advantage of these new skills by using the most accomplished students as facilitators and thus improve the cross-cultural interactions on their own campus.

NOTES

1. See Craufurd D. Goodwin and Michael Nacht, *Abroad and Beyond: Patterns in American Overseas Education* (New York: Cambridge University Press, 1988), chap. 3, for a typology of foreign-study programs.

2. See Joe K. Fugate, "Kalamazoo College: Study Abroad and Foreign Language Learning," in *Integrating Study Abroad into the Undergraduate Liberal Arts Curriculum*, ed. Barbara Burn (Westport, Conn.: Greenwood Press, 1991), in which the former director of Kalamazoo College Foreign Study Office discusses the foreign language emphasis within the Kalamazoo program, as well as others.

3. Mildred Sikkema and Agnes Niyekawa, *Design for Cross-Cultural Learning* (Yarmouth, Mass.: Intercultural Press, 1987): 3, 4. See also Ronald Fry and David Kolk, "Experiential Learning Theory and Learning Experiences in Liberal Arts Education," in *New Directions for Experiential Learning: Enriching the Liberal Arts through Experiential Learning #6,* ed. (San Francisco: Jossey-Bass, 1979).

4. For more information on cross-cultural simulation games, see R.E. Horn and A. Cleaves, eds., *The Guide to Simulation/Games for Education and Training*, 4th edition (Beverly Hills: Sage, 1980); and Sandra Mumford Fowler, "Intercultural Simulation Games: Removing Cultural Blinders," in *Experiential and Simulation Techniques for Teaching Adults*, ed. Linda H. Lewis (San Francisco: Jossey-Bass, 1986). The author of BaFa-BaFa, R.G. Shirts, has designed a number of games with cross-cultural implications. His firm, Simile 11, can be contacted at Box 910, Del Mar, CA 92014.

5. During the summer of 1992, the Foreign Study Office (which handles the European predeparture orientation and oversees the Africa orientation) began a separate pilot program. If successful, it will be extended to include the Africa orientation, adding field ethnographic exercises, challenging "rope courses" that require students to come to grips with their physical limitations, encouraging them to push through inclination to distrust others about whom they have preconceived notions, and simulations involving male-female relations.

6. For a discussion of the philosophy behind cultural immersion programs, see Goodwin and Nacht, *Abroad and Beyond*, chap. 3.

7. One such training program is administered by the Intercultural Communications Institute. The institute can be reached at 8835 S.W. Canyon Lane, Suite 238, Portland, OR 97225.

8. This difficulty can be attributed to a number of factors: (1) administrators at the college have limited the extent to which the Africa program can expand; (2) financial commitment by Kalamazoo College remains small; and (3) only limited efforts are made by the college admissions office to recruit first-year students on the basis of an interest in the Africa program.

9. For examples of reentry exercises, see Margaret Pusch and Nessa Lowenthal, *Intercultural Interactions: A Practical Guide* (Washington, D.C.: NAFSA, 1988); and Richard W. Breslin et al. *Intercultural Interactions: A Practical Guide* (Beverly Hills: Sage, 1986).

16

"The Walk Liberating": Africa Abroad as an Undergraduate Experience

Joseph W. Pickle, Jr.

With my comments here, we move from one of the oldest, best organized Africa Abroad programs run by a small liberal arts college (Chapter 15) to another program—one of the newest. The organizing and operating approach of this program is different from that of Kalamazoo—though we have learned much from it. The differences are more interesting for this book than are the many similarities and points of indebtedness. So I will tell the story from my personal perspective as one of the founders of the Associated Colleges of the Midwest Zimbabwe Program.

I am not an African. More importantly, I am not an Africanist. Even worse, I'm an old Baptist minister! And so, I start with a text. My text is from a poem by A. R. Ammons, "Corson's Inlet." The poem describes a solitary walk along an inlet. It uses the observations made during the walk as a metaphor for the simultaneous path of reflections on the poet's own thought, work, and self-consciousness. Perceptions of nature and of the mind at work are woven together in a way that rings true to life. I offer it here as a metaphor for a particularly undergraduate, liberal arts approach to study in Africa. Perhaps a few lines can suggest the power of the whole:

> I went for a walk over the dunes
> again this morning to the sea, then turned right along the surf
> rounded a naked headland
> and returned
> along the inlet shore. . . .

> the walk liberating, I was released from forms, from
> the perpendiculars, straight lines, blocks, boxes,
> binds of thought. . . .

> I allow myself eddies of meaning: yield to a direction
> of significance running like a stream through the
> geography of my work. . . .

so I am willing to go along, to accept the becoming
thought, to stake off no beginnings or ends, establish
no walls. . . .

I see narrow orders, limited tightness, but will not
run to that easy victory: still around the looser,
wider forces work: I will try
to fasten into order enlarging grasps of disorder,
widening scope, but enjoying the freedom that Scope
eludes my grasp, that there is no finality of vision,
that I have perceived nothing completely,
that tomorrow a new walk is a new walk.[1]

The themes I want to touch on are suggested by phrases like "the walk liberating," "yield to a direction of significance," "willing to go along," and
"Scope eludes my grasp."

I confess I got into this by accident, and it is a confession of self-in-
dulgence. I wanted to go back, once I had visited Africa. I found ways to
keep going back, and if I can find any more ways, I will. My confession is
also of an active arrogance. My liberal arts education at Carleton College
led me to believe I could learn to do most anything—even to apprehend and
appreciate Africa. And because I believe in liberal education, I could not
see why my liberally educated colleague Solomon Nkiwane (Colorado College) and I could not just set up a program in Zimbabwe. Why not?

Since the essence of liberal education is the cultivation of an "appre-
ciative consciousness,"[2] study of Africa in Africa is particularly fitting.
Such a walk is liberating, not only freeing us and our students from the
shackles of provincialism of politics and culture, but also enabling a double vision, a sense of meaningful difference.

My first trip to Africa was in 1987. I found my way serendipitously to
Zimbabwe and spent time with Solomon Nkiwane and many of his colleagues at the University of Zimbabwe. From that visit emerged an informal link that allowed us to start a tentative faculty exchange to bring several colleagues to Colorado College to teach. Our hope was to find yet
another way to overcome faculty provincialism and continue to internationalize the faculty. We made a little headway. As the college struggled
with issues of divestment and as more of us struggled for a way to respond
to the moral and political controversies in a meaningful, educational way,
the dean of the college suggested that he would be open for a proposal for
a study program in Africa in the summer of 1989. Our tenuous link became
a bond of opportunity.

Dr. Nkiwane and I organized and directed a nine-week program that
had eleven undergraduate participants. Utilizing his contacts and experience as senior lecturer in Political and Administrative Studies and deputy
dean of the Faculty of Social Studies in the University of Zimbabwe, we
were able to establish a close, informal, working relationship and to draw

upon some of the most distinguished lecturers of the university. Our program was intended to be introductory but substantial. We arranged for the students to study Shona (more as a cultural resource than with the expectation that six weeks would bring significant command) and two other courses: Issues of Political and Economic Development (a course directed by Dr. Nkiwane); and Cultural Identity in Independent Zimbabwe (a course coordinated by me). The last three weeks were devoted to independent projects on topics ranging from cave painting to railroads, and from wildlife management policy to the status of women in Zimbabwe.

We tried to connect what our students learned specifically about Zimbabwe to issues in Southern Africa and to contemporary political change in South Africa. We sought to enhance study and research skills in cross-cultural context. My model was the Associated Colleges of the Midwest (ACM) program in Pune, India, in which my son had participated. Solomon Nkiwane's model was his own experience as an international student at Colorado College. Our students benefitted from extended home-stay with African families. We encouraged personal, independent travel throughout Zimbabwe—in Harare on the bicycles we had everyone bring, and outside Harare, by hitchhiking, train, and bus. We encouraged individual travel outside of Zimbabwe as much as possible.

As a first effort, it was successful. The president of the Associated Colleges of the Midwest came to see what we were doing and, with us, became enthused about Zimbabwe and the possibilities of a consortium-wide African studies program. She persuaded us to treat our effort as a pilot project and to plan a full semester program for the consortium. The ACM includes fourteen liberal arts colleges: Beloit, Carleton, Coe, Colorado, Cornell, Grinnell, Knox, Lake Forest, Lawrence, Macalester, Monmouth, Ripon, St. Olaf, and the College of the University of Chicago. In 1991, our first institute had sixteen students; in 1992 there were twenty-three; eighteen in 1993; and we project twenty-four in 1994. Since 1991, we have begun to provide options for service projects or internships at the end of the program. Each year, a faculty member from one of the U.S. institutions serves as visiting co-director, at least in part on the assumption that not only students can benefit from "the walk liberating."

Charles Darwin once observed that it was a good thing that he had not been trained fully as a biologist when he traveled on HMS *Beagle,* else he would have missed much of what he found because he would have "known what to look for." In that sense, one needs to make a virtue of what otherwise might be a devastating weakness. Because I am an amateur (in the strict sense of that word), I had no choice but to "yield to a direction of significance." Because we had to yield, we learned the liberating value of *new* (to us certainly, but also to experts) directions of significance. But it was still hard. Academicians believe they ought to be in control—especially of the content of their courses!

We tried hard not to bring *our* courses to Africa. Even Solomon Nkiwane recognized that he could not simply teach in Zimbabwe the courses he would teach in the United States. And, of course, we did not simply assume that the very slightly modified English curriculum of the University of Zimbabwe comprised significance! We learned that we had to yield to directions of significance that emerged in response to the concatenation of current events, available resources, student dispositions, and surprising new student insights and interests. We have learned to adapt the program to the opportunities as we have moved beyond the university campus, Harare, and Mashonaland into rural areas, Bulawayo, and other cultural communities.

Specifically, that meant calling on *others* (from outside the university as well as from within) to share, from *their* perspectives and contexts, what we, too, knew. It meant using *Zimbabwean* books, magazines, and newspapers. It meant not merely adjusting to the frustrations and inconveniences (telephones, local transportation, bureaucracies, and all the rest), but turning them into occasions of contact and reflection. It meant finding and cultivating new contacts for ourselves and our students, and it meant trusting our students to find directions and significances we had not thought of. A colleague had admonished our first group of students to "let Africa teach you." We found that he was right, and that, if we let go enough, they would.

And so we learned to be "willing to go along, to accept the becoming" possibilities. The University of Zimbabwe was not used to having U.S. undergraduates. We entered into contact with the university in Zimbabwe in a manner and a time different from those in which, I think, either St. Lawrence or Kalamazoo (chapters 14 and 15) began in Kenya. The university was already feeling crowded, with admissions limited to about 10 percent of those technically eligible. Though the vice chancellor welcomed and assisted our program in many ways, the university did not want to have our students in their classes. That has since changed, I think, for a variety of financial reasons.

But they were willing for us to set up programs and provide us with space. All our contacts were developed informally by and through Solomon Nkiwane, and in contacts I developed in regular trips to Harare. We cannot recommend this procedure to those with nervous deans and large institutional bureaucracies, but it worked for us. We were able to accept, more than I would otherwise have been able, the pattern, rhythm, and pace of African ways of working. We found individuals and institutions open and friendly, but we shamelessly drew on all the goodwill and personal contacts we could. (It did not hurt that Dr. Nkiwane had taught in graduate seminars many of the most interesting and effective officials in a number of Zimbabwean government offices!) We also faced the question of alternative models. By the time we returned to the United States with the first ACM group in 1991, not only was there a continuing School for International Training and an occasional Duke University program, but Scripps College had a program, and the California State University system, the University of Michigan, and the University of Richmond were negotiating and establishing undergraduate programs. We were influenced by the experiential model used by the School for International Training, whose Harare-based program I think is quite good. Although that model would not be generally acceptable to the faculties of our constituent colleges, it provided impetus to find our own appropriate ways to enhance the experiential dimension of our Africa program.

The other models—placing students in University of Zimbabwe classes, study tours, composites of independent courses and university courses, and so on—suggest a wide range of possible approaches to undergraduate Study-in-Africa programs. I think that is great. We all ought to explore ways of walking into Africa that are natural and appropriate to us. What we encounter will be much too varied, rich, problematic, and exciting to be grasped in any but a preliminary, promising way. "Scope," in any ultimate sense, "eludes my grasp," and not only mine, that of each of us.

Africanists know "that there is no finality of vision." Undergraduates, and often their teachers, do not. It is hard to wear our moral and political convictions lightly enough to let other ways be seen and heard. One of our students dissolved into tears of frustration and anguish in her final oral exam. She admitted to herself for the first time that she could not reconcile her responses to the radically divergent accounts of her Shona host family and her Ndebele host family concerning the time of troubles in the early 1980s. She longed for something more final, more certain.

We need in various ways to remember that what we undertake is to let Africa in its diversity and richness help us and our students, black and white, come to "accept the becoming thought," come to let go of our ideological and cultural certainties, come to acknowledge that we "have perceived nothing completely." Perhaps then we will be ready to return and share aright in the promise of "a new walk" in Africa.

NOTES

1. A. R. Ammons, *The Selected Poems, Expanded Edition* (New York: W. W. Norton, 1986): 43–46.

2. The phrase is from Bernard Meland's remarkable book, *Higher Education and the Human Spirit* (Chicago: University of Chicago Press, 1953): see especially 48–78.

17

Inside or Outside the University? The Conundrum of U.S. Undergraduates in Africa

Neal W. Sobania

The number of U.S. undergraduates who study abroad as part of their academic experience is small; and the number studying in Africa is smaller still. The Liaison Group for International Education in their 1989 "Exchange 2000 Report" calculated that only 748 students (or 1.2 percent) of the 62,341 who studied overseas in 1988/89 were in Africa. One impact of these numbers is that there are few students returning from study in Africa to encourage their peers to do the same. Set alongside a number of other issues that need to be considered when encouraging students to study in Africa, or developing new programs in Africa, one cannot be overly optimistic about the prospect for substantially expanding these numbers. Still, there is student and institutional interest, and courses on Africa are more widely available on campuses than ever before.

This brief chapter is designed to raise a set of issues for which no easy answers exist. It is not intended to single out particular Study Abroad programs, African universities, or African governments, nor to criticize the choices that they have made or had to make. The continent is enormous; and the variety of circumstances faced by individual countries is broad indeed. Rather, it is intended as one U.S. international education director's perspective of the issues—issues with which I must contend as I actively encourage U.S. students to consider study in Africa. If an institution is going to accept the credit its students earn overseas and allow financial aid to travel to overseas programs (without which most students could not participate), there must be convincing evidence of the quality of the overall experience available to students. Further, options presented to students must be defended to faculty colleagues who are most concerned about the quality of education being provided, especially as the majority are convinced that no one can provide this better than they themselves. And one must respond to parental concerns about where their daughters and sons want to study, especially as regards health and safety.

Who are the students that we have targeted for study in Africa? It is a guiding principle of Study Abroad programming that overseas study must articulate with the on-campus academic experience, but what is the on-campus course base from which we build? In the past, there was an over-riding assumption that few students going to Africa had much background in African studies. As a result, many Africa programs have required a significant on-campus period of course work and orientation (e.g., the programs of Kalamazoo College that prepare students for direct placement in African universities). Other programs are purposefully designed as a broad introduction to Africa. The Zimbabwe program of the Associated Colleges of the Midwest (Chapter 16) and the various field-study programs of the School for International Training represent this model. Each of these programs is essentially an "Africa 101" offering, although each can also accommodate better prepared students. The significant expansion of courses related to Africa in the 1970s and 1980s in the undergraduate curriculum suggests that there should, in fact, exist a significant group of undergraduates who are better prepared to study in Africa. Which programs offer these students an "Africa 301" option? And if these are not the students being attracted to study in Africa, why not? At the very least it would be useful to have research results that suggest what the audience for these programs is or could be, but it is only recently that serious research has found its way into the Study Abroad field.

The study of a language as part of an Africa program (or any Study Abroad program) finds ready endorsement as a necessary, integral component of overseas study. Few will disagree with the need for this if students are expected to gain cultural insights from their experience. But this is based on a model for Study Abroad in Europe in which students carry on the study of languages readily available on the home campus. Offerings of African languages for undergraduates are limited and unlikely to include enough students to sustain a program in many places outside Swahili-speaking areas. If introductory language courses are offered in Africa as part of the Study Abroad program, are there opportunities for students to continue their study of the language once back on the home campus? Does the program have an obligation to assist in this endeavor? If language study ends with the end of the overseas program, what does this have to say about quality?

Ideally one would like to place U.S. undergraduates on the campuses of African universities, and in the past this has been done with confidence: confidence that the education U.S. students would receive was at the very least equivalent to that offered on the home campus. The position of African university education today, however, is not, even in the most prosperous of countries on the continent, what it was ten or twenty years ago. It is no use pretending that it is.

African higher education is at the least underfunded. Governments must make spending choices, and higher education is but a small part of the equation. And because universities represent real sources of political instability and students need to be kept under control, significant portions of university budgets are taken up with funding student housing and food, in part to limit cause for discord. Libraries, laboratories, faculty salaries, and basic maintenance have all suffered; and so, in turn, have research and educational quality. New campus building may suggest otherwise, but these are more often indicators that governments have forced increasing numbers of students upon universities—or that campuses are being decentralized as part of political decisions to keep students dispersed and outside the capital.

At the same time, the procuring of a university diploma has taken on a life of its own, the sine qua non of qualification and promotion. The resulting paper-chase adds further to the politically charged atmosphere in which education operates. To keep secondary school students content, ever increasing numbers find admission to university. To absorb these expanding intakes, class sizes increase; and new universities are established. To keep the campus atmosphere calm, students are promoted and awarded degrees. An everexpanding spiral of awarding diplomas to less-qualified students leads inevitably downward.

Budgets are not expanded; laboratories and libraries are not maintained. Nowhere in the equation are faculty added or their salaries increased to compensate for the increased workload. Faculty who once earned a respectable salary find it necessary to take other jobs to support their families. And as they are among the best and the brightest the countries have to offer, international firms and organizations and overseas-based nonprofits are only too pleased to hire them for research and training, administration, and translation. If these jobs are taken in addition to a faculty appointment, into which job are energies placed? How thinly can one individual be stretched? As trained faculty leave the university, their positions often go unfilled. Periodic recruiting trips for university staff are made to Europe and North America to lure educated citizens home, but there is little with which to lure them. Under such circumstances, even with the best intentions of dedicated faculty and administrators, what kind of quality can be maintained?

The equation is further complicated by the action of U.S. Study Abroad programs that draw off African faculty to teach U.S. students. On the one hand, the U.S. creates an opportunity for faculty because they can use well the dollars offered; but with what impact on their own, African, students? With the decline of quality at African universities, whether real or perceived, U.S. institutions move to establish their own Study Abroad programs. The "island" programs thus established, those in which U.S. students study with other U.S. students, taught by U.S.–based faculty or in a location to which African lecturers come, represent a common Study Abroad format. Such programs have some administrative advantages, and they assuage the concerns of the U.S. faculty over quality of education.

But what happens to the quality of the experience? How much contact can our students have with their African university peers? What happens to the possibilities of participatory learning? How do U.S. students form the friendships through which they learn the cultural and political cues that assist them in adapting to their overseas experience?

These "island" programs often recommend themselves to U.S. parents since they offer a sense of security. Parental ideas about Africa—the stereotypes in the minds of parents—are a factor to contend with in encouraging undergraduates to study in Africa. Not only students, parents, too, are fed by U.S. media coverage of Africa—coups, crime, and corruption, to use words from a cover story in *Time* magazine. To many parents, the more tightly held the student's hand, the more acceptable the program. Without such assurances of security, the parental role is often to urge students to explore options in Europe. A safety net can be built into any program—indeed, they exist even in European programs—but if fears are to be mollified and student numbers increased, clearly a middle-ground needs to be sought. If the conditions and nature of the African classroom experience are not the same as they were and can no longer be relied upon for a total academic experience, then other forms of learning need to be employed. Field studies and opportunities for realistic independent studies need to be developed as part of the overall learning experience.

Another serious issue that needs to be considered is that of credible reciprocity. What is there in our organizing of Study Abroad programs in Africa *for Africa and Africans?* One cannot in good conscience have a program that serves only North American undergraduates. When we place U.S. undergraduates in African universities, our students are taking places that would otherwise provide African students with their only real chance at betterment. How do we respond to that situation? What is our obligation? Too often we focus on balanced reciprocal exchange—a not unusual model in European exchanges—and dismiss it because of the cost. Greater creativity is required, especially when the programs are sponsored by private liberal arts colleges where graduate scholarships for African students are simply not an option. One idea that might be considered is the hosting of junior university staff. Most African universities today train their own M.A. students and often the Ph.Ds, too. This may severely limit the exposure these young faculty have to other educational systems, pedagogical styles, and even models of departmental collegial relations and operation. Programs might therefore want to consider providing short-term visiting faculty positions to colleagues from universities in which a Study Abroad program is located. A number of private liberal arts colleges have small scholarship programs for international students. Do these scholarship programs give priority to students who apply from countries in which Study Abroad programs operate? Is the Study Abroad program actively involved in the identifying of potential students?

Finally, what does the future hold for Study Abroad in Africa? The emerging focus in institutional accreditation on assessment of learning will shortly overtake Study Abroad. This emphasis on student learning outcomes—we know we enhance student learning, but how do we demonstrate we are doing what we claim to do—is in part being driven by parents and legislators who want to know what the return on their investment in education is. What are the goals and learning objectives in Africa programs? And what methods will be used to measure these intended outcomes? Since the goals and objectives for cognitive learning and attitudinal change are different, multiple assessment methods will need to be developed. Assessment affords an opportunity for all those involved—faculty, students, and administrators, Africanists and Study Abroad specialists—to work together openly and in a spirit of cooperation to respond to these issues. Program goals must be made explicit, as must the variety of learning methods. More than ever before, the goals in Study Abroad will have to articulate with the on-campus academic program, and, when they do, undergraduates will be well served.

PART FOUR

THE EVOLUTION OF UNDERGRADUATE PROGRAMS IN AFRICAN STUDIES

18

Africa, Undergraduate Teaching, and Title VI African Studies Centers

James C. McCann

The task is to assess the state of U.S. undergraduate education on Africa. Implicitly, it is to diagnose this education field's failure to thrive on U.S. campuses and to transform U.S. public perceptions and understanding of Africa.

I have two perspectives on this. The first is that of the historian, a view of undergraduate education's evolution over time as a part of the wider growth of African studies since the 1950s. My second vantage point comes from my role as a product of two Title VI African Studies Programs (Northwestern and Michigan State) and my new role as director of a third. Clearly, Title VI centers are not the sum of African studies in the United States, but they have trained a substantial percentage of the professoriat that is teaching undergraduates today, and for forty years have absorbed the lion's share of U.S. federal resources on African studies. Given these perspectives, I want to raise a number of critical issues on the evolution of undergraduate programs in African studies.

TITLE VI AND LEADERSHIP
IN UNDERGRADUATE EDUCATION

The Title VI portion of the National Defense Foreign Language and Area Studies Act of the early 1960s cast federal support for the study of Africa as primarily a function of producing graduate-level competence in language and area studies. The group of programs founded in the early 1960s (Michigan State, Wisconsin, UCLA, Indiana, and Ohio University) evolved in direct response to this federal program. The two oldest programs, Northwestern (founded in 1946) and Boston University (founded in 1953), had already established faculty research and graduate training as their primary missions. Under the federal guidelines funding was competitive and reflected those institutions' ability to train graduate students and

269

to develop new programs according to priorities set in the Department of Education.

Over the years, these emphases and priorities have included language training, development links with professional schools, Outreach (K–12), and underdeveloped fields of social science (economics, sociology) and the natural sciences. Within these priority areas, only language training had a potential impact on undergraduate pedagogy, and even in that area the intent of African language development was the production of area studies expertise at the graduate level. Undergraduate enrollments only became a factor of evaluation in the 1980s. The Department of Education required reporting on undergraduate enrollments and numbers of courses with *Africa* in the course title as necessary but not sufficient criteria for funding. The emphasis on Africa-in-the-title courses pushed the addition of some courses; but it never recognized—and even discouraged—investing resources in the integration of Africa material into existing courses.

Title VI centers did, in fact, offer large numbers of undergraduate courses in African studies and encouraged faculty to expand those offerings. In the late 1960s, many programs introduced large interdisciplinary courses, often using the guest-lecture format as their primary response to increased student interest. Integration of programs, however, came relatively late. Northwestern introduced its Undergraduate Certificate in African Studies in 1973, Michigan State in 1979–1980. Boston University added an undergraduate minor in African studies in 1980. Ironically, these programs came when enrollments in Africa courses were declining. They received little campus visibility. They were also conceptually limited; that is, they served primarily to recognize students who took a requisite number of existing courses, including the core interdisciplinary courses, rather than reexamining or challenging the nature of undergraduate education on Africa itself. Centers tended to see undergraduate training as an administrative rather than an intellectual/pedagological challenge.

This tendency for the Title VI centers to emphasize both graduate education and an intellectual agenda based on research should not be surprising. The selection criteria for funding, though broadly based in assessing total resources, favors large research universities in which undergraduate teaching and innovation ranks relatively low in faculty performance evaluation. Such programs have been the foundation of research, publication, and library resource development on African studies (and area studies as a whole). The major question is whether we can harness and direct those faculty resources and experiences effectively into an infusion of new ideas on teaching Africa to undergraduates. Whatever the record of the past for Title VI centers, any reconception of how to address the task of undergraduate education must take into account the concentration of resources and experience in the major centers.

INTELLECTUAL LEADERSHIP
FOR THE RECONCEPTION OF AFRICA
IN THE UNDERGRADUATE CURRICULUM

I would argue strongly that the basic thrust of changing the role of Africa in undergraduate curricula must be intellectual in its foundations; that is, not be based on administrative restructuring, which comes down to simply adding more courses. This reconception I believe is not likely to emerge from the recent debates over multiculturalism and core curricula in which inclusion of Africa material into undergraduate curricula is mandated from above. Those debates, at their core, are conflicts over power, authority, and ideology within campus politics and U.S. politics in general. They are not, in their essence, about the study and understanding of Africa. Few if any African studies centers and programs are in the forefront of that movement, though many may be in sympathy with its goals. I am in agreement with Stanley Fish, one of the most visible spokespersons for the academic left, who argues that the primary issue in such campus debates is power and not inquiry about and teaching about non-Western societies.

Rather than concentrating on efforts to increase the numbers of Africa courses, I believe there should be a parallel movement to explore and illustrate the extent that the study of Africa can contribute new conceptual frameworks for interdisciplinary approaches to problems in social sciences and new critical frameworks for the humanities. These approaches should have their impact on already existing courses and in thematic curricula, not merely area specific courses. In the same way in which Outreach goals have shifted—from addressing stereotypes and adding Africa units to K–12 curricula to making Africa "normal"—undergraduate curricula need to include Africa not only in specialized area studies courses but to infuse Africa into a broad spectrum of courses.

The Contribution of Africanist Scholarship

My point here is best illustrated by looking at the ways in which Africanist scholarship has affected disciplinary paradigms in a number of fields and pioneered interdisciplinary research methodology as a whole. This has particularly been the case in explorations of the relationship between art, language, and literature, on the one hand, and social change on the other. Scholars have come to understand social life, culture, and politics as organized around symbols whose meaning must be studied in order to make sense of, and identify, the organization and its underlying principles.

African studies has a long history of contributions to this form of understanding that can link the humanities with social science. The Social

Science Research Council in the late 1980s began to explore these relationships. In that effort, anthropologist/historian Timothy Weiskel argued that Africanist scholarship has been fundamental to interdisciplinary scholarship in general. He pointed out that Africanist, sociocultural anthropologists' classic work on kinship and family structure—and more recent studies of gender—has been the foundation for larger theoretical literature in anthropology, social history, and challenges to neoclassical microeconomics.

In the field of linguistics, research on African languages has been important for understanding a range of important issues in noun class formation, tone and aspect, and sociolinguistics. Joseph Greenberg's classic *Language, Culture, and Communication* draws extensively on Africanist research to derive generative approaches to linguistic phenomena. Jack Goody's work on literacy and orality based on his field work in Ghana has become the standard work on the role of literacy in social and political change.

It is in the humanities—art, literature, music, religion, classical studies—and their interdisciplinary study that Africa has the greatest potential to enrich undergraduate curricula. Here, Clifford Geertz's notion of "blurred genres" has both testified to and advocated a more holistic approach to understanding the worlds of symbol and metaphor that connect art and literature, music and religion. Of all the disciplines in the humanities, literature is the largest and most powerful in its role in undergraduate teaching. Departments of English, which are among the largest on any campus but have been the site of fractious debates over method, will need to reassess their teaching in light of the waning of the postmodern, deconstructionist perspective. Work in the new historicism has led to a renewed interest in connections to the social sciences—a context that is already familiar ground to African humanities and analysis of African material culture, music, and religion. Unlike social science approaches to Africa (which can be problem-oriented and ahistorical) humanities materials—novels, film, plays, art—provide richer texts for undergraduate classrooms and can emphasize more universal experience. Moreover, in most programs, humanities and the arts have been traditionally underrepresented in faculty appointments and course coverage.

In a period when there appears to be some expansion in the funding and perhaps the numbers of Title VI centers, it is important to rethink the directions of Africa in the undergraduate classroom. Given their special access to off-campus resources and concentrations of activities, outreach programs, and so forth, Title VI centers can take a leadership role in expanding the teaching of Africa humanities curricula. The most productive approach, I believe, will be to infuse Africa into existing curricula, not just enlarge the number of Africa courses. This will require an explicit outreach effort across the campus and region to train and engage humanities faculty in discussions about the African humanities. The most effective mechanisms for this will be summer seminars (funded on campus or through NEH or Title VI Outreach Priority funds), team-teaching, and sponsoring an intellectual debate on teaching in the humanities that addresses Africa's past exclusion from teaching of the classics, modern literature, music, and so on. Obviously, the effort will also require that university administrations be convinced of the value of team-taught courses, tolerance for low enrollments in initial stages, and willingness to shift evaluation criteria from research to innovation in teaching. These criteria may be less easy at major research universities than liberal arts colleges, but will nonetheless likely be a sine qua non for success.

19

Accidents in African Studies: Africa in the Curriculum at the University of Richmond

Louis Tremaine

The accidents my title refers to are those by which Africa has slipped onto the campus and into the curriculum of the University of Richmond. They have been, by and large, happy accidents, though it is only recently that I have come to see them in that way. For several years now, the university has been lurching and stumbling toward what may, in the not-too-distant future, become a formal African studies program. My intent is not to express relief that we have survived the accidents, nor to speak about the program to come: it is to discuss the benefits these accidents have brought to intellectual and academic life on our campus, for both faculty and students, and to consider how we might safeguard those benefits, should such a program ever befall us.

The view I present is my own: I do not speak as a representative of my institution. Some of my colleagues share my interpretation of our recent collective history; others emphatically do not. We are, with respect to African studies and related questions, a university struggling with itself, and this is, of course, the case with many colleges and universities. The struggle I want to describe, however, is not the usual story of shifting institutional priorities and competition for scarce resources; rather, it is a struggle of ideas—one that has strengthened rather than sapped our overall effectiveness as a faculty, and, therefore, one that should be encouraged.

The setting for this struggle, the University of Richmond, is a private, primarily undergraduate institution of about three thousand students. The endowment is strong and climbing steadily. The student body is overwhelmingly white, well-to-do, politically conservative, academically successful, and oriented toward careers in business, medicine, and law.

Our story of accidents in African studies begins with me. I was the first accident. When I joined the Department of English in 1981, I was the only Africanist on the faculty. And I was hired despite my interest in Africa, not because of it, though I was permitted to teach one course in African literature every three semesters. A couple of years later, when the

275

Political Science Department advertised for someone to teach its methods course, it, too, turned up an Africanist—and she, too, produced a course on Africa. Although she moved on after a couple of years, and her course was expunged from the catalog, this pattern has continued. Through some recent hirings, our faculty now includes Africanists in history, political science, sociology, English, French, and anthropology (in one case, Africanist-in-the-making would be a better description). Three of these are Africans. In every one of the searches that brought these people to us, the job description either made no mention of Africa or listed Africa as one of two or more optional areas of interest. You could say that we just got lucky.

But it was more than just luck (and not merely accidental) that most of these people, unlike me, began work at Richmond in a climate that actively encouraged them to help expand our offerings on Africa. For in the meantime, someone had begun asking questions about what we were doing to promote something called "international competence" in our students, and the question got asked often enough that a committee was empaneled to look into the matter. The particular charge given this committee, as it turns out, was important in determining the direction we have traveled since. We were not asked in this committee to create an international studies program (though we subsequently did), or to establish a series of area studies programs. We were not, in fact, asked to create anything at all. Rather, our charge was to study several related questions:

- What is international competence?
- Can undergraduates acquire it as part of their college training and experience?
- If so, are our undergraduates acquiring it?
- If they are not, what might our university be capable of doing to help them acquire it?

The upshot, after two years of discussion and another year of implementation, was an Office of International Education with a full-time director and assistant. These people coordinate Study Abroad, recruit and support international students, organize cocurricular programs, assist in bringing foreign scholars-in-residence to campus, organize annual faculty study tours abroad, and administer a major in international studies. The 140 or so students in this single, interdisciplinary major select one or another of several tracks or concentrations, defined by region or by a combination of disciplines, and take relevant courses in the various departments. But they also take two courses in common:

1. An introductory course that explores issues regarding the production of knowledge about other cultures and about relations between cultures

2. A senior seminar in which students in all the tracks, nearing completion of their studies, pool their training and perspectives to work together on a common problem

We have, then, institutionalized something called "international studies" at the University of Richmond. But what I want to draw attention to is that the model by which we have done so is one that resists enclosure, both institutional and intellectual. The International Studies Program is administered within the same office that manages all international activities on campus, and consequently international studies majors interact often and significantly with students outside the program. Within the program, there are strong connections among the various tracks, preventing their becoming isolated as separate programs. Responsibility for the major is exercised jointly by the director and a committee comprising the faculty advisors in the various tracks. Both the introductory course and senior seminar include material and focus on problems relevant to all. Many of the same departmental courses satisfy requirements in more than one track, again encouraging in students a range of perspectives brought to bear on common problems. At the same time, members of the faculty teaching these courses are discouraged from thinking of themselves as attached institutionally to one of these area interests as separate from the others. By design, students in this program think of themselves as internationalists with an area concentration, rather than, for example, as Asianists or as Latin Americanists.

Or, to return to our subject, as Africanists. No, there is not an Africa track, not yet. I think that it is coming and that it will, with perhaps a couple more happy accidents, replace the current Third World track fairly soon. But Africa is very much present in the program, both through the specialized courses we do offer and, just as significantly, through its extensive incorporation into the common courses.

Why is that incorporation important? To answer that question I want to trace a different line of development in the Richmond curriculum—one larger in scale but consistent with the first in its outcome and effects. We have recently implemented a fundamental revision of our general education curriculum. As a part of that revision, we have instituted a First-Year Core Course. In this course, students engage in research and reflection on fundamental issues in human experience through the reading of primary works drawn from a variety of historical periods and cultural traditions. Currently, the course examines different ways of formulating questions about order and change, breaking these two related concepts down into categories such as moral order, social order, and so on, and bringing to this study various sorts of texts from Europe, East Asia, the Middle East, and Africa.

This, as readers might already have anticipated, is where the struggle came in, and it is an instructive one. The initial proposal for the new course came from the faculty Curriculum Committee. It reads in part as follows (readers will notice significant differences from the course I have just briefly described):

> [T]he two-semester core course would use primary texts to focus on central questions regarding self, society, and cosmos in selected periods in Western history, and would contrast the treatment of those questions with analogous discussions from a non-Western culture. . . . The Western tradition will be a constant focus and backbone for the core course, if only because it is the tradition of the overwhelming majority of our students and faculty. For the first several years of implementation, a different, non-Western culture will be selected each year to serve as the second, contrasting focus for the course. . . . We envision that year by year we will introduce such cultures as those found in China, Africa, Japan, Latin America, and India.

The Curriculum Committee passed this proposal to the Office of International Education for assistance in developing "other culture" modules for the grant application that was then being prepared. In doing so, the committee understandably assumed that the idea would delight the hearts of the international studies faculty, whose efforts in multicultural education would here find support and, indeed, be placed at the core of the new curriculum. Instead, a debate was opened regarding two difficult issues:

1. One issue was not simply whether the West is superior to the rest, but rather how difficult it is not to teach it as if it were. As noted above, the initial proposal not only describes Western culture as "ours," but characterizes every other culture as "non-Western" and casts it in the explicit role of contrasting case. Any non-Western culture could be substituted freely for any other, indeed, would be, as the course developed. All are defined by absence, negation, and their quality of being alien: by what they are *not* as compared with what the West *is* and to what *we* are.

2. The other issue was: What are we doing when we use the word *culture* to divide human experience into categories to be thought about? And, therefore, what are we doing when we "teach" these categories? The language of the original proposal treats such non-parallel terms as Japan, Africa, and the West as equally monolithic categories of culture that can be meaningfully compared on the basis of a few selected texts.

These are hardly new issues. Yet in the situation I have described, they had a kind of effective reality. They posed a concrete, and indeed urgent, dilemma. Some of us said to ourselves, "I'm happy to see Africa introduced at long last into the curriculum, but do I want it at the price of unintentional but inevitable denigration and distortion?" The reaction of some of my colleagues was to want to tell the committee, "Keep Western Civilization and give us a separate program so that we can teach Africa *right*."

As I have noted above, the international studies effort at Richmond has, so far, resisted such enclosure. Instead of expressing such thoughts, the internationalists offered a counterproposal to the committee. The result was that, by this accident in curriculum development, area studies specialists found themselves engaged in a conversation with colleagues from very different fields and a broad range of disciplines about what it means to teach a world that includes Africa. Instead of creating a self-contained module and turning it over to an expert to handle, all these faculty were thinking about just why it is important that students attend to cultural products coming from Africa.

There was much discussion. The consequence was the course I have described. That course now eschews all claims to be teaching or comparing cultures—not because cultures should not be taught or compared, even by us, but because this course is not the place to do it. Instead, its objective is a kind of intellectual training that teaches, among other things, that students should turn as readily to the work of African, Asian, or Middle Eastern thinkers as they would to that of Europeans or North Americans when they are faced with challenging intellectual problems.

The questions do not end there, of course. We have come around to asking students to compare ideas rather than cultures. But ideas arise within cultures and within history—are we not dangerously decontextualizing? I think the answer is that we are—and that every educational move we make has its intellectual dangers and trade-offs. In this case, those dangers are regularly examined and debated by faculty in the process of course development. Each spring semester and early summer, faculty preparing to come into the course in the fall meet in a seminar to discuss the texts and the purposes of the course. When the seminar incorporated African texts into its syllabus for the first time—in 1991/92—these texts produced ongoing debates on several matters that the participants perceived to be problems:

1. We are forced to deal with these texts without a thorough appreciation of their historical and cultural background
2. In choosing texts with oral sources we are dependent on problematic mechanisms of transmission and translation and cannot, therefore, guarantee the authenticity of our materials
3. Both (1) and (2) above raise additional questions as to how representative these texts and their authors are
4. Some texts may undermine the positive image of Africa that we might like to promote

These debates are salutary for at least two reasons. The first is that they force us to define our purposes very carefully, for ourselves and for our students, focusing on what we can do well and responsibly in the course and articulating carefully what we are not attempting to do. The second reason lies closer to my theme. It is that the context of the seminar (as of the course itself) leads us to do several things:

1. Ask why we are raising these issues in regard to African texts and not to others
2. Put the same questions to the texts of what we consider more familiar sources
3. As a result, either to defamiliarize those sources in some very constructive ways or to discern the flaws in the questions themselves

These details are enough, I think, to demonstrate the pattern that has emerged at Richmond with regard to the teaching of Africa. Through a series of what I have called accidents, both in hiring and in selection of course materials, Africa has increasingly established a presence in our undergraduate curriculum. But it is an uncontained presence, acting in such a way as to touch meaningfully all of our students and a very large proportion of our faculty and to take a significant part in the research and reflection that we consider central to our work as an academic community.

With some of my colleagues, I am currently designing an international studies concentration on Africa. I think that it is important to do this: it will establish a stronger base for claiming institutional resources; it will provide a framework for the sort of study that does require contextual understanding; and it will encourage more extended study of Africa. But another rationale often cited, the need to "legitimize" Africa as an area of study by assigning it an institutional niche, does not apply at Richmond. That work will already have been undertaken by the very different sort of institutional engagement with Africa that I have described. As an accidental development becomes an increasingly intentional one, therefore, our challenge will be not to lose sight of what we have gained by letting Africa run loose in our curriculum.

20

Underdevelopment and Self-Reliance in Building African Studies: Some Pedagogical, Policy, and Practical Political Issues at the College of Charleston

Jack Parson

A committee-led initiative created a minor in African studies and thereby modestly institutionalized African studies at the College of Charleston in Charleston, South Carolina, in 1992. This development resulted from processes of decision making and implementation dealing with three inter-related sets of issues: pedagogical, policy, and political. Decisions had to be made about the design and articulation of courses in the African studies curriculum as well as about how to deliver these courses to students; decisions had to be made about the governance of the minor and its relationship to other programs on campus; decisions had to be made about the purpose and role of the new program in the wider community.

This chapter reflects upon the process leading to the establishment of the minor, drawing out of that process perspectives and conclusions that are more widely applicable. The elements in this reflection include the context within which the process unfolded, a narrative on the unfolding debate and steps in decision making, and a consideration of pedagogical issues related to undergraduate African studies. A main conclusion is that the application of minimal resources, combined with a careful packaging of the existing curriculum, created a worthwhile, if modest, institutionalization of African studies. This institutionalization, in turn, provided a point of further organization within the college and local community.

INTERNATIONAL STUDIES AT CHARLESTON

It is important to contextualize the process of creating and implementing an African studies presence. Institutions vary tremendously in size, mission, and status (whether public or private). These variations condition the sources and availability of financial resources as well as the socioeconomic composition of the student population. The composition, experience, and orientation of the faculty are similarly conditioned by these variations. The demographic, economic, and political complexion of the wider community served by the institution is an additional factor.

The College of Charleston goes back more than two hundred years, laying claim to being the oldest municipal college in the United States.[1] Its most recent history begins in 1970, when it was a financially pressed, 450-student, private, segregated college. It was saved from extinction by a state-level decision to develop a public, four-year college to service the South Carolina low-country centered on Charleston, where the Civil War began—and where, it seems at times, it never ended. Since 1970, now a public institution, the college has grown rapidly. There were about five thousand students in 1980 and about nine thousand in 1992. Its academic programs continue to be primarily undergraduate.

The college almost completely missed the so-called revolution of the 1960s in undergraduate education, retaining what is now sought by many schools—a strict set of general degree requirements that create a solid liberal arts foundation. All students at the college must complete two years of a foreign language, a year of a laboratory science, a year of mathematics, a year of English, twelve semester hours of humanities courses, six of social science, and a year of European history (often referred to incorrectly as a year of Western Civilization). It is generally assumed that these requirements arise from the accumulated wisdom of mankind and, therefore, are unavailable for amendment. For some faculty, this package is unavailable for discussion. While this package of liberal arts requirements ensures an exposure to a significant slice of the human experience, it also has a rigidity about it, working against the incorporation of experiences different from those already incorporated. Its disciplinary base also works against the development of interdisciplinary courses and experiences.

The curriculum, resources, "traditions," and many faculty of the institution are organized and occupied in the service of this idea of the liberal arts undergraduate curriculum—a noble endeavor, no doubt, in the context of a state university with a minuscule endowment and subject to state funding in an economically disadvantaged state. Classes are still relatively small, are taught by a "real" professor, and are numerous. The teaching load is normally twelve semester hours (four classes), often with three preparations each semester, at least in the social sciences.[2] To use a wartime metaphor, these are the trenches of undergraduate teaching in the United States.

The history of these programs is heavily white and focused on the United States. The non-U.S. liberalizing component consists almost entirely of an exposure to Western European history and English (British) literature and, for the most part, the European literature of the language studied.[3] A student can graduate without ever being systematically exposed to any non-Western or minority experience. My impression is that most do just that.

This does not mean that there is no interest in international studies. There is an international studies minor and an administrative office responsible for international programs, essentially Study Abroad (mostly to Europe), and looking after the roughly 125 international students who are at the college. Moreover, certain departments are international in focus, particularly a large Languages Department. But the curriculum, even in these departments, tends to be skewed toward Western European studies. The History Department, indeed, offers courses for all areas of the world; but because virtually everyone must spend the majority of their teaching time in History 101 and 102, European History, the department for the most part has been unwilling to recruit faculty who do not offer Europe as a strong area.

I do not think this situation is unique to the College of Charleston, not by any means. But it is contradictory, that what appears as a well-rounded, broad, liberal arts background is geographically and temporally narrow in curricular terms. At worst, it sends the message that a well-educated person is the one who knows certain details of the Western European and U.S. experience. All other experiences are therefore either derivative from this experience or irrelevant to it. Moreover, this institutionalizes a conservative view of what is and is not a legitimate avenue of inquiry down which students should proceed. It idealizes the worth of the Western European tradition and devalues other experiences, even those which may have been the foundations for Western European history. Had the college imbibed more deeply of the critique of the Eurocentric tradition in the 1960s, it is possible that the Eurocentric view would not be taken so much for granted. On the other hand, I would note that, at places such as UC–Berkeley where there was much turmoil, there is now a lively debate about "multiculturalism" and "political correctness."

It appears to me that some of the senior academic officers of the college more readily recognize these limitations to the undergraduate experience than do many departments and their chairs. The academic officers, of course, do not have the same vested interest in the curriculum status quo as the faculty. They are more responsive to external stimuli—the community, the corporate environment, and trends abroad in the land that are brought to their attention mainly in the *Chronicle of Higher Education.* In relation to African studies at Charleston, the more important influences on the senior administrative environment are community-based. The population of the Charleston community is approximately 40 percent African-American. The student body at the college is about 7 percent African-American. While this proportion has remained fairly constant over the past few years, the growing student body meant an absolute increase in the African-American presence, and it has begun to approach a critical mass. Beginning in 1990, some African-American students articulated a demand for more relevant courses and programs, particularly the regular teaching of African-American history. This subject had not been regularly offered for several years. African-American students also formed an increasing student constituency in Africa-based courses.

Also contextually important is the fact that the Avery Research Center is associated with the college. Avery's mandate includes research and programs on low-country African-American life and history. By 1991, an important dimension to this work was research establishing an important connection between the rice-growing culture of the low-country in the nineteenth-century era of slavery and rice-growing cultures on the Western African coast; hence, an intellectual and political linkage between African-Americans and Africans and between African-American studies and African studies.

DEVELOPING AN AFRICAN STUDIES DIMENSION

This intellectual, institutional, and political environment was the one in which an organized African studies dimension began to develop in 1990. The core faculty involved were the two Africanists on campus (myself and a colleague in African history, who is African) and a colleague in French (a Nigerian) with a strong interest in African literature and the creation of an African focus on campus. By 1992, this committee grew to seven, with the inclusion of two additional members from the French section of the Languages Department, one from the Spanish section (who is from Ghana), and a linguist who is now in the English Department.

The original core committee discussed and drafted a proposal creating an African studies *program*, a component of which was a minor in African studies. The minor would be composed of a new, freshman-level, interdisciplinary, required course entitled "Introduction to African Civilization;" two semesters of African history; and three additional elective, Africa-based courses, which in practice were composed of existing courses I taught in political science; additional courses offered in history; a course in anthropology; and less-frequently offered courses in African literature. The original program proposal also included: (1) the development of international exchange and linkage programs with African scholars and/or universities (particularly capitalizing on the historical association between the low-country and West Africa); (2) the facilitation of research through bringing to campus Africanist scholars for public presentations and research seminars and developing a link with the Avery Research Center; (3) the encouragement of the internationalization of the broader college curriculum; and (4) engagement in community outreach activities, including in the local school districts. The estimated annual budget to maintain a minimal program was $15,000 per year. This figure included provision for a one-course reduction and "tenth month" salary for a director, money to pay for offering two sections of the new course each semester, and for one Africanist scholar to be invited to campus each semester.

In a meeting with senior academic officers, it became clear that, while there was sincere intellectual support for this initiative, little material support was available. A number of worthy programs were forming (e.g., women's studies), and all needed support. There were not enough resources to support them all so none could be adequately supported. Had we portrayed the program as specifically meeting the needs of African-American students and the African-American community, in the name of African-American studies, there might have been more immediate interest in the proposal (see below).

The upshot was that the committee had to decide whether to go forward with a more or less unfunded minor or do nothing. The decision to go ahead involved a significant commitment to add work to already hard-pressed schedules, but that was the decision made. It was feasible only because the dean of the School of Humanities and Social Sciences agreed to fund the offering of one section of the new course each semester for two semesters. After that, it was expected to pay for itself through full enrollments.

There was a particular, local necessity for the funding of the new course: it is difficult to offer interdisciplinary courses in an institution very firmly organized around disciplinary departments. Department faculty positions are related to the number of students enrolled in departmental courses. Anyone teaching a course outside a department, therefore, hurts the department's enrollments, although collegewide there is no such effect. This does mean that, in releasing a faculty member to teach a nondepartmentally based, interdisciplinary course, a department expects that compensation will be paid in the form of an adjunct replacement salary. The way around the situation is to cross-list an interdisciplinary course as a departmental course. This is often done, but it distorts the departmental curriculum and sends a mixed message to students, who soon think of it as a departmental course.

The committee insisted on maintaining the integrity of the 101 course as an interdisciplinary offering, and fortunately the dean agreed to provide two adjunct course salaries for 1992/93. Without that commitment, we could not have proceeded to create even a minor without undermining that first course. No other resources were made available in the form of released time, other budgetary support, or compensation. Additional activities and planning depend on the goodwill and time of the faculty involved and serendipitous funding by the administration. In the present, restrictive budgetary climate, it is likely that in the immediate future we can expect little support. The proposal for a minor wound its way through the faculty governance procedure and was approved in late 1991. The introductory course (and minor) was first offered in the fall of 1992. By spring 1994, full enrollment (thirty students) had been achieved, and the new course seemed to be securely established. A grant proposal titled "Making Connections: Strengthening African Studies in the Liberal Arts Curriculum" was submitted for possible funding to the Undergraduate International Studies and Foreign Language Program of the U.S. Department of Education. Growing course enrollment and the possibility of external funding may allow the development of additional curriculum components and new activities envisaged in the original proposal for an African studies *program,* not merely a *minor.*

This process raised several issues. First, we had to make a basic policy decision during the conceptualization phase about the articulation of African to African-American studies. Our discussions took place at a time when the long-felt need for some sort of African-American studies was receiving new attention, partially because students were pressing, rightly, for it—particularly students in the History Department. The African studies committee unanimously supported this development. The question was, what should be the relationship between African and African-American studies? The African studies drafting group made a conscious decision to create an African studies dimension organizationally and academically distinct from African-American studies. Simultaneously, we created the principle that those involved in both areas (in practice most of us were involved in planning in both areas) should, in their planning, identify all of those points at which the programs intersected and create joint and/or coordinated means for working together at those points. We reached this decision for two main reasons.

First, while all members of the committee were supportive of developing a program in African-American studies, and recognized the role of an African studies curriculum in conjunction with a program of African-American studies, none of us had any specific training directly related to offering African-American studies and little experience in teaching in programs of African-American studies where African studies was an integral component.[4] In addition, the college did not at that time have any African-American studies specialists. The Avery Research Center was not a teaching department. Without expertise, we felt it would be a disservice, and arrogant, to create a program that purported to be in African-American studies when in fact it was devised and offered exclusively by Africanists.

Second, aware of this limitation, in a context where the need for an African-American studies program was palpable, we were concerned that we might be forced to portray our work as meeting this demand. Therefore, we insisted that this was African, not African-American studies. This left no room for anyone at the college to assert that here was the program specifically meeting the needs of African-American students. We were not prepared to let the college curriculum and public relations operation off of that particular hook. I believed, and still do, that the potential process of empowerment possible with the creation of an African-American studies program would be undermined if the program identified for that purpose became that process's main obstacle—as an undiluted African studies program would surely be.

So we decided that the African studies component should be independent and distinct. But this, in our thinking, created the need to see to it that the development of African-American studies should be simultaneously stimulated, and that this process should include the articulation of African and African-American studies. Each of us had been invited to serve on a working party on African-American studies chaired by an African-American emeritus professor of English. This group also included staff from the Avery Center as well as interested faculty from college departments. There being only a handful of African-Americans on the faculty and staff, a majority of members were non-African-Americans. However, African-Americans provided the leadership. The result was the drafting of a document for an African-American studies program that included a minor in African-American studies incorporating Africa-based courses. The resulting relationship at Charleston is a very healthy one. African and African-American studies have distinct identities and purposes, but they are also intimately related. Faculty approval for the minor in African-American studies was completed in late 1992. During 1993/94, the college began recruiting for a new director for the Avery Research Center, who will also be the director of African-American studies at the college. With this appointment, we believe the state will be set to render considerable service to both students and the surrounding community.

I will mention two additional perspectives on this experience of establishing a minor in African studies. First, that while organized African studies is now part of the curriculum, its existence is precarious. The emperor, while not completely naked, is at best barely preserving his modesty. No staff members have on-load time to either teach in or manage the minor and develop new dimensions to it. Funding for the new basic course is not secure. This is another way of saying the minor has no budget. And it is unlikely that funding for African studies will be a high priority. Faculty resources at Charleston are thinly spread, and the loss of such resources, even for short-term sabbaticals, can be crippling.

The precarious nature of the effort leads directly to a need to seek external assistance. That search assumes that, if we can generate even modest curriculum development through new courses in departments, there will be a growing student FTE generated by African studies courses. If this happens, those departments will begin to have a vested interest in African studies. From a college administration point of view, the minor will then pay for itself. This would result in institutional commitment, normalization of the program—and a budget!

My second take on the experience is that, despite the difficulties and stress involved in negotiating the creation of the minor, it was worth it.

The minor meets a real student need and demand. It increased the legitimacy accorded to the study of the non-European experience by institu-
tionalizing it in the curriculum; and it has created a network among those
on campus who have an interest in Africanist scholarship. These achievements are permanent, enriching the intellectual life of the institution and
furthering its mission.

SELECTED PEDAGOGICAL ISSUES

An important ancillary component to the development of African studies
at the College of Charleston was a discussion of pedagogical issues. Many
of these issues are well known, but I will reprise them in the context of my
experience. I highly value the experiential component of certain courses
taught at Charleston.

For nearly twenty years, I have taught a one-semester-long undergraduate course on contemporary African politics to U.S. students. I also
teach a variety of more specialized courses, particularly dealing with the
Southern African region. This continues to be a frustrating business. I have
come to the conclusion that there are three, sometimes related, problems to
be faced in the United States for teachers and students of basic African
courses: the image of Africa, the U.S. context, and the lack of resonance.
The stereotypes of Africa in the context of U.S. history and culture often
stand in the way of imparting/absorbing knowledge. And the content of
most basic courses lacks resonance in the lives and minds of students.

The most easily recognized part of the problem is the existence of
powerful and pervasive stereotypes of Africa that students bring—often
not very consciously—to African courses. When students approach texts,
lectures, and other material, there is a tendency to refract what they read,
hear, and see through the prism of these stereotypes—what they already
"know" about Africa. Typically this "knowledge" insists that Africa is a
"country" that is, in this image, either gloriously romanticized or hopelessly mired in primitive barbarism. If a lecturer teaches that, in Buganda,
traditional house construction is of mud and wattle and that, done correctly
and maintained well, it will provide good accommodation efficiently and
cheaply, students may "learn" that natives still live in mud huts. The
image of the either happy or immiserated savage is, therefore, reinforced.
Students do not always learn what we teach. Many students learn in the
context of what they already "know," and this is often negative knowledge. Teachers tend to think that the mind of the average student in an
African survey course is a tabula rasa; in fact, it may be a black hole into
which has already been sucked, and then imbedded, an enormous quantity
of distorted mis- and disinformation. New information is then evaluated
against the "known." Information that conforms to or reinforces preexisting

notions is accepted; information that does not is rejected. Rejected material may be discredited on the grounds of a professor's liberal (or other) biases. What we think we teach is not always what students learn.

My second observation is on the matter of context. We often forget, or try to ignore, the fact that we teach African courses in the United States of America. This enveloping historical and cultural context we often treat as an epiphenomenon unrelated to our academic endeavor. We like to think that, within the confines of "our" Africa course, we can forget about the cultural context in which it is offered. Most Africanists wish to convey an African experience to students, which means endeavoring to shut out, as best we can, the culture of the country within which our course is taught.

The truth, of course, is that we cannot divorce the content of courses, and the processes of learning in those courses, from the wider culture, from the institutions and the society in which the teaching happens. Like it or not, African survey courses taught in the United States are offered in a culture with a continuing history of racism—a culture in which "Africa" has had a special, though contradictory, place. African-Americans may sometimes appropriate for themselves the culture of the African continent and make it an undifferentiated reference point of identification and nostalgia. And why not? In the same way that a Kennedy (or a Reagan) appropriates the culture and identification of Ireland. For many African-Americans, such an affiliation with, and even expropriation of, "Africa" is an important piece of political identification, and sometimes of action in the United States. The Back to Africa movement, at least for the purpose of discovering and cultivating roots, is a positive, for many indispensable, feature of African-American life in coping with and confronting racism. On the other hand, for many whites the Back to Africa movement means sending "them" back to Africa where they belong! White racism is reflected in the Tarzan image. It is very powerful, very pervasive, and very American.

Each of these perspectives—that on context and that on stereotypes—is distortive. One is constructive and positive, the other negative and destructive. Both are directly related to the study of Africa; and both are very American. Both find a place in the minds of the student constituencies I know best—not in all of them, but in most of them. These perspectives result from the fact that there is a significant layer of racism in U.S. society, and this racism itself affects the process of learning about Africa. Courses on Africa cannot of themselves change society; but that society should not be ignored in teaching those courses. If we ignore the racism of U.S. society and the emotive symbolism of "Africa" in it, it may operate as a sore that can fester and grow to gangrenous proportions.

I mentioned a third problem in introductory African courses: the lack of resonance between what is taught and the daily lives and thoughts of students. Students do not always make the connection between the common humanity of Africans and themselves. Of all the genetic material of all the people in all the world, 99 percent of it is the same and it creates a common set of basic needs. Our common biology leads to needs for food, shelter, health care, clothing. The commonality of human existence leads to common underlying social, economic, and political issues: how to structure social interaction, how to produce the goods needed for life, how to live collectively in relative harmony. Africans, too, want to live comfortably, educate their children, perform worthwhile and creative labor, and enjoy in peace the fruits of their effort. They laugh and cry, rejoice in birth, and mourn at death. Too often, our common predicament and condition goes unrecognized. This absence of empathy, of ability to place oneself in someone else's shoes and vicariously experience the life and feelings of another, is an obstacle; and as long as it exists, there will be an impenetrable wall between what students learn about Africa and the reality of life in Africa. After years of grappling with these issues, I have concluded that there is no magic bullet with which to make the problems go away. I cannot quickly change the societal context in which I offer classes. But also I cannot afford to ignore that context. Hence, I want to discuss three techniques I regularly incorporate into teaching. I will concentrate on one of these: the use of simulations.

In basic courses, I always deal with stereotypes about Africa, first in general. Then, in particular, I deal with the role of images of Africa in relation to racial politics in the United States. First, I try to make students conscious of the stereotypes. At the first class meeting, and without explaining the purpose, I ask students to free-associate the first thing that pops into their minds when Africa is mentioned. We do this as a group, and two lists of words are created on the blackboard. One list contains words which convey positive images, and the other is negative characteristics. The students are not told the rationale for why some words are put in one list rather than the other. The negative list is always longer than the positive list. Then the word *Europe* is mentioned, and the names of one or two countries, usually including *England,* and another pair of lists is created. The lists on Europe and European countries are almost always 100 percent positive.

Having explicitly developed the stereotypes, we discuss their content as "knowledge." This is broadened to a discussion of stereotypes in general and their widespread importance in day-to-day life. The means through which such stereotypes are reproduced and their use in the context of political power are also discussed, which allows for a discussion of the stereotypical images of Africa in the context of U.S. society and its politics. The desired outcome, not ever perfectly achieved in practice, is a classroom environment where the stereotypes and images are very conscious, creating in students a healthy skepticism in relation to what they read, see, and hear. It is also a healthy beginning in encouraging students to see the relevance of Africa and African studies to their own lives.

This process encourages students to relate their lives to a broader world; but it is only a beginning in tackling the problem of the lack of resonance between the students' lives and the African experience. It is important that what students learn about Africa should not be placed by students in a separate category of human experience, unrelated to their own. One technique here is to discuss with students the vocabulary used to describe things African. For example, it is important that students think of Africans as people, not as "natives," and as people who have important ethnic identities beyond their tribal membership. The vocabulary used in discussing these issues turns out to be very important.

This development of a common vocabulary to discuss life in African countries leads to being able to discuss issues of political, economic, and cultural development in comparative terms. Analogies and metaphors rooted in the past understanding and experience of students are developed. For example, when discussing ethnic conflict in Africa, one can draw on the historical development of European nations rooted in ethnic identities. In current affairs, the situation in the former Yugoslavia is tailor-made for a discussion of tribalism and the historical reasons why politics may become interethnic. The use of current examples from Europe not only illustrates the general point that ethnicity may be an important means of political mediation; it also demonstrates that these issues are alive and well in the contemporary, so-called developed world and are not to be regarded as indicative of societies at a lower or earlier stage of development.

A comparative perspective may be introduced into many aspects of a survey course. The topic of political stability and instability is always of interest to students. It is an important topic. Students tend to think of African polities as somehow inherently and wrongly unstable. When there is such need for economic progress, why can't this divisiveness be put aside? In this context, I find it useful to sketch, briefly, almost to the point of caricature, the earlier history of the United States—the facts, inter alia, that it was formed as a result of armed rebellion, created a constitution (the Articles of Confederation) that failed miserably within a decade of independence and was replaced by a constitution that, with the society as a whole, contained the seed of what became a bloody civil war seventy-five years after the rebellion against Britain. The path of the United States to relative political stability was long and difficult. Most African countries are around thirty years old. Few have experienced anything like the social disorder represented by the U.S. Civil War. Moreover, it is important to deal with the concept of political stability and unity in the *current* circumstances of the United States. Civil rights issues, for example, still define a society as yet unable to resolve inequities in the economy and polity.

Such an approach has the virtue of encouraging students to consider the long-term as well as current history of Africa as part of a broad human experience not unlike their own. The danger, of course—as pointed out in an earlier chapter—is that it implicitly encourages students to think that the issues being faced in Africa are the same as those in the United States. If this happens, one loses the distinctive, historical, structural, and cultural contexts of African countries. To avoid this, I try to indicate through the comparative material, which is scattered throughout the course, that we should be thinking that the problems of development are more or less universal and then develop the African material on those problems, only reprising the comparative perspective.

The most effective technique I have used in teaching about political, economic, and social development in Africa is that of the simulation. Simulations force students to develop and play out a role as an African. They are required to shed their personal and national identities in order to approach becoming someone different from themselves. They can, and most do, begin not only to think within but also to feel the situation of another whose life, at first blush, is unfamiliar and even exotic.

I have used simulations in two course settings. A brief description of each may be helpful in illustrating the utility of such experiences. One is entitled "The Politics of Revolutionary Change in South Africa," offered during the Maymester term. Maymester takes place during the last three weeks of May. One course is a full-time load for both faculty and students—each course meets five days a week for three and one-half hours each day. So, the students are a captive audience. They can be expected to fix all of their attention on one subject. They can be expected to eat, live, and breathe that one course. With three and one-half hours each day, the students quickly get to know each other and the professor. A corporate feeling about the class is quickly established.

In May 1992, at the second meeting of the class, each student was assigned a character or role, such as Nelson Mandela or F.W. de Klerk. (The total number of roles depends upon both the current situation and the number of students in the class.) The assignment of roles was done by random drawing.[5] Class meetings leading up to a four-day simulation were designed to accomplish two things. One was to develop the context for the contemporary situation (in May 1992, the context was the ongoing CODESA talks in South Africa). The second objective was to assist students in developing their assigned character through reading, class discussion, and film. All students read both standard history and political science literature, but greater attention was given to biographical and autobiographical work and film. A good deal of class time was spent watching and then discussing documentary and theatrical productions. In Maymester 1992, the list of films viewed included *Last Grave at Dimbaza*, *Generations of Resistance*, *A World Apart*, *Cry Freedom*, *A Dry White Season*, and *Destructive Engagement.* The biographical, autobiographical, and film material was an in-your-face educational experience that forced students to confront situations in both intellectual and personal terms. This created a context in which they could develop not only the factual content of their character or role; they also developed a stake in their character's personality. Later this facilitated the simulation.

At the close of the period of preparation, each student presented his/her character's political personality orally to the class. They also presented a written paper to me as class leader. These presentations punctuated the transition from role development to the acting-out of those roles. The oral presentations gave each student the opportunity to be the character they would portray in the simulation, increasing their confidence. It also provided the opportunity for all the characters to reflect on the personality of their character in relation to the others.

In Maymester 1992, the simulation itself ran over four days for three and one-half hours each day. The issues were limited to the more important debates in the CODESA talks, such as whether a constituent assembly would write a new constitution, what kind of interim government could be created, and what institutions would be written into a new constitution. The situation and parameters for the meeting were communicated through a mock issue of the *Weekly Mail,* a newspaper that was used throughout to guide and shape the simulation. While CODESA participants met, non-CODESA roles observed from a distance. Non-CODESA roles could, of course, communicate with participants directly, either overtly or privately. And all participants could issue press releases that might, or might not, be picked up by the *Weekly Mail* for publication. The role of editor of the newspaper is filled by faculty, who are also available for consultations with characters who are unsure of their positions. Direct interventions are to be avoided: they can best be handled through the newspaper. At the beginning, the students are always unsure of themselves. The temptation for faculty (a temptation to be resisted) is to intervene too often and too directly. My experience is that, after an initial rocky start, students quickly get into their roles, and the simulation takes on a life of its own.

The period of the simulation is very intense and stressful. It becomes real. For the teacher it is nonstop and action packed. But the payoff is watching average students turn into characters of which they had no knowledge a few short weeks before. For the group collectively, the outcome is often a relatively comprehensive and nuanced understanding of the current situation. While the simulation is not in itself very good at developing a sophisticated conceptual perspective, it is good at getting students to deal with the nitty-gritty of practical politics and at involving them in that in a very personal way. Incidentally, the simulations often offer a déjà vu sense later, if events unfold in reality along the lines of the simulations. In May 1992, we found in our simulation that if the Third

Force (see note 5) remained active and covertly worked with Inkhata, the CODESA talks broke down. Within two months, the reality in South Africa was that this happened. Students are always impressed when something like this occurs. Current events reinforce for students the value of what they learned during the simulation. Frequently, students call me, months after such a simulation, to talk about how the real situation unfolded and their perspective on why the simulation was or was not therefore realistic. The ability of students to undertake that sort of analysis is for me significant reinforcement to continue developing the use of simulations. They are a valuable learning experience.

A second experiential learning event, in which I have regularly participated since 1981, is the National Model Organization of African Unity (OAU), held yearly at Howard University in Washington, D.C. The model OAU was founded in 1980 by Michael Nwanze, of the Political Science Department at Howard. Working with faculty advisors, he has continued to develop it. The model OAU simulates a meeting of an international organization—not unlike the UN—the members of which are nation-states. The "characters" in the simulation are, therefore, national delegations. *Unlike* a model UN, the model OAU puts Africa and African issues at the center of debate and discussion. For those interested in teaching about Africa, it offers a unique opportunity to immerse students in such discussions. Student delegations composed of from five to seven students represent the member states of the OAU. The model OAU is structured into four commissions (economic, social, liberation and defense, and mediation), and over a period of two and a half days the gamut of developmental and political issues are discussed. A final day is then devoted to a plenary assembly of heads of state and government to pass final resolutions. A council of ministers meets concurrently with the commissions to deal with crisis situations. The crises build upon existing situations and then allows the council to deal with them. In 1992, the council dealt with two crises, one in Liberia and the other in South Africa. The fact that the venue is Washington D.C. allows students to be given a briefing at the embassy of the country they represent—a key experience.

This is a four-day immersion in thinking and talking about Africa and African issues. Students are forced to identify, defend, and promote the national interests of the country they represent, sometimes in cooperation with other countries and sometimes in conflict. By the end of the four days, students are prepared to go to the wall for causes that to them a few short weeks before were only vague ideas, if they thought about them at all. Students see the world through African eyes, however imperfectly and haltingly. They always achieve some level of empathy. Such learning is permanent.

Participation in the model is the payoff for the teaching process that has taken place at home universities. (The *Faculty Advisors' Handbook* for the model describes it as an "extension of the classroom.") The preparatory period, before the model takes place, is excellent for developing student interest and interdisciplinary skills. At Charleston, the "delegations" I advise are enrolled in a three-credit-hour course entitled "International Regional Organizations." This course was custom created for this purpose.[6] The syllabus is the history, culture, economics, politics, and international situation of the country represented. The class meets as a late-afternoon seminar. Except for the earliest meetings, it is student-led, each student having been assigned to one or another commission or the council of ministers. The commission agenda structures individual research, the results of which are shared with the entire delegation. The goal of this preparation is to develop knowledge of the character of the country, enabling students better to portray particularity as diplomats from that country at the meeting of the OAU.[7]

The period of preparation, reinforced by an embassy visit and followed by the model itself, constitutes the most satisfying teaching I have ever done. I feel I have had more of an impact on students through this than in any other way. Students temporarily become diplomats from Ghana or Botswana or Mozambique. It is often necessary afterwards to remind students that this experience was not "real," that it was acting. For weeks afterwards, students will stop by to talk about something related to their experience at the model. I have remained in touch with some of these students for years.

I admit to an unabashed enthusiasm for using simulations in teaching—and in particular for the model OAU. These are the best means I have found to reach average students. My enthusiasm is tempered only by the recognition that there are limitations to what is taught and learned in the simulation process. It is not a substitute for a structured curriculum that teaches development theory and abstract analytical skills. It is also not appropriate if one firmly believes that social science should be taught as a cold, objective exercise: simulations generate passion toward social, economic, and political issues. The biggest difficulty for teachers is the fact that simulations are labor intensive and time consuming. You cannot teach large lecture sections in a simulation. They require a lot of time with relatively small groups. It does not generate large numbers of FTEs.

The national model OAU is, of course, a premier event; but it is possible to scale it back for use on campus. I once did a Maymester course in which there was a simulation of a meeting of the Southern African Development Coordination Conference (SADCC). Any regional grouping can be used for a small-scale simulation. Even the OAU could be run on a single campus with only a few modifications to the rules and preparatory material for the national model.

Simulations can also carry learning about Africa into the K–12 school system. I twice ran simulations from Ed Bigelow's *Strangers in Their Own*

Country, presenting material on apartheid to middle-school students. In the spring of 1992, I worked with a social studies teacher in a rural middle-school in McClellanville, South Carolina, to simulate a SADCC meeting with a hundred or so sixth-grade students. Incidentally, this social studies teacher had graduated from the college in about 1987 and had been a delegate to the model OAU while a student. Simulations such as these have lasting impact beyond that of a mere presentation on Africa. Having run such a simulation once, teachers can subsequently do so on their own.

WORK IN PROGRESS

I am not at all sure that I wish to write a conclusion to this chapter. African studies at the College of Charleston and my experience in pedagogical tinkering are works in progress. My hope is that these will remain in the "forthcoming" category for a long time because that will mean that the institution and I are still spending energy on improving the teaching of African studies. But I will reach this conclusion: I believe we have been relatively successful, in our curriculum and teaching, because of a solid appreciation of the context in which we work. The minor in African studies was realistic in relation to the institution's resources and commitments. The minor's curriculum accepted the limitations of existing course offerings but also identified opportunities for development as resources might become available. My teaching perspective recognized—even if it did not always successfully overcome—the realities associated with teaching at Charleston and in the U.S. context. Successful change began with a sound appreciation of the parameters that structured change and the opportunities to develop within those parameters, including the opportunities that might ultimately change the parameters themselves.

NOTES

1. This perspective on the college, its programs, African studies, and everything else is a professional but personal one. It in no way should be taken as a reflection of the official views of the college, its board of trustees and officers, or of the committee that coordinates the African studies minor.

2. Obviously the faculty are overworked. This, however, does not appear to be obvious to the commission on higher education, the state legislature, or the board of trustees.

3. The two most popular languages are French and Spanish. Faculty in the French and Spanish sections incorporate non-European sources in French and Spanish, particularly Spanish from Latin and South America.

4. Such experience was not entirely absent. In a visiting capacity, I, for example, taught African courses in the Black American Studies Department at Southern Illinois University at Carbondale during the 1979/80 academic year.

5. In May 1992, the class consisted of thirteen students. The roles assigned were: the National Party/State President (F.W. de Klerk), the State Bureaucracy/Security System/Third Force, White Public Opinion, The ANC (Nelson Mandela), the ANC (Cyril Ramaphosa), the ANC (Comrades), the Democratic Party, the Inkhata Freedom Party (Chief Buthelezi), the Pan Africanist Congress, the Azania Peoples' Organization, the Conservative Party, the Afrikaaner Resistance Movement (AWB), and the United Democratic Front (UDF) and its successors.

6. There is also the Model Organization of American States (which also meets in Washington, D.C.), and one of my departmental colleagues at Charleston regularly takes delegations to these simulations.

7. The knowledge gained about African countries and issues is the key reason for the model OAU. But other types of learning occur as epiphenomena of this main purpose. Among these is a working knowledge of parliamentary procedure, negotiating skills, diplomatic behavior, and how to handle stress and frustration. For delegations from the College of Charleston and similar schools, there is also an educational payoff from the venue being at Howard University. Some of my delegates are white, and for them it is always their first, always instructive, experience at being a racial minority. It offers them an interesting, if unpredictable, opportunity to deal with the politics of race in the United States. For African-American students on the delegation, it is equally illuminating to be comfortable as a majority in an institution of higher education. For me, it is a subsidiary but important teaching experience to work with students, mostly from South Carolina, in these circumstances. It is not without significant stress, but it is worthwhile.

21

Program Building:
Some Principles and Lessons

Arthur D. Drayton

African studies at the University of Kansas (KU) has enjoyed measurable success in recent years. I want, in this chapter, to share some of the strategies that have served us in good stead.[1] But simply recounting the measures we took, in addition to being tedious, might give the misleading impression that it was all a neat succession of coolly calculated happenings. Overtures and experiments were not uniformly successful, and some things had to be tried twice and three times. To be sure, conscious planning had to be done as if it were a campaign, and every now and then one grew tired of this insistent need to strategize. But equally, not a little of what we did was done because they appeared to be things that ought to be done, often for the sake of the program, but not seldom for the sake of the college or the institution.

I want to present our experience in a way that also suggests some of the principles that informed our strategies. I therefore begin by pointing to an important if obvious principle: one must be prepared whenever necessary to step forward in the best interest of the institution, even if doing so might indicate a temporary setback for one's own nascent program.

The challenge facing any lonely Africanist, any group or committee of Africanists, any embryonic Africa program seeking to enhance the study of Africa on the campus, will vary according to circumstances. Factors that determine the nature of the challenge include the size of the institution, its ethnic profile, its geographical location and the sociopolitical implications of that, and, of course, one's objectives. I will, therefore, provide a little of the background of the specific situation at KU.

A large, white institution in the Midwest with a student body of about 29,000, KU has witnessed a falling-off in its African-American student population from about 6 percent to about 3 percent. Although in the past few years the minority population as a whole has been on the increase, no noticeable growth is to be found in the African-American component. The decline, however, has been halted. We are not blessed with the kind of demography that can, by itself, sometimes generate and even sustain a viable level of interest in Black studies.[2] Not only does the Midwest not have a particularly large concentration of African-Americans, but Kansas in particular is not exactly where you will go to find them, and in Kansas, not Lawrence.[3] Yet Lawrence was not immune from the civil restiveness of the country in the late 1960s and early 1970s, and in 1970 a Department of African Studies came into being at KU as a result of those pressures.

When this department came into being, the University of Kansas already had well established area studies programs—among them the Latin American program, already well known for being the first in the nation to have a Central American focus. Yet what KU dubbed African studies was in reality a Black studies program responding to the immediate needs and pressures of the time. The name of the program notwithstanding, it appears that the existence of area studies programs on the campus did not quicken any commitment to the study of Africa per se. What was initiated in the classrooms in 1971 was a Black studies program embracing continental Africa and the African diaspora, intended to create at KU "an opportunity to extend the field of intellectual inquiry" in directions hitherto neglected, and constituting, as did all Black studies programs at that time and since, a challenge requiring "a complete reorganization of the intellectual life and the historical outlook of the United States."[4] No doubt the initiators of the program worked in the space they were allotted (or, more likely, had succeeded in creating). A genuine effort was made to provide as rich an array of courses as the few Africanists and African-Americanists on the faculty made possible. "Instructors" were identified to complement faculty resources, as were graduate teaching assistants. Nonetheless, it must have been a kind of lottery, as it must needs be in the absence of any institutional commitment to a timely and well-timed schedule for the recruitment and deployment of resources adequate for the realization of clearly defined objectives. Few Black studies programs were so blessed at the time of those nervous beginnings. It is to the credit of the program and the college that there was an effort to contain the ardor of the time in a meaningful structure, even if there was little evidence that the university was serious about providing muscle. These two, potentially centrifugal, realities had predictably contrary results. On the one hand, some courses, mercifully, recurred fairly frequently; on the other, too many others were dependent on who happened to be on the ground in any given semester. While the open structure of the major could accommodate that situation to some extent, the potential for a mishmash had to be frighteningly real.[5]

That at any rate was the situation when I inherited the program in 1981, and something had to be done if adequate student participation and faculty commitment were to be ensured. Part of the strategy, it seemed to me, was to make Africa a visible and discrete component of the program. That fall, the number of African courses available, including my own

African literature course, was two. Clearly if Africa was to be effectively studied we had to make immediate headway; and we did, even if at first it was nothing that might be termed spectacular. As an interdisciplinary studies program we were necessarily dependent on resources in other departments, but the number of Africanists, or for that matter African-Americanists, was very few. It was certainly the case that some of them were very committed to the program, but there was not any widespread enthusiasm such as would, for instance, ensure that we would get to know about suitable, available courses without some detective work on our part. Indeed, how else will one know what courses are out there, suitable for cross-listing and cross-referencing? True, one might put in place a mechanism whereby other departments may routinely offer this information. By all means do it, but don't make the mistake of relying on it. Every semester it is necessary to get out there and dig up that information anew. Still, networking surely helps.

It therefore did not take us long to recognize that we had to rebuild our network. But networking must go beyond discovering what exists and seek to identify potential and try to actualize it. In this latter endeavor, it helped to be able to make the case for the inclusion of African content in a given department's curriculum independent of the existence of an African studies program: in other words, that Africa does have a claim on that department's international track—which is patently demonstrable for most social science disciplines and not a few in the humanities. This was a position already adumbrated in the philosophy that gave birth to the program, though weakened by submerging Africa in the broader field of Black studies. From this position, however, it becomes easier in due course to persuade departments to keep African studies' needs in mind when recruiting. Even so, little of this can be achieved if the program does not first catch fire and offer some vision of real possibilities. At such a juncture, when one seems viciously circled in dilemma, much imagination, creativity, and especially persistence and sacrifice are required, for how else can one make the program exciting and imbue it with potential in order to attract the kind of faculty participation that would have done it for you in the first place.

It is prudent, of course, that from the very beginning there be a concern not only with the availability of instructors but also of students. Here, too, looms the shadow of that vicious circle. On the one hand, the number, range, and quality of courses are particularly important if we are to attract students and especially quality students. On the other hand, Africanists resident in other departments who are needed to generate that curricular variety and quality are understandably preoccupied with the politics of preferment in their own departments and accordingly have other priorities. A lot of work is needed to pry them out of that posture, and it helps to be able to hold out the prospect of a crop of bright students keen to cultivate the faculty's very own area studies interests in an interdisciplinary context. The challenge of fulfilling these two conditions, each apparently a prerequisite for the other, can be daunting. Ultimately it requires a lot of leverage throughout the system, and for this a department is usually much better placed than a coordinating committee, better even than the conventional area studies program, which often has few if any budgeted faculty, and, therefore, for all practical purposes is in effect a committee. The lonely Africanist or the small group of pioneers should seriously consider this option, at least as an ultimate objective. Basically the more autonomy, the better the chances of building and sustaining a program of sufficient range and quality.

How, then, might the status of "department" help? Indirectly, among other ways. Being a department naturally confers on the program's leadership the status of a college "manager," meaning by this no more than the opportunity and privilege that chairs may have in assisting the dean in shaping the affairs of the college. Where this opportunity exists, and to some extent it must in most institutions of scale, chairs make "leadership" contributions to the institution both from within their departments and without. Done responsibly and selflessly, this can make networking easier. There is a world of difference in the effect on a struggling program between having, on the one hand, a chair who places his or her intelligence, experience, and innovativeness at the service of colleagues and the school, and, on the other, one who inhabits the sidelines and turns up only when it is time to beg, threaten, or cajole. One does not have to be a department chair to do the former; a struggling program should at all times avoid having as leader someone inclined to be the latter. Respect for the program can turn on this.

Departmental autonomy is important in other ways too. The committee and the committee-based program must necessarily depend entirely on resources in other departments. On the other hand, being a department in your own right gives you control of your own resources, and, just as significantly, the right to negotiate those resources. Many factors have to be present, of course, for successful negotiation; but you cannot continue to be a department and always come away empty-handed from that table. Nor can one maintain departmental status and be forever dependent on other departments for one's academic program. As a department you identify (and defend) your resource needs—and, of course, enter into competition for them. To the extent that you obtain those resources, you are in control of your curriculum, and this is an important asset.

But there is a flip side to this, and it is that departments are not forever. We had a sharp reminder of this fact during a program review in the early 1980s when the board of regents raised the possibility of our dismantlement. What saved the day was a coalition of the college, the university administration, and the department, which obviously constituted a

new level of commitment to the program. For me, this near-adversity became a new point of departure. It was proof that we were doing something
right and an assurance that we were by then already projecting a credible
vision of the future. For this, we were obviously indebted to renewed student interest, to a growing body of faculty sympathetic to our activities,
though not necessarily teaching for us, and lots of philosophical support.
From that point on we were no longer in the business of proving that we
had a place at KU, but concentrated on occupying it fruitfully.

The work that had brought us to this position included the development of four levels of networking, among students, faculty, chairs, and administrators. While it remains true that a black student population is not a
prerequisite for an African studies program, there are several reasons why
such a program is vital to them. If they are on campus, they are therefore
a natural constituency. But it is sometimes the case that African-American students see their mission on campus as eschewing "black" courses if
they are to breach the barriers that have stood between them and the white
dispensation. Perhaps even more strangely, African students can sometimes show a stupendous lack of interest in the African curriculum, as if
by virtue of their origin they know all that is to be known about their continent. And yet, for most of them, it will be their only opportunity to study
Africa at this level. So we held meetings with the Black Students Union
and the African Students Association, together and separately; and spoke
at their functions when invited. I even traduced my principles and performed the duties of a judge at one of their beauty contests. We also
brought representatives from their association into our advisory board. But
student leaders are a fugitive population, and the work usually has to be
done all over again every year or two. The aim, however, was twofold: to
build a political constituency, and to get them to identify lacunae that, if
corrected, might make the program more attractive—perhaps even irresistible to them.

At the same time, individual faculty with anything remotely approximating an interest in African or diaspora affairs—be it by virtue of past
residence or a visit, or cultivated but now unpracticed expertise, or present
expertise smothered by departmental priorities—all were encouraged to
get involved. They were invited to our faculty seminars, to meet and make
use of our visitors, to give guest lectures in our classes or invite our colleagues to do so in theirs, to be involved in our projects, and so on. I met
with chairs of core disciplines one-on-one; and when this seemed to be
getting us nowhere, I asked the then dean to call a meeting of chairs at
which he and I could discuss with them ways in which their departments
might more effectively contribute to the program. There were two such
meetings: very urbane, very understanding, endorsing all our objectives,
and even the principle of cooperation on which our argument was based.
But none of this produced any early hard results. A few semesters later,

however, when the real breakthrough began, I was to recognize the absolute value of all that earlier legwork. I recall that my mother used to test the quality of flour by tossing a little to the wall: if it was flour of good quality, some would stick to the wall (and I got to clean it off!). Like good flour, those years of effort left their mark. Perseverance in a good cause usually pays off in the end, if you can stay the course.

Just as untiringly, we worked on the quality of the program. Persuading faculty in other departments to make their courses available to our students as part of our program is more easily done if in their view the students are capable and serious. Unfortunately, as late as the early 1980s there were too many students who saw African studies as a soft option, and our handful of majors boasted too many athletes without the ability and/or time necessary to negotiate the degree. There were, of course, very many students who took our courses to satisfy general education requirements, but it would have been perilous to rest our future on being a service department. So we had to do something to attract good students in larger numbers, which meant that we had to do something about the major: developing a program is more than the politics of the enterprise. However small the beginnings, the program must be excellent enough to earn the respect of students, faculty, and administrators alike.

The academic viability of our program was therefore a top priority. To understand how we proceeded in this respect it might be useful first to recall that the program I inherited was essentially Black studies, with no clear identity as African-American or African and no guarantee of constant balance. I am not sure that the question of a complete conversion to African studies proper ever arose. Nor could there be any question of reducing, let alone removing, the African-American content. Nonetheless, it seemed to me that the time had come to offer students a degree that would be more marketable by virtue of a more sharply defined area of study. At a time of shrinking financial resources, in a white university in Kansas (and perhaps anywhere else in the Midwest), it would have been foolhardy to ask the institution to support two Black programs. Nor was it our intention to reduce the vision of the original founders of the program, who had seen the wisdom of placing Africa as well as Afro-America and the Caribbean in the KU curriculum. We therefore signalled our intention, not only to strengthen all three elements, but formally to recognize the triad in a new name. As it turned out, we received an even stronger signal from the board of regents that we would be spreading ourselves too thin. *Verbum sapientibus satis*: we settled for African and African-American Studies as name and focus. The Caribbean, included in the program from the outset, was not removed or diminished, but it would not compete for resources. The yoking or separation of the two curricular areas of African and African-American continues to be debated in many circles. I thought I would explain the very pragmatic reasons why, in our case, they comprise an integral whole. I should add, however, that several of our courses encourage an exploration of linkages across the diaspora, which I hope is more than making a virtue of necessity.

We also took steps to reconstitute our governance to reflect this clear duality. In keeping with our status as a department, the advisory board was encouraged to advise rather than run the program. This is not likely to be an option generally available to nascent programs, in which case care should be taken to build the kind of relationship between the coordinating committee and the individual charged with its leadership that would permit the latter ample space for initiative. There is no adequate substitute for the vision and energy that an individual can provide, and the nursing of fragile relationships requires a perseverance that is more likely to come from a creative and committed individual than from committee meetings. Further, we reconstituted our advisory board so that it rested on two "subject committees"—African and African-American, with the criteria for membership being determined accordingly and the board having the option of meeting as a whole or in its separate committees, as the needs of the moment dictate.

This restructuring of governance mirrored the alterations in the major itself. Because we were loth to proclaim a major that we could not make functionally available, we introduced our changes in two stages, timing each stage by the progress we made in putting into place those faculty resources needed for what we had in mind. The final product provides for discrete concentrations in African *and* African-American, with an adequate number of courses, increasing in range and variety every year, to make such a choice both possible and rich.[6] In addition, several courses were made more rigorous, and colleagues were encouraged to enforce that rigor in both instruction and examination.

We also rewrote our mission statement to make it abundantly clear that our program had an essential and integral place in the institution. Our mission statement rested on the premise, foreshadowed back in 1970 in the philosophy of the program's founding parents, that a comprehensive university such as the University of Kansas has an obligation to undertake the study of the nation's largest and second-oldest minority, that that study was not the business only of members of that minority, and that it could not be satisfactorily conducted without ample knowledge of that minority's origins. Further, as a flagship institution in a part of the country that feeds the world, KU owed it to its students and to the region to include Africa in the curriculum. Finally, the mission statement implied that graduates of this university, whether citizens of Kansas or not, should not be denied the opportunity to compete for certain jobs in the diplomatic, international, and related fields by virtue of any failure on the university's part to make its curriculum more inclusive. I considered this to be a basic, irrefutable position, and seized every opportunity to expound it. It became my *Carthago delenda est*! As a corollary to all this and in keeping with our founders' determination not to "withdraw into the 'sandtrap' of provincialism," we reaffirmed that we would not permit, or worse yet be ourselves responsible for, the ghettoization of our program, for that way lies extinction.

I imagine that, even as one feels the loneliness of the long-distance runner, one continues to expend energy in anticipation of that time when the stadium swims into view, when the several pieces of the puzzle begin to come together. Moreover, unlike the long-distance runner, one is not likely to be at one's loneliest as the finish line approaches. This is particularly so because, in addition to all the strategizing, the building of coalitions, and so on, you are, above all else, striving to *be* a program. You develop and teach courses with whatever resources are available; you put your students first, whether or not you have a major (and most certainly if you do); you sponsor conferences and seminars and workshops; you bring in Fulbrighters (and encourage your colleagues to use that program to go to Africa); you try to get the university to accommodate the odd African scholar on sabbatical; you engage in outreach; you do these and other things that make Africa real and relevant to the campus and the larger community. In short, if you cannot be a program, you try to be one, if in all but name. This level of activity, perhaps aided by small grants, will have placed you, as it placed us, in an excellent position to apply for medium-size and large grants.

For us, a number of things began to fall into place in the late 1980s. Incidents and grievances on campus sparked a greater engagement with issues affecting minorities, and that at a time of growing concern across the nation. At that time, too, the nation's educators began to increase their interest in the globalization of the curriculum—and these are two issues that feed one another. KU was fortunate to have a cohort of administrators committed to these objectives, or at least responsive to the concern. The college had also recruited a new dean, whose credentials included these visions and a verifiable track record. A few departments began shortlisting minorities, and soon enough began hiring some. Both Africa and Afro-America thus began to be provided for in a few key departments in the college, or to be better provided for. In sum, the climate was distinctly different, and it is conceivable that our long years of advocacy on behalf of both the African and African-American curricula contributed a little to this. By far more important, however, was the fact that this climate facilitated the consultations and negotiations that were necessary for the preparation of our grant application to the Title VI Undergraduate International Studies & Foreign Languages Program.

Entitled "Toward a Functional Balance of African Studies," our proposal sought funds to enable us to fill crucial gaps in the traditional African core so that we might offer students a more balanced and more functional curriculum in the African concentration of the major. Fourteen new or revised courses were anticipated, including the introduction of Hausa, African art history, African theater, and African geography.[7] Two new full-time faculty were to be added to the department and one part-time. Three other departments had to be involved in hosting some of these courses, and others could be direct beneficiaries. Moreover, since it would be pointless to diversify the curriculum in this way if it were all to come to an end upon expiration of the grant, a commitment had to be secured to preserve at least the two full-time positions as tenure-track lines and to continue offering everything else made possible by the grant. Consultation therefore had to be undertaken with chairs, the dean, and individual colleagues. The new climate helped tremendously, as did the new level of commitment in the college administration and academic affairs. But the bona fides of the department was a crucial element: the quality of the flour on the wall told in the pudding.

Among other things, consultations were designed not only to secure an enduring commitment in the departments and the college office, but to generate a synergy that would secure African studies both in our department and others. And that is precisely what has happened. Space continues to be made for Africanists in the departments, the level of cooperation between our department and others has risen dramatically, and African content is beginning to be integrated into existing courses and departments where it was difficult to obtain this before. The grant having expired, not only have the two full-time positions been converted into tenure-track lines, but the offerings in African art history by our part-time instructor have been augmented, and several additional courses have been created through the new access of strength in our department and others. The Department of Geography is collaborating with us in finding ways to increase both graduate study and instruction in African geography. Response to an initiative by the dean of International Studies to stimulate the development of courses for the international curriculum has begun to produce results for African studies. Long contemplated, the category of courtesy professors in African and African-American studies has now been instituted, and already one of these colleagues has succumbed to the lure of a sabbatical in Africa. Perhaps most important of all has been the lift that these developments have given to our students. Already, there has been a new quality to the relationship between the students and the program; and while it may be yet too soon to see (or even to expect) a surge in enrollments as a direct result of the grant, there is no denying the improvement in the quality of students who are now attracted to the program.

One can, of course, be a victim of one's success, and in academia there are two intractable areas in which this affliction is guaranteed to strike. I refer to space and staffing, which never keep pace with other, supposedly more difficult, advances. Rising programs need to keep this phenomenon in mind—and to hope. There can be no question, however, that African studies at KU has arrived at a plateau from where we can confidently envisage a leading role in building the discipline in the region. Our present plans are predicated on this. Internally, we seek to move the program to an enhanced capability in developmental issues and problems in contemporary Africa. Faculty and curriculum development is a central component in this undertaking, as are the exchange of scholars with African institutions, a KU presence in Africa, and fieldwork and other opportunities to buttress this development with prime scholarship. The outcome we hope for is a further transformation of our curriculum, the infusion of in-service teacher training with a more immediately engaging approach to Africa, and generally the ability to better serve the region and beyond.

NOTES

1. This chapter is my personal interpretation of the KU experience over the past dozen years. It does not represent the views of either my department or my institution.

2. It is important, however, not to buy into the proposition that an African-American environment, or even an African-American student population, is a prerequisite for an African studies program.

3. The largest and fairly substantial concentrations of African-Americans are to be found in metropolitan Kansas City, a half-hour's drive to the east of Lawrence, and in Wichita, some two and a half hours to the southwest. A small but discernible concentration is also to be found in the capital, Topeka, a half-hour to the west of Lawrence. However, it appears that neither of the nearby black populations (Kansas City and Topeka) has exerted any pressure on KU politically or in terms of student numbers.

4. From University of Kansas, *1971–1973 University of Kansas Bulletin: Liberal Arts and Sciences* B20. We are probably justified in concluding that the fact that many of these programs are still struggling for acceptance is an indication that academia has, on the whole, failed to rise to that challenge.

5. The major in African (read Black) studies at first required two approved courses in each of African, Afro-American, and Afro-Caribbean areas, a practicum (fieldwork), and three electives for a total of thirty credit hours. Students were encouraged to choose their electives with an eye to a field of concentration. The mainstays of the program over the first ten years (i.e., courses offered on a very regular basis, sometimes every semester) were, in descending order of frequency: "Introduction to African [read Black] Studies," "African History," "Introduction to Jazz," and "Intercultural Communication: the Afro-American." Close behind these were courses offered between six and eight times over this early period. These were, in descending order of frequency: "The Rhetoric of Black Americans," "The Psychology of Women" (later, "The Black Woman"), "Black Nationalism," "Peoples of Africa," "Black Theater," "Southern African History," and "Introduction to African Art." Also taught, at least five times, were "African Music," "African Literature," and "African and Western Cosmologies." Several other courses were taught once only, or at best a few times. There was, of course, the practicum requirement that was made available every year.

6. At least twenty-seven hours are required for the major, consisting of six hours of freshman/sophomore preparation, twelve hours of core courses, and nine elective hours. Only two courses are common to both concentrations, "Peoples of Africa" and "African Traditional Religion & Thought." One upper-level course must deal with the black experience outside the geographical area of the concentration. Three languages are available, and majors are expected to satisfy their language requirement through one of them: Hausa, Kiswahili, and Haitian. Three additional hours in an honors course plus grade point average criteria are necessary to graduate with honors in the major. Opportunities exist for both fieldwork and independent research, and one of these upper-level options must be included in the major.

7. These courses were:

- Elementary Hausa I
- Elementary Hausa II
- Intermediate Hausa I
- Intermediate Hausa II
- African Traditional Religion & Thought (revised)
- Comparative Studies of Religions in Africa
- The Missionary Impact on Africa
- African Theater & Drama
- Readings in Comparative Black Drama
- African Art History
- Introduction to the Geography of Africa
- The Geography of [an African country or region]
- Another African language or language-related course in culture, history, or linguistics
- Economic Development of African Countries (revised)

22

Tufanye Kazi Pamoja: The Association of African Studies Programs

Thomas A. Hale

When I ask an Africanist if his or her institution is a member of the Association of African Studies Programs (AASP), the response sometimes comes in the form of a question: What is the difference between the AASP and the African Studies Association? Most Africanists in this country and many of their foreign counterparts are familiar with the African Studies Association (ASA), an organization of approximately 2,500 members that holds the largest annual meeting of its kind in the world. The ASA is an important forum for scholarly exchange. For the isolated Africanist at a small undergraduate institution it serves as a lifeline to colleagues with common interests.

But the winds of change in academia today have enabled many of these same scholars to assume a more prominent role in both the general studies curriculum as well as in programs offering majors and minors. Many institutions are now launching small African or Africana studies programs, and some of those that have already embarked on this path are now seeking to build larger units. A recent issue of *The Chronicle of Higher Education* revealed that Dartmouth College, an Ivy League institution best known for housing a highly vocal band of conservative students, is now increasing its investment in African and African-American studies. And at Penn State, our Black Studies Program has just become the Department of African and African-American Studies.

There are, however, problems. Not all of our colleagues in other fields are happy to see these new interdisciplinary units appear on the academic scene; and there is no guidebook on how program directors should go about establishing and operating them. By contrast, heads of English and foreign-language departments find continuing guidance in the Association of Departments of English (ADE), or the Association of Departments of Foreign Languages (ADFL).

We do, of course, have large-scale models to follow in the National Resource Centers in African Area Studies, funded by the Title VI Program

at the Department of Education. Their significance stems from a broad involvement in the field that includes support for faculty research and graduate study as well as undergraduate African studies instruction. They also
provide a variety of outreach assistance both to secondary schools as well
as to other institutions.

But it is unlikely that many second- or third-tier research universities
or even small liberal arts institutions can emulate the National Resource
Center model. It would require an investment of between $500,000 and
$1,000,000 in new positions just to prepare a proposal that might have a
chance against Michigan State, UCLA, Indiana, and the other federally
funded centers.

If the difference in scale and resources between the large African studies centers and the small programs or committees at liberal arts colleges
will always remain vast, the goals of Africanists at all of these institutions
remain fundamentally the same: to build a strong foundation in African
studies at the undergraduate level. For the past two decades, the Association of African Studies Programs has attempted to support that goal by
bringing together representatives of both large and small African studies
units for two meetings per year.

One of these meetings is a short, morning session at the African Studies Association annual gathering in the fall; the other is an intensive, two-
day marathon in Washington, D.C., in the spring. The AASP's goal is to
promote African studies at all levels. We work toward this goal in several
ways. The most useful means is simply to exchange information informally and in special sessions at our meetings. But we also represent to
other groups our collective views on issues affecting African studies' support in this country; and the AASP coordinates activities that strengthen
African studies.

For many, a most valuable information-exchange event is when we
meet in Washington, each year, with representatives of agencies interested
in Africa. Most of these agencies, among them the USIA, the Ford Foundation, and the Social Science Research Council, fund activities in Africa.
The focus of their presentations, each limited to one hour, is on both the
current status of continuing support programs for African studies and information on new ones. Other agencies involved are the State Department,
the Congress, and the World Bank. At these meetings, members can interact with administrators and policymakers. We want to hear what they have
to say, especially about funding, and they want our views as administrators
and scholars. In most cases the sessions are sympathetic; occasionally they
have become slightly adversarial. At all times, both parties have benefited.

For the chairman of a small, ongoing African studies committee, such
as the one we have had for years at Penn State, these meetings help to keep
things in perspective. I acquire a clearer sense of where the support money

is, what kind of investment, small or large, is needed by my institution to make a competitive proposal, and how to plan my strategy for building. For example, one of my goals is to obtain a Title VI undergraduate program-strengthening grant for African area studies at Penn State. At the meeting in Washington I have heard presentations by the program officers from the Department of Education; I have read proposals, to learn how others have succeeded; and I am now in the process of building the kinds of basic programs, and lobbying for the kinds of positions, that we will need at Penn State to compete for a grant.

Newcomers to the AASP have described the encounter with these diverse agencies as a powerful eye-opener. A good example of what can come out of an AASP meeting is the case of Georgia Southern University. GSU's François Manchuelle learned at an AASP meeting about the Title VI Undergraduate Language and Area Studies grant program, secured institutional support, and submitted a successful application.

The AASP has other functions. AASP is the coordinating body for its larger members when they submit proposals for summer-intensive language programs in Africa to the Group Projects Abroad program at the Department of Education. For years, the department has been unwilling to fund more than two proposals per year in African languages. We have many member-institutions who could submit such proposals. We try, therefore, to coordinate the submissions so that they do not compete with each other. The organization also has a voice in national discussions on area and language studies. In April 1993, the AASP took a strong position on the need for changes in the National Security Education Act (the Boren Bill) urging legislation to distance funded programs from the Defense Department and open the selection procedures to academic peer review. Other area studies organizations praised AASP for its principled approach and followed suit. Now implemented as the National Security Education Program (NSEP), this legislation has the potential to make a major impact on area studies education. In December 1993, the AASP reaffirmed its stance against the NSEP in its current form.

The AASP serves as a sounding board for government agencies as they shape new programs. In 1991, for example, USIA officials, preparing new exchange programs to respond to the wave of democratization in Africa, met with AASP members in Washington for an informal, give-and-take discussion. Out of this, and their consultation with others, has come a series of innovative initiatives to support the process of democracy in Africa. The AASP has also met with those who implement or influence U.S. foreign policy in Africa to talk about national goals for the continent. For many years we have sponsored a luncheon with the chairman of the House Foreign Affairs Subcomittee on Africa. We also meet with the assistant secretary of state for Africa and/or one of the deputy assistant secretaries.

I should add that as we seek a higher profile for Africa in our society, the AASP and its sister organizations are dwarfed by the far greater financial resources of those who support other area studies groups—for example, Asian studies scholars.

The opportunities we do have to engage in discussion with those involved in foreign policy decisions help to attune us more effectively to current issues. They also contribute, I think, to making us more effective in our own efforts at diplomacy in our home institutions. For many of us, the most recalcitrant, narrow-minded people we must deal with are not our students and not even university administrators, but colleagues who cannot understand why the institution should offer a three-course sequence in Swahili, or why the retiring African history professor should be replaced. Most of us have faced these problems, and we have devised individual solutions to them based on the cultural dynamics of our own institutions. But by working more closely together, we can advance more effectively the cause of African studies for undergraduates.

AASP is not able to provide the kind of one-stop, one-call services that are needed for program directors in African studies today. We remain far from that goal. We are a small organization (approximately sixty members) with extremely limited resources. We serve more as a facilitator than initiator of change. What is needed in the near future is better communication. The AASP distributes minutes of its annual meeting, but they are a mere record of what happened. The chairperson responds to phone calls, letters, and even electronic mail when he figures out the software. In the next five years, I hope to see day-to-day exchange of information by electronic bulletin board, founded on existing networks, the Title VI centers, the ASA, and the AASP membership. This would enable every Africanist and program director to obtain current information on visiting scholars, performers, programs, course design, funding, access to archives, and, perhaps most importantly, a means of contacting colleagues in Africa. We have seen promising steps in this direction: the efforts of a computer group that meets regularly at the African Studies Association meetings as well as from the remarkable work of Patricia Kuntz at Wisconsin, who launched the Wisconsin Bulletin Board; and initiatives by the American Association for the Advancement of Science to improve contact with African colleagues.

As a guide for the future, we might borrow a proverb from Chinua Achebe's novel *Things Fall Apart*. A minor character named Nwakibie reminds Okonkwo about Eneke the bird, who says that since men have learned to shoot without missing, he has learned to fly without perching. To survive and prosper in the face of the budget cutters, and the increased competition from other area studies units, we must find strength in unity and better communication. We know how to perch each year for our palaver, but unless we learn to communicate on the fly twenty-four hours a day, we may find it more difficult to respond in a timely and aggressive manner to those whose image of Africa lives on in the form of Tarzan. As they say in Swahili, *tufanye kazi pamoja*—let us work together.

PART FIVE

CONCLUSION

23

Concluding Remarks

David Lloyd & Ahmed I. Samatar

If the concerns of the scholars in this volume echo some of the sentiments of the Africanist community in the United States and abroad, the nature and direction of African studies are at a major crossroads. Both reflection and debate need to be pushed further, and the chapters in this book appear in that spirit. All of them in various ways confront the question, "Whither African studies?" To distill their salient insights, as well as weave in an editorial perspective, is not easy. One strives to disentangle the issues most appropriate for the study and teaching of African studies at the undergraduate level in relation to the field as a whole. Perhaps this should not be unexpected, given recent seismic shifts in academia and a world in the throes of massive change.

To make this a manageable undertaking, these concluding remarks focus on five core issues that emerge from these essays:

1. The ambiguous image of Africa
2. The recent efforts to internationalize undergraduate curricula
3. The growing debate about African studies
4. The relationship between African and African-American studies
5. The efforts to construct cross-cultural experiences

We will then close with a few suggestions for future directions.

THE IMAGE OF AFRICA

A central concern in this book is the ambiguous image of Africa that permeates both popular culture and the "official mind"—and even the field of African studies.[1] On the one hand, Africa is portrayed as a lost continent, its peoples striving unsuccessfully to stop a downward spiral that threatens the very necessities of life and sociopolitical structures—the essential bulwarks against chaos and conflict. The essays in this volume can only suggest the broad parameters of this portrayal, perhaps understating the current crises facing the continent. Most Africanists would agree that both the dislocation and marginalization involved in this image are far from fully understood or appreciated.

On the other hand, there is a contending image, perhaps as equally underresearched, of a vibrant, resilient Africa; a place where human populations have met formidable challenges successfully for millions of years. Africa is a continent with the deepest of human history, a rich cultural diversity, a youthful population, and large reservoirs of untapped natural resources. The continent's present plight, therefore, is not an accurate reflection of its past, nor a basis for projecting its future. There are, arguably, human and natural resources that will arrest, and ultimately reverse, the grim prognosis. How to assess and present these images remains one of the fundamental challenges confronting those studying and teaching African studies. Such a challenge constitutes one of the connecting threads in these chapters.

However, the contributors' main task was to delineate the manifold configurations in the study and teaching of African studies in the undergraduate arena. To contextualize this entails taking cognizance of recent developments in higher education in the United States.

INTERNATIONALIZING
UNDERGRADUATE CURRICULA

Institutions of higher learning across the United States are aspiring to become more international in their missions, program planning, faculty development, student selection, and opportunities for student learning on campus and abroad. In many of them there has been an intensive effort, in particular, to reappraise and restructure their undergraduate curricula.[2]

Some educators feel that we lack a clear understanding of what has been happening. In the words of Sven Groennings, a former director of the Fund for the Improvement of Postsecondary Education, "Like the scientific revolution, internationalization is leading to a ubiquitous, pervasive and permanent redirection of the intellectual framework. Yet, like the early scientific revolution, it is disorderly development, lacking clear definition, boundaries, and agreement. It is a many splendored chaos with momentum."[3] Perhaps the most obvious consensus from these essays about this "momentum with chaos" is that our visions and efforts must be better informed than they have been so far by an understanding of multiple forces both inside and outside the academy.

It is not enough to focus on our local institutional context; how successful we will be in establishing and sustaining African studies will be ineluctably tied to how well we connect with these broader developments.[4]

Among the many forces stimulating this recent emphasis on internationalism are the creation of numerous new states in the wake of decolonization, with the resultant intensification of political competition, and the rapidly globalizing nature of the international economy, creating intense pressures for countries to reassess their often unequal relationships. Many more voices and interests have been heard in the past few decades as a global community is forged—but not without tremendous pain and discord. After World War II, there were serious efforts to develop U.S. expertise to cope with the challenges emerging in this disparate, often discordant new world. These efforts were located almost exclusively within graduate education. Unprecedented university, federal, and private resources were directed toward establishing international programs at a handful of U.S. universities.[5] Tens of thousands of students educated there subsequently found positions within our colleges and universities, government, and numerous areas of the private sector. Many of those graduates have become a critical force for change at our undergraduate institutions, particularly as they have helped to raise and then grapple with the question of how most effectively to internationalize the curricula. What has become evident throughout all sectors of the U.S. educational system most recently, however, is that international education has been moving beyond the production of experts— toward general education for global citizenship.[6]

THE DEBATE ABOUT AFRICAN STUDIES

The struggles unfolding on our campuses around internationalizing the curricula involve deeply contentious issues, as evidenced in several of the chapters in this volume. Central among these are how knowledge is created and transmitted; and who are the key players in that process. This is intricately connected to the growing debate, at both graduate and undergraduate levels, over the rationale for African studies, how best to develop and teach African studies, and whose voices are legitimate in these efforts.

The initial rationale for area studies, particularly within major U.S. graduate centers, was constructed along two broad lines. Some saw these centers as part of a strategy to train the experts needed to maintain U.S. global hegemony in the post–World War II era. For others, they were environments for creative exploration of other cultures—part of a serious effort to understand those cultures on their own terms and as much as possible through their own voices. Many educators in this latter approach saw their primary responsibility as mediators, as cultural interpreters and brokers, who made the case that U.S. and African interests were not necessarily congruous or convergent. The possibility that "we" could learn anything from "them" that could help to improve Western societies seems to have been scarcely perceived in either approach.

While these two approaches have characterized much of the study and teaching in African studies over the past few decades, the possibility of understanding the *other* as a means to our own improvement is forcefully vying at present for serious consideration.

At the same time, a new crisis obtrudes into the conception of area studies, provoking an intense debate over the very survival of African studies. In the view of some scholars, U.S. "triumphalism," underpinned by a revived modernization theory in conjunction with competing claims on diminishing resources, threatens to marginalize or even destroy African studies, a perception aptly presented by Joel Samoff in Chapter 2. As Africa and Africans become marginalized in contemporary geostrategic configurations and U.S. policy interests, why should the fate of African studies be any different? Also threatening African studies is the contention of other scholars that even the cultural brokerage approach to African studies has not been very effective in promoting understanding of a world that, though it be increasingly integrated, yet remains largely estranged culturally, economically, and politically. In brief, these scholars assert there is the need for a radically new role for African studies.

This role has not yet been clearly defined, but recent debates have begun to suggest some new directions. A particularly contentious point is the call to move toward the attenuation, if not abandonment, of disciplinary scholarship. Some scholars, such as William Martin in Chapter 3 of this book, argue the necessity of a "unidisciplinary stream of scholarship" focused on broad processes of intercultural penetration. Others still see a critical role for a more focused area-studies approach that systematically studies Africa, albeit along more interdisciplinary lines in which African scholars and perspectives play a much larger part. At the heart of the matter is the relationship between disciplinary and interdisciplinary scholarship. Academic disciplines have been the bedrock of our institutional structures and the means through which most of the status, rewards, and achievements of faculty are recognized. Are recent interdisciplinary developments perceived as deviations from the "real" intellectual and professional responsibilities of faculty? Some faculty will agree that students need interdisciplinary approaches and multiple perspectives to understand world problems; but they think undergraduates need to gain that insight through the rigor and conceptual tools located within the established disciplines. These faculty contend that disciplines alone are able to provide the depth of knowledge, theoretical understanding, modes of analysis, and substantive building blocks for interdisciplinarity. How much is this a valid prescription for moving toward interdisciplinarity? And how much is it a rationale to safeguard the existing structures? This is one of the most contentious current issues.

Most contributors to this volume affirm the continuing centrality of disciplines in African studies at the undergraduate level. But they also demonstrate that there have been numerous efforts to cross disciplinary lines and innovate new institutional structures. In some cases, faculty, although attached to disciplinary departments, are given considerable latitude to interact with other internationally focused faculty, with mandates to innovate new structures such as area studies, interdisciplinary minors, and international majors or certification. In other instances, the major thrust is toward diffusing international material across the curriculum through retraining existing faculty and stimulating more team-teaching to enable them to incorporate more non-Western materials into their courses. In the best of cases, area studies remain viable sources of expertise to facilitate these processes; at worst, they are perceived as redundant and unnecessarily competitive for scarce institutional resources.

Despite many such efforts to cross disciplinary lines, however, area-studies faculty, particularly within African, Asian, Latin American, and Caribbean areas, have not been able to build many cross-communicating linkages. These specialists face serious risks of "ghettoization." The critical challenge is how to gain acceptance of these efforts as integral to the interests of the department and discipline as well as to build wider university linkages. Some help on how to do this has begun to appear, mostly drawn from personal and institutionally based experiences, within the past few years.[7] Nevertheless, how to construct and institute these "unidisciplinary" or "interdisciplinary" approaches within the academy remains vague. Those proposing such approaches need to do much more to define them and delineate what is at stake.

While restructuring and repositioning African studies in the academy, there is also the need to give more attention to fundamental concepts and ideas that underpin the field. Here, too, there is ambiguity. Should the primary focus be on a deeper awareness of historically constructed, transcultural relationships? Some scholars, while empathetic to understanding broader and more abiding linkages, perceive such an approach as a "universalizing" quest that threatens to overlook much of the value, and underestimates the tenacity, of cultural heterogeneity. In making such an approach, what are the risks with regard to moving toward reductionism and minimizing the importance of intracultural developments? Contemporary events, testifying to the resurgence of micronationalism among diverse ethnic groups heretofore merged within multiethnic states, would suggest that such heterogeneity is a powerful force ignored only at great peril.[8] Can these two approaches be better melded?

Others argue that the way forward is through a new synthesis out of the engagement of old adversaries. This new synthesis would evolve from an unprecedented conversation on the relationship between and among at least the following related areas: modernization and Marxism, tradition and Enlightenment, and problem-solving and paradigm-building. If the Enlightenment brought forth the ascendance of science and calculating rationality, its legacy includes atomization, ecological wreckage, and the objectification of the *other*. A new dialogue with tradition, or indigenous knowledge, could validate what is intellectually remarkable about the Enlightenment and at the same time underscore the limits of both. The interface of cultural conciousnesses could set a new epistemological ambience. Here, developmental paradigms of (neo)modernization and (neo-)Marxism would need willingly to shed their by now familiar and public deficiencies—deficiencies that partly grew from a mutually impoverishing cold war with each other. Such an attempt at cross-fertilization of their thinking would help to redefine the nature of the African condition and imagine new strategies for survival and renewal. The distressed world of Africa is desperately calling for new collaborations that could usher in new vistas for scholarly exploration and action. To meet this task requires a transcendance of the great intellectual rifts of the past—a transcendance that is daring and experimental while avoiding the seductions of academic fads or unnecessary epistemological conflicts.

AFRICAN AND AFRICAN-AMERICAN STUDIES

One of the most sensitive issues arising out of these essays is the relationship between African and African-American studies on U.S. undergraduate campuses. There has been a troubled history of linkage over the last few decades, most emphatically dramatized at the Montreal joint meeting of the U.S. and Canadian African Studies Associations in 1969. Charges of institutional racism, white-male domination, and discriminatory practices in competition for research funding, among others, led many educators to leave—some to form new associations, such as the African Heritage Studies Association. Some contend that the roots of this schism go much deeper and have been explored most profoundly by Afrocentrists and a generation of African and African-American scholars before them. While valuing the work of these scholars, others also see as important the interplay among scholars of various racial and ethnic backgrounds. Given the history of institutionalized racism in many U.S. academic and professional circles, many argue that Afrocentrists, in particular, have not been given a fair and thorough hearing. Part of the result can be seen today as increasing numbers of faculty and students from diverse cultural backgrounds, as well as faculty and students with cross-cultural experiences, confront these issues with unprecedented vigor. Most would agree that these issues remain far from resolved.

For many undergraduates, particularly those lacking overseas or cross-cultural experience, racial tensions appear to be looming ever larger. Flashpoints erupt on U.S. campuses with disturbing frequency. Many contend that there has not been much progress—perhaps, even, an overall deterioration. Some university administrations have attempted to contain African-American issues by encompassing them within African studies programs; other institutions have tried to create more inclusive Africana studies programs or Black studies concentrations. Some scholars see these as complementary fields of study that have distinctive justifications—while readily admitting that more permanent linkages need to be built. Where African studies and African-American studies intersect, and what their positioning is within larger internationalizing currents, are issues at the heart of many campus debates. For many, these are healthy stirrings, even though the outcome is uncertain. Hopefully, mutual concern will foster a climate of interaction and lead to a more equitable community. We all have a long way to go.

CROSS-CULTURAL EXPERIENCES

A fifth important issue revolves around efforts to construct opportunities for firsthand cross-cultural experiences for North American and African students. Studies indicate that only a handful of U.S. institutions have established such programs; and only about 2 percent of U.S. undergraduates have a Study Abroad experience. Very few of these go to a non-Western area. Events indicate that there is a movement to increase these percentages substantially. A national task force organized by the Association of International Educators (NAFSA), the Council on International Educational Exchange (CIEE), and the Institute of International Education (IIE), have called for a goal of 10 percent of U.S. undergraduates to have cross-cultural experience abroad by the turn of the century. Similar goals have been established by many European and Southeast Asian countries. In addition, the National Security Education Act of 1991 has tripled federal funding for undergraduate study abroad and increased funds to support program initiatives in international and area studies and foreign languages.[9]

Some of the goals, approaches, and constraints of these Abroad programs are discussed in this volume. What is still not clear to many faculty and institutions is both the significance of these programs and how well they meet their goals. Many faculty remain skeptical about the quality of the courses offered abroad, as well as how to measure the effects of Study Abroad on students. Reports indicate that students who do go abroad experience substantial personal difficulties; that many programs have minimal impact on the existence of cultural stereotypes; and that the salience of gender, race, and ethnicity issues do not get the attention they deserve.[10] The significance of these programs, for both hosts and the United States, needs to be explored more. Are they really mutually beneficial? Some of the most candid assessors argue that there often remains a disturbing disjuncture between the goals and presumed benefits of these experiences. Hard-hitting assessments are acutely lacking. In the best cases, assessments from host institutions, faculty, and students are not only solicited, they become a vital source for change.

THE FUTURE

Undeniably, this book raises far more questions than it answers. This suggests the need for more conferences focused on African studies at the undergraduate level. Particularly critical is the need to probe the relation between African studies and African-American students and African-American courses. More opportunities to investigate the numerous issues of pedagogy are also needed. Among these, the following are especially important:

1. What are the most effective ways to stimulate participatory, problem-centered learning and to get African and American students working together?
2. How do we connect an experience abroad to university coursework? How can students be reintegrated into U.S. campuses in ways that will impact more forcefully on internationalizing efforts? And how can African students be involved in such efforts?
3. African languages and African arts courses offer students the chance to learn through direct participation. What are the best strategies for developing stronger commitment to these courses?
4. What are the benefits of building networks among students after they graduate? Do networks usefully enable students and institutions to assess the impact of intercultural training on careers?

Permeating all these issues is the search for more effective ways of encouraging students to take leadership roles and work in collaboration with faculty.

These efforts must go beyond the holding of conferences. Faculty need to structure better ways to assess their work, both at institutions and within professional organizations. Telecommunications advances such as electronic mail are beginning to play a larger role in this. Most faculty are involved with professional organizations (the African Studies Association, the Association of African Studies Programs, the Association of American Colleges, the Association for the Study of Higher Education, Educational Resources Information Center, and Clearinghouse on Higher Education) that are engaging these issues.

These organizations could make a more concerted effort to meet the challenges facing African studies at the undergraduate level. This should become a more clearly defined objective of the African Studies Association and the Association of African Studies Programs. Appropriate resources and structures should be developed, similarly with African studies centers and regional organizations. At least a few institutions should consider creating research centers. Out of this an intercommunicating network might emerge. The fate of African studies hinges in large measure on how well the individuals engaged construct bridges between themselves, the wider academic community, and the global community.

NOTES

1. Many scholars have discussed this image. Recent work on it includes Jacques Attali, *Millenium: Winners and Losers in the Coming World* (New York: Times Books, 1991); Jennifer S. Whitaker, *How Can Africa Survive?* (New York: Council on Foreign Relations Press, 1988); Basil Davidson, *Black Man's Burden* (New York: Times Books, 1992); Douglas Rimmer, ed., *Africa 30 Years On* (London: James Currey, 1991); Richard Sandbrook, *The Politics of Africa's Economic Recovery* (New York: Cambridge University Press, 1993); and Breyten Breytenbach, *Return to Paradise* (Winchester, Mass.: Faber & Faber, 1993).

2. Several chapters in this volume help to identify some of the most useful materials available in this effort. Cf. also Barbara Turlington and Sarah Pickert, *Internationalizing the Undergraduate Curriculum: A Handbook for Campus Leaders* (Washington, D.C.: American Council on Education, 1992); Philip H. Coombs, *International Studies Funding and Resource Book: The Education Interface Guide to Sources of Support for International Education*, 5th ed. (New York: Apex Press, 1990).

3. Sven Groennings, "Higher Education, International Education, and the Academic Disciplines," in *Group Portraits: Internationalizing the Disciplines*, ed. Sven Groennings and David Wiley (New York: American Forum for Global Education, 1990): 11–31.

4. Cf. Association of American Colleges, *Integrity of the College Curriculum: A Report to the Academic Community* (Washington, D.C.: Association of American Colleges, 1985); Ernest L. Boyer, *College: The Undergraduate Experience in America* (New York: Harper and Row, 1987).

5. Cf. Robert McCaughey, *International Studies and the Academic Enterprise* (New York: Columbia University Press, 1984); Sarah Pickert, *Preparing for a Global Community: Achieving an International Perspective in Higher Education* (Washington, D.C.: George Washington University, 1992).

6. Cf. American Council on Education, *International Studies and the Undergraduate* (Washington, D.C.: American Council on Education, 1989); David Engerman and Parker Marden, *In the International Interest: Contributions and Needs of America's International Liberal Arts Colleges* (Beloit, Wis.: International Liberal Arts Colleges, 1992).

7. Cf. Robert Bates, Jean O'Barr, and V.Y. Mudimbe, eds., *Africa and the Disciplines* (Chicago: University of Chicago Press, 1993); Sven Groennings and David Wiley, *Group Portraits.*

8. Edmond J. Keller, "Towards a New African Order?" (presidential address to the 1992 annual meeting of the African Studies Association) *African Studies Review* 26 (Sept. 1993): 1–10.

9. Cf. Barbara Burn, *Integrating Study Abroad into the Undergraduate Liberal Arts Curriculum: Eight Institutional Case Studies* (Westport, Conn.:

Greenwood, 1991); B. Burn, L. Cerych, and A. Smith, eds., *Study Abroad Programmes,* Higher Education Policy Series, no. 11, vol. 1 (London: Jessica Kingsley, 1990); and Pickert, *Preparing for a Global Community.*

10. Cf. S. Opper, U. Teichler, and J. Carlson, *The Impact of Study Abroad Programmes on Students and Graduates,* Higher Education Policy Series, 11, vol. 2 (London: Jessica Kingsley, 1990); and J. Carlson et al. *Study Abroad: The Experience of American Undergraduates* (Westport, Conn.: Greenwood, 1990).

The Contributors

Patricia Alden is professor of English at St. Lawrence University and currently coordinator for African Studies. A student of the novel in English, her published work includes *Social Mobility and the English Bildungsroman* (1986) and, more recently, essays on Nuruddin Farah and other African writers.

Sara Berry is professor of History at Johns Hopkins University. Her recent publications include *No Condition is Permanent: The Social Dynamics of Agrarian Change in Sub-Saharan Africa* (1993).

W. Howard Brown is the associate director of the St. Lawrence University Kenya Semester Program and assistant professor of History. His teaching and research interests focus on the social and cultural history of the Swahili peoples of the East African coast.

Gregson Davis was born in Antigua, West Indies, and educated at Harvard and the University of California at Berkeley. He is currently the Goldwin Smith Professor of Comparative Literature and Classics at Cornell University. His books include *Non-Vicious Circle: Twenty Poems of Aimé Césaire* (1984) and *Polyhymnia: The Rhetoric of Horatian Lyric Discourse* (1991).

Arthur D. Drayton, formerly of the University of Ibadan and the University of the West Indies, has been professor and chair of African and African-American Studies at the University of Kansas since 1981. His main research interest is literature and society in Africa and the African diaspora. His most recent publications have focused on the writings of Caribbean authors.

Sandra E. Greene, former director of African Studies and associate provost at Kalamazoo College, is currently associate professor of African

History at Cornell University. She has published a number of articles on the precolonial social history of Africa and has, in press, a book entitled *Gender, Ethnicity and Social Change on the Upper Slave Coast*.

Thomas A. Hale is professor of African, French, and Comparative Literature at Pennsylvania State University. A founder and past president of the African Literature Association, he has completed a two-year term as chair of the Association of African Studies Programs. His research ranges from the Caribbean to Africa, and from the written to the oral tradition. His most recent book, *Scribe, Griot, and Novelist: Narrative Interpreters of the Songhay Empire*, appeared in 1990. He is now writing a book about griots—the musical entertainers of Western Africa.

Lidwien Kapteijns is associate professor of African and Middle Eastern History and chair of Women's Studies at Wellesley College. Apart from coauthoring an introduction to African history in Dutch, she has written several books and many articles about the precolonial and colonial history of Sudan. She is currently working on the history of women and gender relations in the precolonial and colonial history of northern Somalia. Her "Women and the Crisis of Communal Identity: The Cultural Construction of Gender in Somali History," is forthcoming in *The Somali Challenge*, edited by Ahmed I. Samatar.

Neil Lazarus is associate professor of English and Modern Culture and Media at Brown University, where he teaches African and postcolonial literatures, as well as social and literary theory, and cultural studies. He is the author of *Resistance in Postcolonial African Fiction* (1990), and is currently completing a second book, provisionally entitled *Hating Tradition Properly: The Politics of Culture in the Postcolonial World System*.

David Lloyd is associate professor of African History at St. Lawrence University. He joined the faculty in 1985 and was coordinator for African Studies from 1986 to 1993. From 1977 to 1983 he was a lecturer in African History at the University of Calabar, Nigeria, and prior to that conducted field research for his dissertation in Zaire, lectured at the Kisangani campus of the national university of Zaire, and taught in the secondary school system of Tanzania. Most of his training, research, and subsequent writing has been centered on African economic history.

William Martin teaches Sociology and African Studies courses at the University of Illinois at Urbana-Champaign. He is coauthor of *How Fast the Wind? Southern Africa 1975–2000* (1992), editor of *Semiperipheral States in the World-Economy* (1990), and author of numerous articles on regional/world economic relationships. His recent work includes research on transnational relationships in the production of knowledge.

James C. McCann is director of the African Studies Center and associate professor of History at Boston University. He is author of *From Poverty to Famine in Northeast Ethiopia* (1987) and a forthcoming book project *People of the Plow: A History of Agriculture in Ethiopia*. He teaches undergraduate surveys and upper-division courses in African History.

Patrick McNaughton is an associate professor of African Art at Indiana University. He has published many articles and a book on West African sculpting and its many complex contexts, *The Mande Blacksmiths: Knowledge, Power and Art in West Africa* (1988). He is presently working on the history of mask forms in many parts of West Africa, and on the intimate and instrumental relationships between aesthetics as systems of thought and the activities of individual and social groups.

Celia Nyamweru is associate professor of Anthropology at St. Lawrence University, teaching courses on topics related to human ecology and resource-use in Africa. She taught in Kenyan schools, polytechnics, and universities from 1968 to 1991. Her publications include frequent reports on the eruptions of Ol Doinyo Lengai volcano, Tanzania, to the *Bulletin of the Global Volcanism Network* and the *Bulletin of Volcanic Eruptions*.

Jack Parson is professor and chair in the Department of Political Science at the College of Charleston, South Carolina, where he has been since 1980. He spent four years in Uganda and six years in Botswana, teaching and researching aspects of that country's political economy. Most recently he was the editor of *Succession to High Office in Botswana: Three Case Studies* (1990) and contributed the chapter, "Liberal Democracy, the Liberal State and the 1989 General Elections in Botswana," to *Botswana: The Political Economy of Democratic Development*, edited by Stephen Stedman (1993).

Joseph W. Pickle, Jr. is professor of Religion at Colorado College. He is the founding codirector of the Associated Colleges of the Midwest Zimbabwe Program. He is currently collaborating on a book addressing science and religion.

Paul W. Robinson is the director of the St. Lawrence University Kenya Semester Program and is an associate professor of History. His teaching and research centers on traditional survival strategies and recent development trends among pastoralist groups in East Africa.

Ahmed I. Samatar is currently dean of International Studies at Macalester College, St. Paul, Minnesota, and formerly associate professor of Government/African Studies at St. Lawrence University. His fields of expertise include international and comparative studies and African development studies, and he has taught courses in international political economy, social and political theory, and African politics and development. His most recent publication is *The Somali Challenge: From Catastrophe Toward Renewal?* (forthcoming).

Joel Samoff is affiliated with the Center for African Studies at Stanford University. A student of African politics and education, he is currently completing a book on the politics of education reform in Tanzania. He has recently worked extensively with the Ministry of Education and Culture in Namibia and managed the research program of an ILO–UNESCO Task Force concerned with the impacts on education and training of financial crisis and structural adjustment. In 1992 and 1993, he was visiting professor of Education at the University of California, Los Angeles.

Ann Seidman is adjunct professor at Clark University in both International Development and Social Change and in the Boston University Law School. She was formerly the president of the African Studies Association (1990–1991) and is currently chair of the Task Force for Sustainable Development in Africa. She taught and did research for eleven years at universities in Africa, and has authored, coauthored, and edited a dozen books and many articles on problems relating to African development.

Neal W. Sobania is director of International Education and associate professor of History at Hope College in Holland, Michigan. His research focuses on the history of pastoral production systems in Kenya and Ethiopia. He is the author of *A Background History to the Mt. Kulal Region of Northern Kenya* (1979), coeditor of a modern history of Kenya (in preparation), and has published widely on history, ecology, and socioeconomic relations in nineteenth-century East Africa.

Thomas Spear is professor of African History at the University of Wisconsin-Madison and previously taught at La Trobe University in Melbourne, Australia, and Williams College in Massachusetts. He has written histories of the Ngoni, *(Zwangendaba's Ngoni,* 1972), the Mijikenda of Kenya *(The Kaya Complex,* 1974), eastern Kenya *(Kenya's Past,* 1981), and the Swahili *(The Swahili,* 1985—with Derek Nurse); edited, with Richard Waller, a book on Maasai ethnicity *(Being Maasai,* 1993); and is currently completing a social and economic history of the Arusha and Meru peoples of northern Tanzania.

Paul Stoller, professor of Anthropology at West Chester University, has, for more than twenty years, researched the religion and social life of several Songhay communities in Niger. His most recent books include *The Cinematic Griot: The Ethnography of Jean Rouch* (1992) and *Fusion of* *the Worlds: An Ethnography of Possession Among the Songhay of Niger* (1989).

Louis Tremaine is associate professor of English at the University of Richmond. His teaching and research are primarily in modern African literature and cultural studies. He has translated Mohammed Dib's *Qui Se Souvient de la Mer* (1985) and written on Maghrebian and South African literature. He is director of the University of Richmond's summer program in Zimbabwe.

Gretchen Walsh is head of the African Studies Library, Boston University. Her recent publications include: "African Language Materials: Challenges and Responsibilities in Collection Management" in *Africana Resources and Collections: Three Decades of Development and Achievement. A Festchrift in Honor of Hans Panofsky*, edited by Julian W. Witherell (1989); "Reading for a Free South Africa," *Choice* (July/Aug 1989); *Publishing in Africa: A Neglected Component of Development* (1991); and "The Book Famine in Africa and the Role of American Academic Libraries," in *The Role of American Academic Libraries in International Programs* (1992).

Ben Wisner is the Henry R. Luce Professor of Food, Resources and International Policy at Hampshire College, Amherst, Mass. Through teaching, research, and program support, he attempts to strengthen nongovernment actors working for the satisfaction of basic human needs, environmental justice, and sustainability.

About the Book

This collection of critical debates—intended for teachers of African studies and others interested in incorporating non-Western perspectives in the undergraduate liberal arts curriculum—reflects the changing educational and sociocultural contexts of the last decade.

Representing a range of disciplines, the contributors address four areas of concern: the role of African studies in fostering interculturalism in the general curriculum; the presuppositions and interests of students with respect to Africa; the redesign of courses and pedagogy in light of theoretical development in key disciplines; and the need to develop reciprocal models of cultural exchange.